YAMATONADESHIKO SHICHIHENGE

Tomoko Hayakawa

Translated and adapted by
David Ury

Lettered by
North Market Street Graphics

Ballantine Books · New York

The Wallflower, volume 11 is a work of fiction. Names, characters, places, and incidents are the products of the author's imagination or are used fictitiously. Any resemblance to actual events, locales, or persons, living or dead, is entirely coincidental.

A Del Rey Trade Paperback Original

Published in the United States by Del Rey Books, an imprint of The Random House Publishing Group, a division of Random House, Inc., New York.

Publication rights arranged through Kodansha Ltd.

First published in Japan in 2004 by Kodansha Ltd., Tokyo, as Yamatonadeshiko Schichihenge.

ISBN 978-0-345-49475-7

Printed in the United States of America

www.delreymanga.com

9 8 7 6 5 4

Translator/Adaptor—David Ury
Lettering—North Market Street Graphics

Contents

A Note from the Author

I went to Disneyland for the first time in ten years. I went because they had temporarily turned the Haunted Mansion into a *Nightmare Before Christmas*–themed ride. I was so excited (too excited). Jack looked really cute. ♥ ♥ I'm gonna go as many times as I can while the *Nightmare* stuff is still up. ♥ I wish they'd just keep the *Nightmare* theme forever instead of just having it for a limited time. I love it!

—**Tomoko Hayakawa**

Honorifics

Throughout the Del Rey Manga books, you will find Japanese honorifics left intact in the translations. For those not familiar with how the Japanese use honorifics and, more important, how they differ from American honorifics, we present this brief overview.

Politeness has always been a critical facet of Japanese culture. Ever since the feudal era, when Japan was a highly stratified society, use of honorifics—which can be defined as polite speech that indicates relationship or status—has played an essential role in the Japanese language. When addressing someone in Japanese, an honorific usually takes the form of a suffix attached to one's name (example: "Asuna-san"), or as a title at the end of one's name, or appears in place of the name itself (example: "Negi-sensei," or simply "Sensei!").

Honorifics can be expressions of respect or endearment. In the context of manga and anime, honorifics give insight into the nature of the relationship between characters. Many English translations leave out these important honorifics, and therefore distort the feel of the original Japanese. Because Japanese honorifics contain nuances that English honorifics lack, it is our policy at Del Rey not to translate them. Here, instead, is a guide to some of the honorifics you may encounter in Del Rey Manga.

-*san*: This is the most common honorific, and is equivalent to Mr., Miss, Ms., Mrs. It is the all-purpose honorific and can be used in any situation where politeness is required.

-*sama*: This is one level higher than "-san." It is used to confer great respect.

-*dono*: This comes from the word "tono," which means "lord." It is an even higher level than "-sama" and confers utmost respect.

-kun: This suffix is used at the end of boys' names to express familiarity or endearment. It is also sometimes used by men amongst friends, or when addressing someone younger or of a lower station.

-chan: This is used to express endearment, mostly toward girls. It is also used for little boys, pets, and even among lovers. It gives a sense of childish cuteness.

Bozu: This is an informal way to refer to a boy, similar to the English terms "kid" or "squirt."

Sempai/Senpai:
This title suggests that the addressee is one's senior in a group or organization. It is most often used in a school setting, where underclassmen refer to their upperclassmen as "sempai." It can also be used in the workplace, such as when a newer employee addresses an employee who has seniority in the company.

Kohai: This is the opposite of "sempai" and is used toward underclassmen in school or newcomers in the workplace. It connotes that the addressee is of a lower station.

Sensei: Literally meaning "one who has come before," this title is used for teachers, doctors, or masters of any profession or art.

[blank]: This is usually forgotten in these lists, but it is perhaps the most significant difference between Japanese and English. The lack of honorific means that the speaker has permission to address the person in a very intimate way. Usually, only family, spouses, or very close friends have this kind of permission. Known as *yobisute,* it can be gratifying when someone who has earned the intimacy starts to call one by one's name without an honorific. But when that intimacy hasn't been earned, it can be very insulting.

THE wallflower

YAMATONADESHIKO SHICHIHENGE

ヤマトナデシコ七変化♡

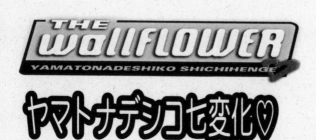

CONTENTS

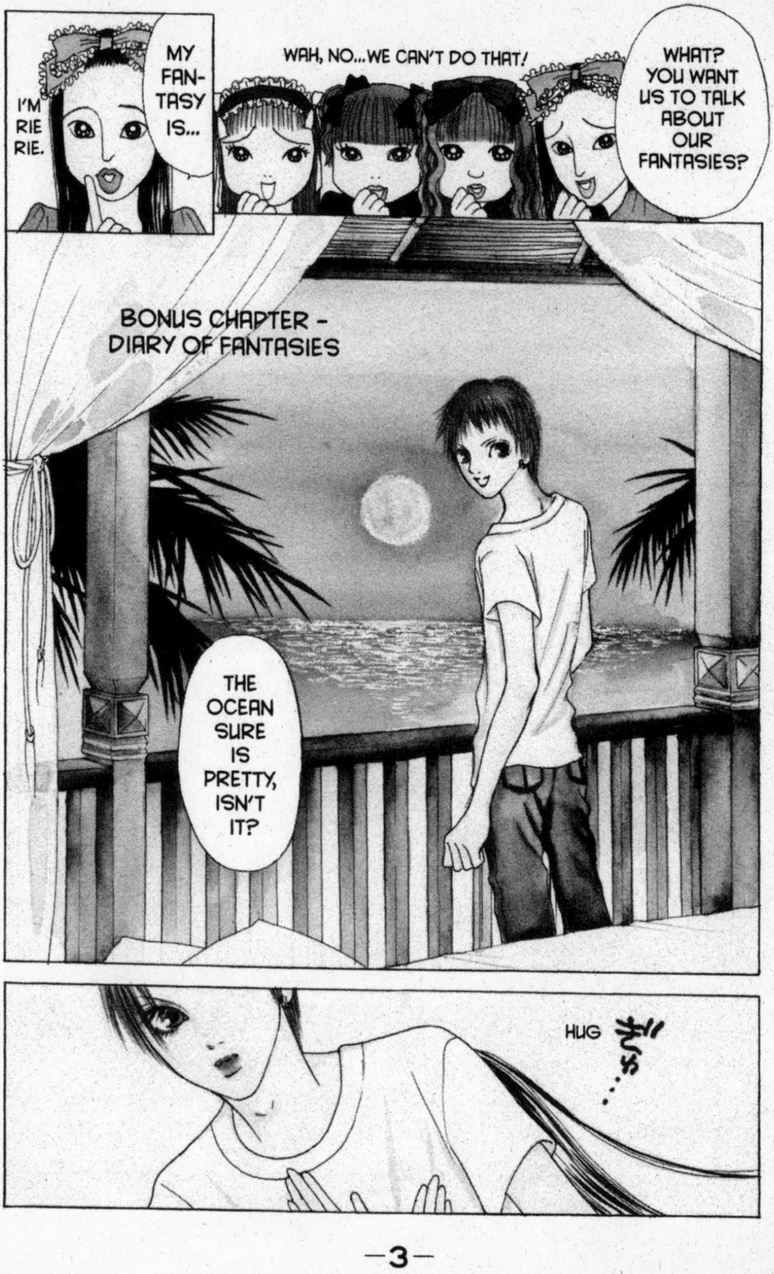
WHAT? YOU WANT US TO TALK ABOUT OUR FANTASIES?
WAH, NO...WE CAN'T DO THAT!
MY FAN-TASY IS...
I'M RIE RIE.
BONUS CHAPTER - DIARY OF FANTASIES
THE OCEAN SURE IS PRETTY, ISN'T IT?
HUG

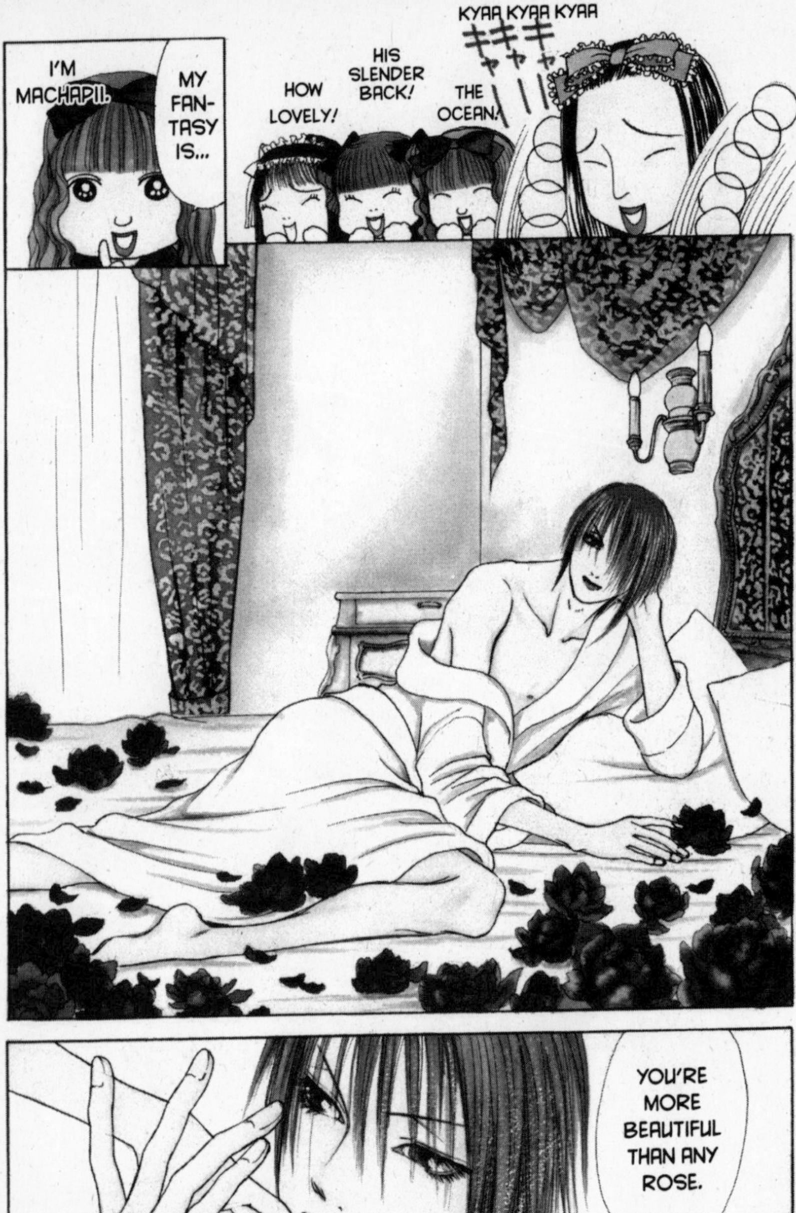
KYAA KYAA KYAA
キャーキャーキャー
THE OCEAN!
HIS SLENDER BACK!
HOW LOVELY!
I'M MACHAPII.
MY FAN-TASY IS...
YOU'RE MORE BEAUTIFUL THAN ANY ROSE.

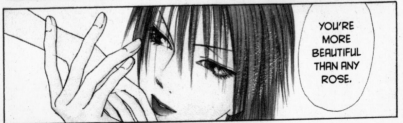

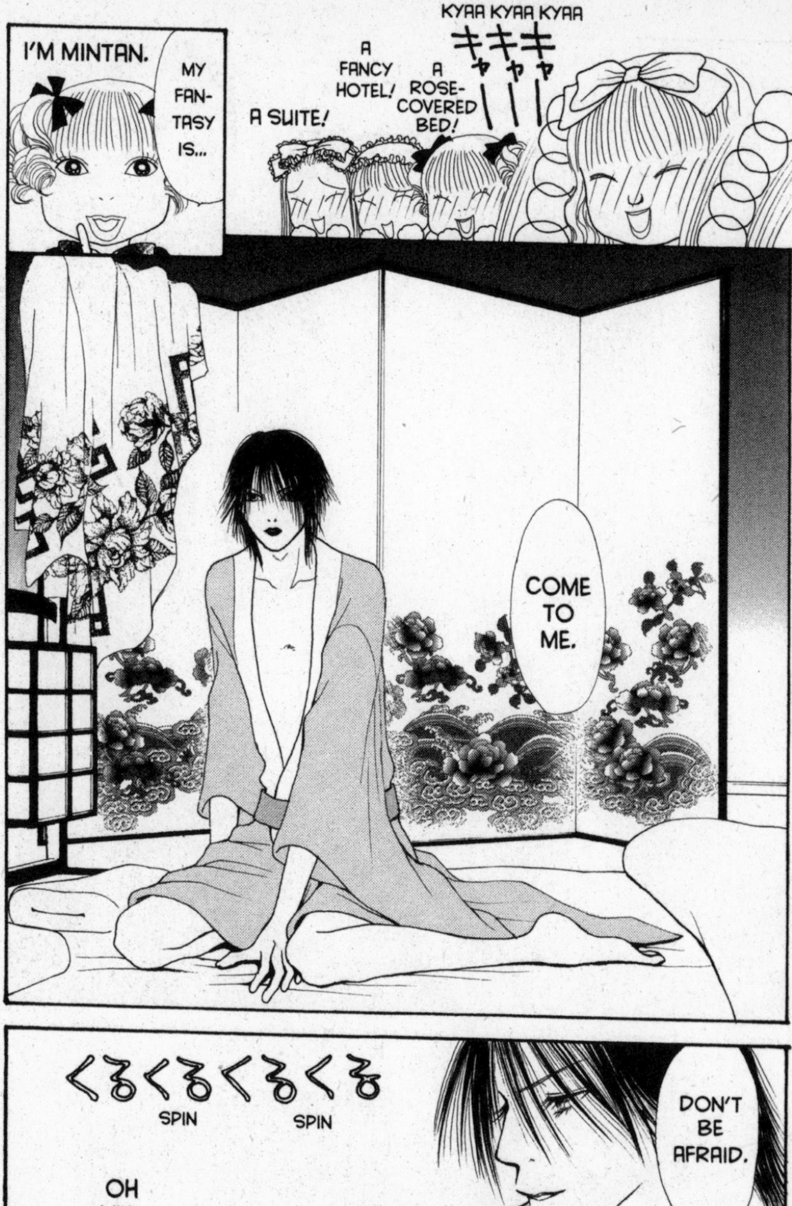

KYAA KYAA KYAA
キャーキャーキャー
A ROSE-COVERED BED!
A FANCY HOTEL!
A SUITE!
MY FAN-TASY IS...
I'M MINTAN.
COME TO ME.
DON'T BE AFRAID.
くるくるくるくる
SPIN
SPIN
OH MY...

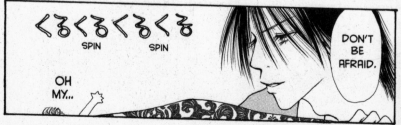

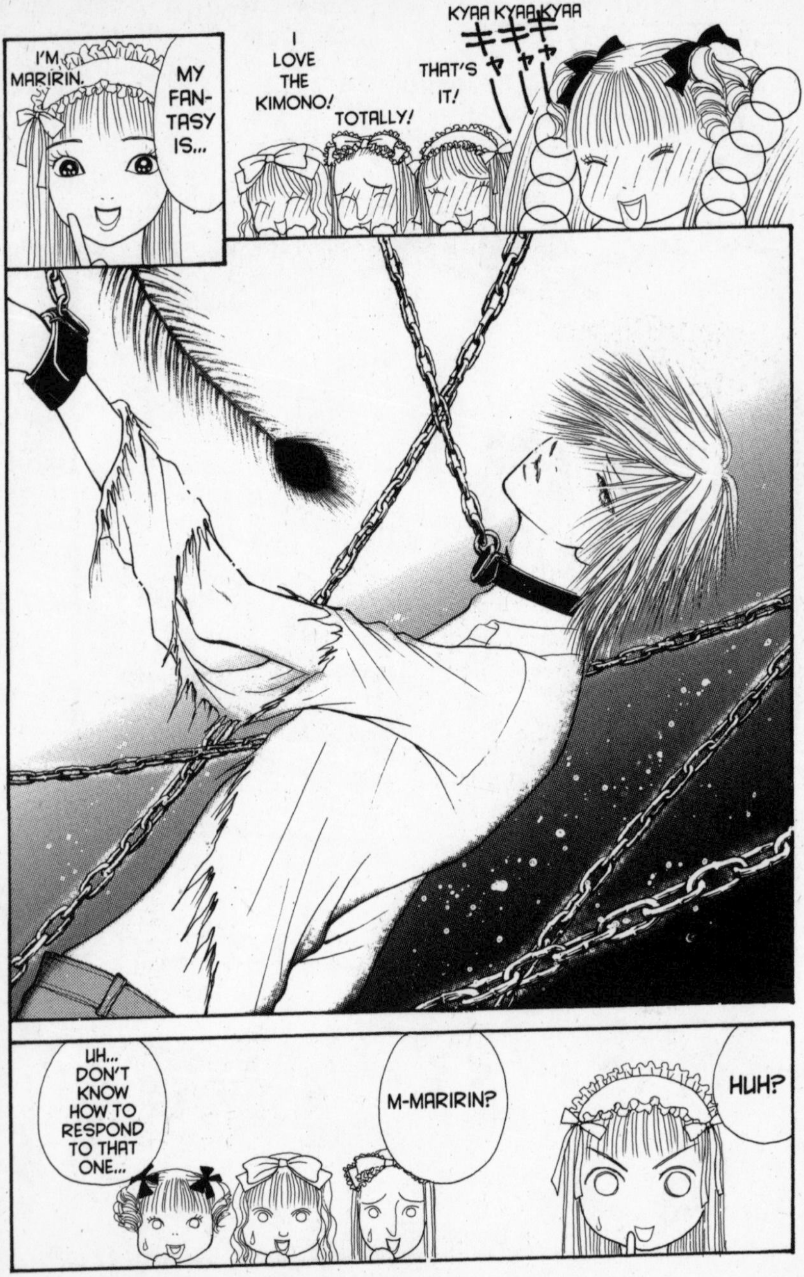
KYAA KYAA KYAA
キャー
キャー
キャー
THAT'S IT!
TOTALLY!
I LOVE THE KIMONO!
MY FAN-TASY IS...
I'M MARIRIN.
HUH?
M-MARIRIN?
UH... DON'T KNOW HOW TO RESPOND TO THAT ONE...

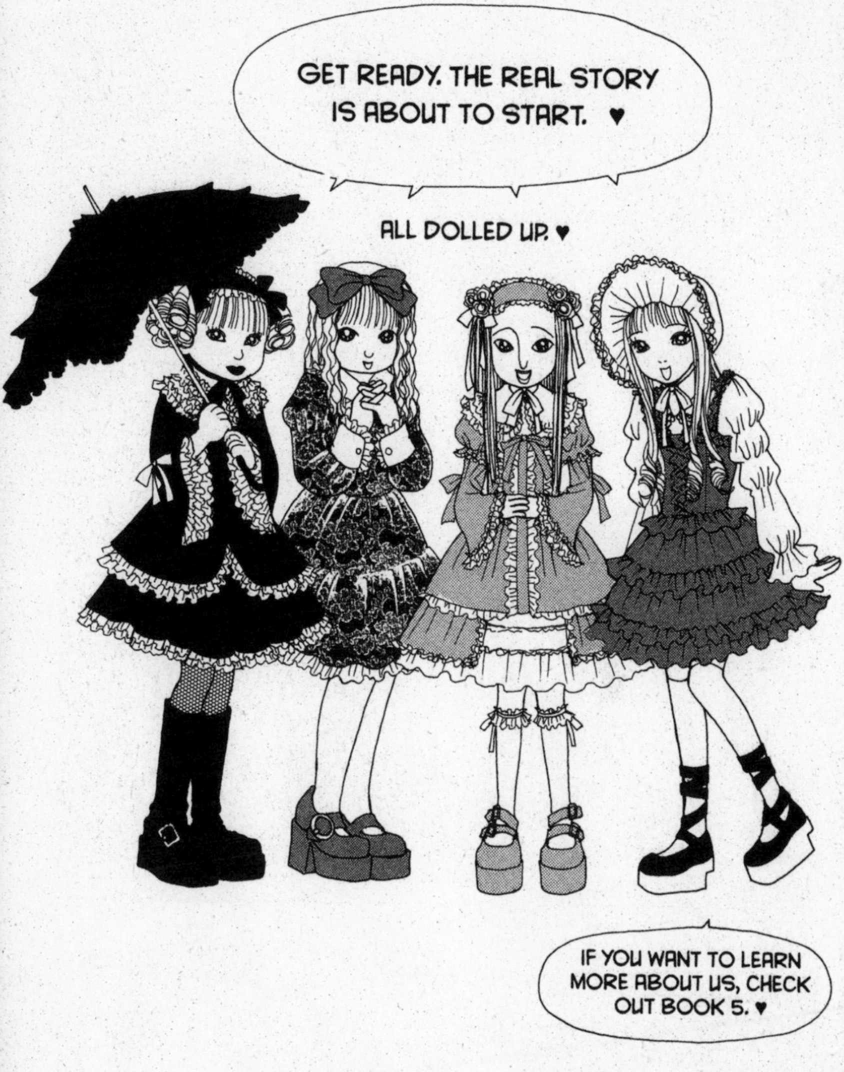
GET READY. THE REAL STORY IS ABOUT TO START. ♥
ALL DOLLED UP. ♥
IF YOU WANT TO LEARN MORE ABOUT US, CHECK OUT BOOK 5. ♥

WALLFLOWER'S BEAUTIFUL CAST OF CHARACTERS (?)

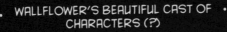

SUNAKO IS A DARK LONER WHO LOVES HORROR MOVIES. WHEN HER AUNT, THE LANDLADY OF A BOARDINGHOUSE, LEAVES TOWN WITH HER BOYFRIEND, SUNAKO IS FORCED TO LIVE WITH FOUR HANDSOME GUYS. SUNAKO'S AUNT MAKES A DEAL WITH THE BOYS, WHICH CAUSES NOTHING BUT HEADACHES FOR SUNAKO. "MAKE SUNAKO INTO A LADY, AND YOU CAN LIVE RENT FREE." AND NOW WITH TAKENAGA'S TRUE LOVE, NOI-CHAN, THE GORGEOUS BISHOJO...AND THAT BEAUTIFUL PRINCESS WHO IS FALLING FOR RANMARU, IT LOOKS LIKE SUNAKO'S WORLD IS GETTING EVEN MORE BLINDINGLY BRIGHT.

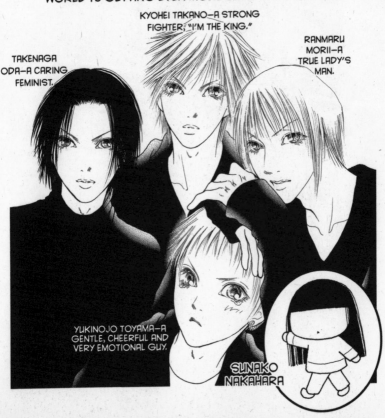

KYOHEI TAKANO—A STRONG FIGHTER, "I'M THE KING."
RANMARU MORII—A TRUE LADY'S MAN.
TAKENAGA ODA—A CARING FEMINIST.
YUKINOJO TOYAMA—A GENTLE, CHEERFUL AND VERY EMOTIONAL GUY.
SUNAKO NAKAHARA

CHAPTER 43 – BRAVO GIRLS!

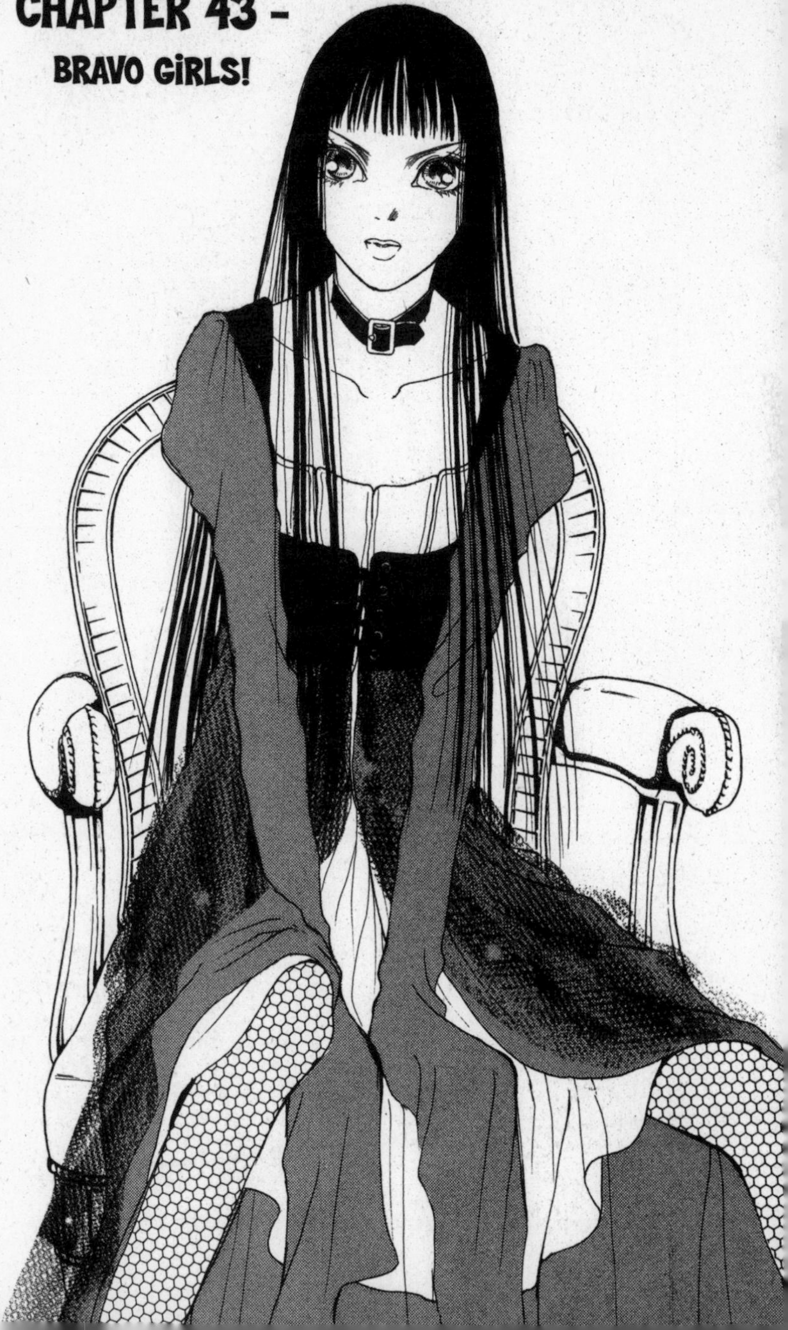

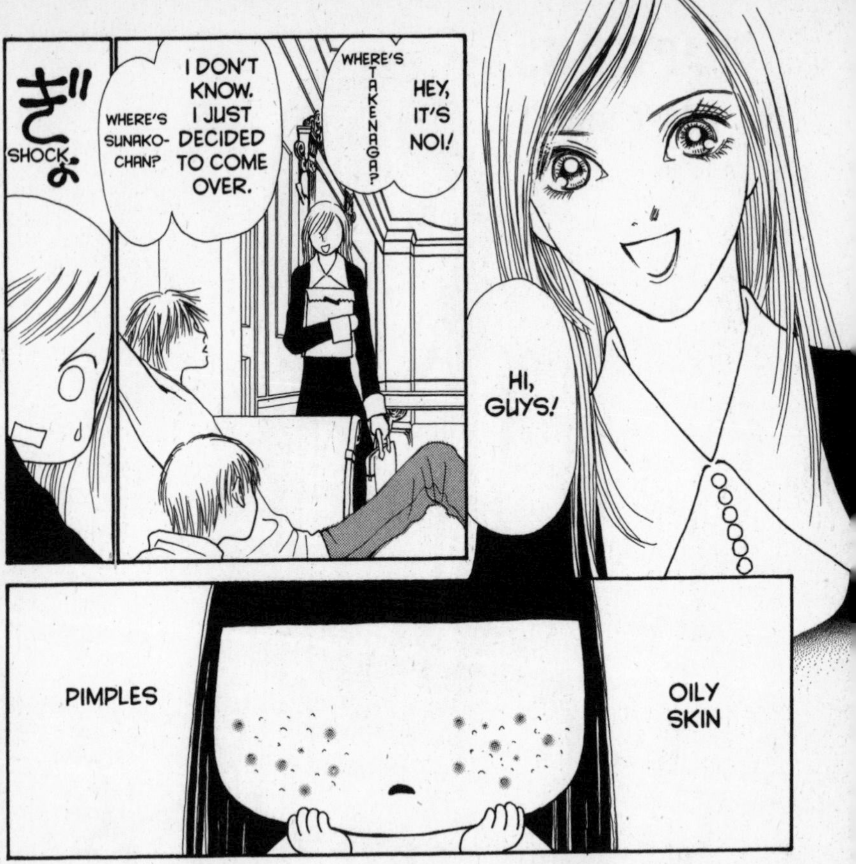
HI, GUYS!
HEY, IT'S NOI!
WHERE'S TAKENAGA?
I DON'T KNOW. I JUST DECIDED TO COME OVER.
WHERE'S SUNAKO-CHAN?
SHOCK
OILY SKIN
PIMPLES

BEHIND THE SCENES

THE STUFF IN THIS BOOK IS ACTUALLY FROM QUITE A WHILE AGO, BUT APPARENTLY, THAT'S THE WAY THE PUBLISHER WANTED IT. (I REALLY DON'T UNDERSTAND WHY, BUT...) RIGHT NOW I'M DOING A BIT BETTER, BUT BACK WHEN I WROTE THESE STORIES, I WAS HAVING A REALLY, REALLY HARD TIME. THE "BEHIND THE SCENES" SECTIONS ARE ALL REALLY NEGATIVE. DON'T PAY TOO MUCH ATTENTION TO THEM.

PLEASE JUST READ THEM AND THINK "ALL THAT SUFFERING AND THIS IS ALL THAT CAME OF IT?" I REMEMBER HAVING SUCH A HARD TIME WITH THIS STORY THAT I BURST INTO TEARS.

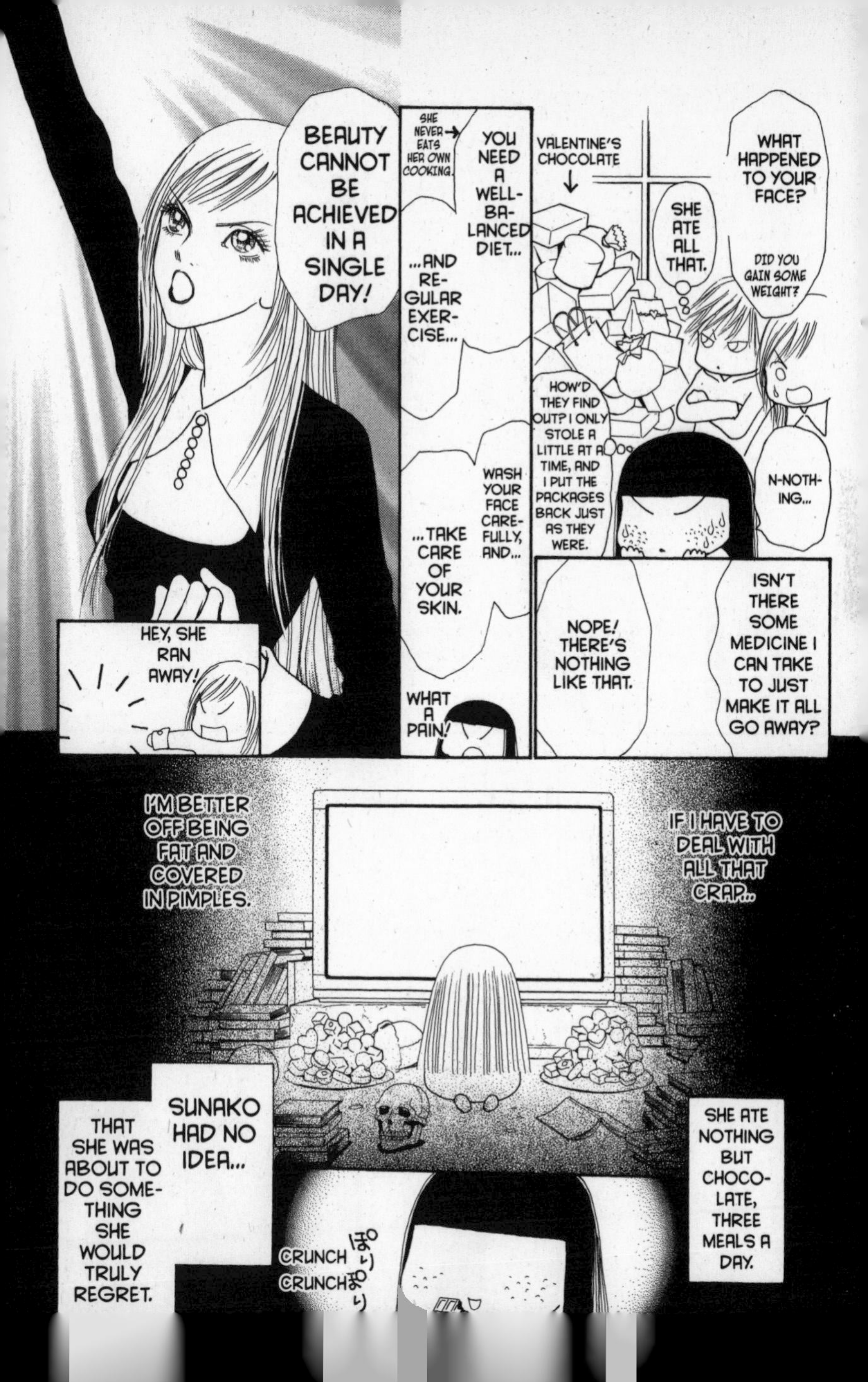
WHAT HAPPENED TO YOUR FACE?
DID YOU GAIN SOME WEIGHT?
SHE ATE ALL THAT.
VALENTINE'S CHOCOLATE
N-NOTHING...
HOW'D THEY FIND OUT? I ONLY STOLE A LITTLE AT A TIME, AND I PUT THE PACKAGES BACK JUST AS THEY WERE.
ISN'T THERE SOME MEDICINE I CAN TAKE TO JUST MAKE IT ALL GO AWAY?
NOPE! THERE'S NOTHING LIKE THAT.
YOU NEED A WELL-BALANCED DIET...
SHE NEVER EATS HER OWN COOKING.
...AND REGULAR EXERCISE...
WASH YOUR FACE CAREFULLY, AND...
...TAKE CARE OF YOUR SKIN.
WHAT A PAIN!
BEAUTY CANNOT BE ACHIEVED IN A SINGLE DAY!
HEY, SHE RAN AWAY!
IF I HAVE TO DEAL WITH ALL THAT CRAP...
I'M BETTER OFF BEING FAT AND COVERED IN PIMPLES.
SHE ATE NOTHING BUT CHOCOLATE, THREE MEALS A DAY.
ぽりぽり
CRUNCH CRUNCH
SUNAKO HAD NO IDEA...
THAT SHE WAS ABOUT TO DO SOMETHING SHE WOULD TRULY REGRET.

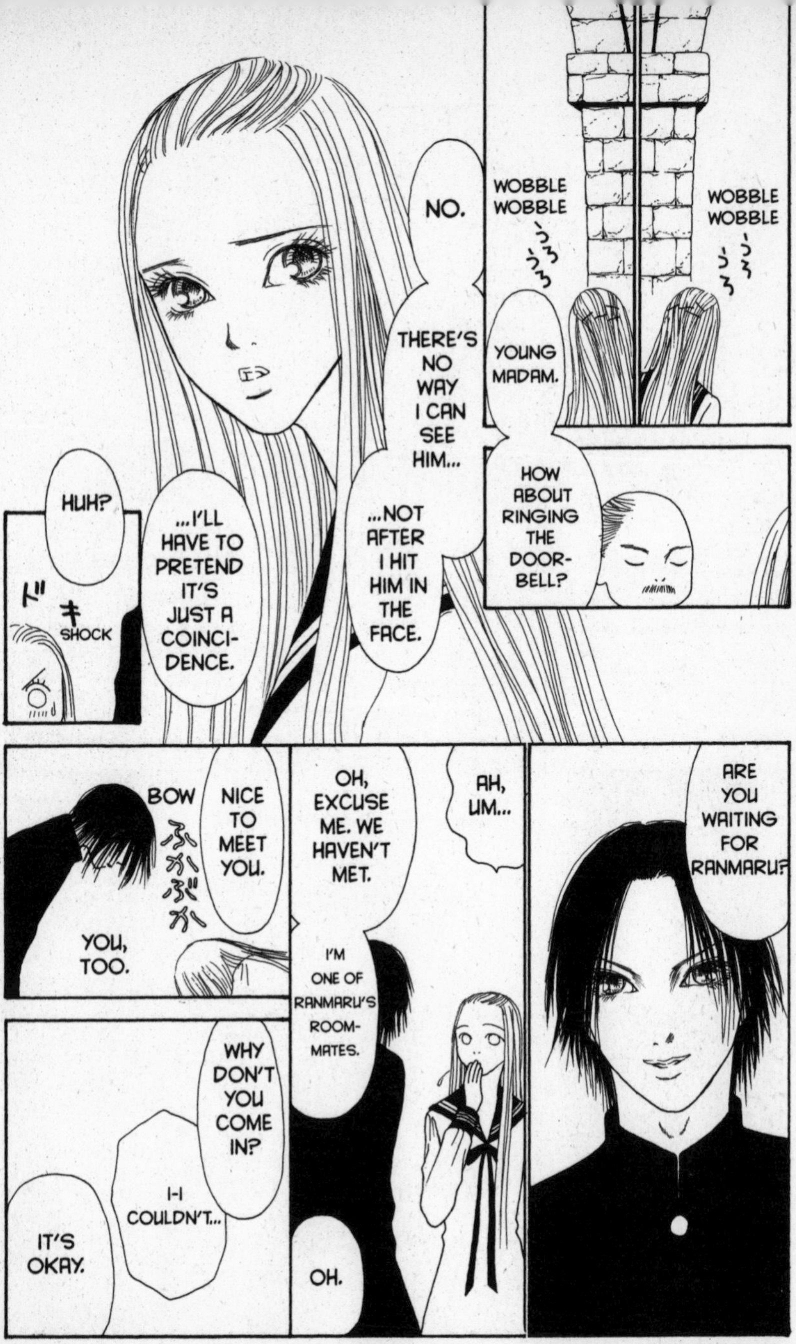
WOBBLE WOBBLE
うろうろ
WOBBLE WOBBLE
うろうろ
YOUNG MADAM.
HOW ABOUT RINGING THE DOORBELL?
NO.
THERE'S NO WAY I CAN SEE HIM...
...NOT AFTER I HIT HIM IN THE FACE.
...I'LL HAVE TO PRETEND IT'S JUST A COINCIDENCE.
HUH?
ドキ
SHOCK
ARE YOU WAITING FOR RANMARU?
AH, UM...
OH, EXCUSE ME. WE HAVEN'T MET.
I'M ONE OF RANMARU'S ROOMMATES.
OH.
NICE TO MEET YOU.
BOW
ふかぶか
YOU, TOO.
WHY DON'T YOU COME IN?
I-I COULDN'T...
IT'S OKAY.

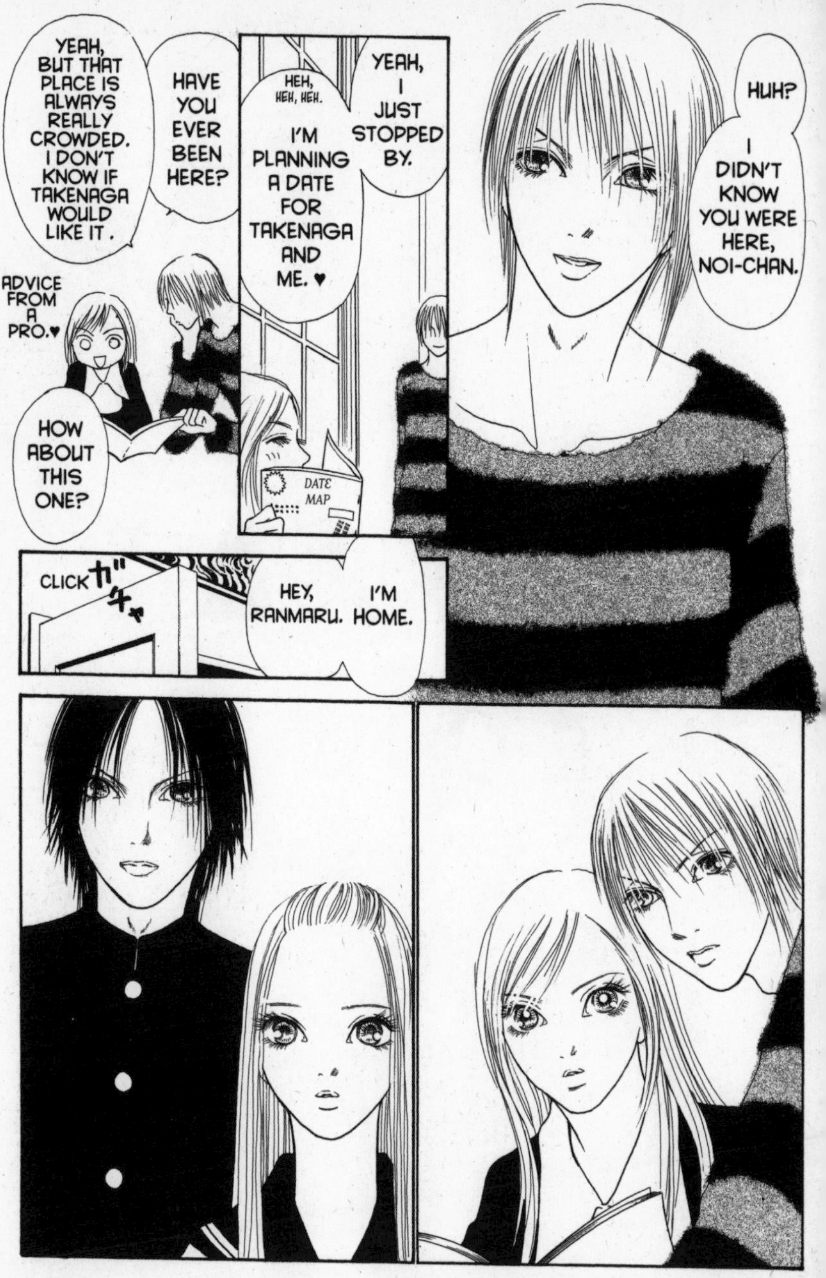
HUH?
I DIDN'T KNOW YOU WERE HERE, NOI-CHAN.
YEAH, I JUST STOPPED BY.
HEH, HEH, HEH.
I'M PLANNING A DATE FOR TAKENAGA AND ME. ♥
DATE MAP
HAVE YOU EVER BEEN HERE?
YEAH, BUT THAT PLACE IS ALWAYS REALLY CROWDED. I DON'T KNOW IF TAKENAGA WOULD LIKE IT.
ADVICE FROM A PRO.♥
HOW ABOUT THIS ONE?
HEY, RANMARU. I'M HOME.
CLICK ガチャ

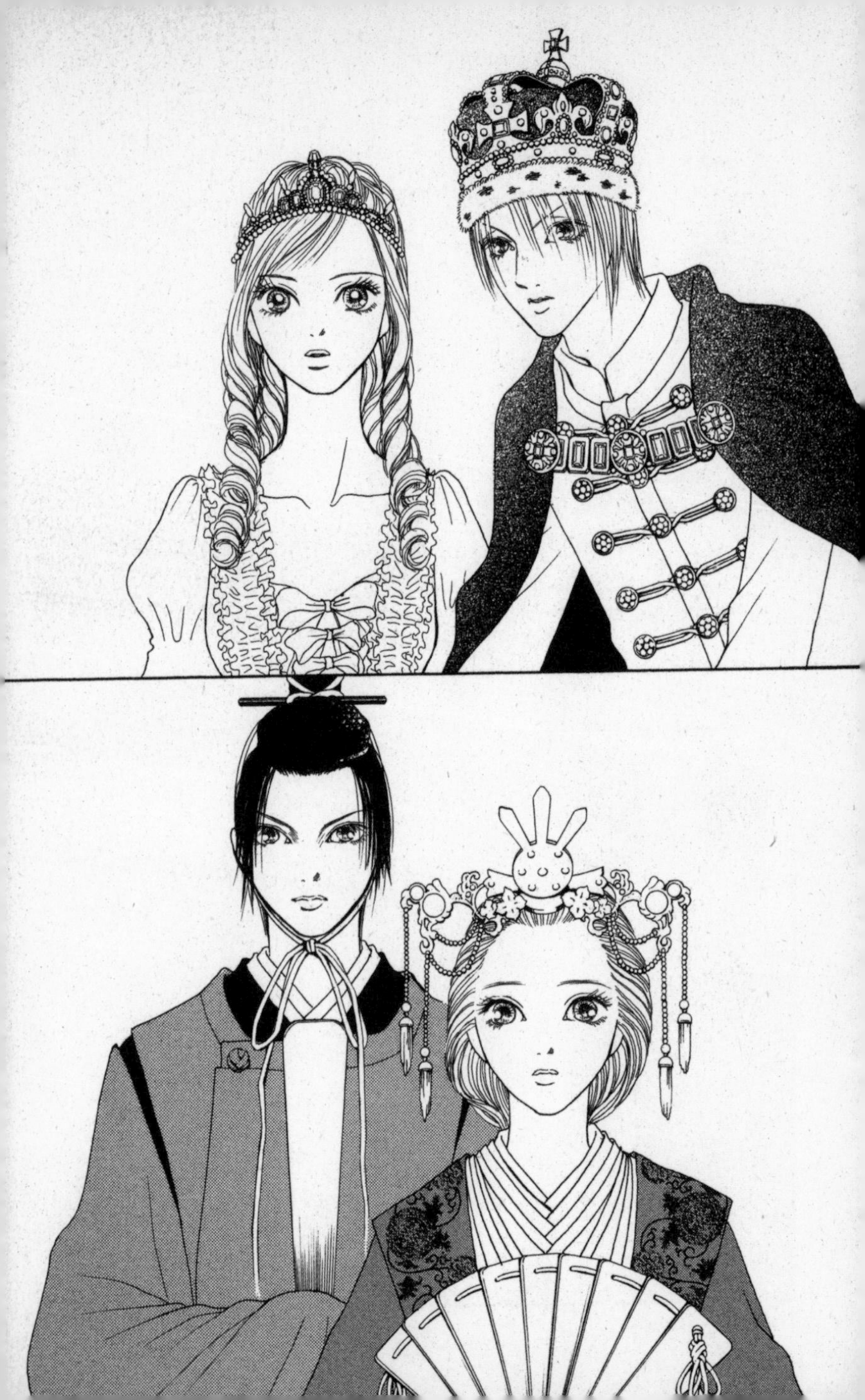

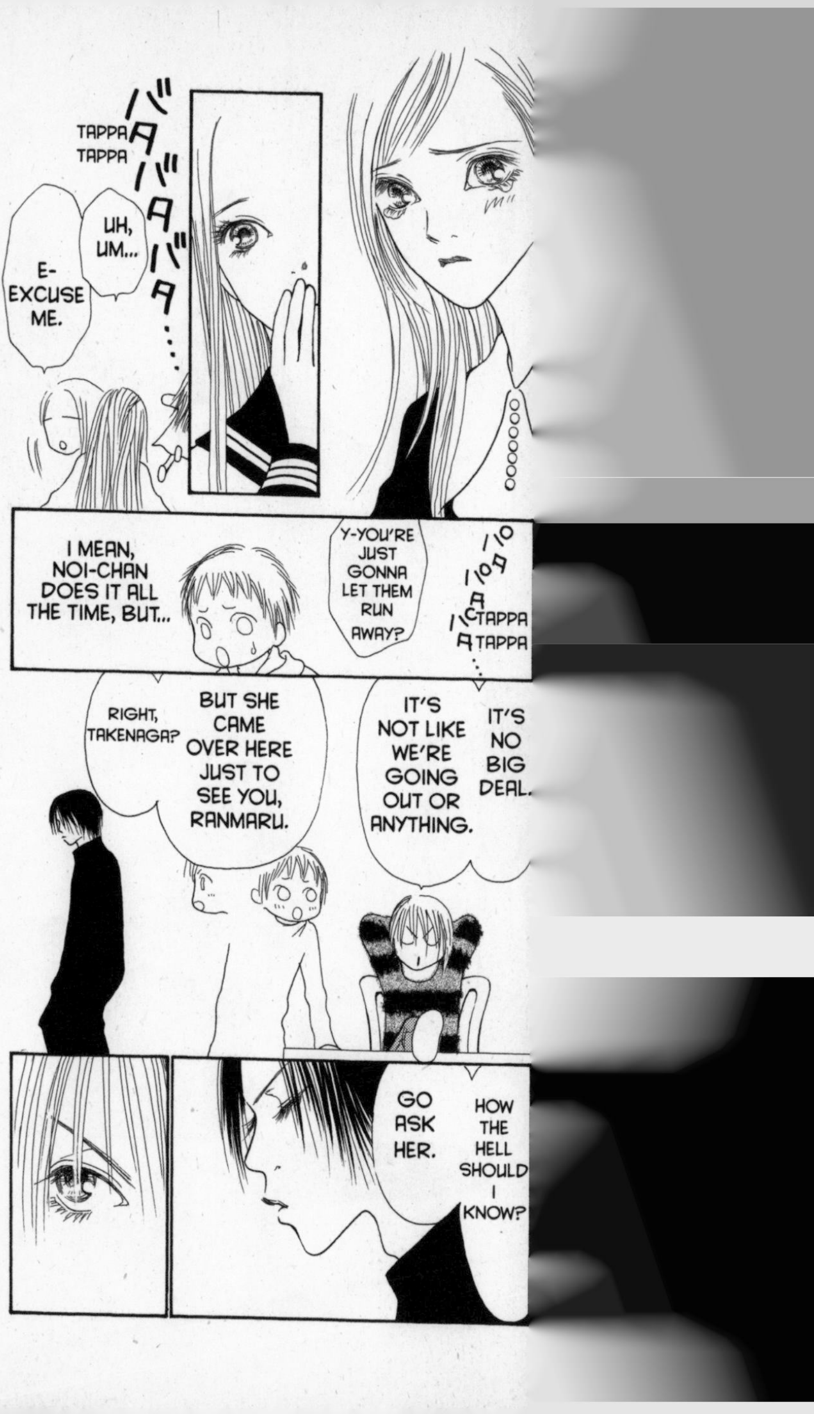
TAPPA TAPPA
バタバタバタ...
UH, UM...
E-EXCUSE ME.
Y-YOU'RE JUST GONNA LET THEM RUN AWAY?
パタパタ...
TAPPA TAPPA
I MEAN, NOI-CHAN DOES IT ALL THE TIME, BUT...
IT'S NO BIG DEAL.
IT'S NOT LIKE WE'RE GOING OUT OR ANYTHING.
BUT SHE CAME OVER HERE JUST TO SEE YOU, RANMARU.
RIGHT, TAKENAGA?
HOW THE HELL SHOULD I KNOW?
GO ASK HER.

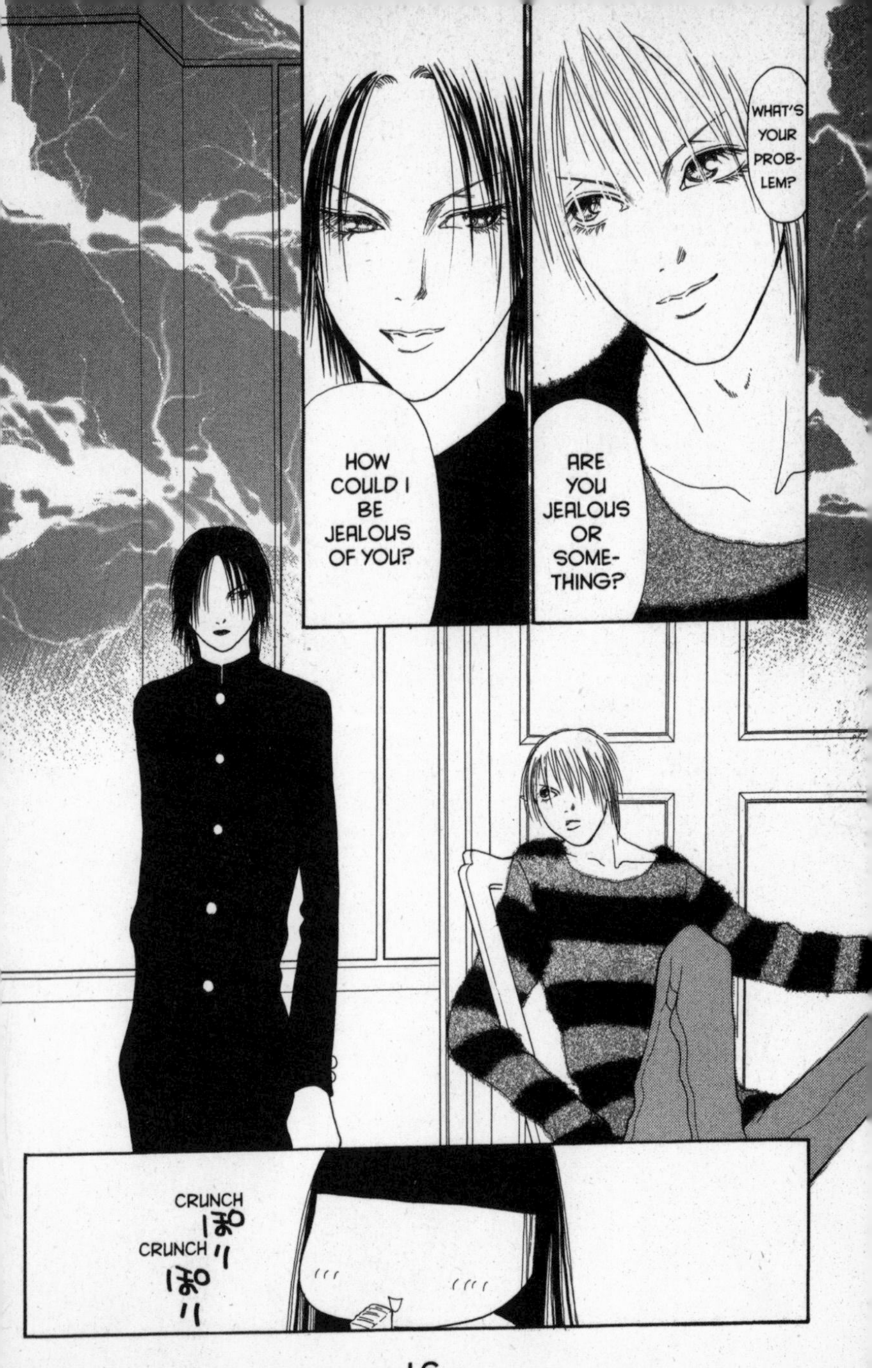

WHAT'S YOUR PROBLEM?
ARE YOU JEALOUS OR SOMETHING?
HOW COULD I BE JEALOUS OF YOU?
CRUNCH ぽり
CRUNCH ぽり

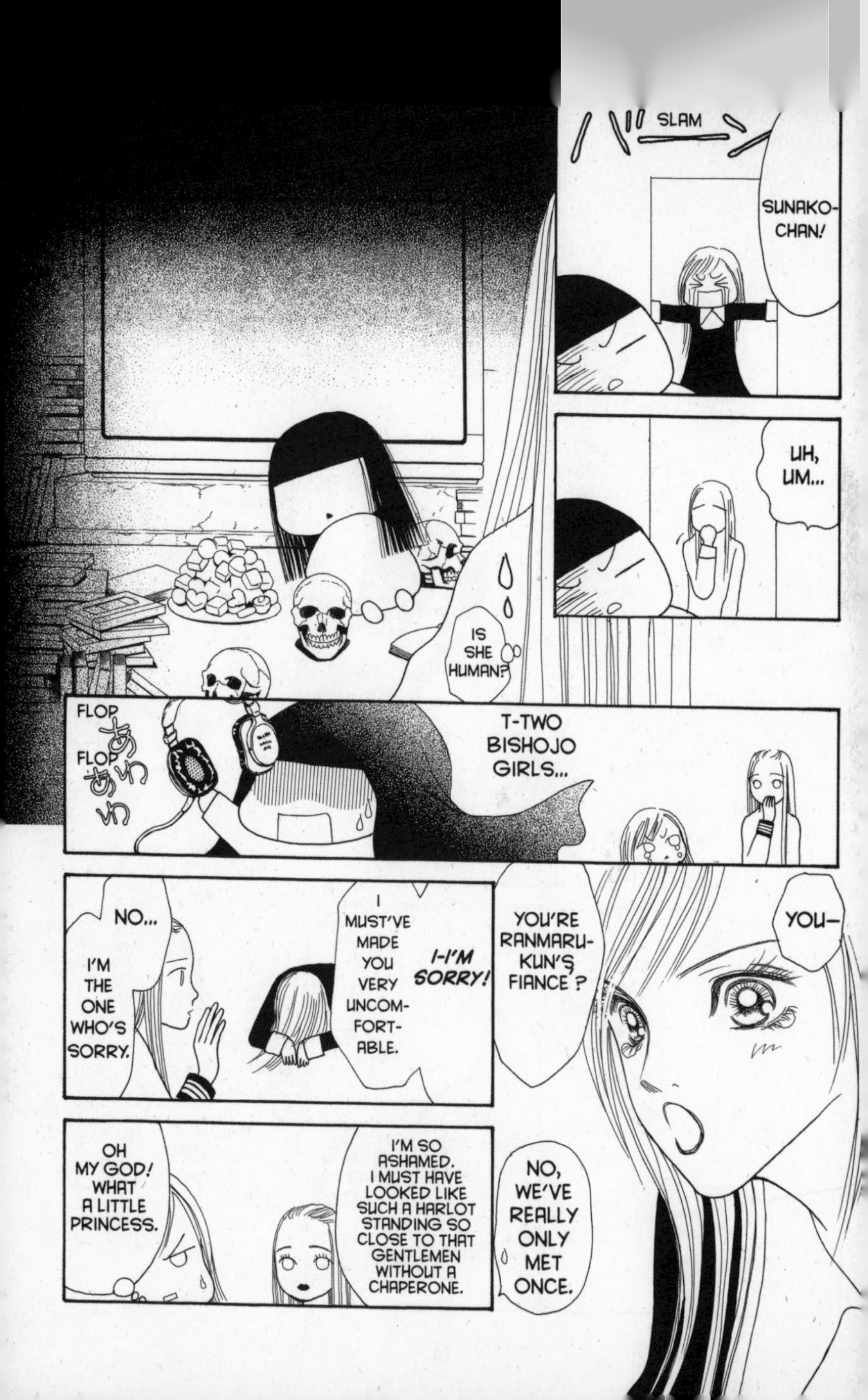

SLAM
SUNAKO-CHAN!
UH, UM...
IS SHE HUMAN?
T-TWO BISHOJO GIRLS...
FLOP FLOP
あわあわ
YOU—
YOU'RE RANMARU-KUN'S FIANCE?
NO, WE'VE REALLY ONLY MET ONCE.
I-I'M SORRY!
I MUST'VE MADE YOU VERY UNCOMFORTABLE.
NO... I'M THE ONE WHO'S SORRY.
I'M SO ASHAMED. I MUST HAVE LOOKED LIKE SUCH A HARLOT STANDING SO CLOSE TO THAT GENTLEMEN WITHOUT A CHAPERONE.
OH MY GOD! WHAT A LITTLE PRINCESS.

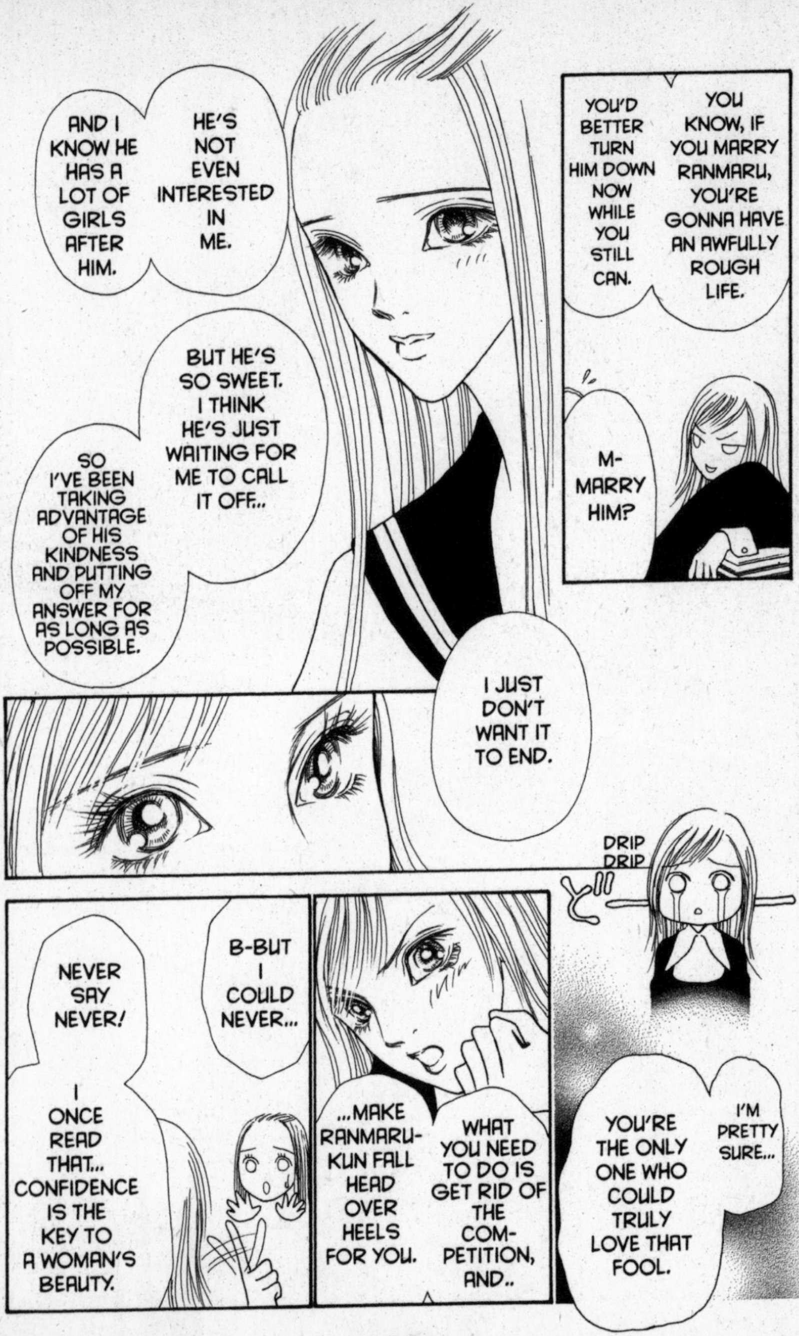
YOU KNOW, IF YOU MARRY RANMARU, YOU'RE GONNA HAVE AN AWFULLY ROUGH LIFE.
YOU'D BETTER TURN HIM DOWN NOW WHILE YOU STILL CAN.
M-MARRY HIM?
HE'S NOT EVEN INTERESTED IN ME.
AND I KNOW HE HAS A LOT OF GIRLS AFTER HIM.
BUT HE'S SO SWEET. I THINK HE'S JUST WAITING FOR ME TO CALL IT OFF...
SO I'VE BEEN TAKING ADVANTAGE OF HIS KINDNESS AND PUTTING OFF MY ANSWER FOR AS LONG AS POSSIBLE.
I JUST DON'T WANT IT TO END.
DRIP DRIP
I'M PRETTY SURE...
YOU'RE THE ONLY ONE WHO COULD TRULY LOVE THAT FOOL.
WHAT YOU NEED TO DO IS GET RID OF THE COM-PETITION, AND..
...MAKE RANMARU-KUN FALL HEAD OVER HEELS FOR YOU.
B-BUT I COULD NEVER...
NEVER SAY NEVER!
I ONCE READ THAT... CONFIDENCE IS THE KEY TO A WOMAN'S BEAUTY.

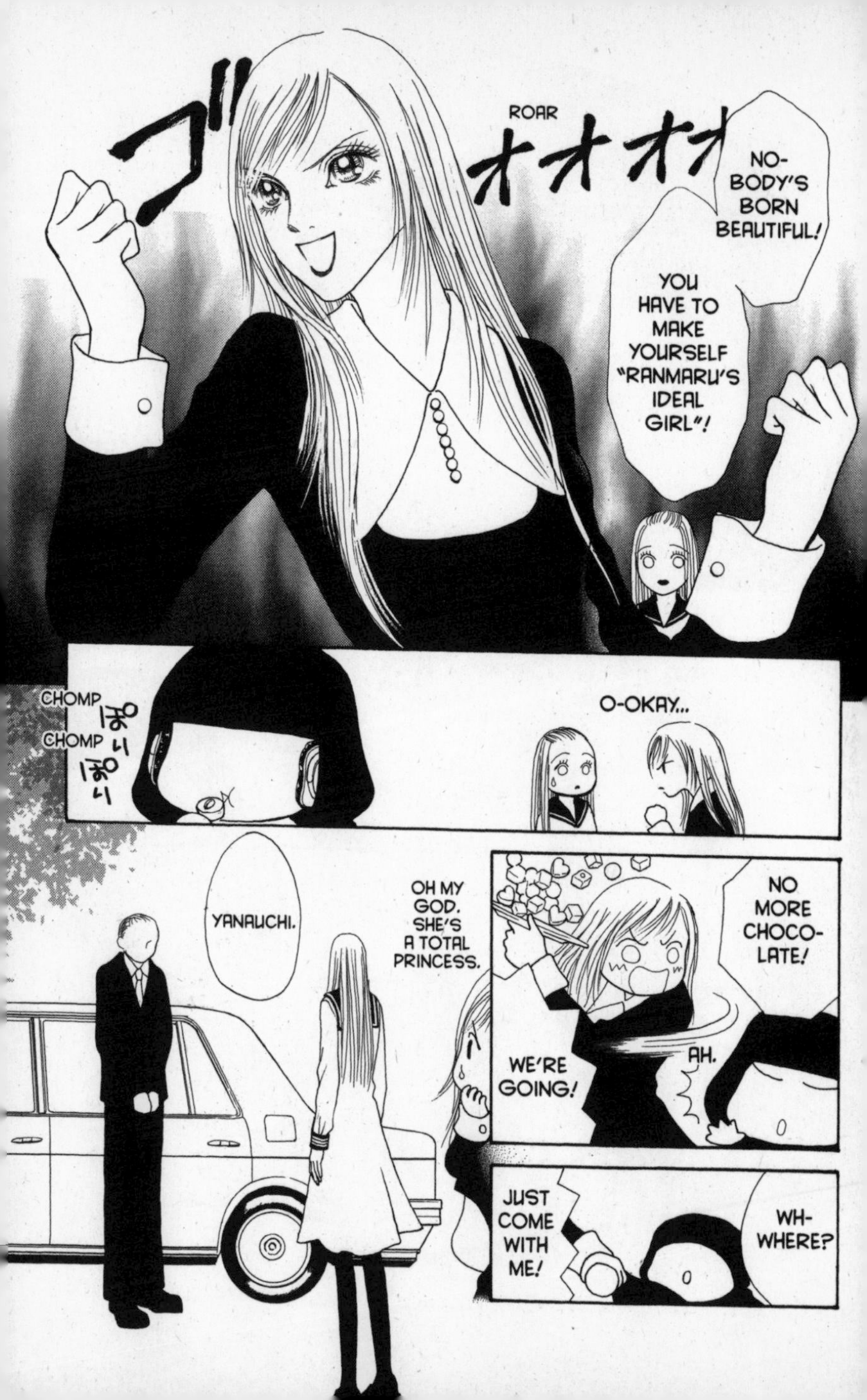
NO-BODY'S BORN BEAUTIFUL!
YOU HAVE TO MAKE YOURSELF "RANMARU'S IDEAL GIRL"!
ROAR
ゴオオオオ
O-OKAY...
CHOMP CHOMP
ぽりぽり
NO MORE CHOCO-LATE!
AH.
WE'RE GOING!
WH-WHERE?
JUST COME WITH ME!
OH MY GOD. SHE'S A TOTAL PRINCESS.
YANAUCHI.

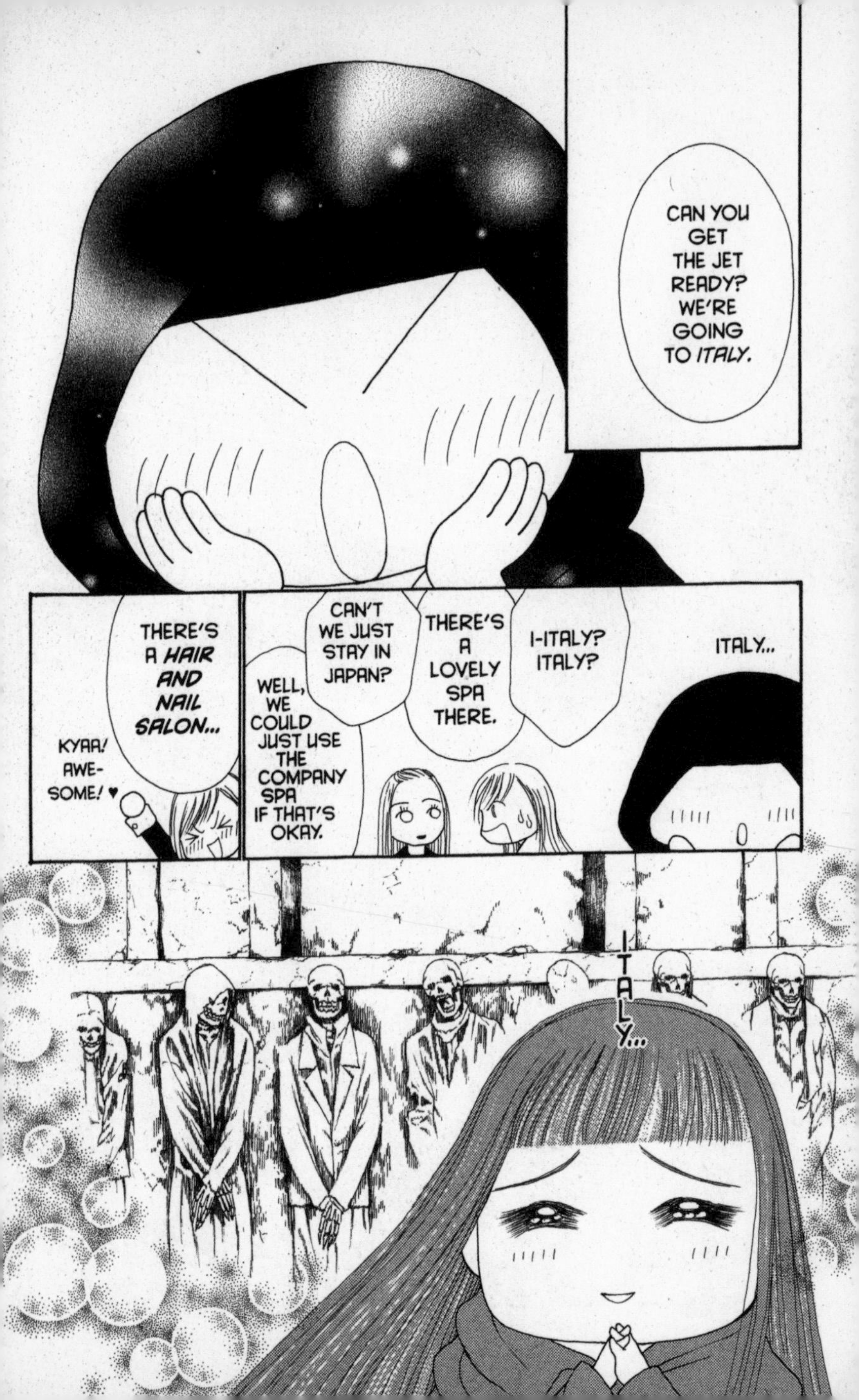
CAN YOU GET THE JET READY? WE'RE GOING TO *ITALY.*
ITALY...
I-ITALY? ITALY?
THERE'S A LOVELY SPA THERE.
CAN'T WE JUST STAY IN JAPAN?
WELL, WE COULD JUST USE THE COMPANY SPA IF THAT'S OKAY.
THERE'S A ***HAIR AND NAIL SALON...***
KYAA! AWE-SOME! ♥
ITALY...

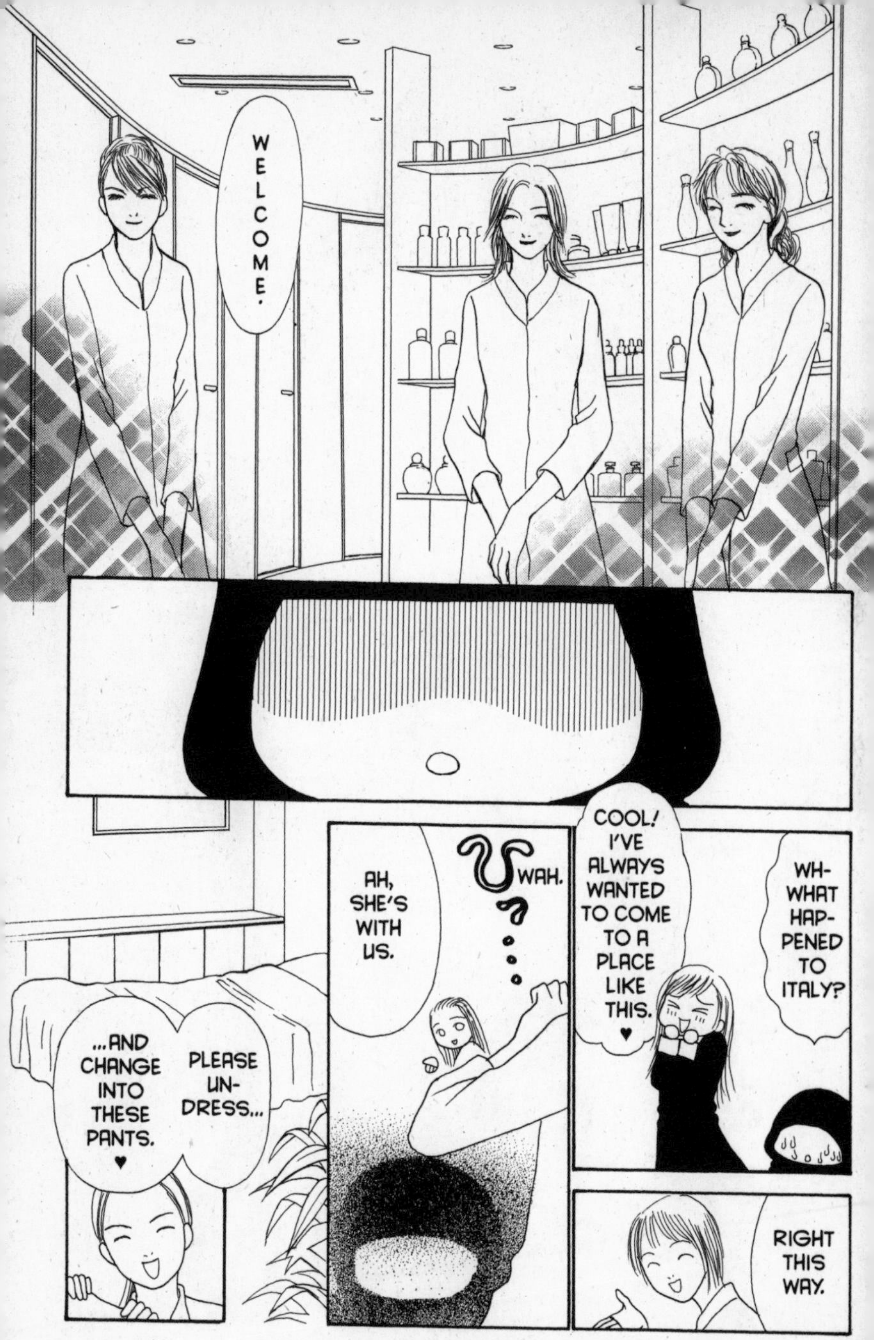
WELCOME.
WH-WHAT HAPPENED TO ITALY?
COOL! I'VE ALWAYS WANTED TO COME TO A PLACE LIKE THIS. ♥
RIGHT THIS WAY.
UWAH...
AH, SHE'S WITH US.
PLEASE UNDRESS...
...AND CHANGE INTO THESE PANTS. ♥

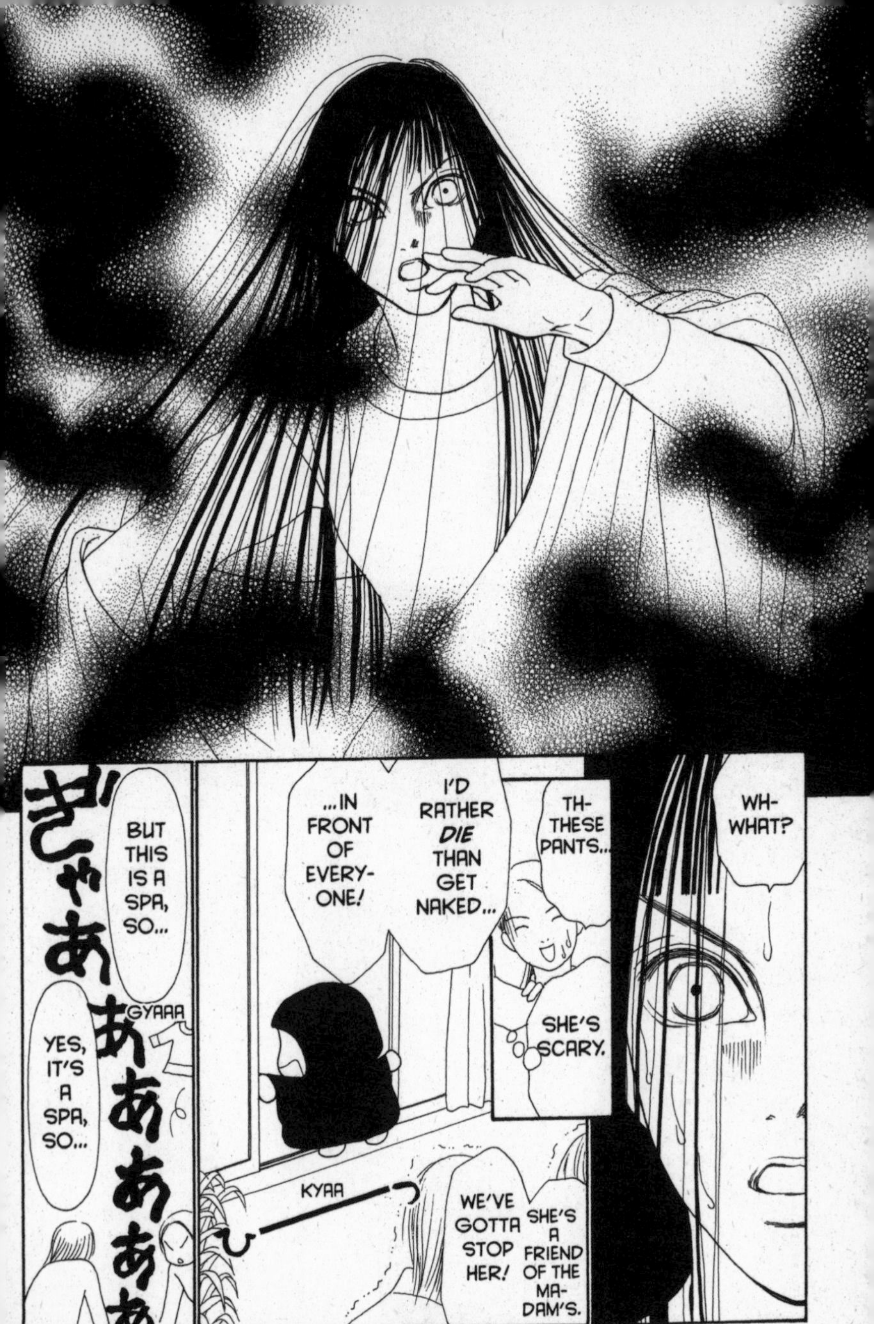
WH- WHAT?
TH- THESE PANTS...
I'D RATHER *DIE* THAN GET NAKED...
...IN FRONT OF EVERY-ONE!
SHE'S SCARY.
SHE'S A FRIEND OF THE MA-DAM'S.
WE'VE GOTTA STOP HER!
KYAA
ぎゃあああああ
BUT THIS IS A SPA, SO...
GYAAA
YES, IT'S A SPA, SO...

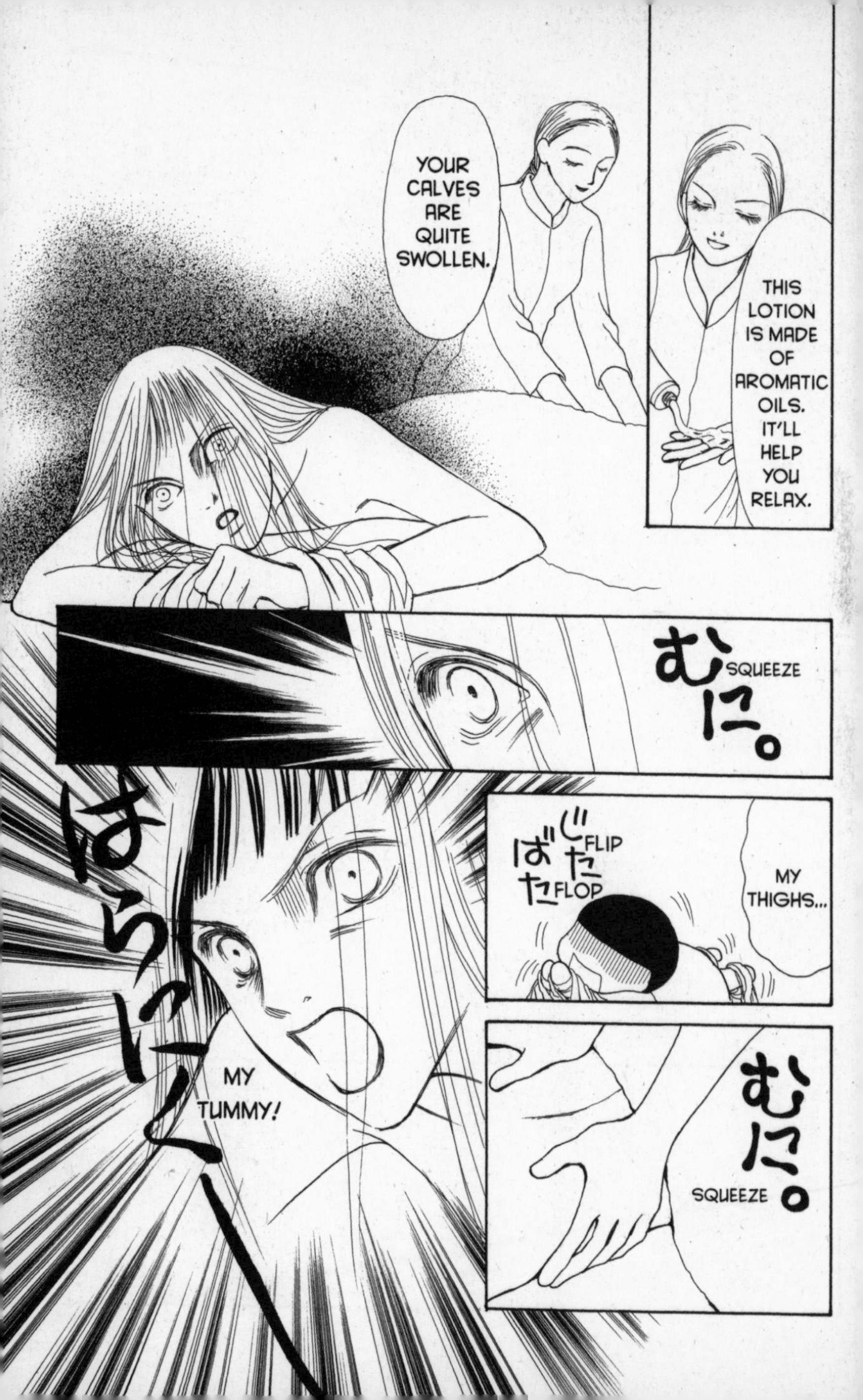
THIS LOTION IS MADE OF AROMATIC OILS. IT'LL HELP YOU RELAX.
YOUR CALVES ARE QUITE SWOLLEN.
むに。
SQUEEZE
MY THIGHS...
じたばた
FLIP FLOP
むに。
SQUEEZE
はらっにくー
MY TUMMY!

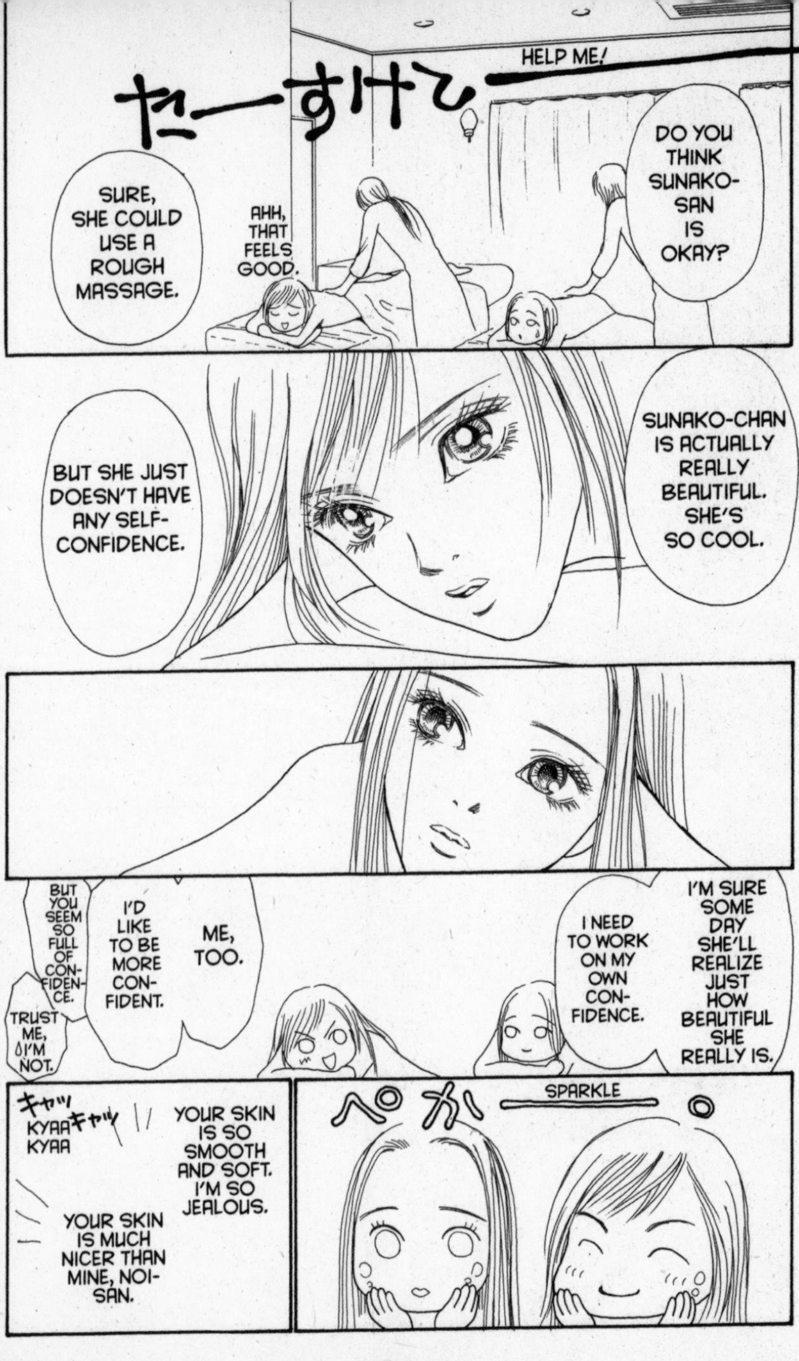
たーすけて
HELP ME!
DO YOU THINK SUNAKO-SAN IS OKAY?
AHH, THAT FEELS GOOD.
SURE, SHE COULD USE A ROUGH MASSAGE.
SUNAKO-CHAN IS ACTUALLY REALLY BEAUTIFUL. SHE'S SO COOL.
BUT SHE JUST DOESN'T HAVE ANY SELF-CONFIDENCE.
I'M SURE SOME DAY SHE'LL REALIZE JUST HOW BEAUTIFUL SHE REALLY IS.
I NEED TO WORK ON MY OWN CONFIDENCE.
ME, TOO.
I'D LIKE TO BE MORE CONFIDENT.
BUT YOU SEEM SO FULL OF CONFIDENCE.
TRUST ME, I'M NOT.
ぺかー
SPARKLE
YOUR SKIN IS SO SMOOTH AND SOFT. I'M SO JEALOUS.
キャッキャッ
KYAA KYAA
YOUR SKIN IS MUCH NICER THAN MINE, NOI-SAN.

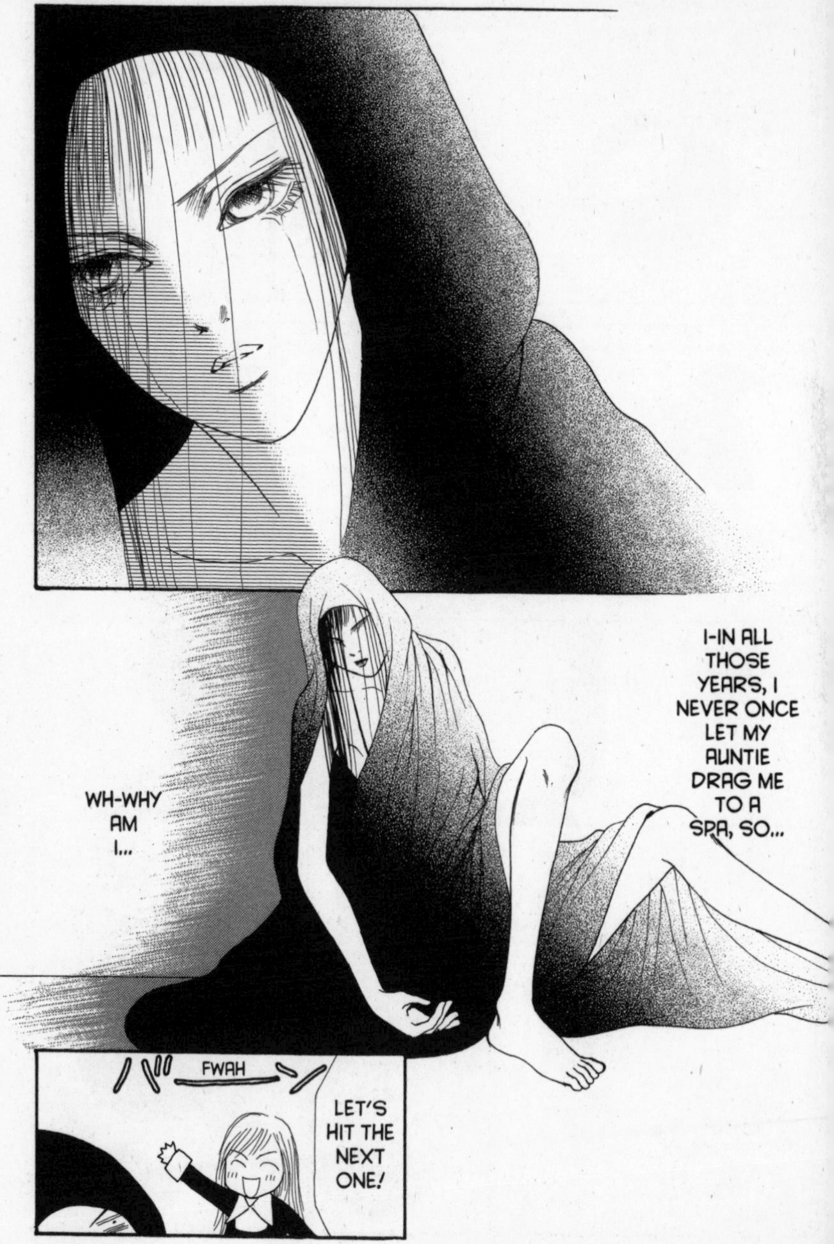
I-IN ALL THOSE YEARS, I NEVER ONCE LET MY AUNTIE DRAG ME TO A SPA, SO...
WH-WHY AM I...
FWAH
LET'S HIT THE NEXT ONE!

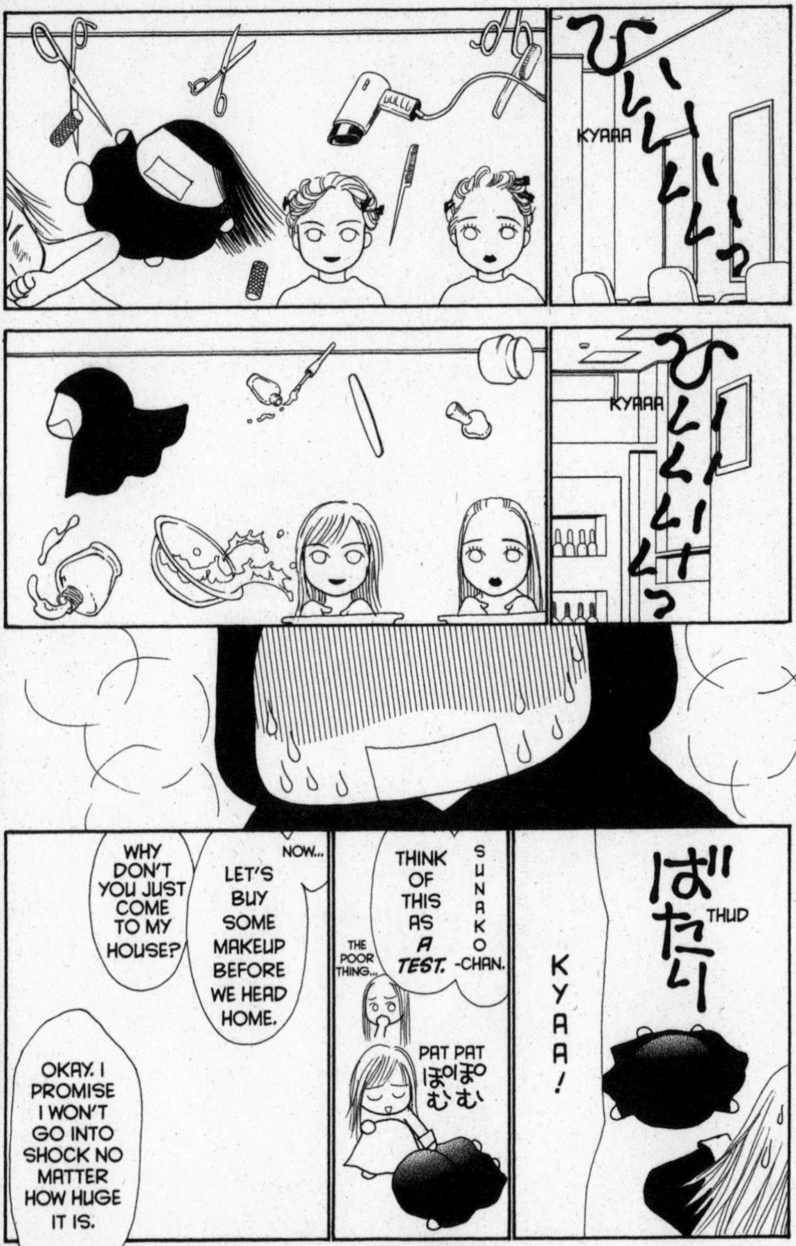
ひぃぃぃっ
KYAAA
ひぃぃぃぃっ
KYAAA
ばたり
THUD
KYAAA!
SUNAKO-CHAN.
THINK OF THIS AS *A TEST.*
THE POOR THING...
PAT PAT
ぽむぽむ
NOW...
LET'S BUY SOME MAKEUP BEFORE WE HEAD HOME.
WHY DON'T YOU JUST COME TO MY HOUSE?
OKAY. I PROMISE I WON'T GO INTO SHOCK NO MATTER HOW HUGE IT IS.

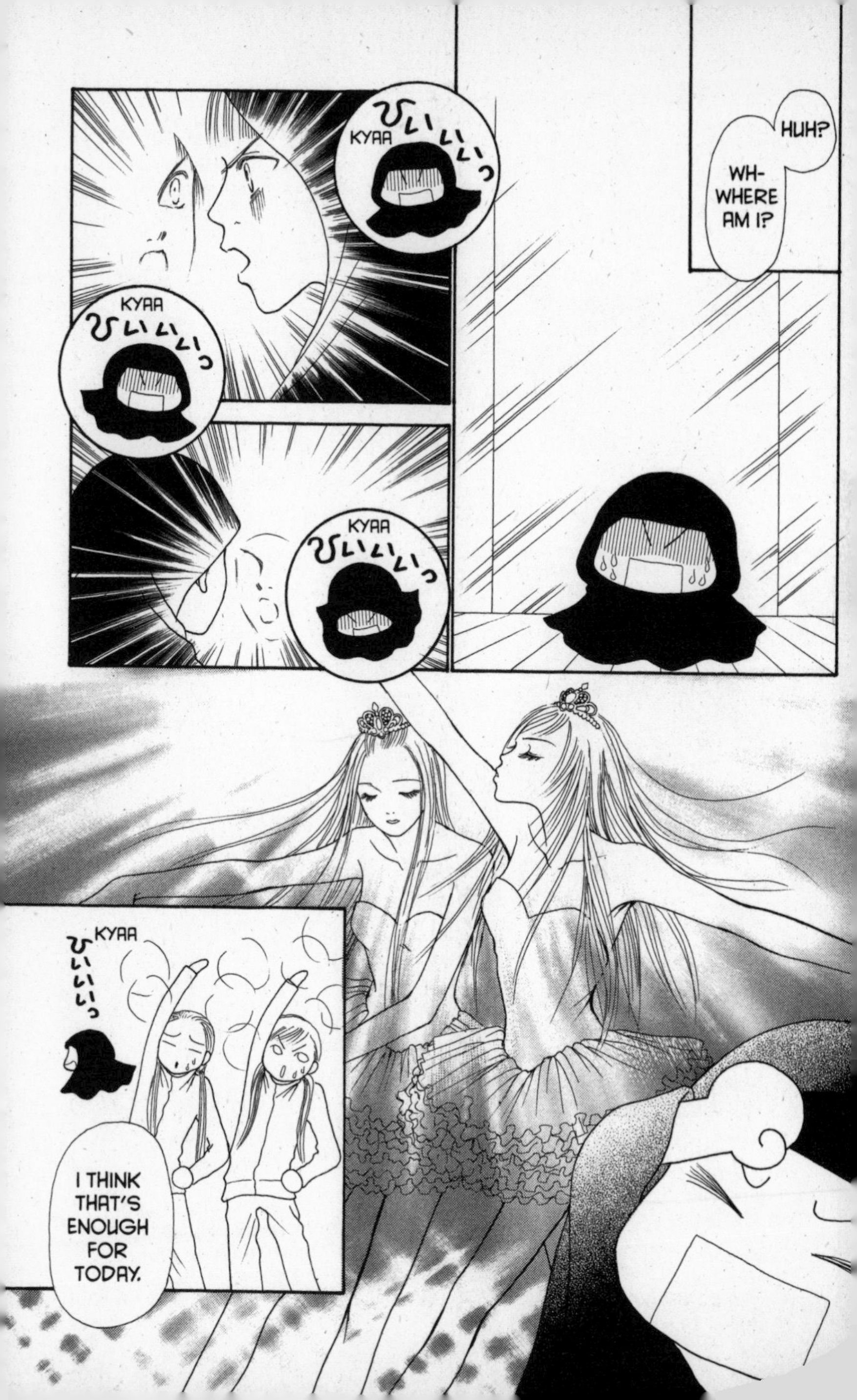
HUH?
WH-WHERE AM I?
KYAA
ひいいいっ
KYAA
ひいいいっ
KYAA
ひいいいっ
KYAA
ひいいいっ
I THINK THAT'S ENOUGH FOR TODAY.

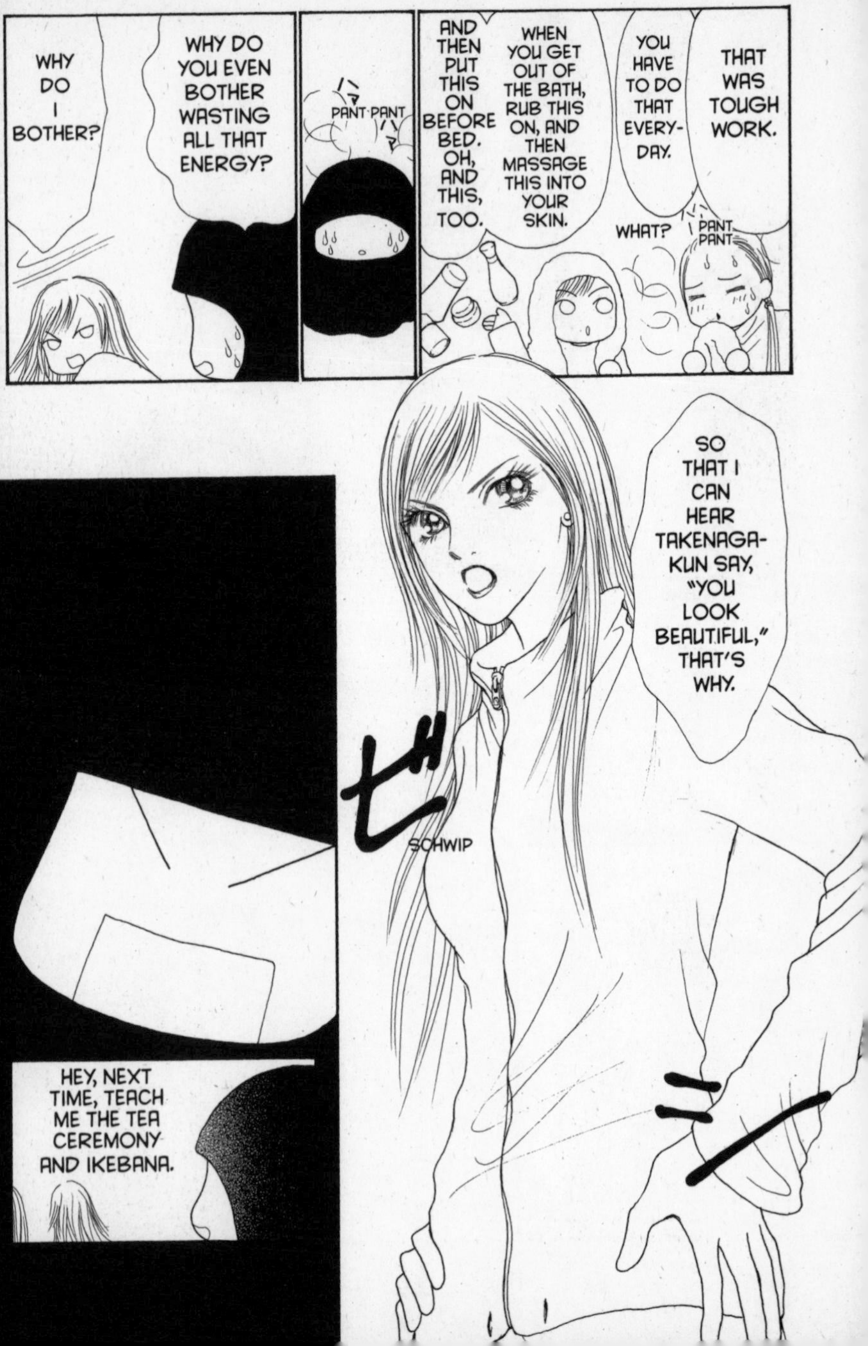
THAT WAS TOUGH WORK.
YOU HAVE TO DO THAT EVERY-DAY.
WHEN YOU GET OUT OF THE BATH, RUB THIS ON, AND THEN MASSAGE THIS INTO YOUR SKIN.
AND THEN PUT THIS ON BEFORE BED. OH, AND THIS, TOO.
PANT PANT
WHAT?
PANT PANT
WHY DO YOU EVEN BOTHER WASTING ALL THAT ENERGY?
WHY DO I BOTHER?
SO THAT I CAN HEAR TAKENAGA-KUN SAY, "YOU LOOK BEAUTIFUL," THAT'S WHY.
SCHWIP
HEY, NEXT TIME, TEACH ME THE TEA CEREMONY AND IKEBANA.

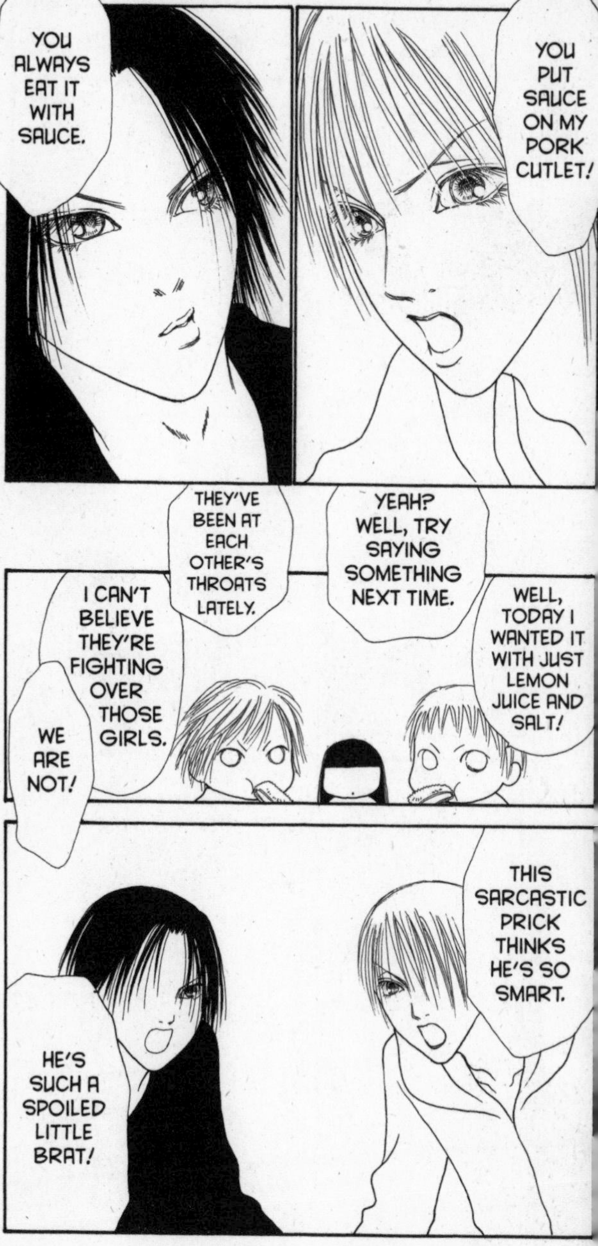
YOU PUT SAUCE ON MY PORK CUTLET!
YOU ALWAYS EAT IT WITH SAUCE.
WELL, TODAY I WANTED IT WITH JUST LEMON JUICE AND SALT!
YEAH? WELL, TRY SAYING SOMETHING NEXT TIME.
THEY'VE BEEN AT EACH OTHER'S THROATS LATELY.
I CAN'T BELIEVE THEY'RE FIGHTING OVER THOSE GIRLS.
WE ARE NOT!
THIS SARCASTIC PRICK THINKS HE'S SO SMART.
HE'S SUCH A SPOILED LITTLE BRAT!

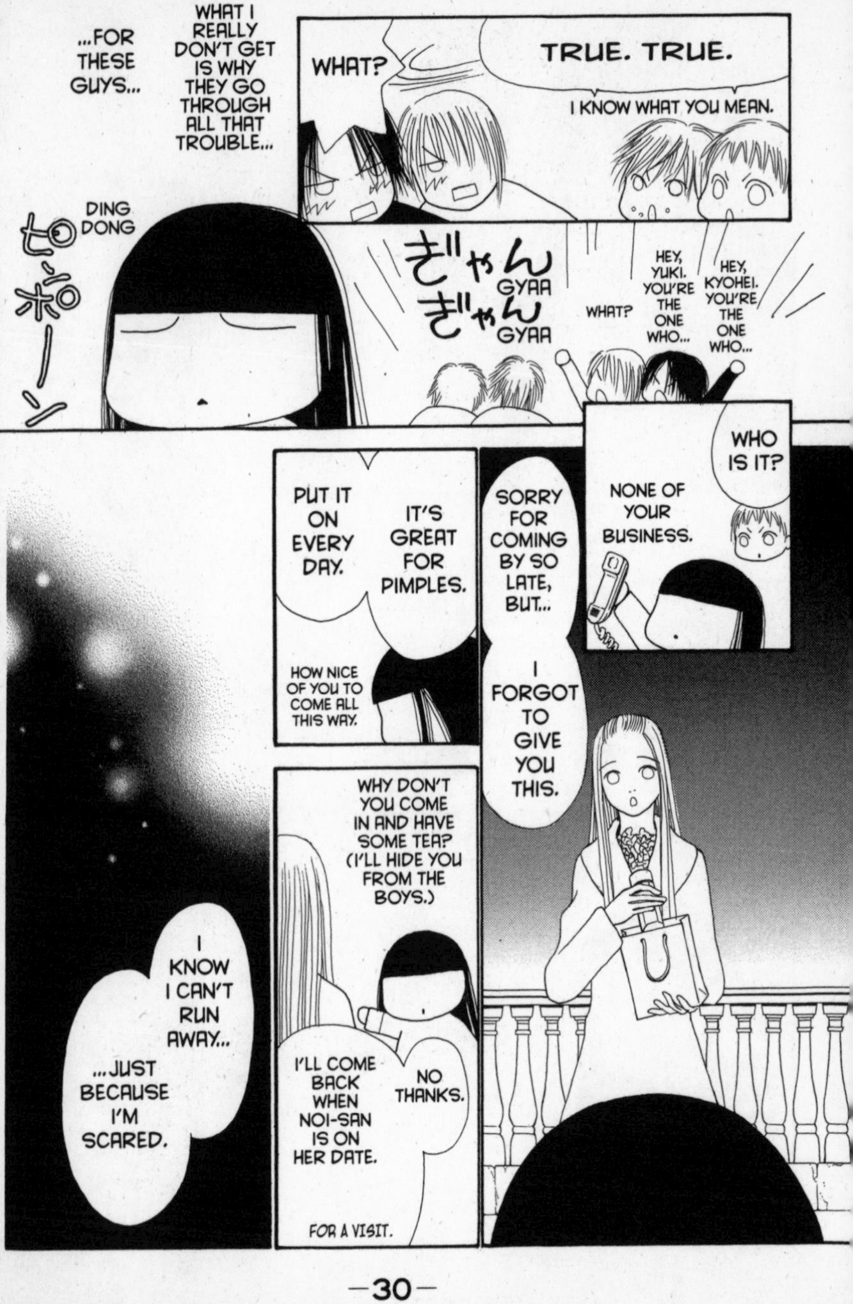
TRUE. TRUE.
I KNOW WHAT YOU MEAN.
WHAT?
WHAT I REALLY DON'T GET IS WHY THEY GO THROUGH ALL THAT TROUBLE...
...FOR THESE GUYS...
HEY, KYOHEI. YOU'RE THE ONE WHO...
HEY, YUKI. YOU'RE THE ONE WHO...
WHAT?
ぎゃんぎゃん
GYAA GYAA
ピンポーン
DING DONG
WHO IS IT?
NONE OF YOUR BUSINESS.
SORRY FOR COMING BY SO LATE, BUT...
I FORGOT TO GIVE YOU THIS.
IT'S GREAT FOR PIMPLES.
PUT IT ON EVERY DAY.
HOW NICE OF YOU TO COME ALL THIS WAY.
WHY DON'T YOU COME IN AND HAVE SOME TEA? (I'LL HIDE YOU FROM THE BOYS.)
NO THANKS.
I'LL COME BACK WHEN NOI-SAN IS ON HER DATE.
FOR A VISIT.
I KNOW I CAN'T RUN AWAY...
...JUST BECAUSE I'M SCARED.

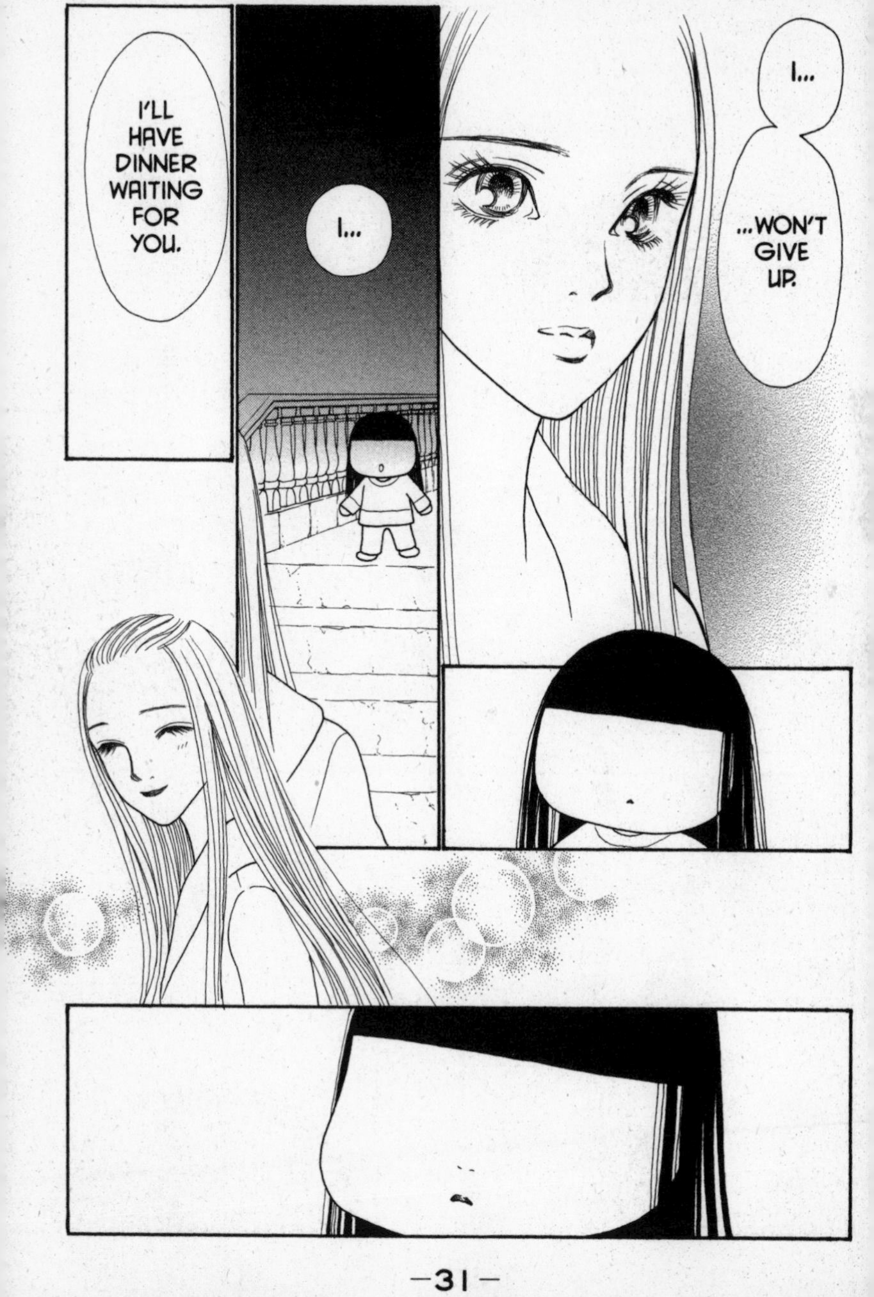
I...
...WON'T GIVE UP.
I...
I'LL HAVE DINNER WAITING FOR YOU.

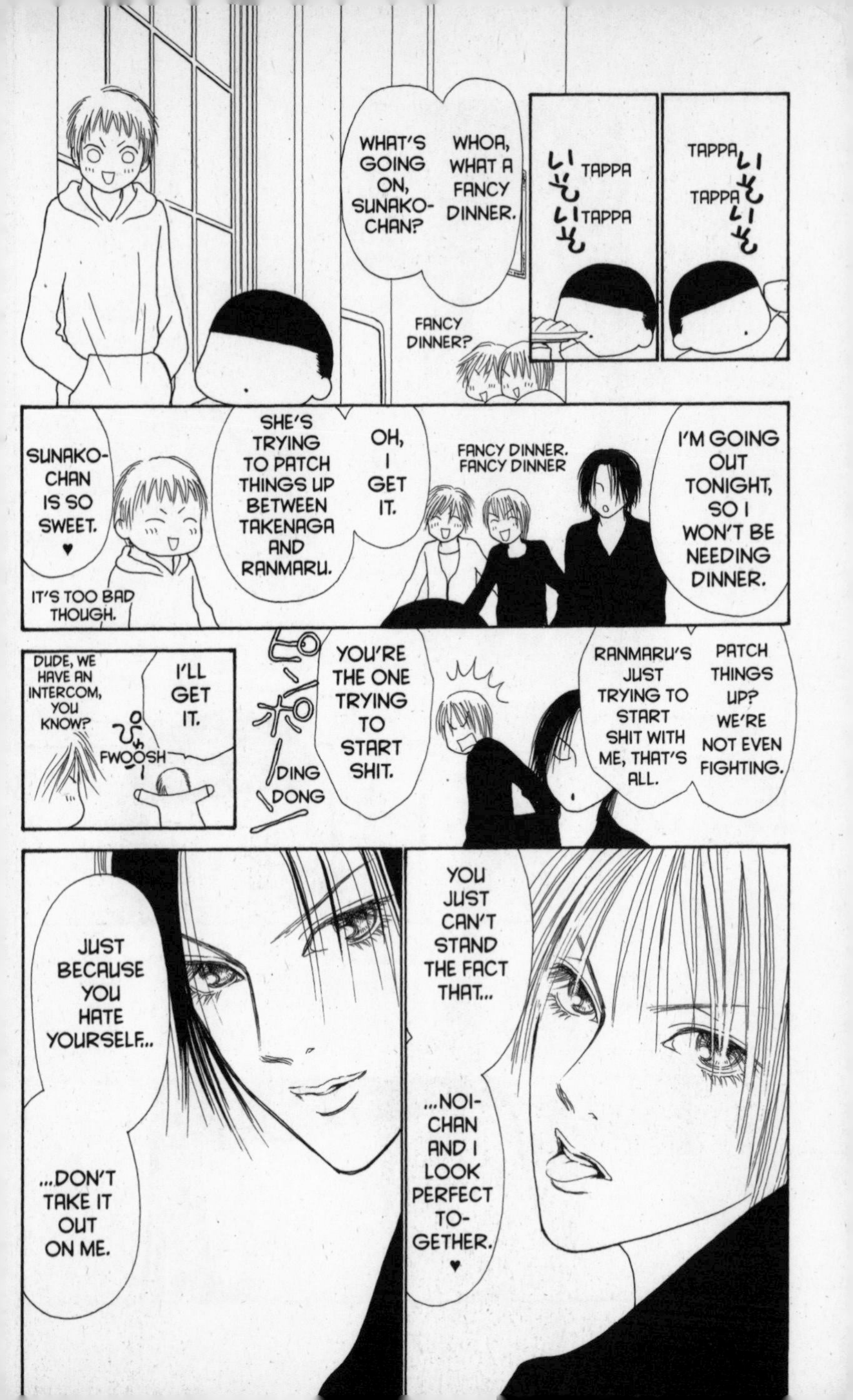
いそいそ TAPPA TAPPA
いそいそ TAPPA TAPPA
WHOA, WHAT A FANCY DINNER.
WHAT'S GOING ON, SUNAKO-CHAN?
FANCY DINNER?
I'M GOING OUT TONIGHT, SO I WON'T BE NEEDING DINNER.
FANCY DINNER. FANCY DINNER
OH, I GET IT.
SHE'S TRYING TO PATCH THINGS UP BETWEEN TAKENAGA AND RANMARU.
SUNAKO-CHAN IS SO SWEET. ♥
IT'S TOO BAD THOUGH.
PATCH THINGS UP? WE'RE NOT EVEN FIGHTING.
RANMARU'S JUST TRYING TO START SHIT WITH ME, THAT'S ALL.
YOU'RE THE ONE TRYING TO START SHIT.
DING DONG
I'LL GET IT.
FWOOSH
DUDE, WE HAVE AN INTERCOM, YOU KNOW?
YOU JUST CAN'T STAND THE FACT THAT...
...NOI-CHAN AND I LOOK PERFECT TOGETHER. ♥
JUST BECAUSE YOU HATE YOURSELF...
...DON'T TAKE IT OUT ON ME.

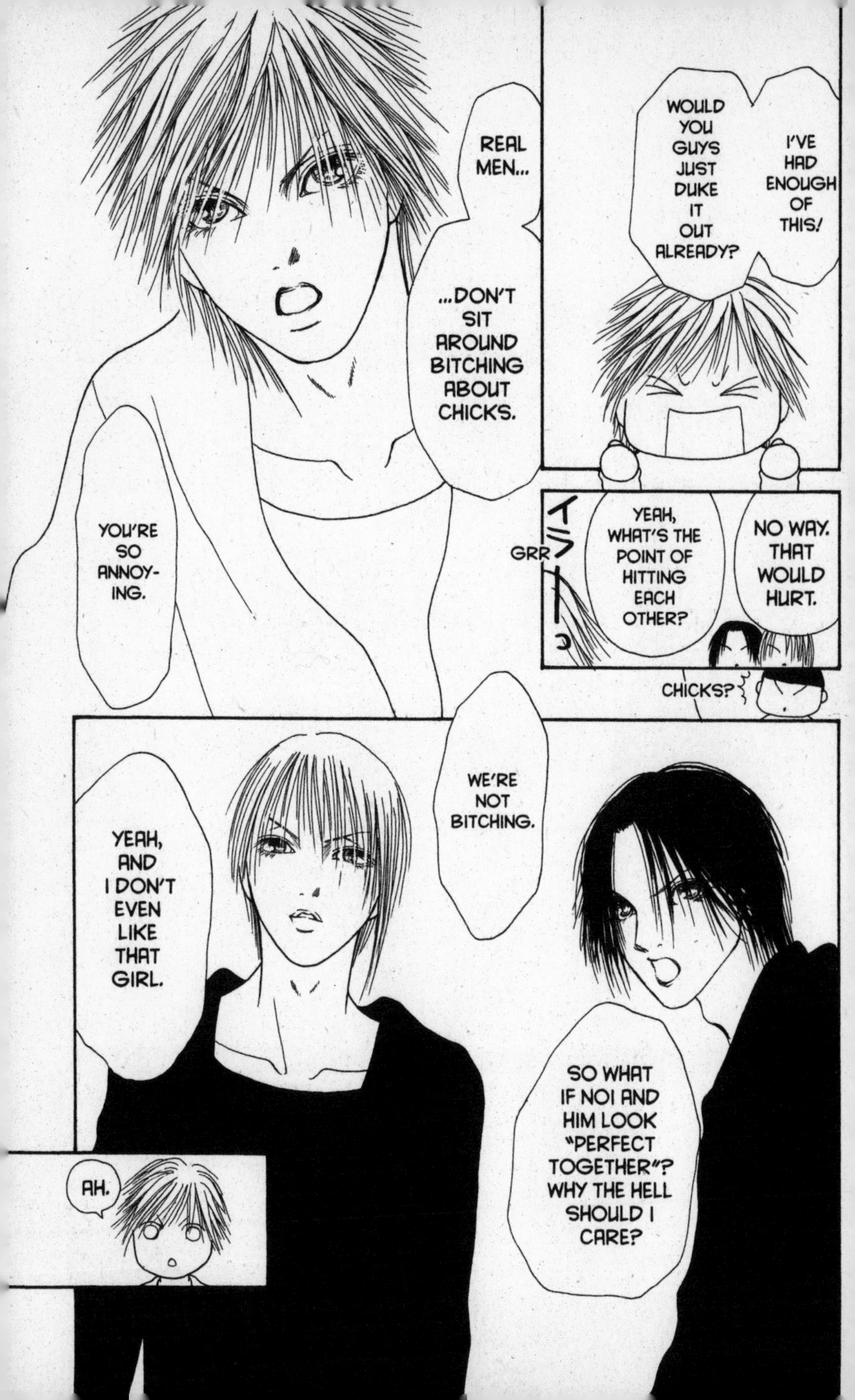
I'VE HAD ENOUGH OF THIS!
WOULD YOU GUYS JUST DUKE IT OUT ALREADY?
NO WAY. THAT WOULD HURT.
YEAH, WHAT'S THE POINT OF HITTING EACH OTHER?
GRR
CHICKS?
REAL MEN...
...DON'T SIT AROUND BITCHING ABOUT CHICKS.
YOU'RE SO ANNOY-ING.
WE'RE NOT BITCHING.
YEAH, AND I DON'T EVEN LIKE THAT GIRL.
SO WHAT IF NOI AND HIM LOOK "PERFECT TOGETHER"? WHY THE HELL SHOULD I CARE?
AH.

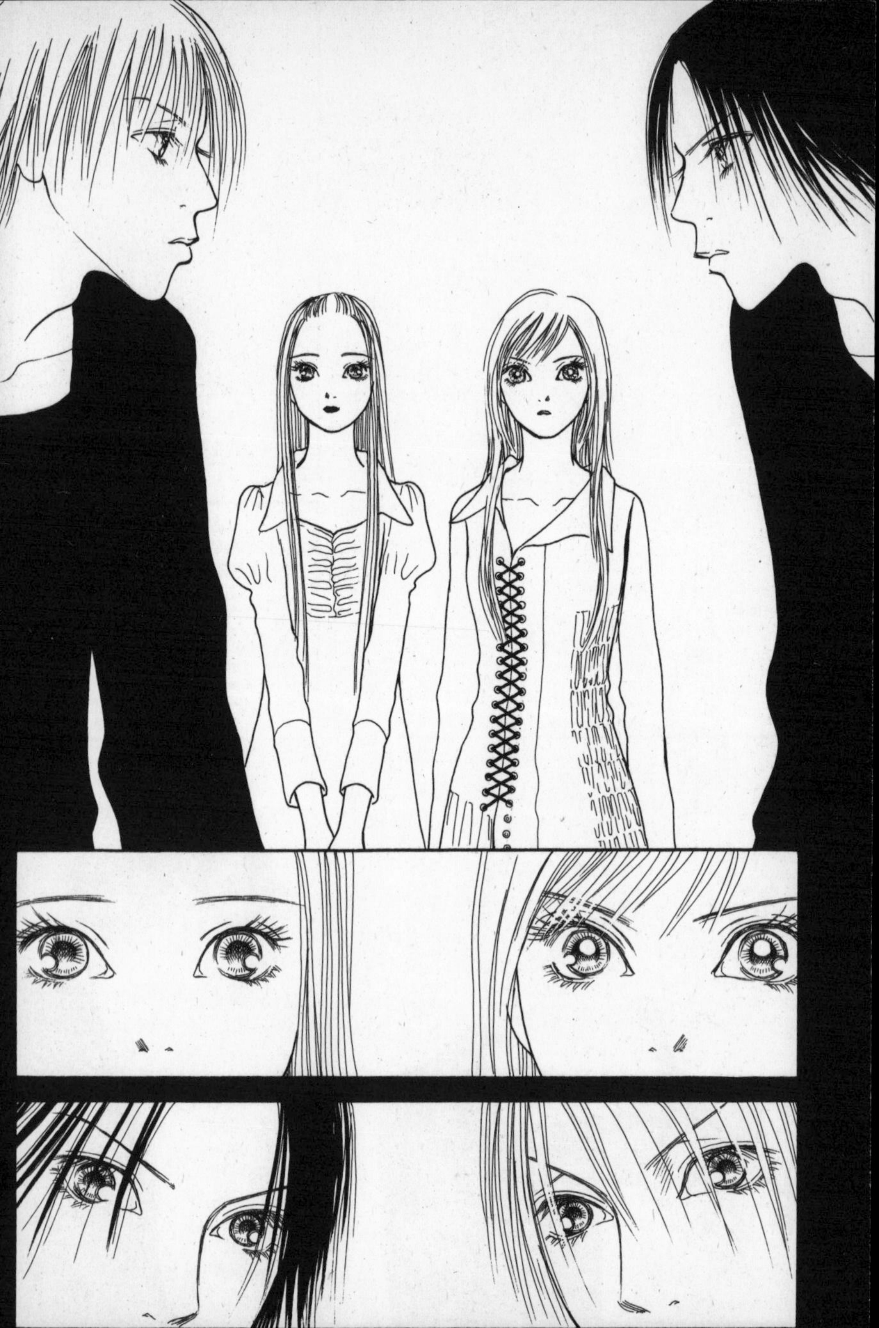

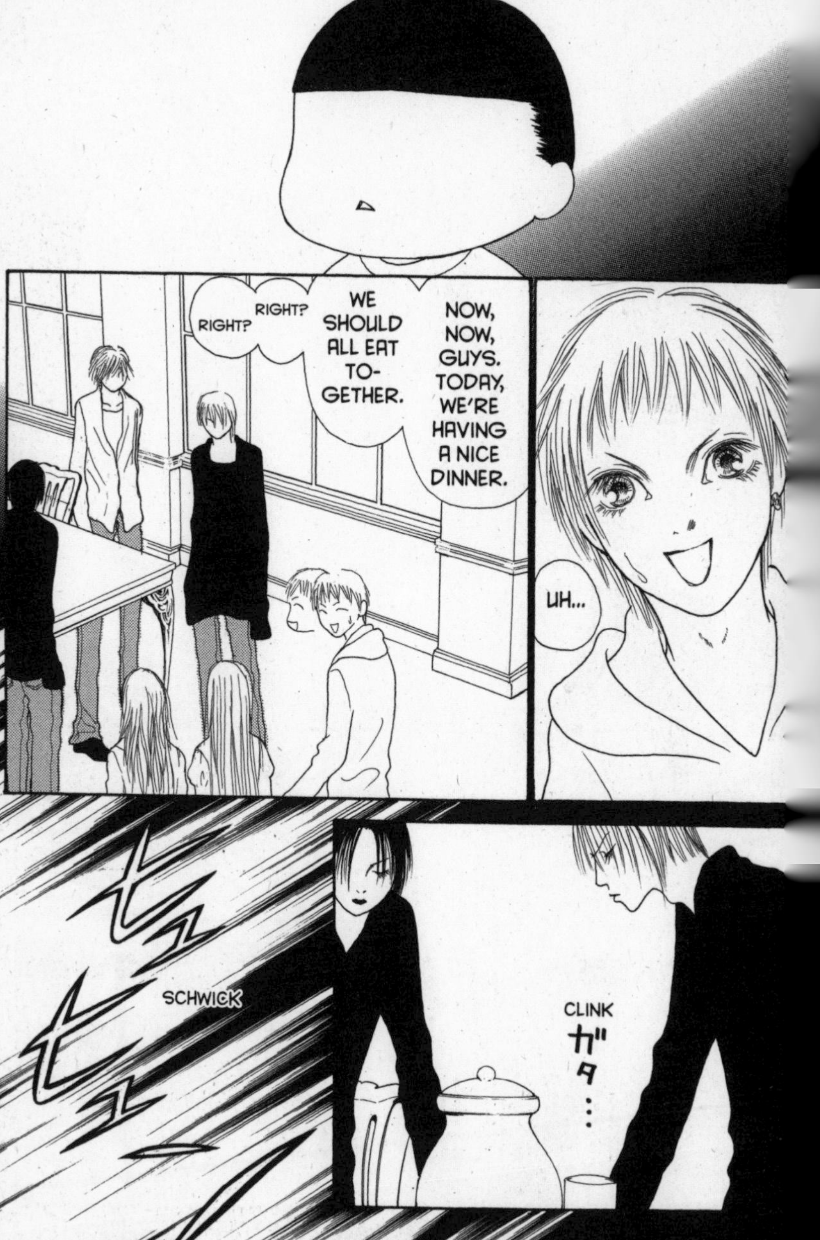
UH...
NOW, NOW, GUYS. TODAY, WE'RE HAVING A NICE DINNER.
WE SHOULD ALL EAT TO-GETHER.
RIGHT?
RIGHT?
CLINK
ガタ…
SCHWICK

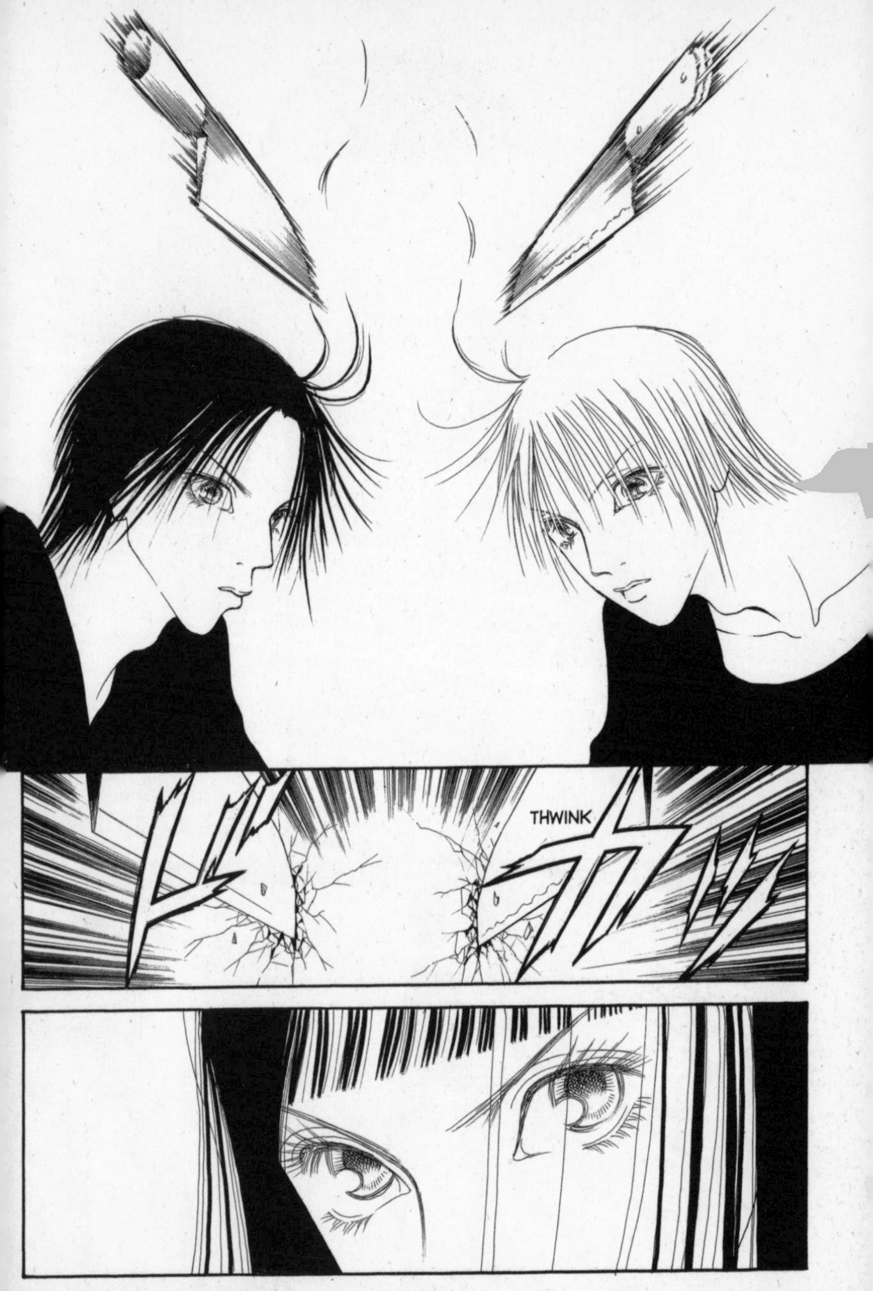
THWINK

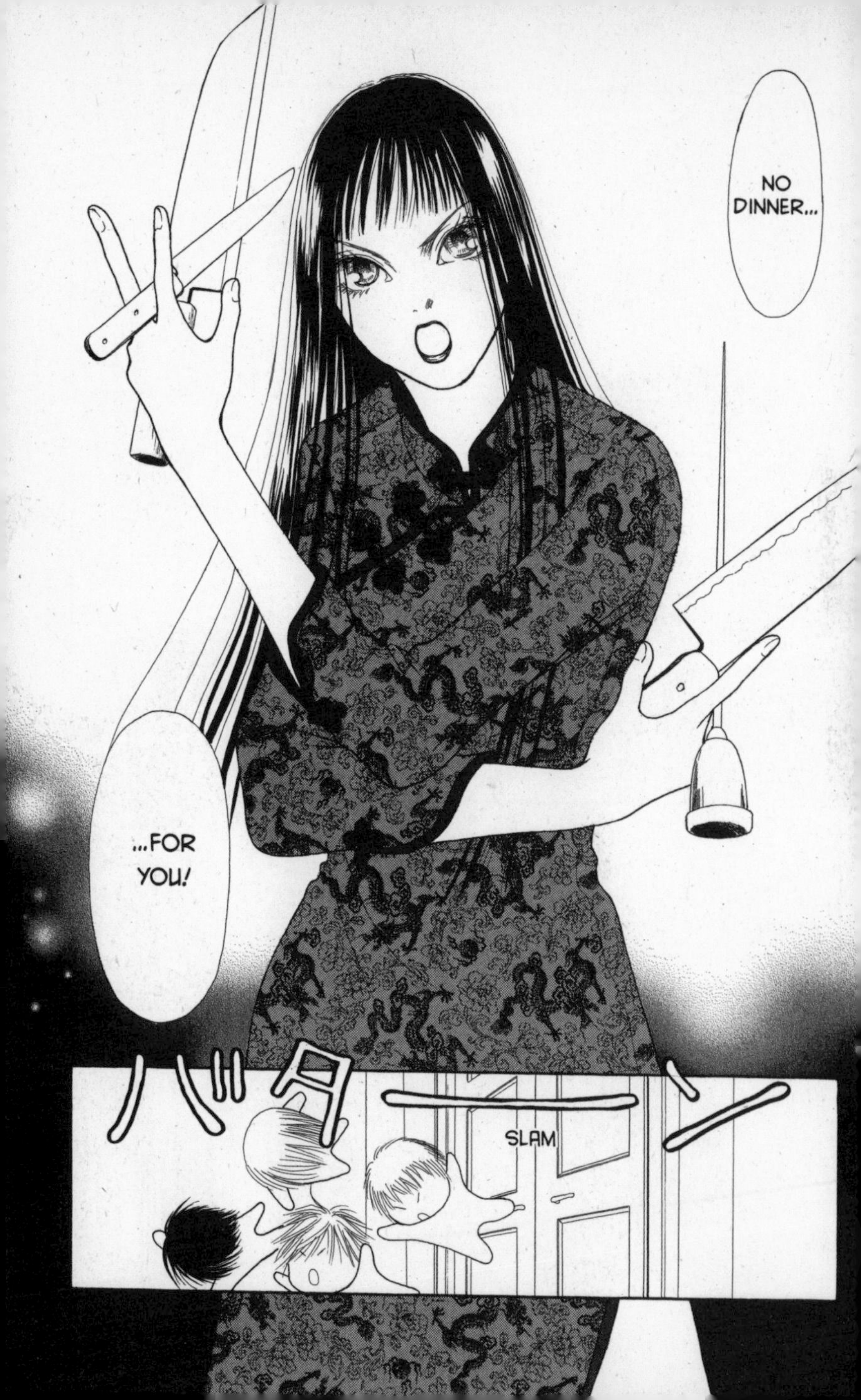
NO DINNER...
...FOR YOU!
SLAM

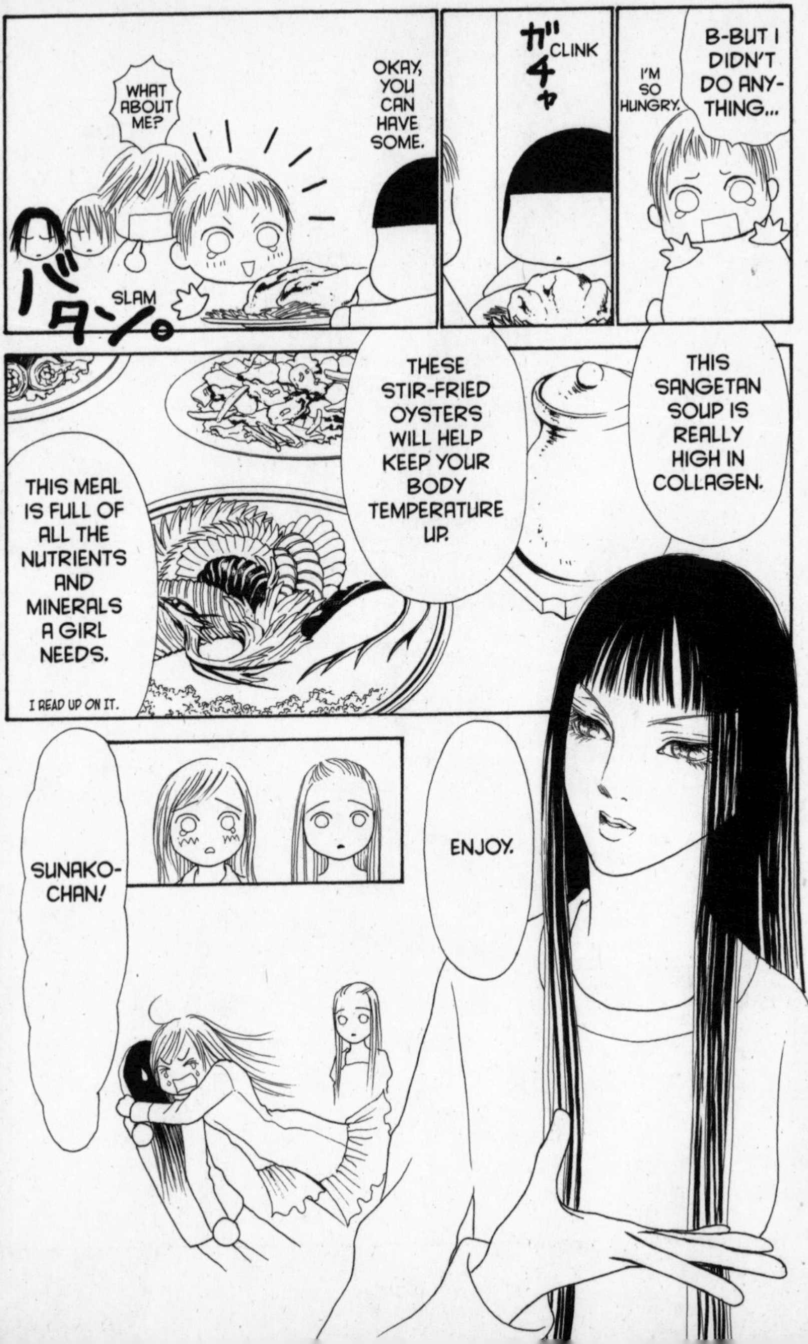
B-BUT I DIDN'T DO ANY-THING...
I'M SO HUNGRY.
ガチャ
CLINK
OKAY, YOU CAN HAVE SOME.
WHAT ABOUT ME?
バタン。
SLAM
THIS SANGETAN SOUP IS REALLY HIGH IN COLLAGEN.
THESE STIR-FRIED OYSTERS WILL HELP KEEP YOUR BODY TEMPERATURE UP.
THIS MEAL IS FULL OF ALL THE NUTRIENTS AND MINERALS A GIRL NEEDS.
I READ UP ON IT.
ENJOY.
SUNAKO-CHAN!

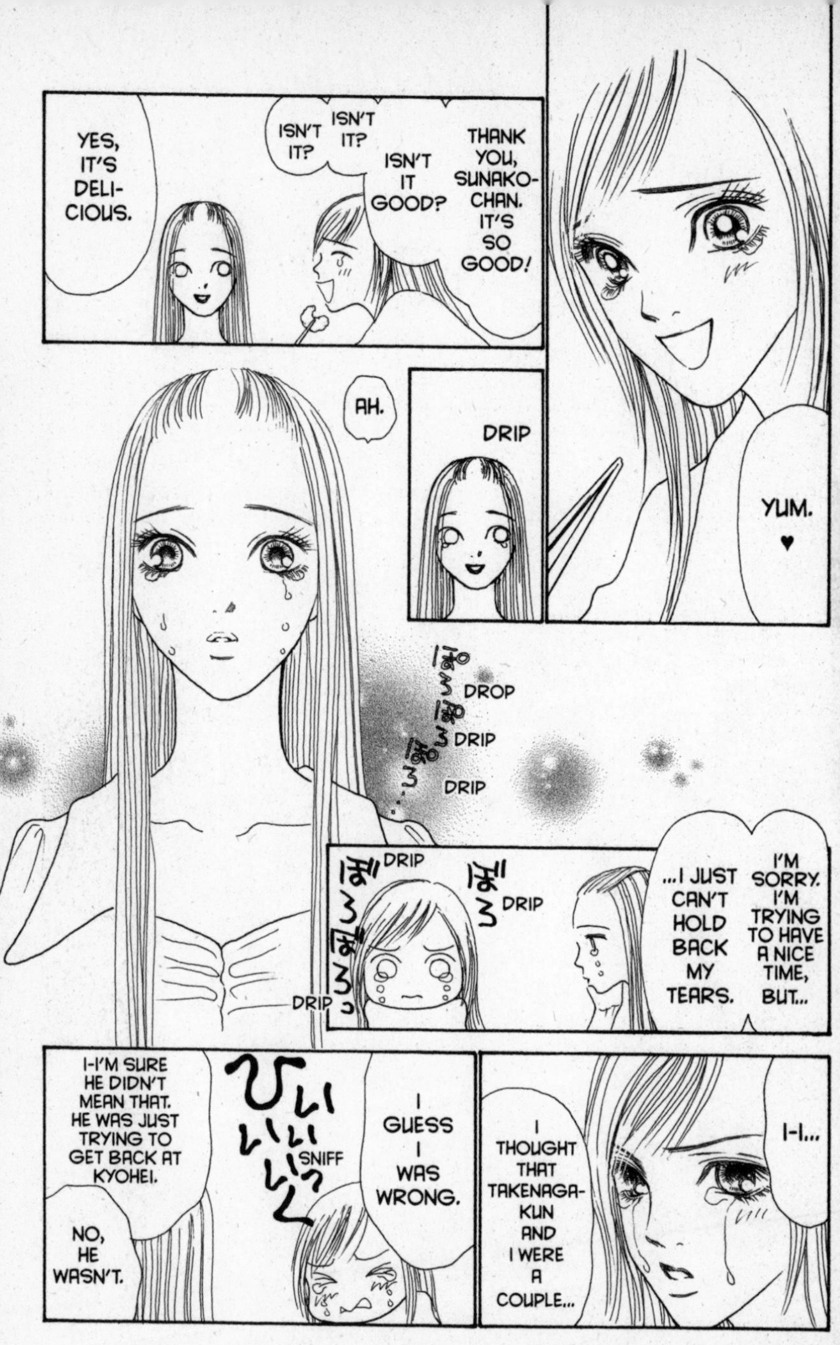
YUM. ♥
THANK YOU, SUNAKO-CHAN. IT'S SO GOOD!
ISN'T IT GOOD?
ISN'T IT?
ISN'T IT?
YES, IT'S DELICIOUS.
DRIP
AH.
DROP
DRIP
DRIP
I'M SORRY. I'M TRYING TO HAVE A NICE TIME, BUT...
...I JUST CAN'T HOLD BACK MY TEARS.
DRIP
DRIP
DRIP
I-I...
I THOUGHT THAT TAKENAGA-KUN AND I WERE A COUPLE...
I GUESS I WAS WRONG.
SNIFF
I-I'M SURE HE DIDN'T MEAN THAT. HE WAS JUST TRYING TO GET BACK AT KYOHEI.
NO, HE WASN'T.

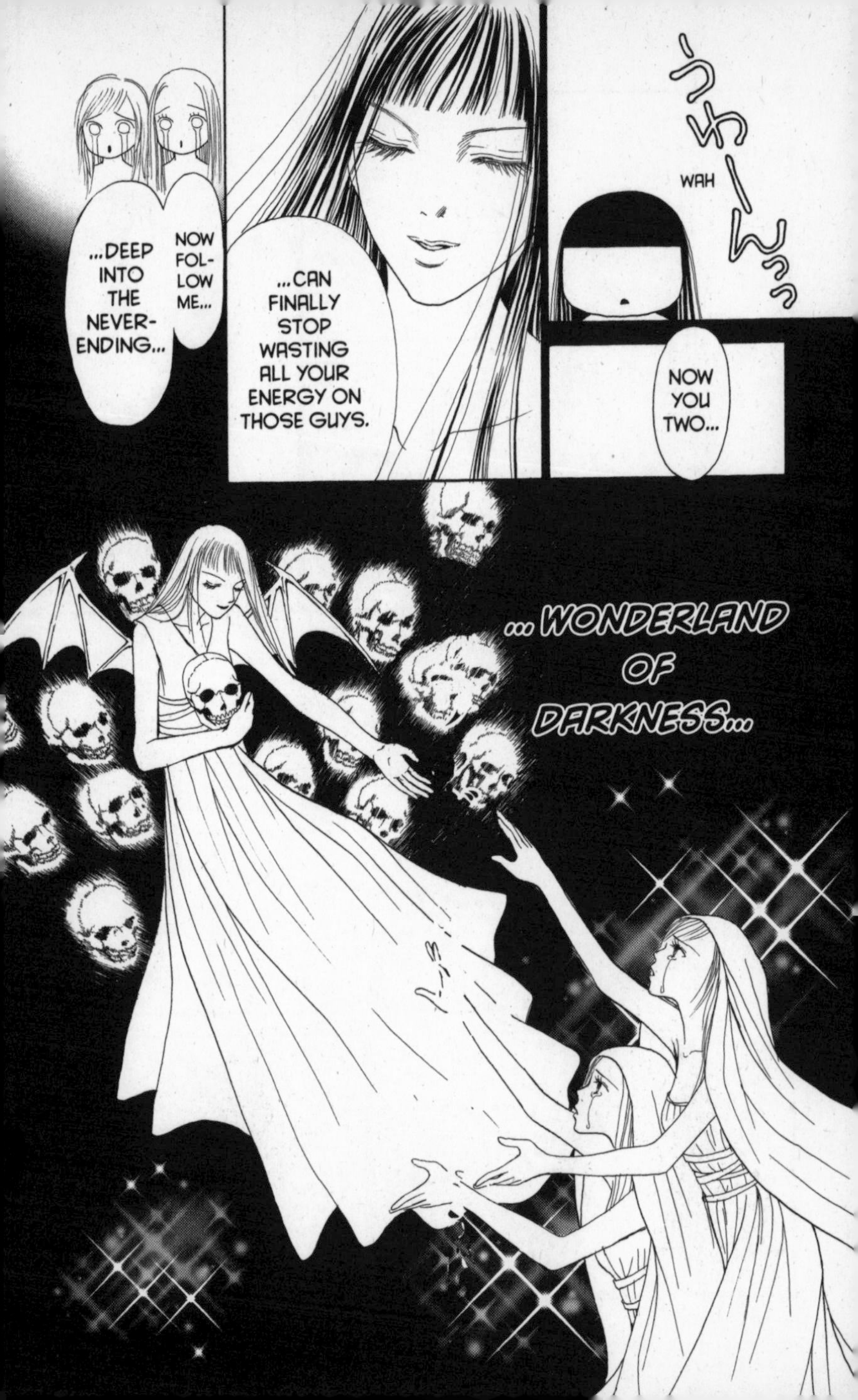
うわーんっっ
WAH
NOW YOU TWO...
...CAN FINALLY STOP WASTING ALL YOUR ENERGY ON THOSE GUYS.
NOW FOL-LOW ME...
...DEEP INTO THE NEVER-ENDING...
...WONDERLAND OF DARKNESS...

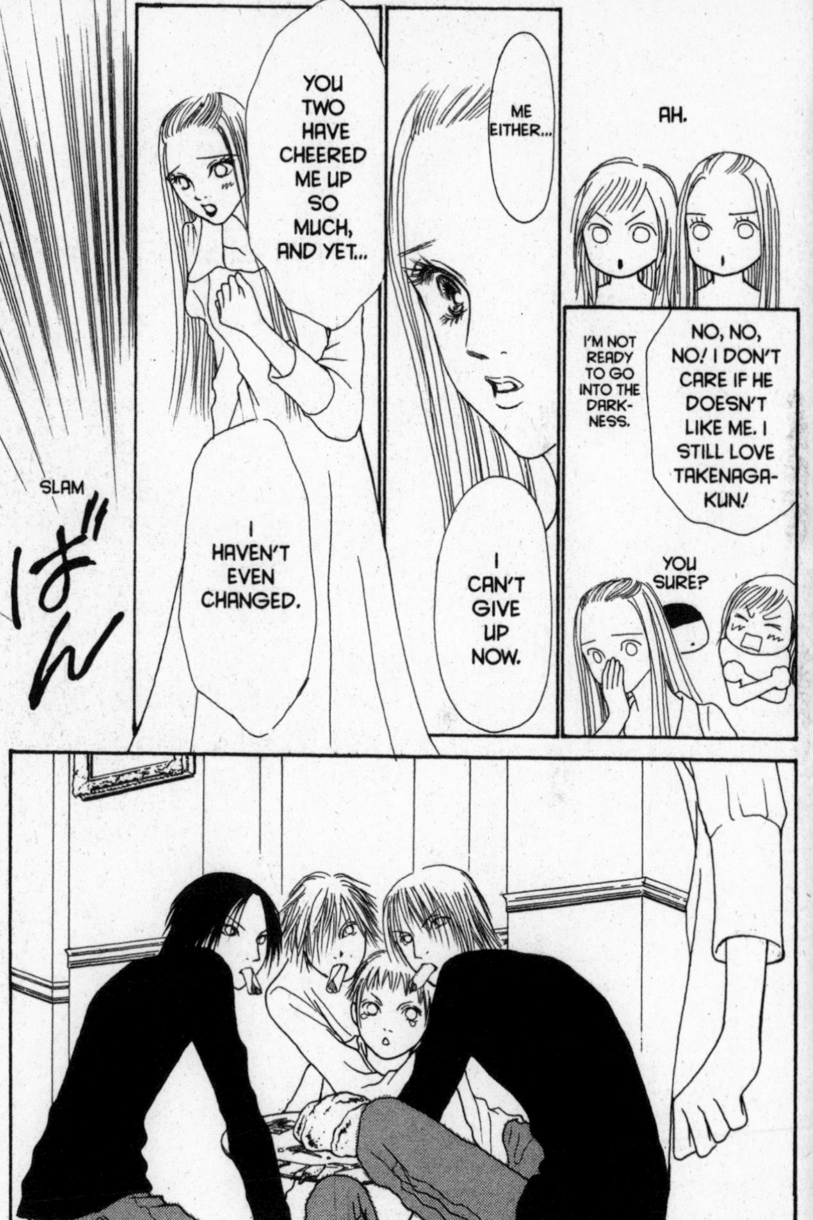
AH.
NO, NO, NO! I DON'T CARE IF HE DOESN'T LIKE ME. I STILL LOVE TAKENAGA-KUN!
I'M NOT READY TO GO INTO THE DARKNESS.
YOU SURE?
ME EITHER...
I CAN'T GIVE UP NOW.
YOU TWO HAVE CHEERED ME UP SO MUCH, AND YET...
I HAVEN'T EVEN CHANGED.
SLAM
ばん

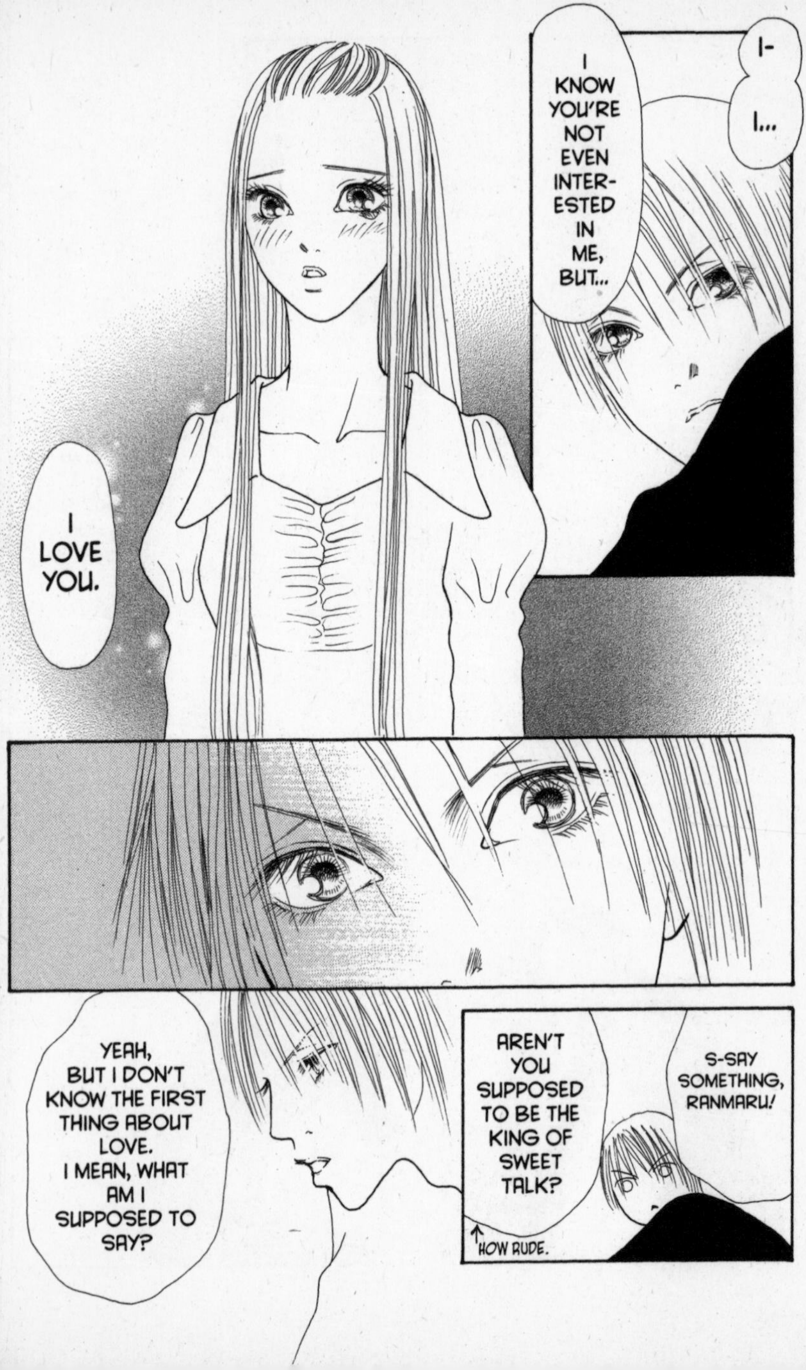
I-
I...
I KNOW YOU'RE NOT EVEN INTERESTED IN ME, BUT...
I LOVE YOU.
S-SAY SOMETHING, RANMARU!
AREN'T YOU SUPPOSED TO BE THE KING OF SWEET TALK?
↑HOW RUDE.
YEAH, BUT I DON'T KNOW THE FIRST THING ABOUT LOVE. I MEAN, WHAT AM I SUPPOSED TO SAY?

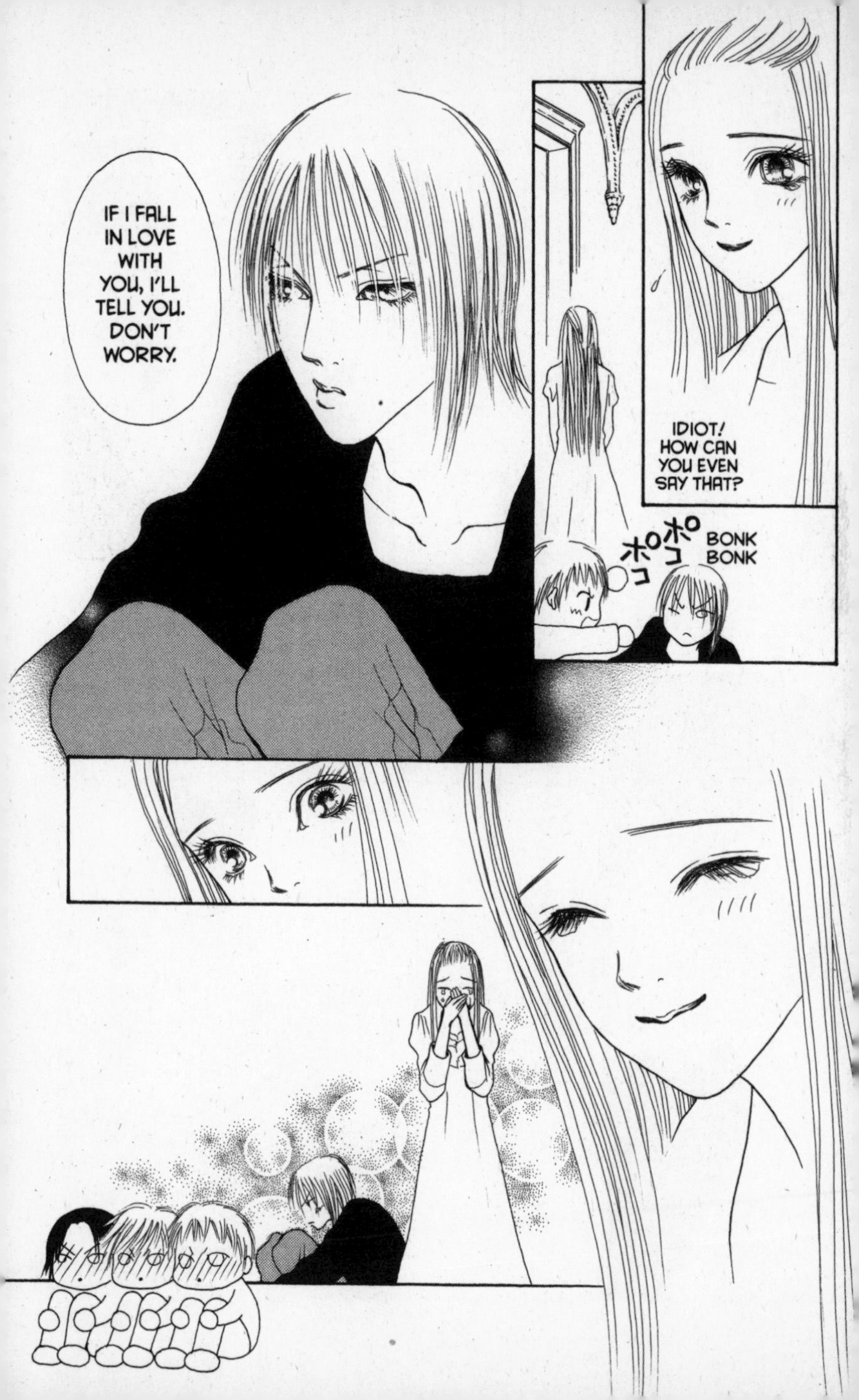
IDIOT! HOW CAN YOU EVEN SAY THAT?
ポコポコ
BONK BONK
IF I FALL IN LOVE WITH YOU, I'LL TELL YOU. DON'T WORRY.

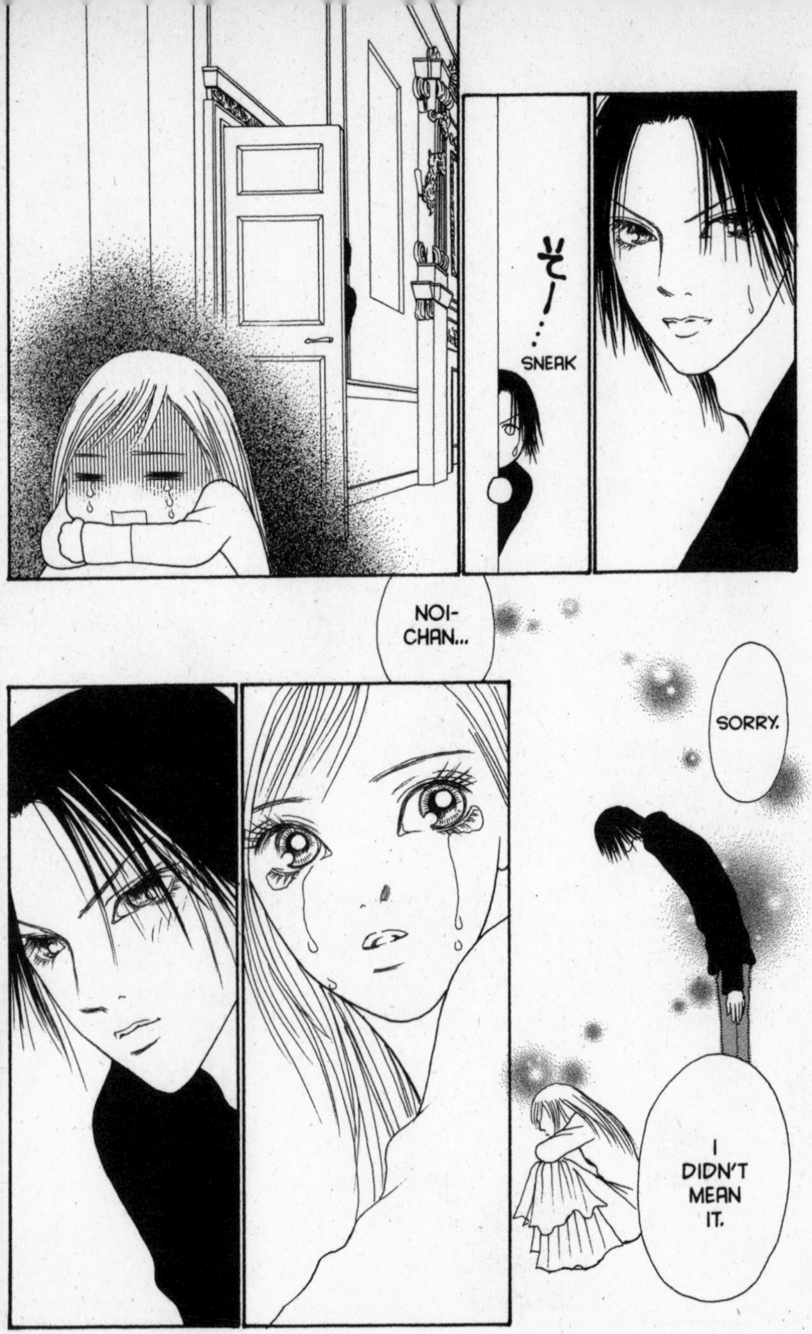
そー…
SNEAK
NOI-CHAN...
SORRY.
I DIDN'T MEAN IT.

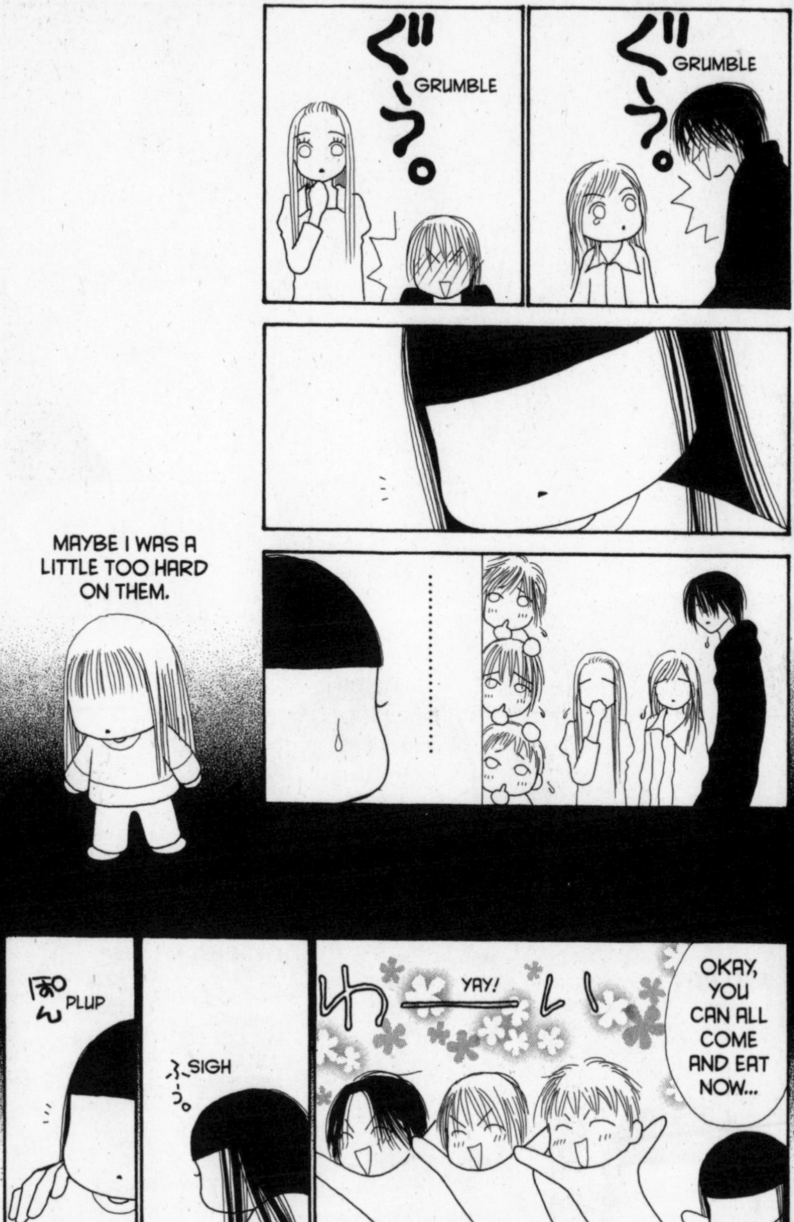
ぐぅ。
GRUMBLE
ぐぅ。
GRUMBLE
……
MAYBE I WAS A LITTLE TOO HARD ON THEM.
OKAY, YOU CAN ALL COME AND EAT NOW...
わーーい
YAY!
ふぅ。
SIGH
ぽん
PLUP

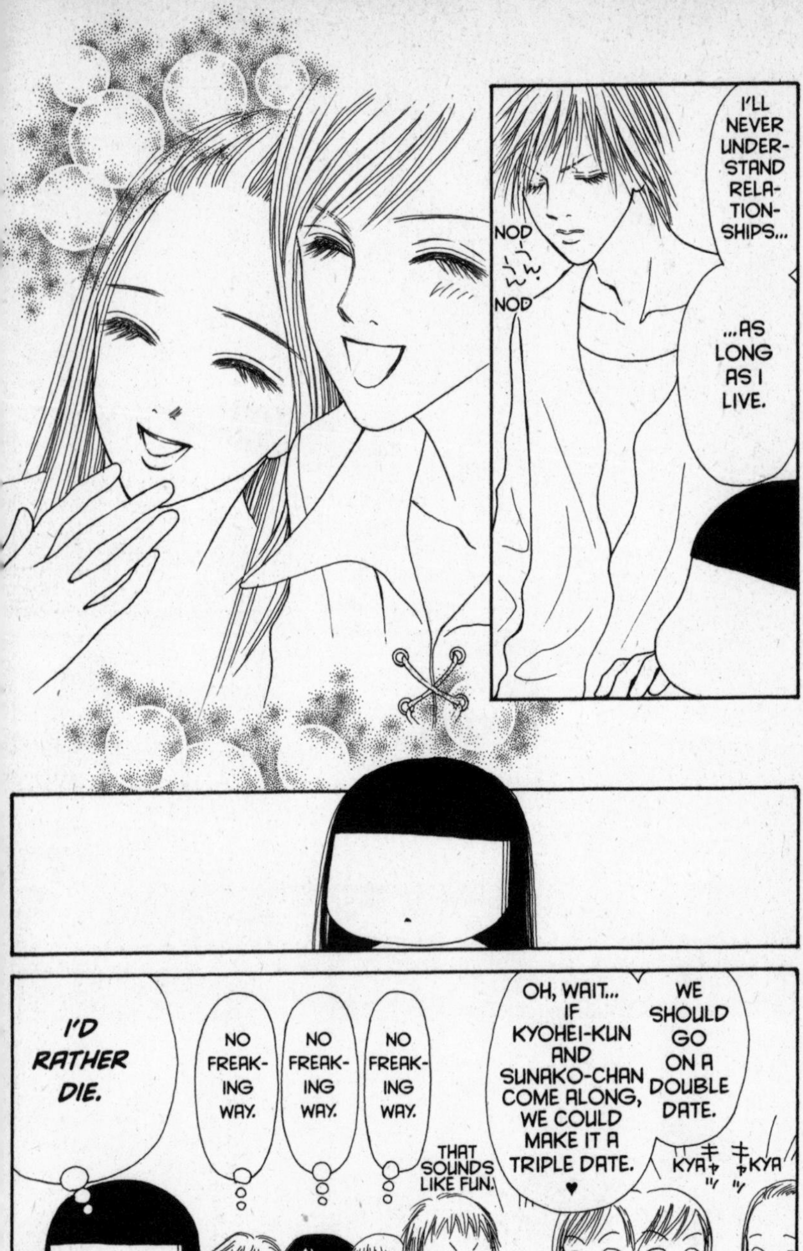

NOD NOD
I'LL NEVER UNDERSTAND RELATIONSHIPS...
...AS LONG AS I LIVE.
WE SHOULD GO ON A DOUBLE DATE.
OH, WAIT... IF KYOHEI-KUN AND SUNAKO-CHAN COME ALONG, WE COULD MAKE IT A TRIPLE DATE. ♥
KYA KYA
THAT SOUNDS LIKE FUN.
NO FREAKING WAY.
NO FREAKING WAY.
NO FREAKING WAY.
I'D RATHER DIE.

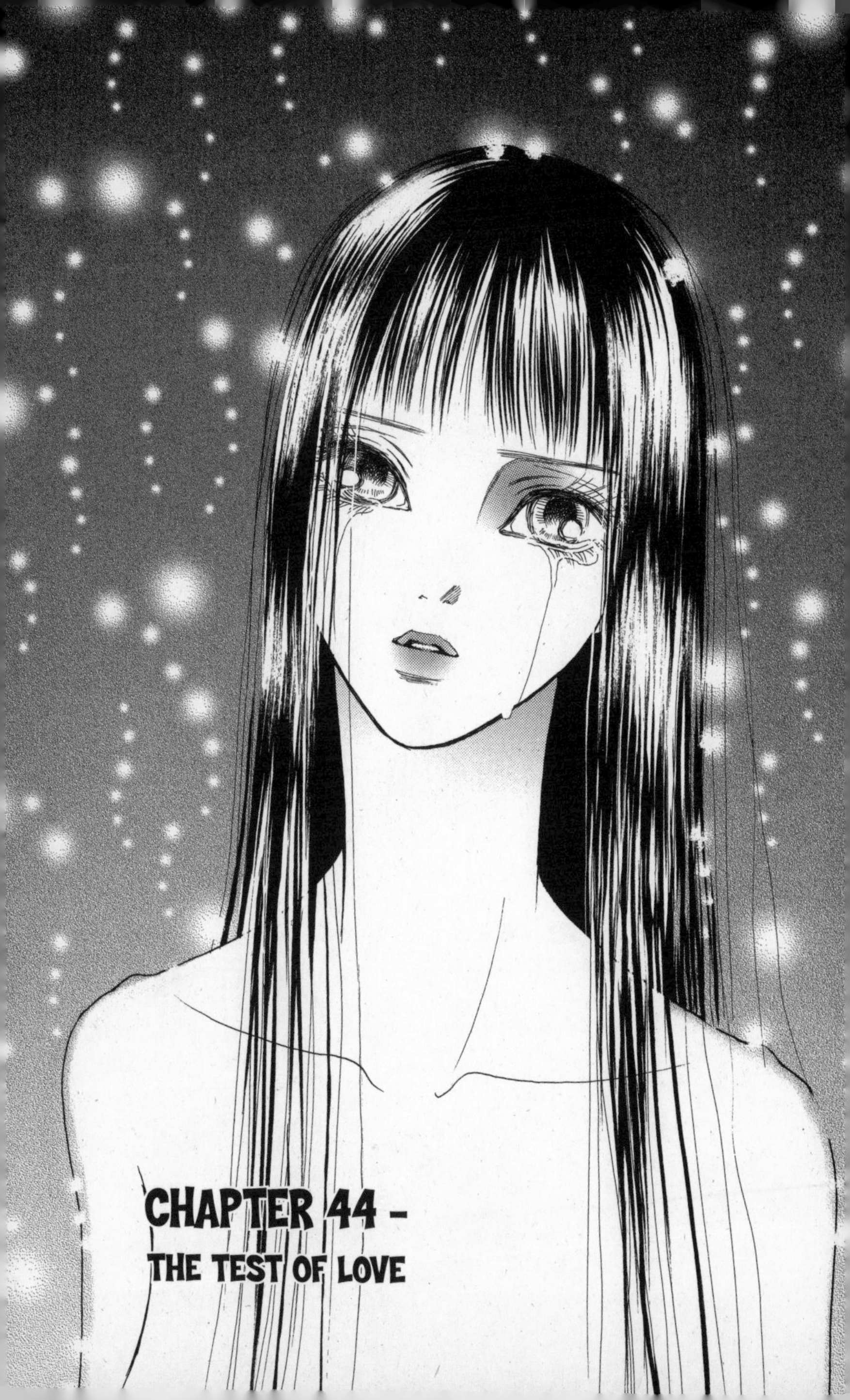
CHAPTER 44 –
THE TEST OF LOVE

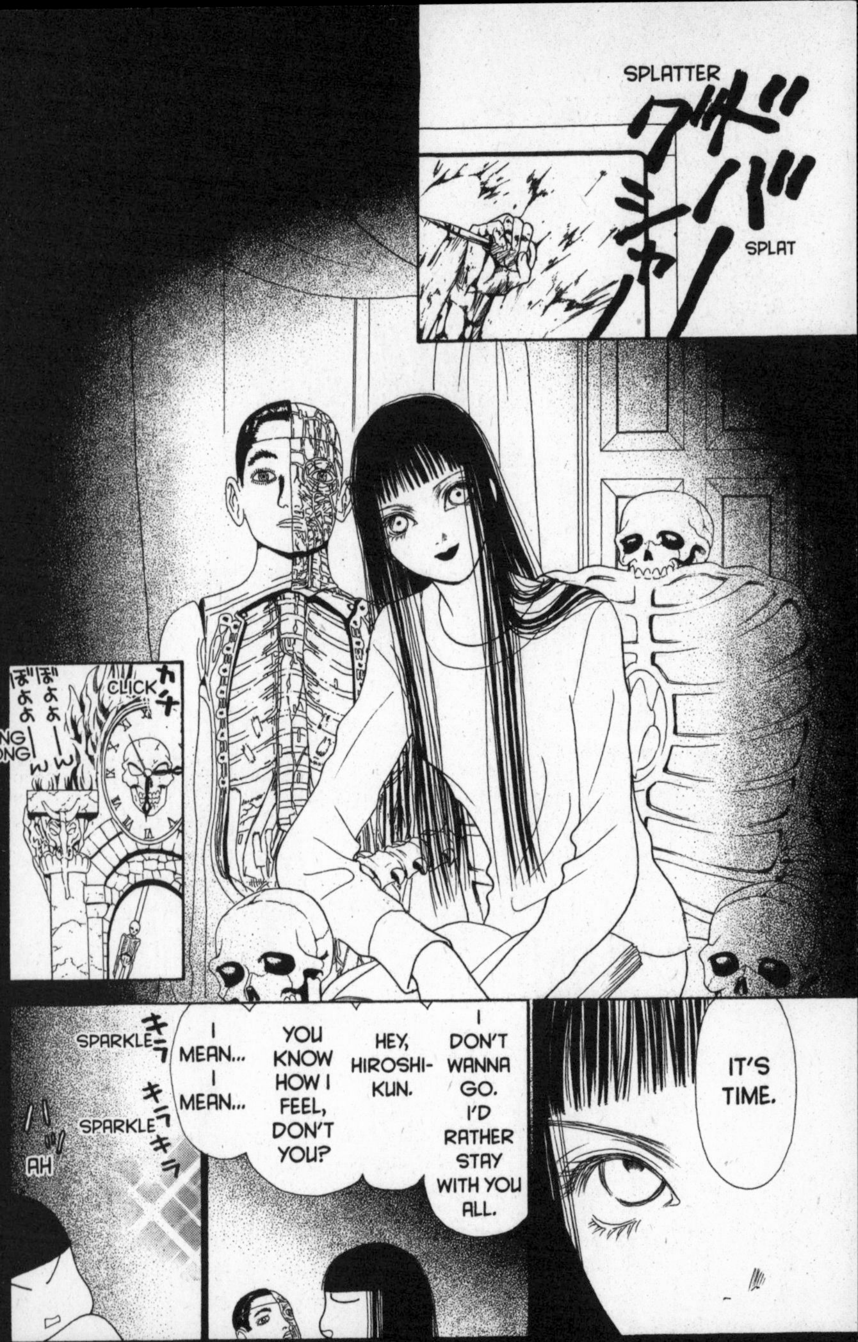
SPLATTER
SPLAT
CLICK
DING DONG
IT'S TIME.
I DON'T WANNA GO. I'D RATHER STAY WITH YOU ALL.
HEY, HIROSHI-KUN.
YOU KNOW HOW I FEEL, DON'T YOU?
I MEAN... I MEAN...
キラ
SPARKLE
キラキラ
SPARKLE
AH

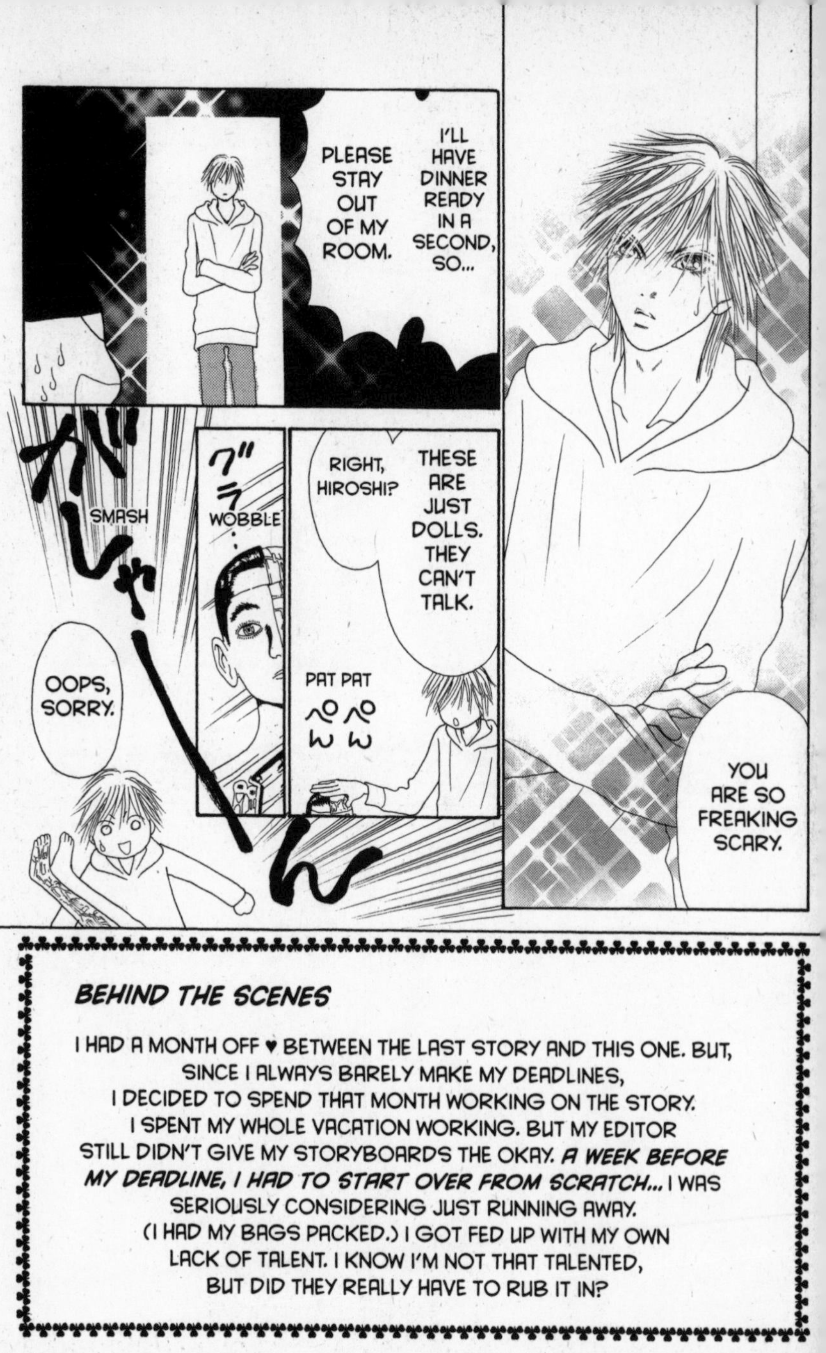
YOU ARE SO FREAKING SCARY.
I'LL HAVE DINNER READY IN A SECOND, SO...
PLEASE STAY OUT OF MY ROOM.
THESE ARE JUST DOLLS. THEY CAN'T TALK.
RIGHT, HIROSHI?
PAT PAT
グラ
WOBBLE
がしゃーん
SMASH
OOPS, SORRY.

BEHIND THE SCENES

I HAD A MONTH OFF ♥ BETWEEN THE LAST STORY AND THIS ONE. BUT, SINCE I ALWAYS BARELY MAKE MY DEADLINES, I DECIDED TO SPEND THAT MONTH WORKING ON THE STORY. I SPENT MY WHOLE VACATION WORKING. BUT MY EDITOR STILL DIDN'T GIVE MY STORYBOARDS THE OKAY. ***A WEEK BEFORE MY DEADLINE, I HAD TO START OVER FROM SCRATCH...*** I WAS SERIOUSLY CONSIDERING JUST RUNNING AWAY. (I HAD MY BAGS PACKED.) I GOT FED UP WITH MY OWN LACK OF TALENT. I KNOW I'M NOT THAT TALENTED, BUT DID THEY REALLY HAVE TO RUB IT IN?

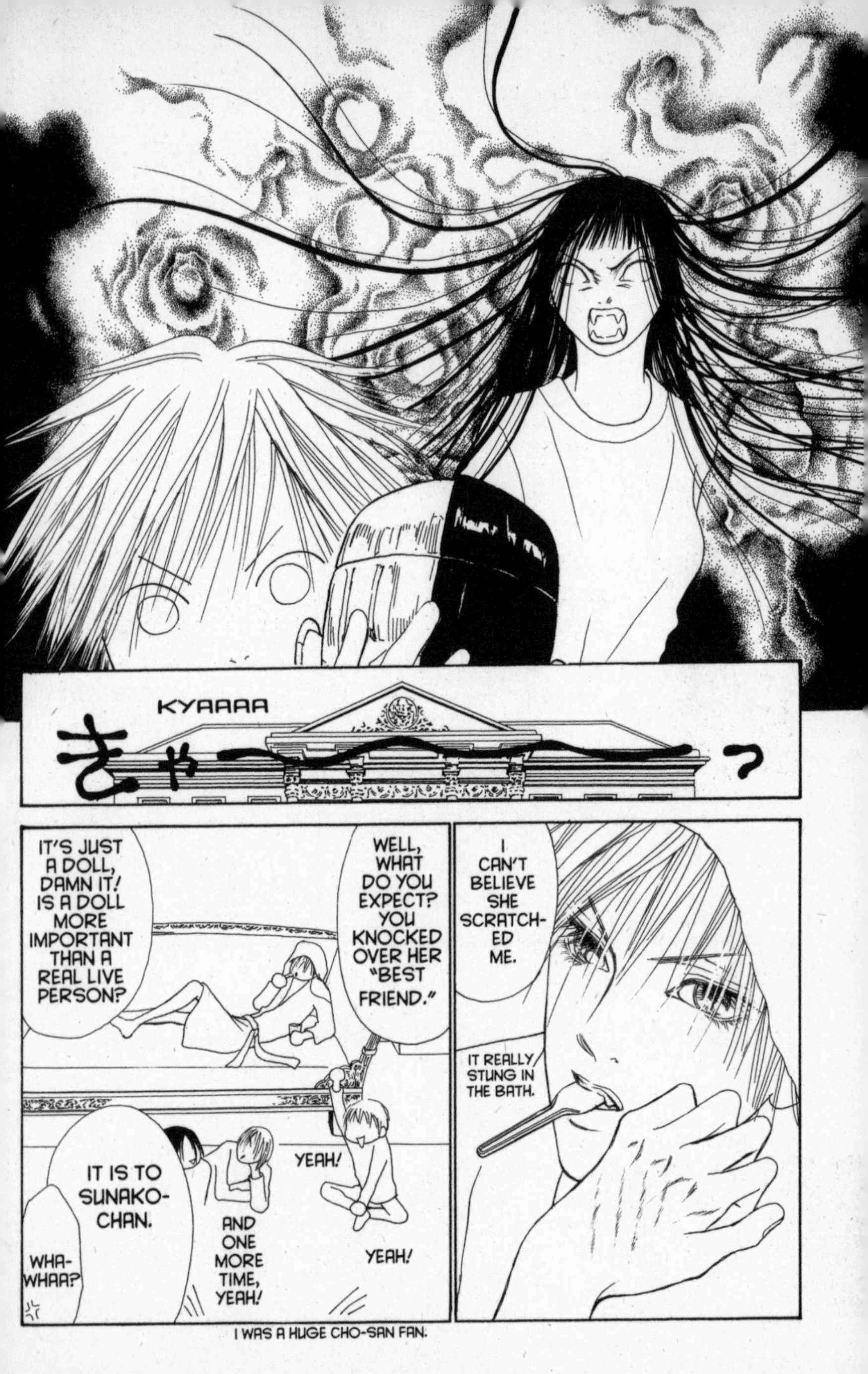
KYAAAA
きゃ————っ
I CAN'T BELIEVE SHE SCRATCHED ME.
IT REALLY STUNG IN THE BATH.
WELL, WHAT DO YOU EXPECT? YOU KNOCKED OVER HER "BEST FRIEND."
IT'S JUST A DOLL, DAMN IT! IS A DOLL MORE IMPORTANT THAN A REAL LIVE PERSON?
IT IS TO SUNAKO-CHAN.
WHA-WHAA?
YEAH!
AND ONE MORE TIME, YEAH!
YEAH!

I WAS A HUGE CHO-SAN FAN.

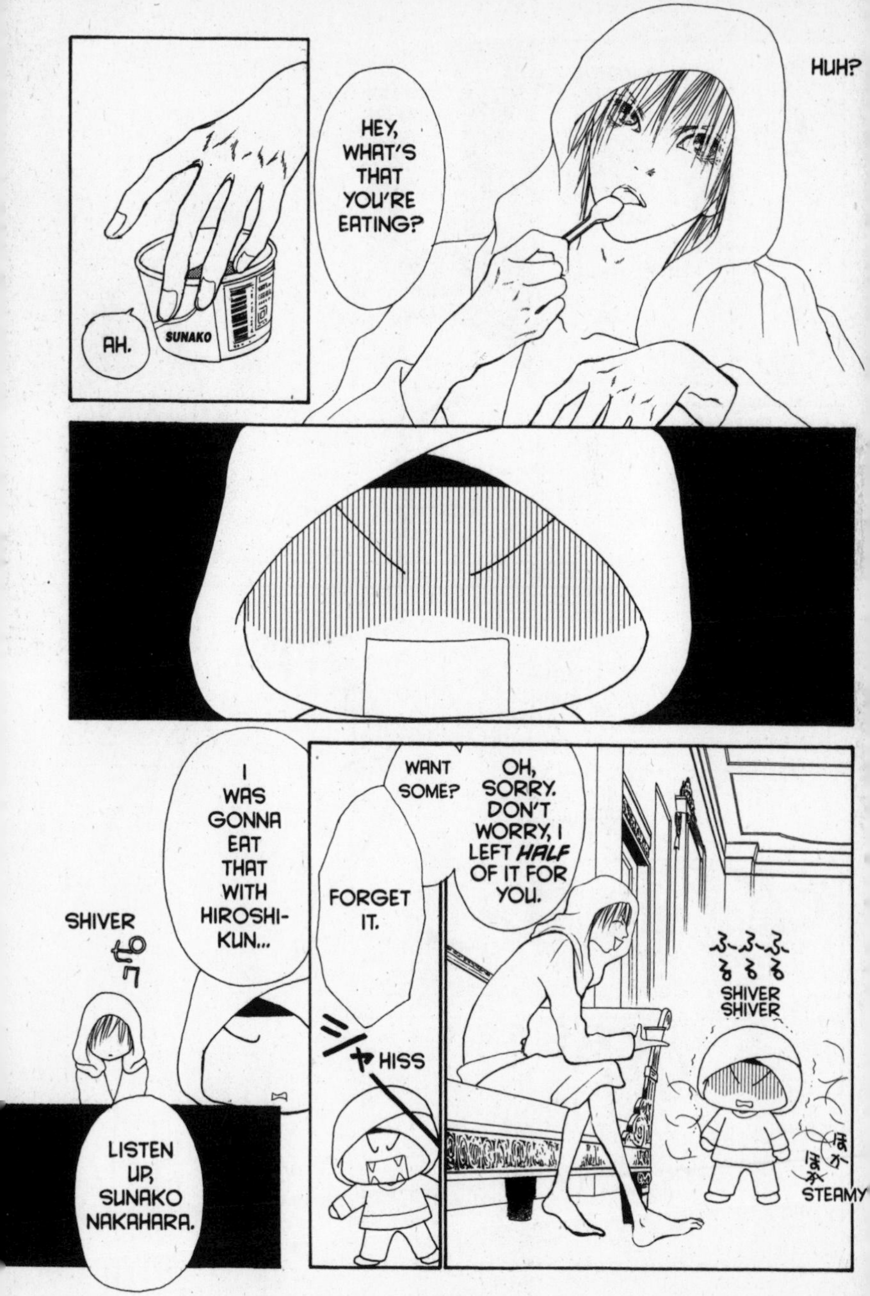
HUH?
HEY, WHAT'S THAT YOU'RE EATING?
SUNAKO
AH.
OH, SORRY. DON'T WORRY, I LEFT *HALF* OF IT FOR YOU.
WANT SOME?
FORGET IT.
ふるふる ふるふる ふるふる
SHIVER SHIVER
ほか ほか
STEAMY
シャ
HISS
I WAS GONNA EAT THAT WITH HIROSHI-KUN...
SHIVER
LISTEN UP, SUNAKO NAKAHARA.

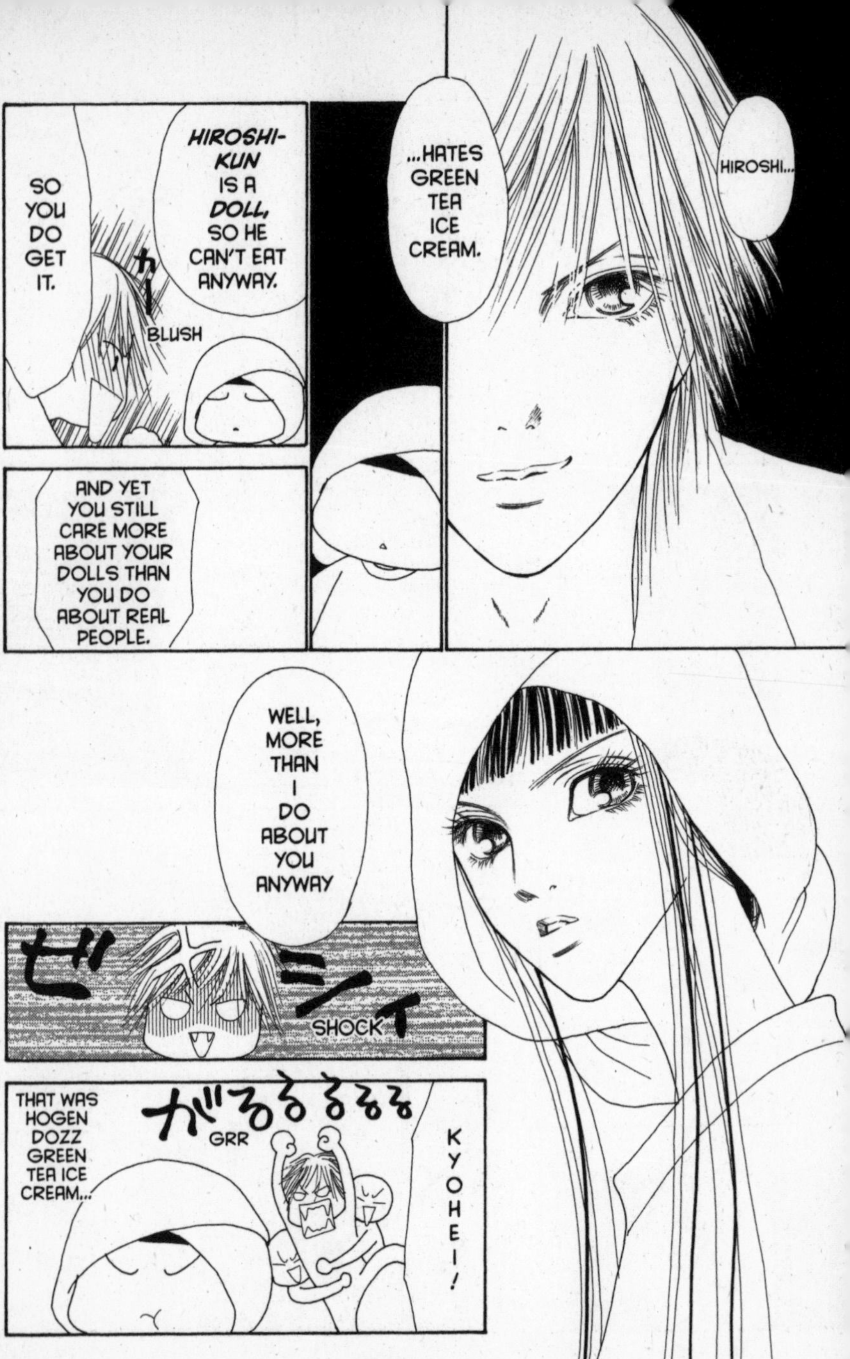
HIROSHI...
...HATES GREEN TEA ICE CREAM.
HIROSHI-KUN IS A DOLL, SO HE CAN'T EAT ANYWAY.
SO YOU DO GET IT.
BLUSH
AND YET YOU STILL CARE MORE ABOUT YOUR DOLLS THAN YOU DO ABOUT REAL PEOPLE.
WELL, MORE THAN I DO ABOUT YOU ANYWAY
SHOCK
KYOHEI!
GRR
THAT WAS HOGEN DOZZ GREEN TEA ICE CREAM...

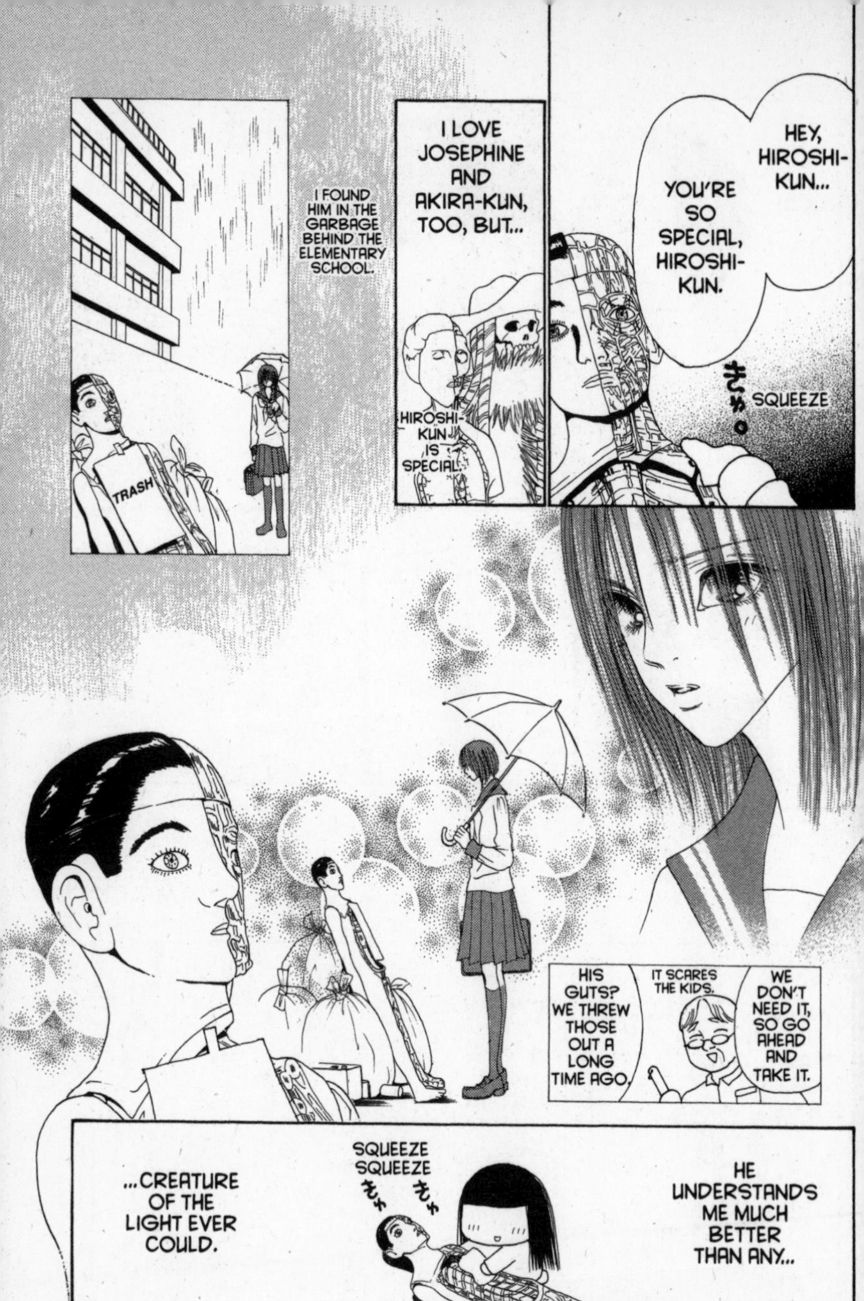
HEY, HIROSHI-KUN...
YOU'RE SO SPECIAL, HIROSHI-KUN.
きゅ。
SQUEEZE
I LOVE JOSEPHINE AND AKIRA-KUN, TOO, BUT...
HIROSHI-KUN IS SPECIAL.
I FOUND HIM IN THE GARBAGE BEHIND THE ELEMENTARY SCHOOL.
TRASH
WE DON'T NEED IT, SO GO AHEAD AND TAKE IT.
IT SCARES THE KIDS.
HIS GUTS? WE THREW THOSE OUT A LONG TIME AGO.
HE UNDERSTANDS ME MUCH BETTER THAN ANY...
SQUEEZE SQUEEZE
きゅ きゅ
...CREATURE OF THE LIGHT EVER COULD.

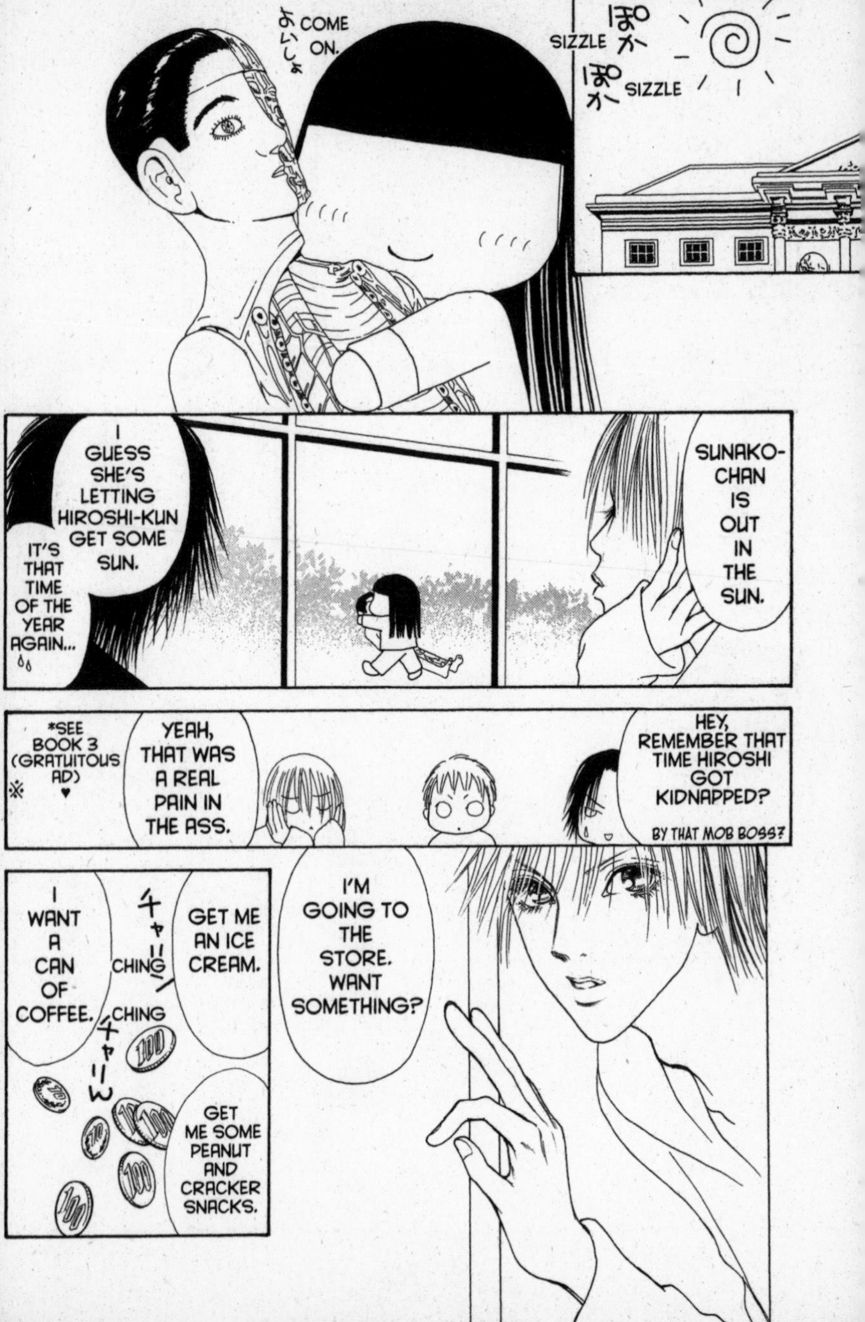
ぽか ぽか
SIZZLE SIZZLE
よいしょ
COME ON.
SUNAKO-CHAN IS OUT IN THE SUN.
I GUESS SHE'S LETTING HIROSHI-KUN GET SOME SUN.
IT'S THAT TIME OF THE YEAR AGAIN...
HEY, REMEMBER THAT TIME HIROSHI GOT KIDNAPPED?
BY THAT MOB BOSS?
YEAH, THAT WAS A REAL PAIN IN THE ASS.
*SEE BOOK 3 (GRATUITOUS AD) ♥
I'M GOING TO THE STORE. WANT SOMETHING?
GET ME AN ICE CREAM.
チャリン CHING
チャリン CHING
I WANT A CAN OF COFFEE.
GET ME SOME PEANUT AND CRACKER SNACKS.

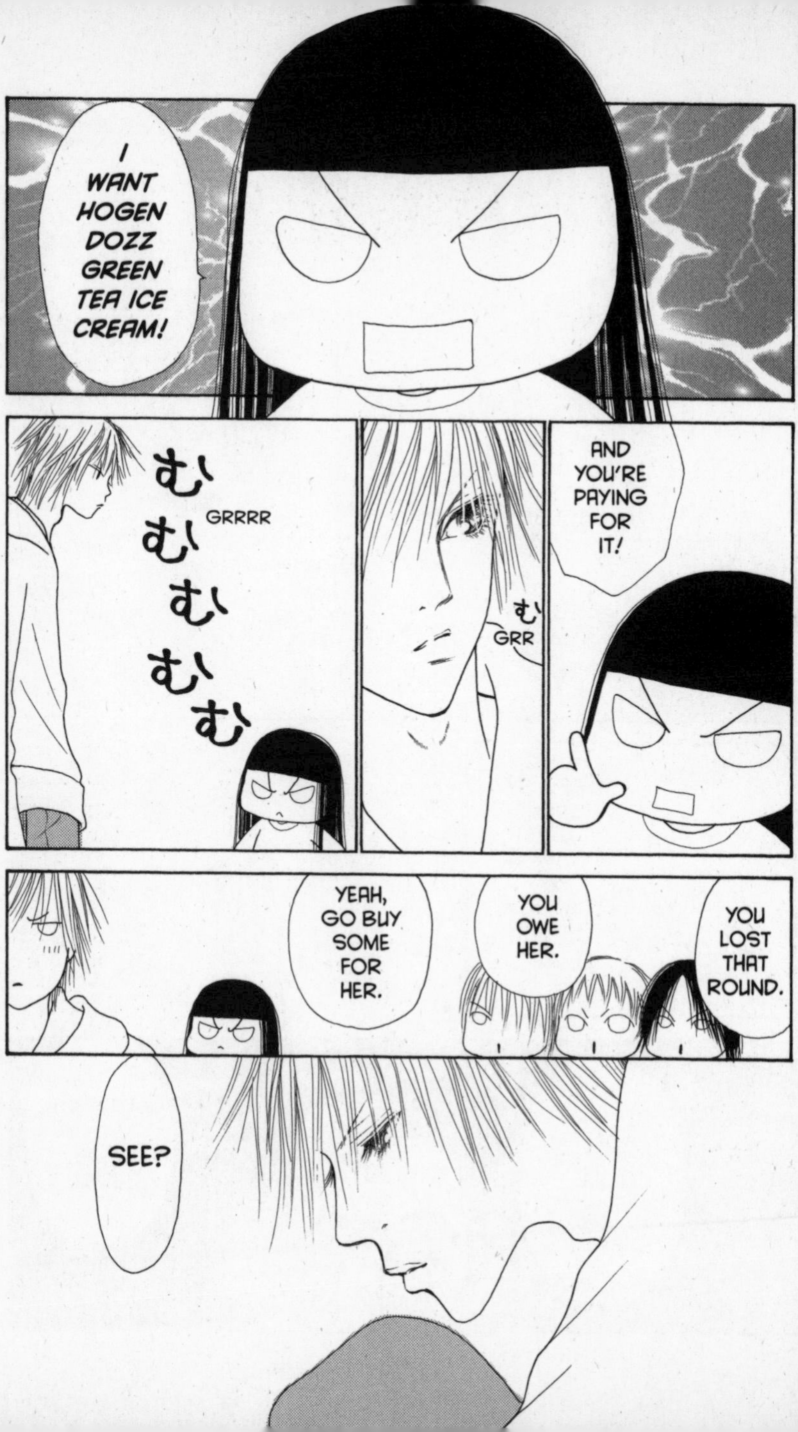
I WANT HOGEN DOZZ GREEN TEA ICE CREAM!
AND YOU'RE PAYING FOR IT!
む
GRR
むむむむむ
GRRRR
YOU LOST THAT ROUND.
YOU OWE HER.
YEAH, GO BUY SOME FOR HER.
SEE?

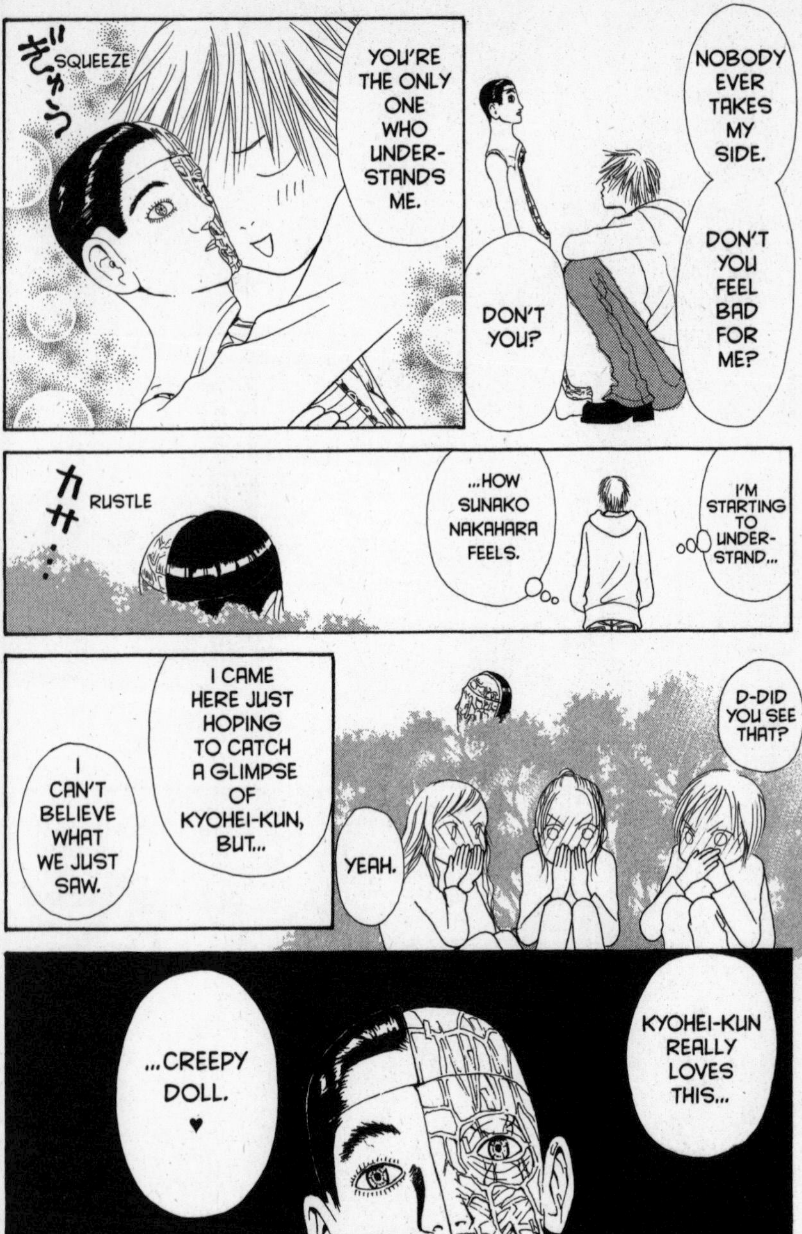
NOBODY EVER TAKES MY SIDE.
DON'T YOU FEEL BAD FOR ME?
DON'T YOU?
YOU'RE THE ONLY ONE WHO UNDER-STANDS ME.
ぎゅう
SQUEEZE
I'M STARTING TO UNDER-STAND...
...HOW SUNAKO NAKAHARA FEELS.
カサ...
RUSTLE
D-DID YOU SEE THAT?
YEAH.
I CAME HERE JUST HOPING TO CATCH A GLIMPSE OF KYOHEI-KUN, BUT...
I CAN'T BELIEVE WHAT WE JUST SAW.
KYOHEI-KUN REALLY LOVES THIS...
...CREEPY DOLL. ♥

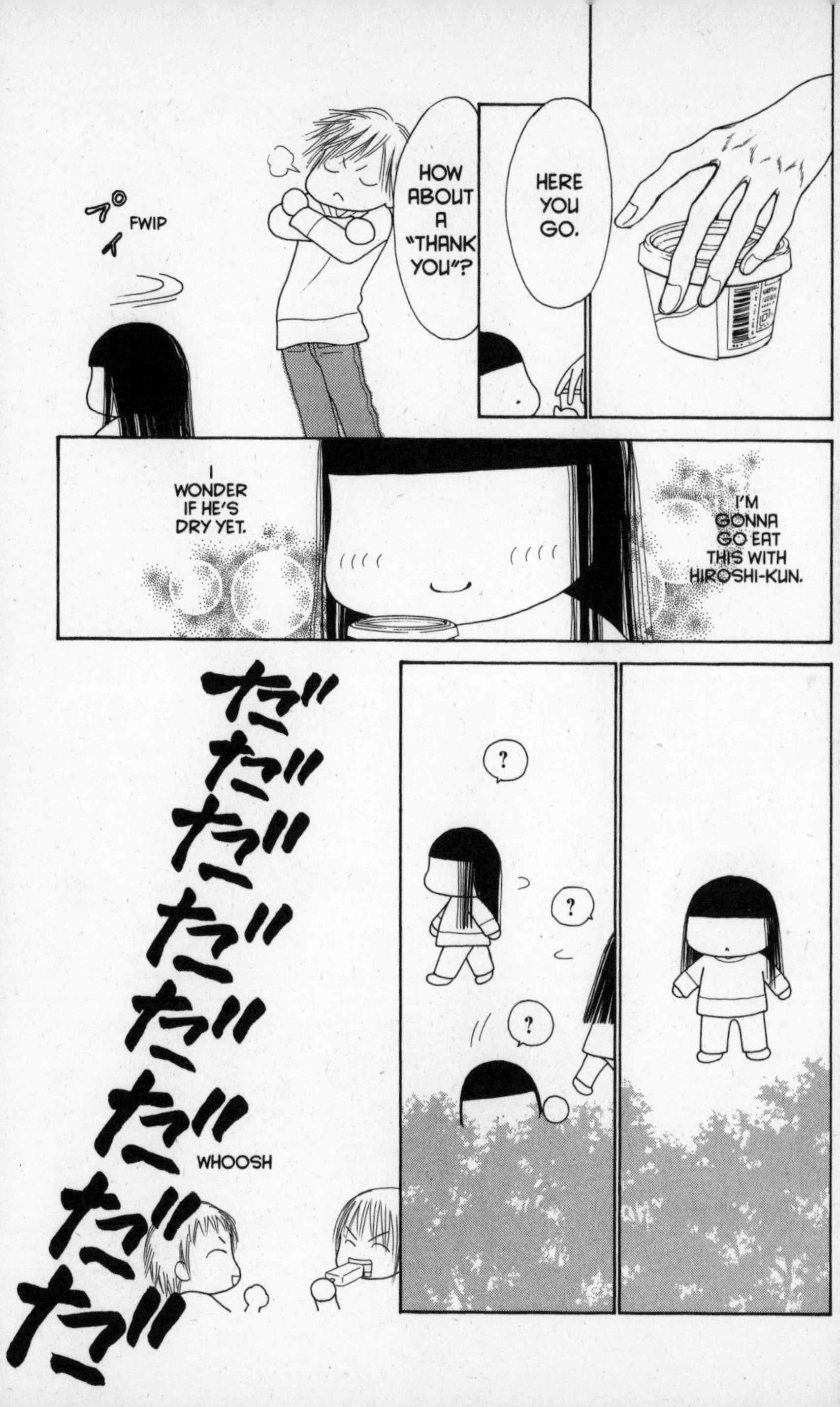
HERE YOU GO.
HOW ABOUT A "THANK YOU"?
ポイ
FWIP
I'M GONNA GO EAT THIS WITH HIROSHI-KUN.
I WONDER IF HE'S DRY YET.
?
?
?
WHOOSH

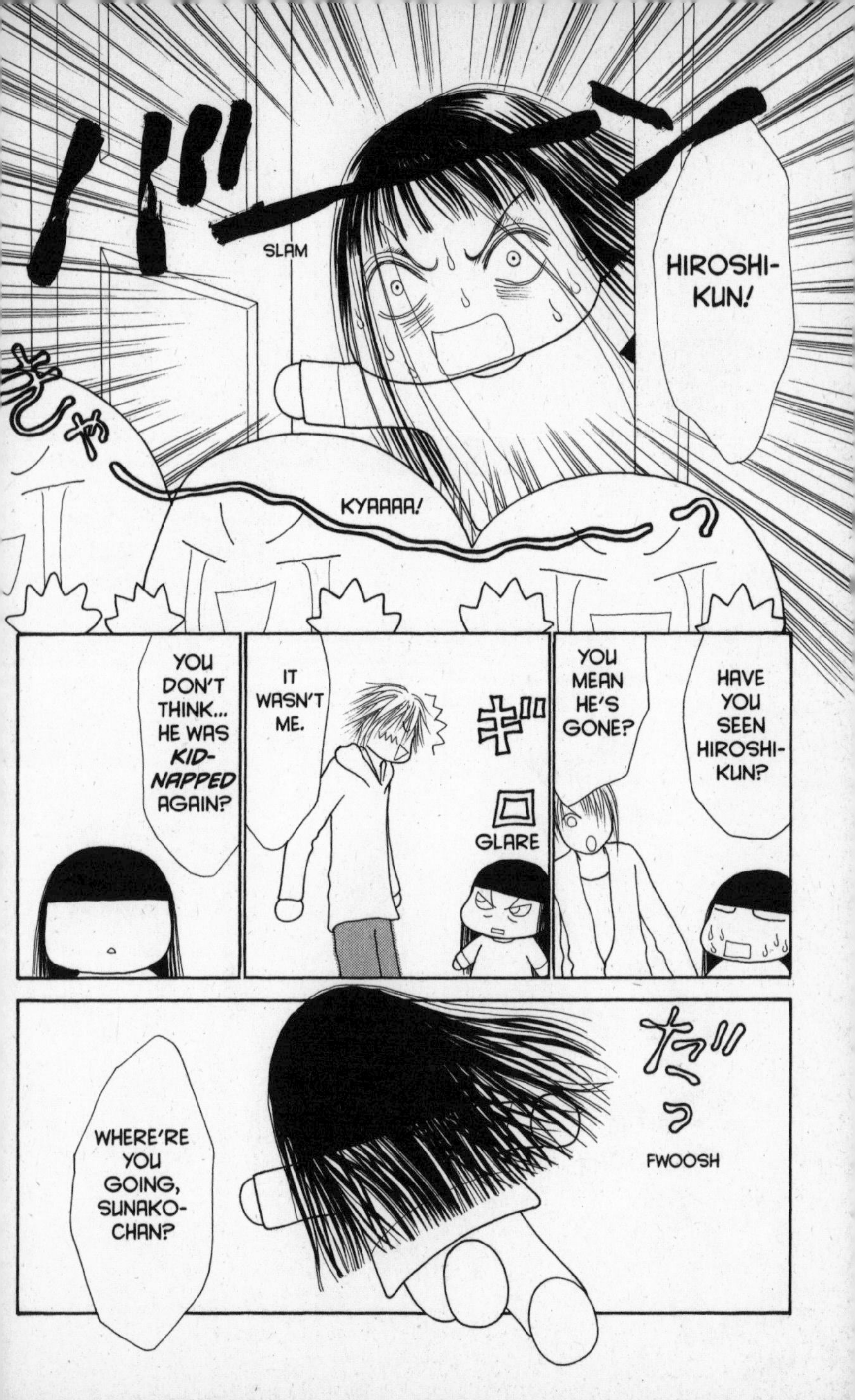
HIROSHI-KUN!
SLAM
KYAAAA!
HAVE YOU SEEN HIROSHI-KUN?
YOU MEAN HE'S GONE?
GLARE
IT WASN'T ME.
YOU DON'T THINK... HE WAS *KID-NAPPED* AGAIN?
FWOOSH
WHERE'RE YOU GOING, SUNAKO-CHAN?

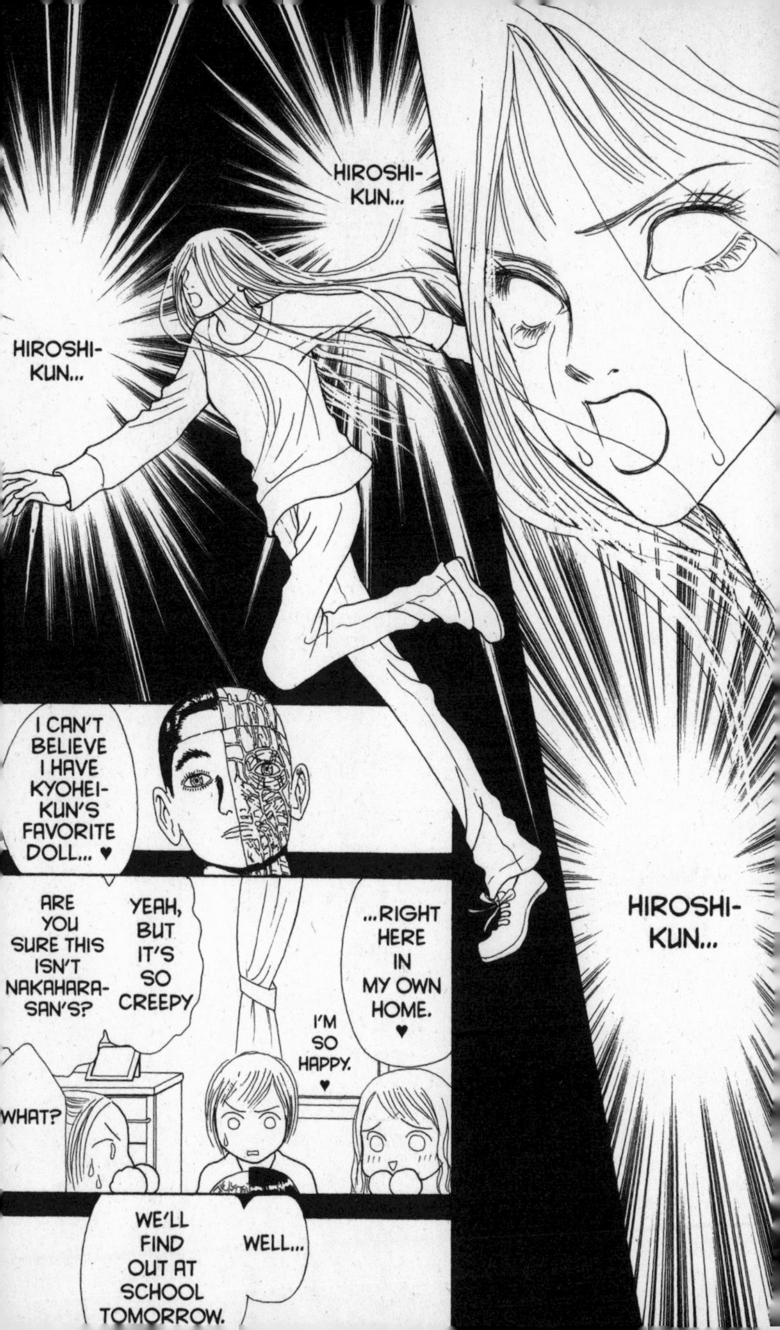
HIROSHI-KUN...
HIROSHI-KUN...
HIROSHI-KUN...
I CAN'T BELIEVE I HAVE KYOHEI-KUN'S FAVORITE DOLL... ♥
...RIGHT HERE IN MY OWN HOME. ♥
I'M SO HAPPY. ♥
YEAH, BUT IT'S SO CREEPY
ARE YOU SURE THIS ISN'T NAKAHARA-SAN'S?
WHAT?
WELL...
WE'LL FIND OUT AT SCHOOL TOMORROW.

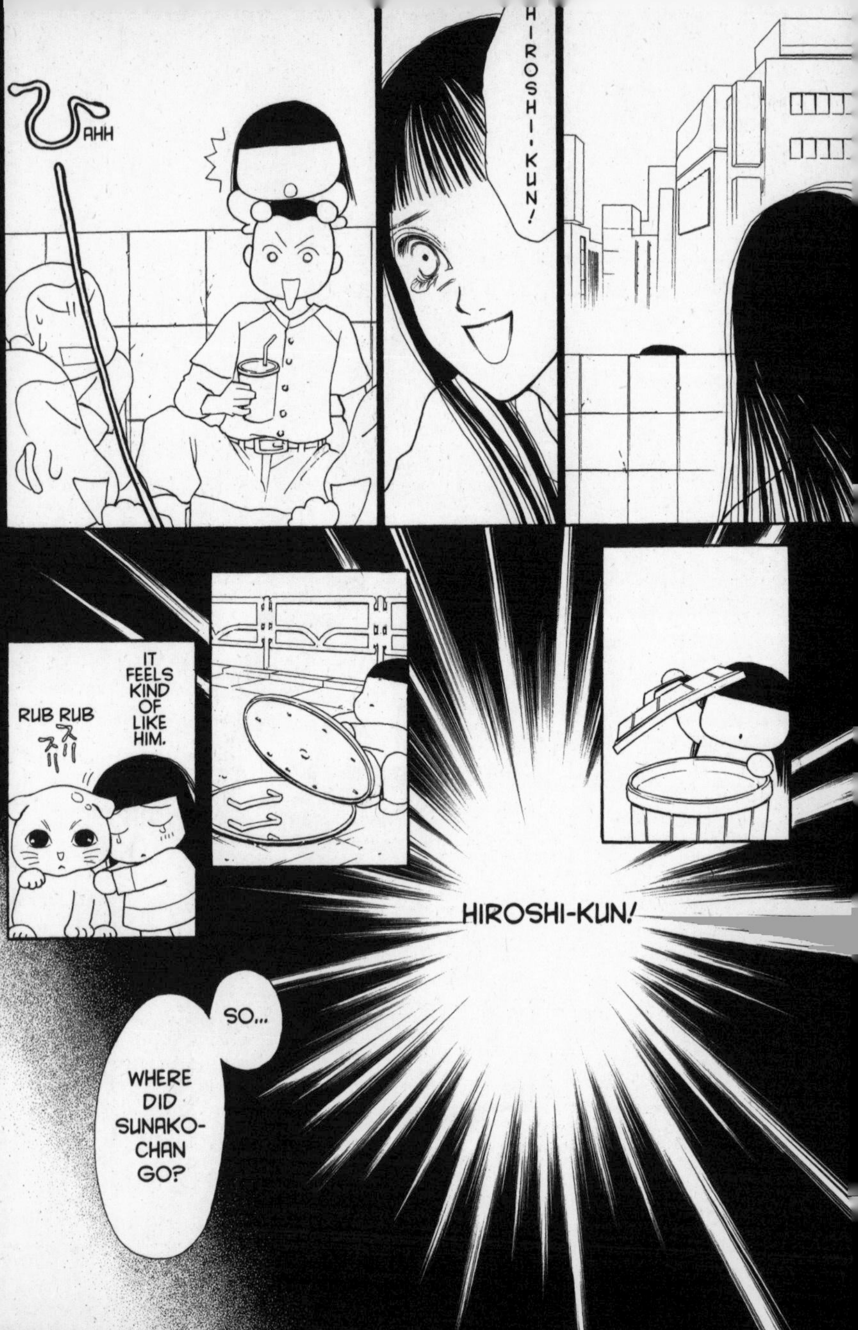
HIROSHI-KUN!
AHH
IT FEELS KIND OF LIKE HIM.
RUB RUB
HIROSHI-KUN!
SO...
WHERE DID SUNAKO-CHAN GO?

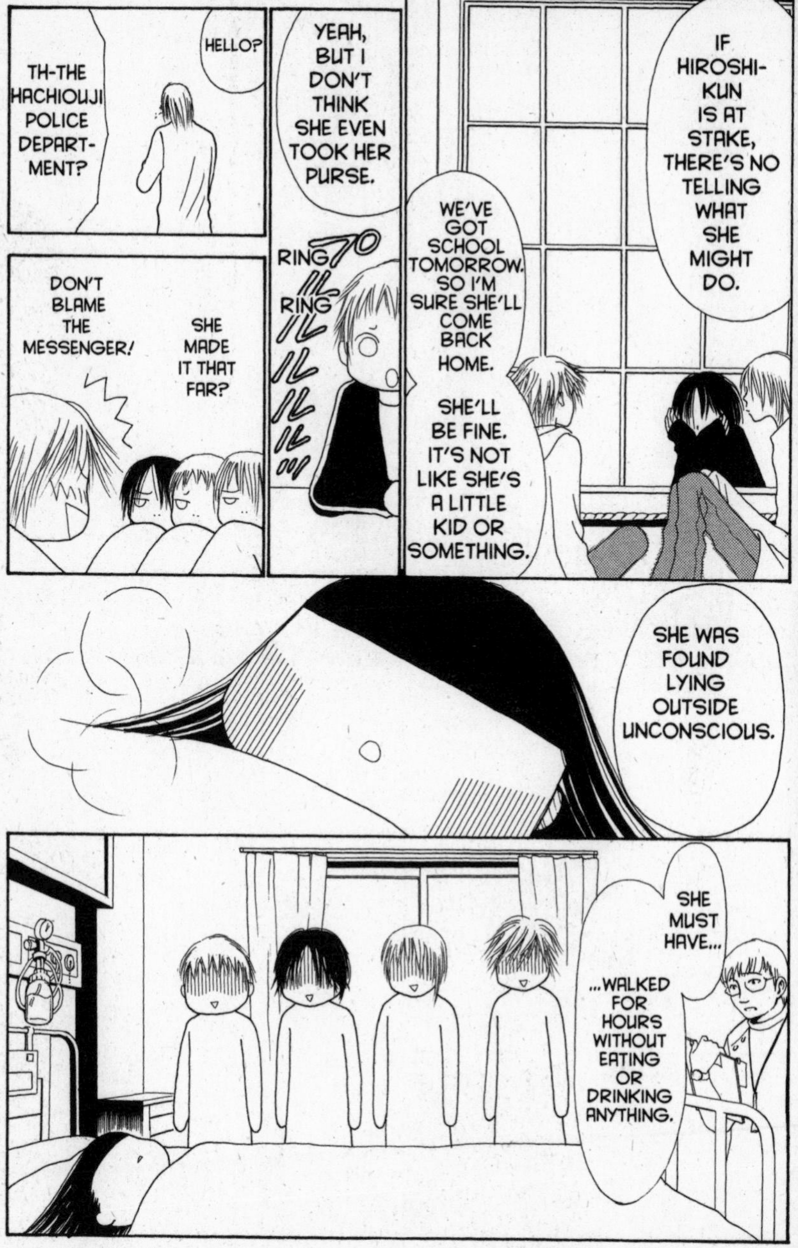
IF HIROSHI-KUN IS AT STAKE, THERE'S NO TELLING WHAT SHE MIGHT DO.
WE'VE GOT SCHOOL TOMORROW. SO I'M SURE SHE'LL COME BACK HOME.
SHE'LL BE FINE. IT'S NOT LIKE SHE'S A LITTLE KID OR SOMETHING.
YEAH, BUT I DON'T THINK SHE EVEN TOOK HER PURSE.
RING RING
HELLO?
TH-THE HACHIOUJI POLICE DEPARTMENT?
SHE MADE IT THAT FAR?
DON'T BLAME THE MESSENGER!
SHE WAS FOUND LYING OUTSIDE UNCONSCIOUS.
SHE MUST HAVE...
...WALKED FOR HOURS WITHOUT EATING OR DRINKING ANYTHING.

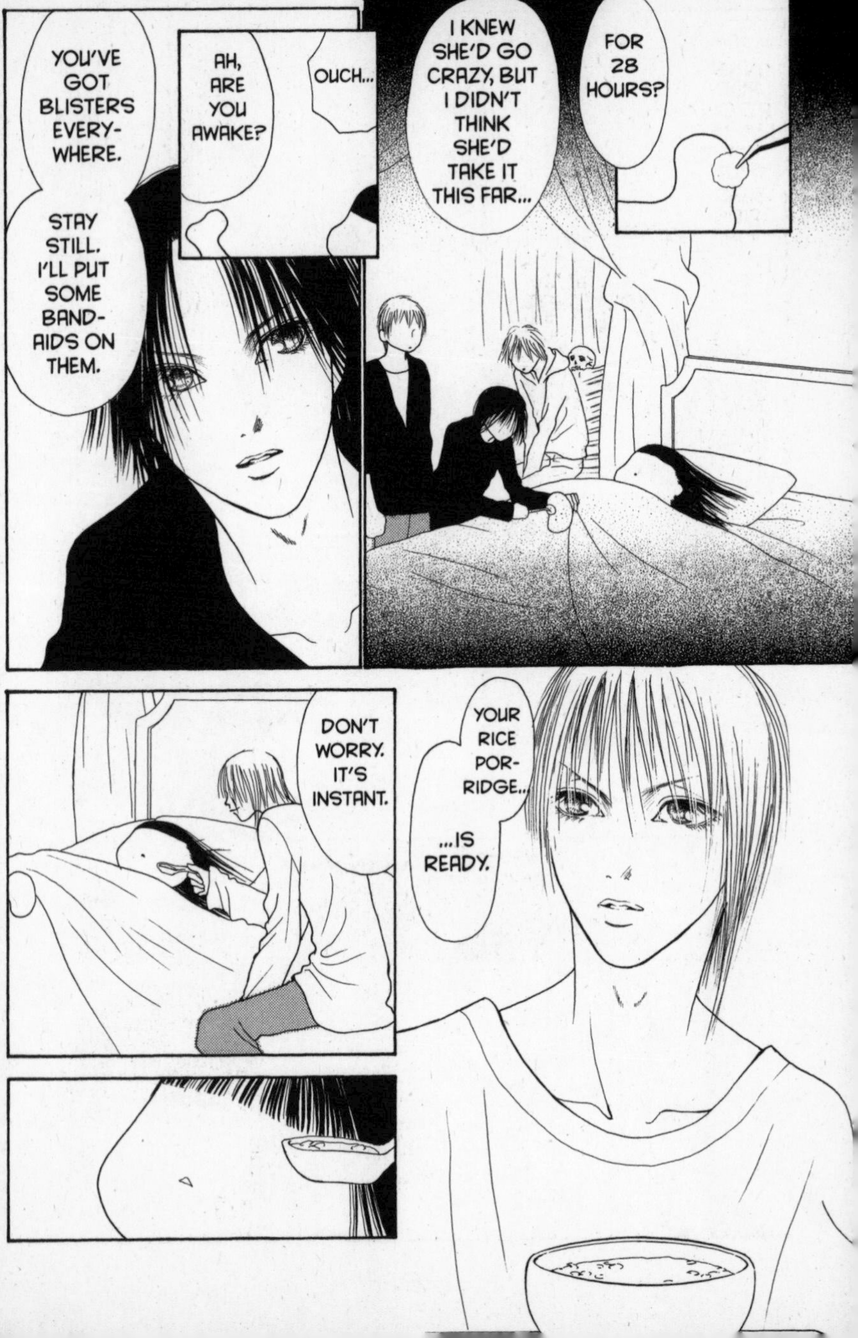
FOR 28 HOURS?
I KNEW SHE'D GO CRAZY, BUT I DIDN'T THINK SHE'D TAKE IT THIS FAR...
OUCH...
AH, ARE YOU AWAKE?
YOU'VE GOT BLISTERS EVERY-WHERE.
STAY STILL. I'LL PUT SOME BAND-AIDS ON THEM.
YOUR RICE POR-RIDGE...
...IS READY.
DON'T WORRY. IT'S INSTANT.

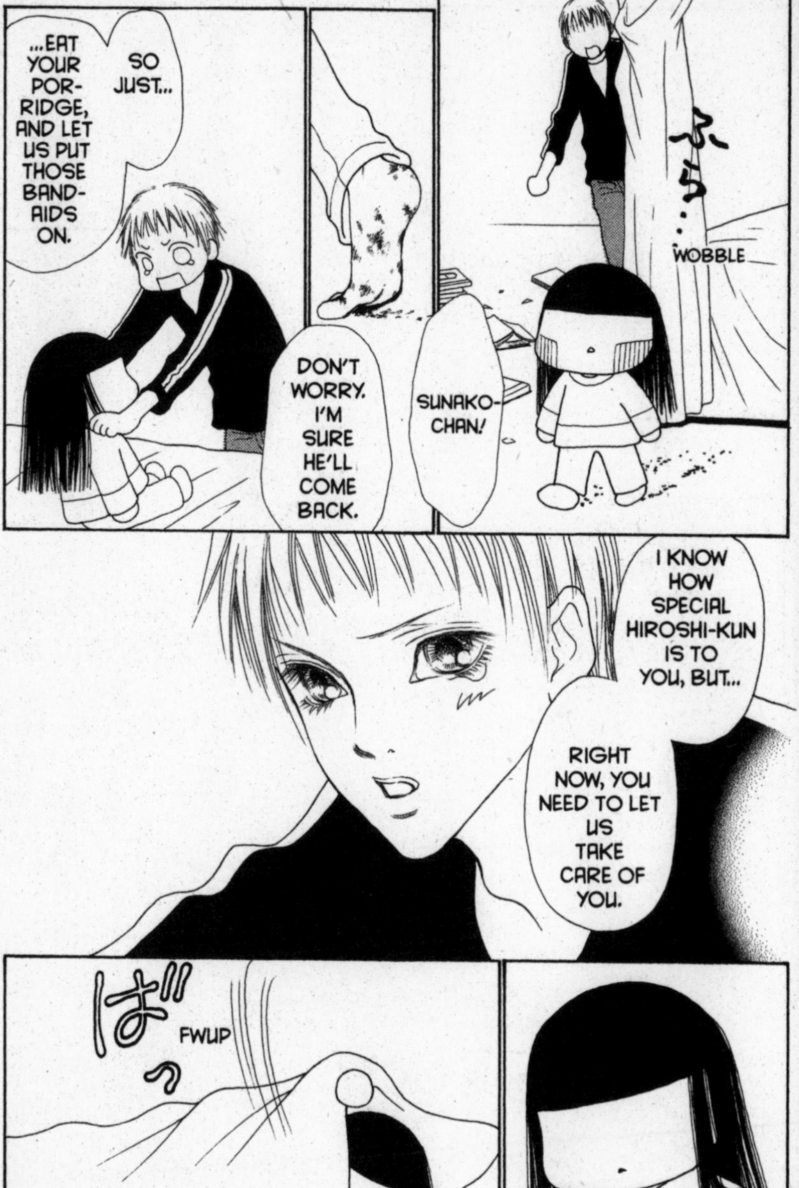
ふら…
WOBBLE
SUNAKO-CHAN!
DON'T WORRY. I'M SURE HE'LL COME BACK.
SO JUST...
...EAT YOUR PORRIDGE, AND LET US PUT THOSE BAND-AIDS ON.
I KNOW HOW SPECIAL HIROSHI-KUN IS TO YOU, BUT...
RIGHT NOW, YOU NEED TO LET US TAKE CARE OF YOU.
ばっ
FWUP

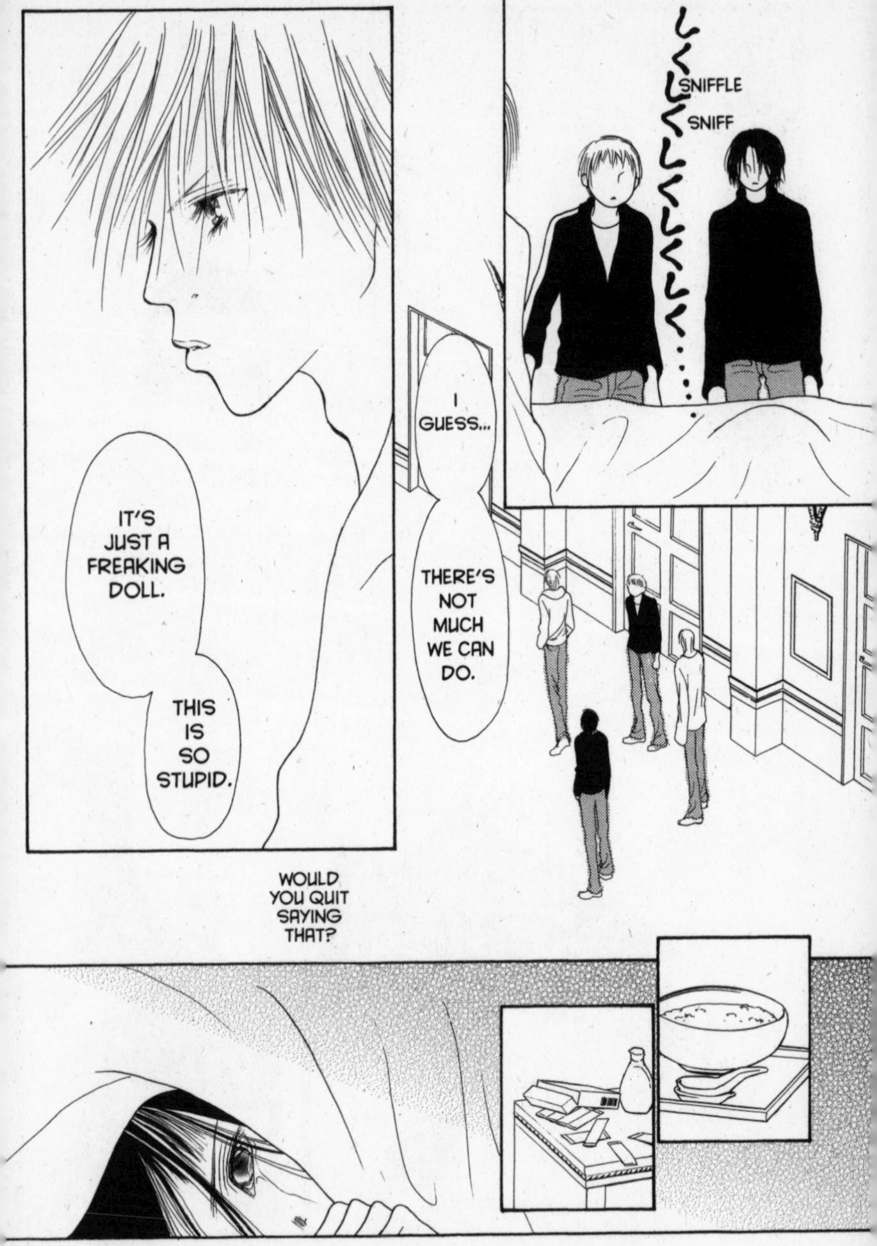
SNIFFLE
SNIFF
I GUESS...
THERE'S NOT MUCH WE CAN DO.
IT'S JUST A FREAKING DOLL.
THIS IS SO STUPID.
WOULD YOU QUIT SAYING THAT?

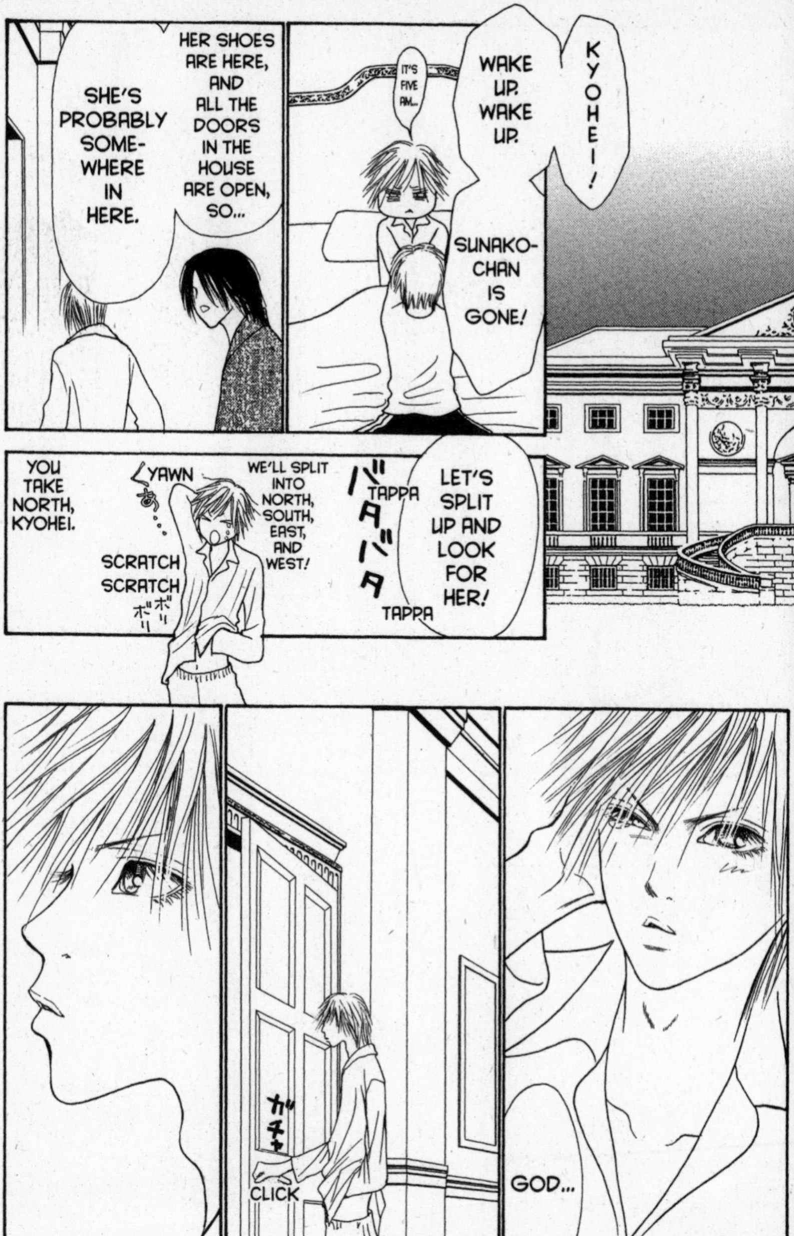
KYOHEI!
WAKE UP. WAKE UP.
IT'S FIVE AM...
SUNAKO-CHAN IS GONE!
HER SHOES ARE HERE, AND ALL THE DOORS IN THE HOUSE ARE OPEN, SO...
SHE'S PROBABLY SOMEWHERE IN HERE.
LET'S SPLIT UP AND LOOK FOR HER!
バタバタ
TAPPA
TAPPA
WE'LL SPLIT INTO NORTH, SOUTH, EAST, AND WEST!
くあ
YAWN
ボリボリ
SCRATCH SCRATCH
YOU TAKE NORTH, KYOHEI.
GOD...
ガチャ
CLICK

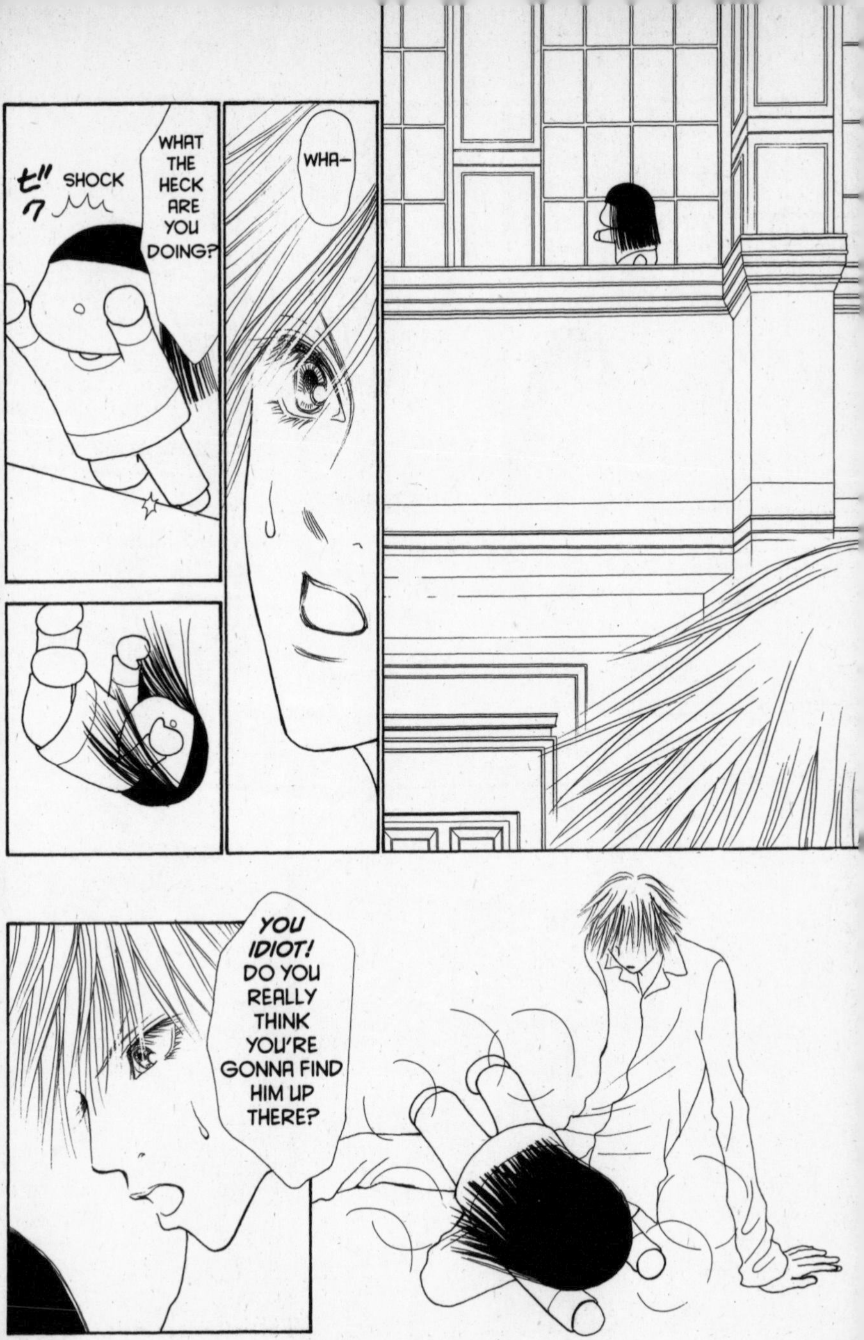
WHA-
WHAT THE HECK ARE YOU DOING?
SHOCK
YOU IDIOT! DO YOU REALLY THINK YOU'RE GONNA FIND HIM UP THERE?

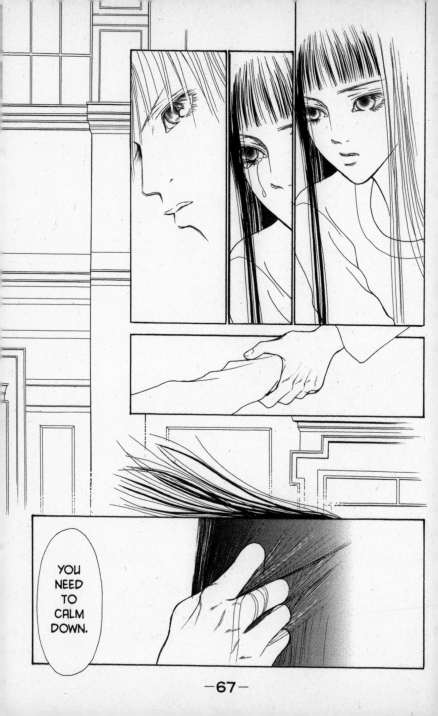

YOU
NEED
TO
CALM
DOWN.

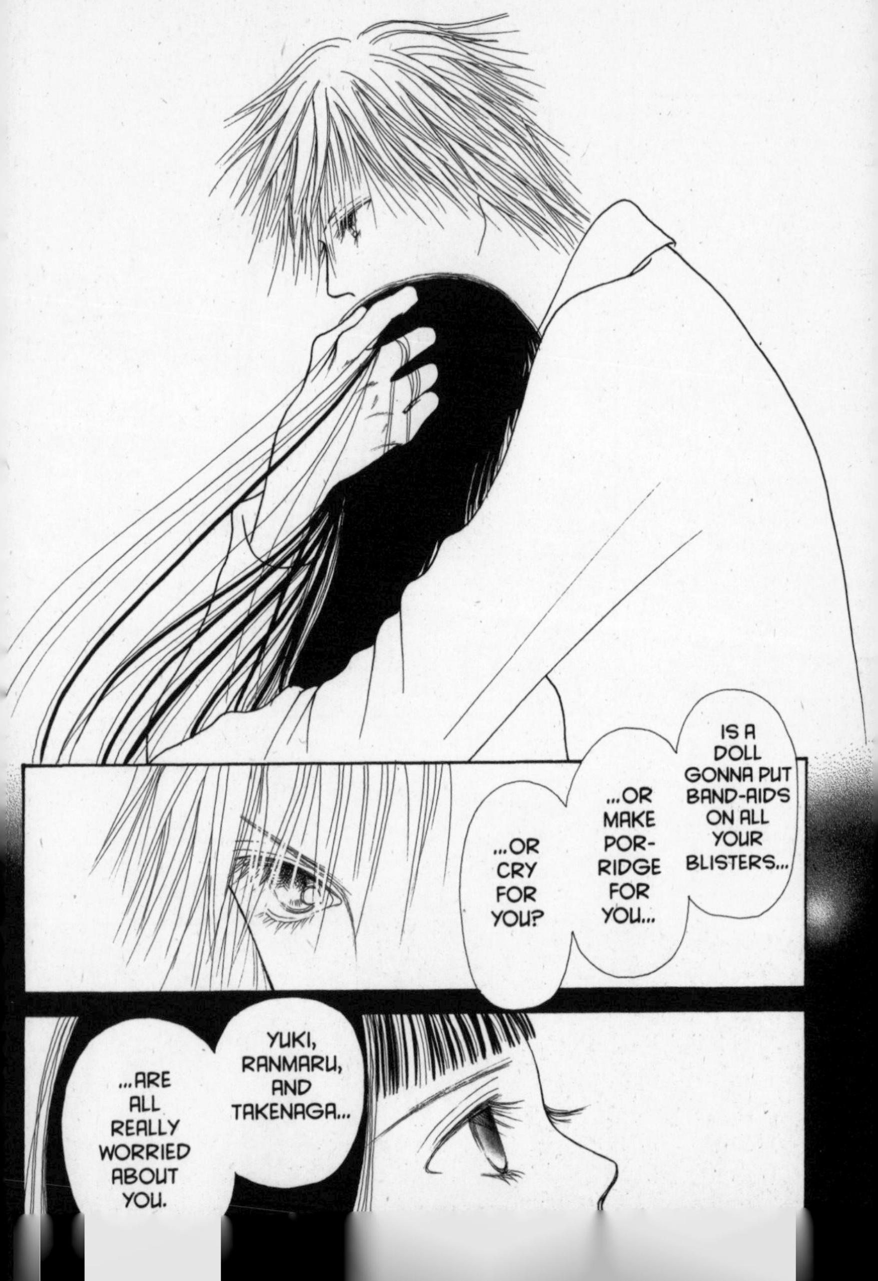
IS A DOLL GONNA PUT BAND-AIDS ON ALL YOUR BLISTERS...
...OR MAKE POR-RIDGE FOR YOU...
...OR CRY FOR YOU?
YUKI, RANMARU, AND TAKENAGA...
...ARE ALL REALLY WORRIED ABOUT YOU.

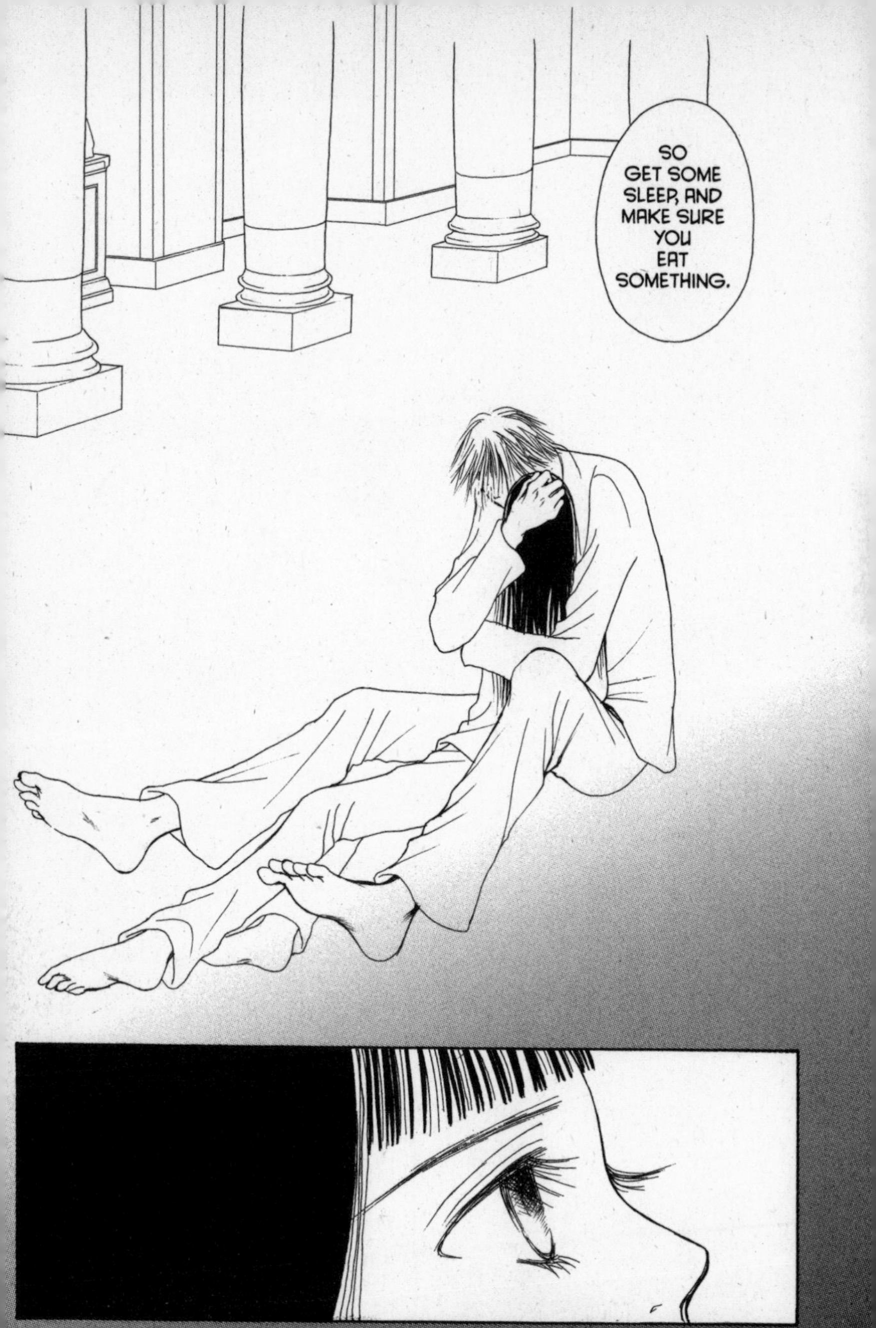
SO GET SOME SLEEP, AND MAKE SURE YOU EAT SOMETHING.

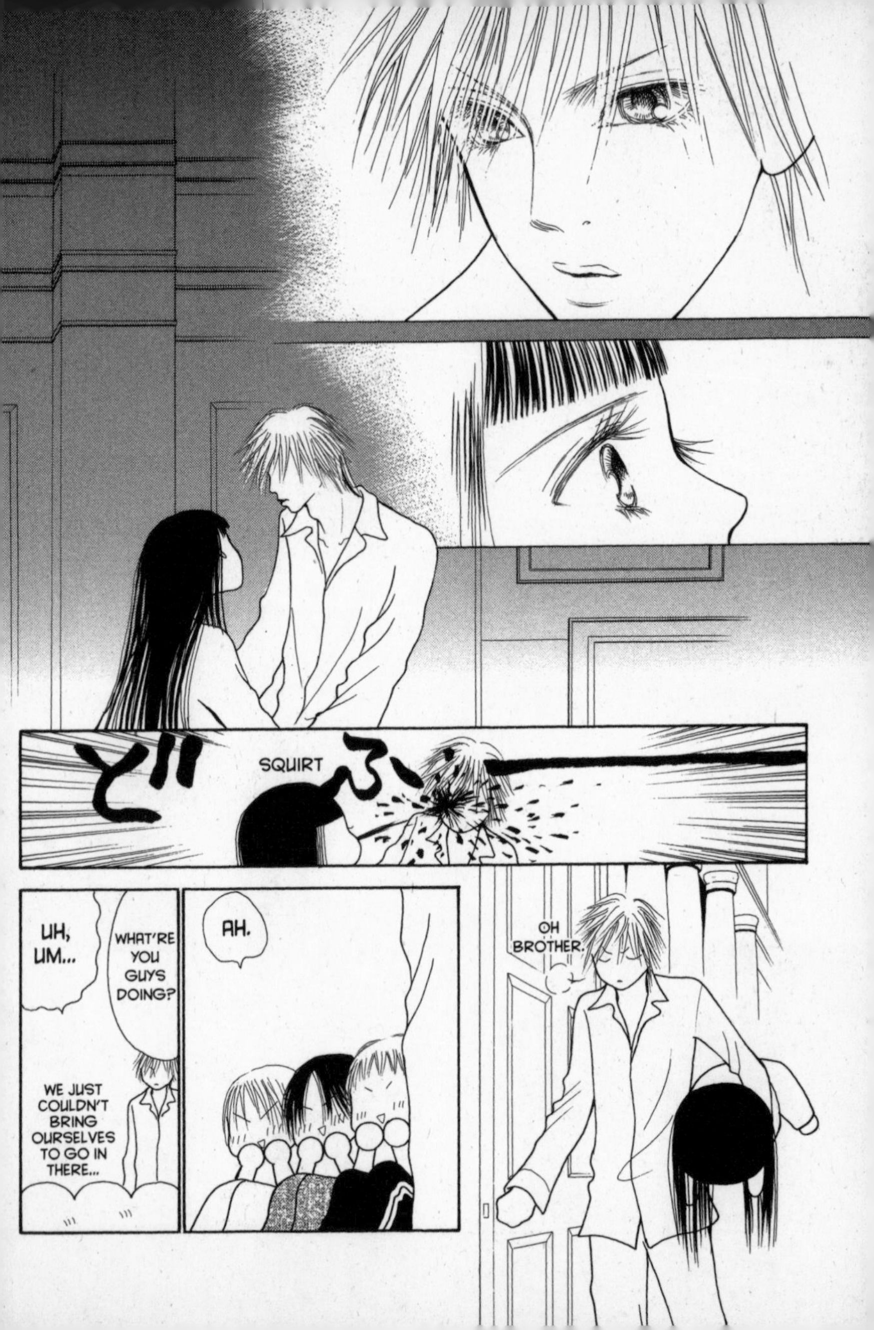
SQUIRT
OH BROTHER.
AH.
WHAT'RE YOU GUYS DOING?
UH, UM...
WE JUST COULDN'T BRING OURSELVES TO GO IN THERE...

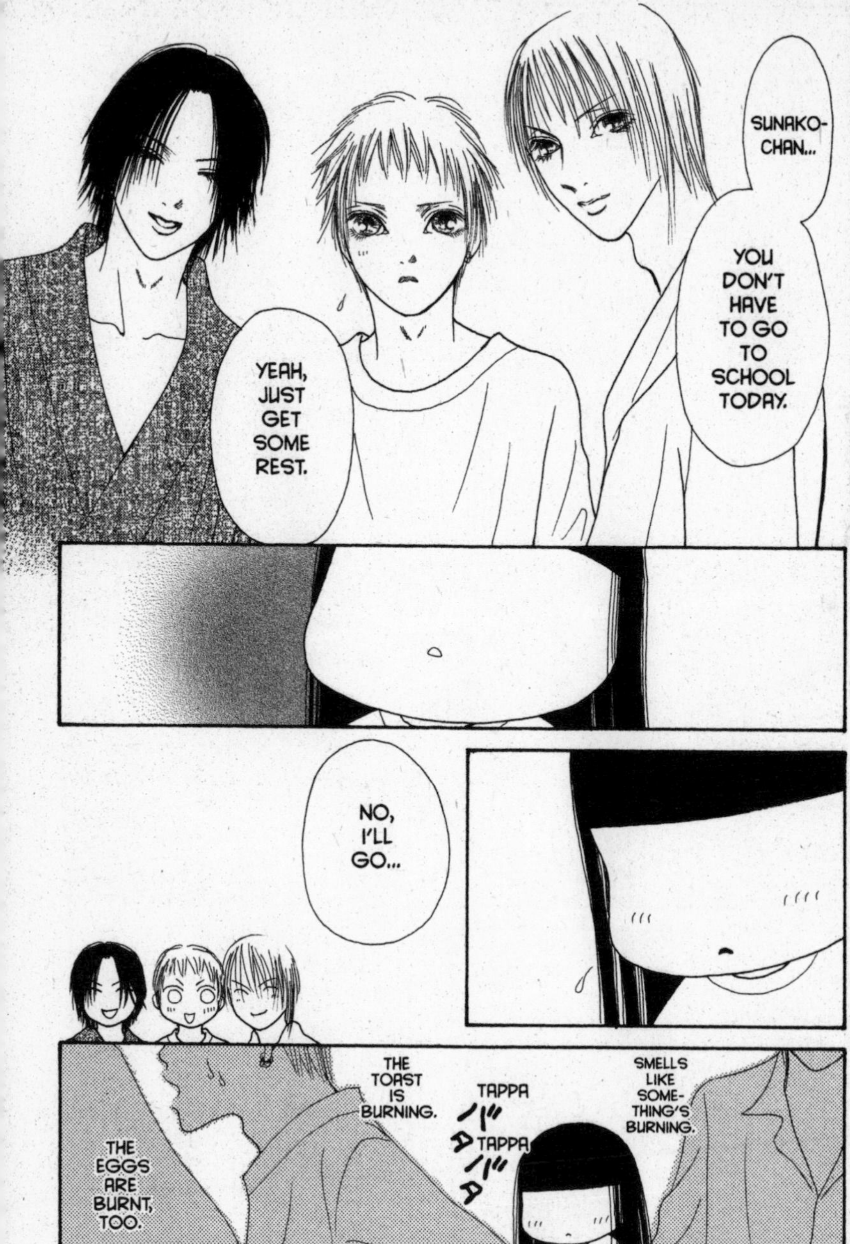
SUNAKO-CHAN...
YOU DON'T HAVE TO GO TO SCHOOL TODAY.
YEAH, JUST GET SOME REST.
NO, I'LL GO...
SMELLS LIKE SOME-THING'S BURNING.
TAPPA
TAPPA
THE TOAST IS BURNING.
THE EGGS ARE BURNT, TOO.

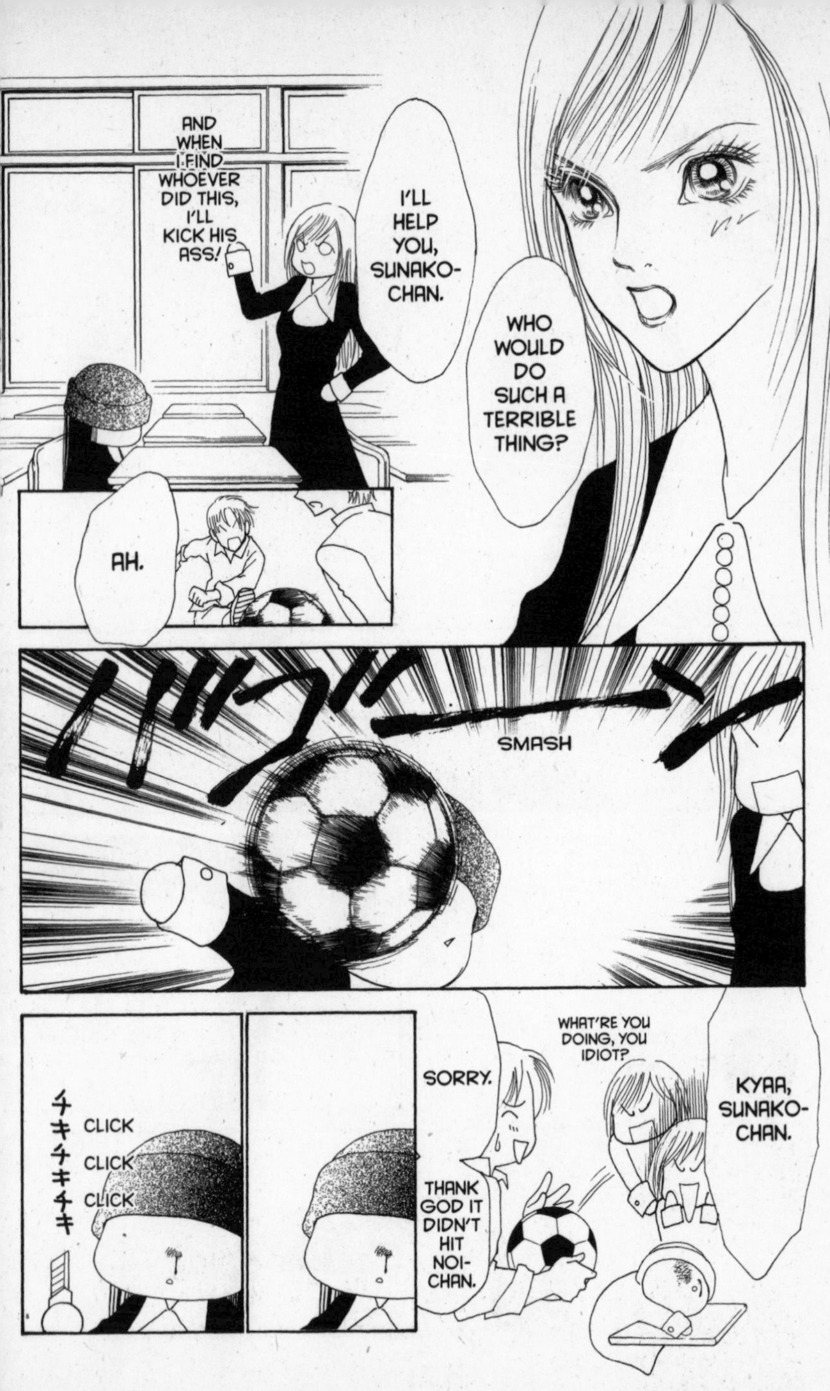
WHO WOULD DO SUCH A TERRIBLE THING?
I'LL HELP YOU, SUNAKO-CHAN.
AND WHEN I FIND WHOEVER DID THIS, I'LL KICK HIS ASS!
AH.
SMASH
KYAA, SUNAKO-CHAN.
WHAT'RE YOU DOING, YOU IDIOT?
SORRY.
THANK GOD IT DIDN'T HIT NOI-CHAN.
チキチキチキ
CLICK
CLICK
CLICK

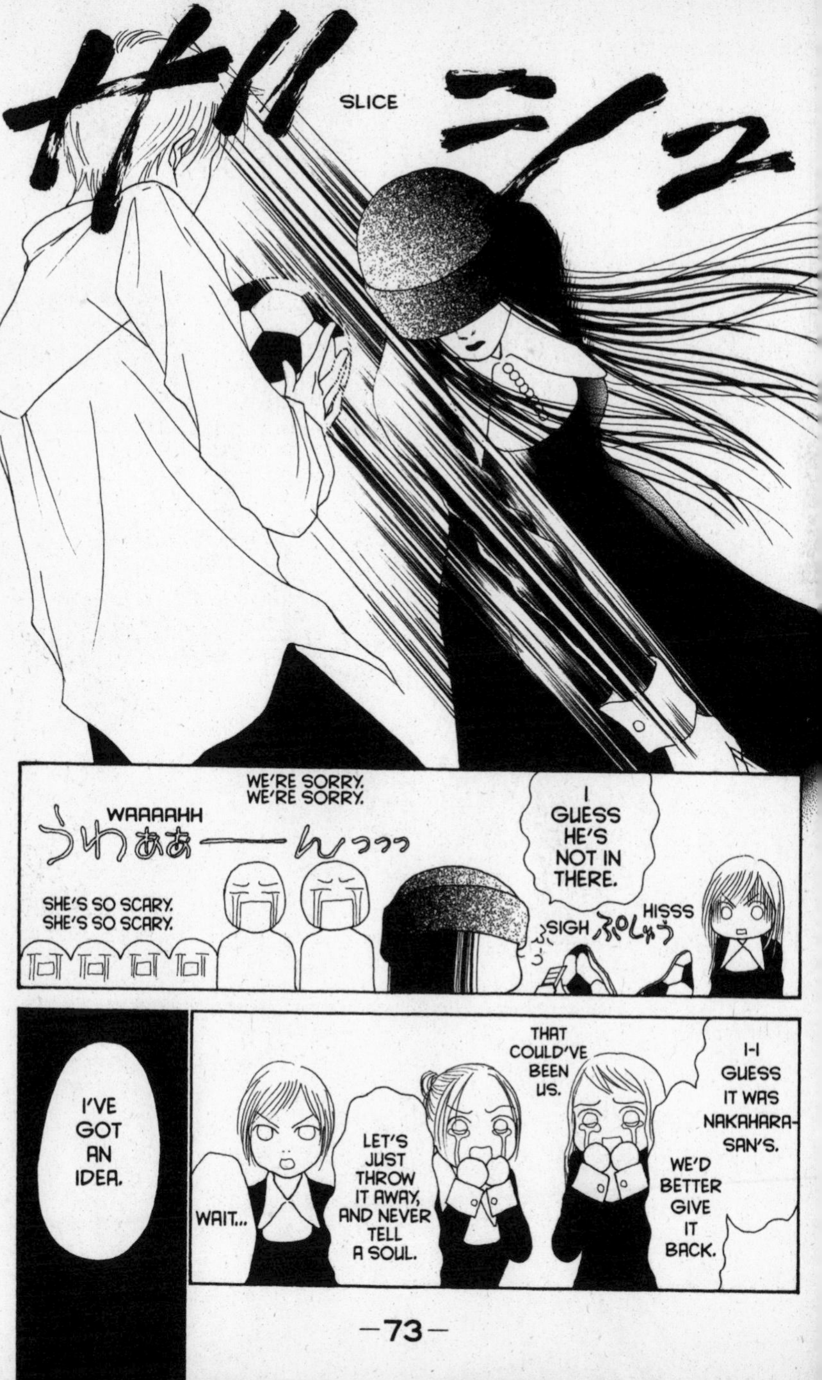
SLICE
I GUESS HE'S NOT IN THERE.
HISSS
SIGH
WE'RE SORRY. WE'RE SORRY.
WAAAAHH
SHE'S SO SCARY. SHE'S SO SCARY.
I-I GUESS IT WAS NAKAHARA-SAN'S.
WE'D BETTER GIVE IT BACK.
THAT COULD'VE BEEN US.
LET'S JUST THROW IT AWAY, AND NEVER TELL A SOUL.
WAIT...
I'VE GOT AN IDEA.

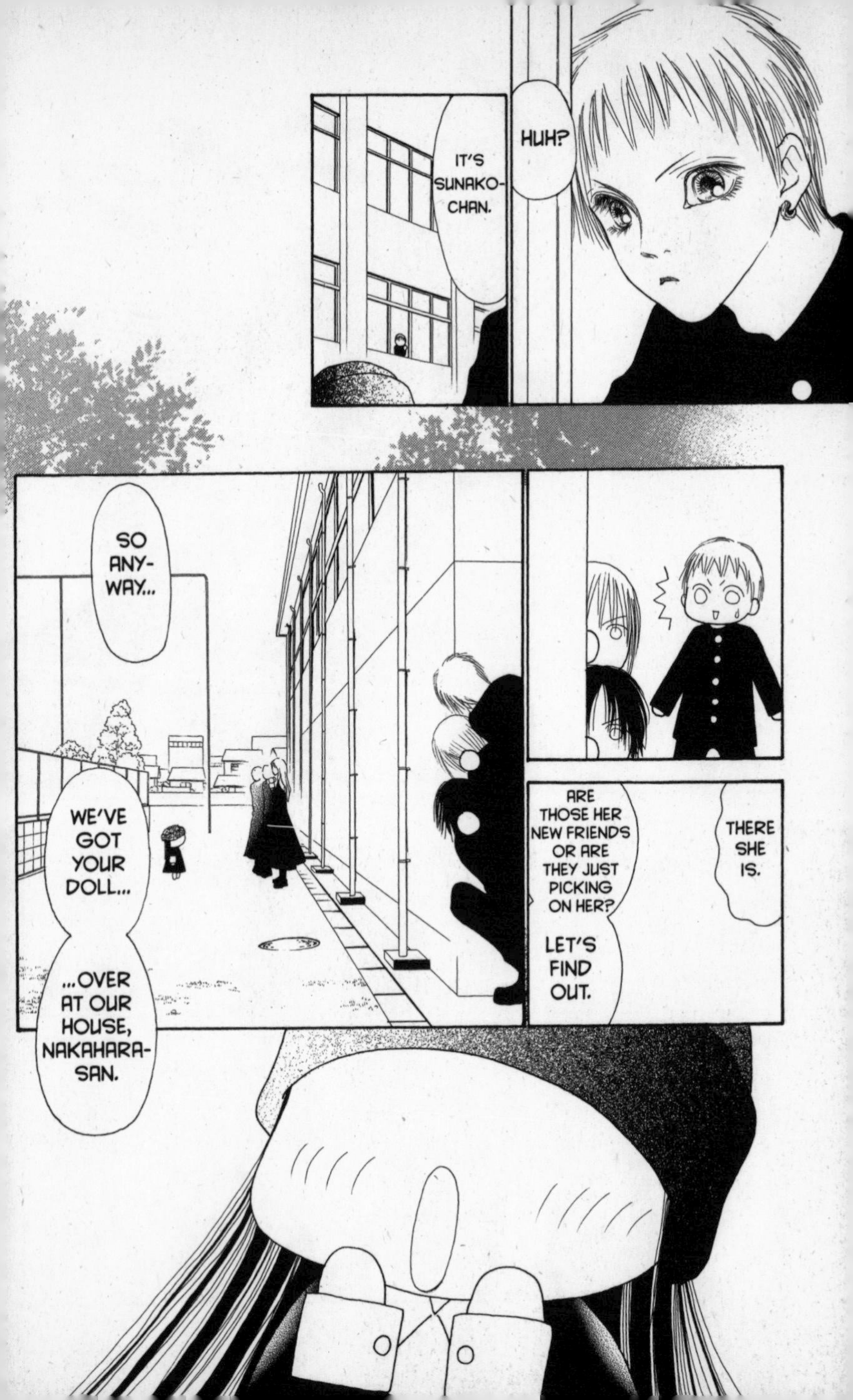
HUH?
IT'S SUNAKO-CHAN.
THERE SHE IS.
ARE THOSE HER NEW FRIENDS OR ARE THEY JUST PICKING ON HER?
LET'S FIND OUT.
SO ANY-WAY...
WE'VE GOT YOUR DOLL...
...OVER AT OUR HOUSE, NAKAHARA-SAN.

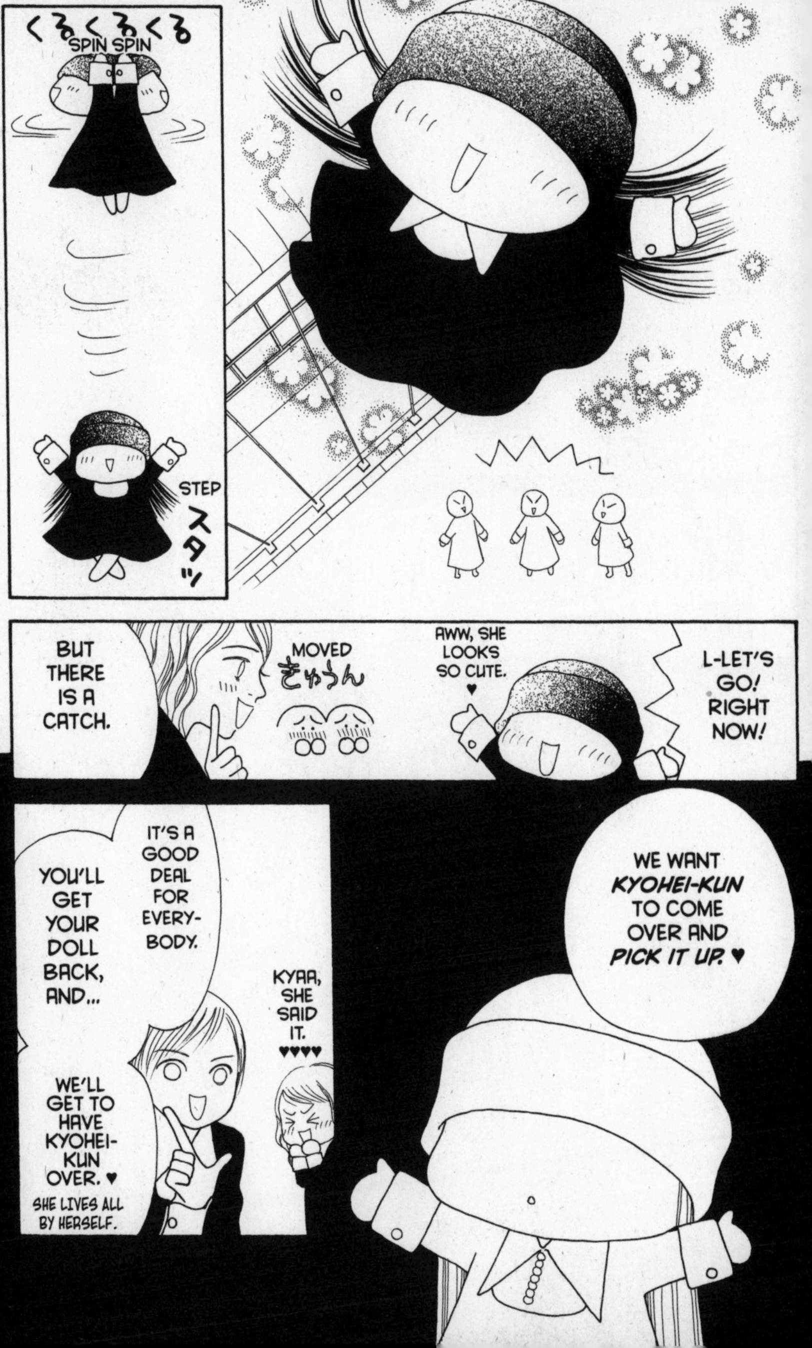
くるくるくる
SPIN SPIN
STEP
スタッ
L-LET'S GO! RIGHT NOW!
AWW, SHE LOOKS SO CUTE. ♥
MOVED
きゅうん
BUT THERE IS A CATCH.
WE WANT *KYOHEI-KUN* TO COME OVER AND *PICK IT UP.* ♥
IT'S A GOOD DEAL FOR EVERY-BODY.
YOU'LL GET YOUR DOLL BACK, AND...
KYAA, SHE SAID IT. ♥♥♥♥
WE'LL GET TO HAVE KYOHEI-KUN OVER. ♥
SHE LIVES ALL BY HERSELF.

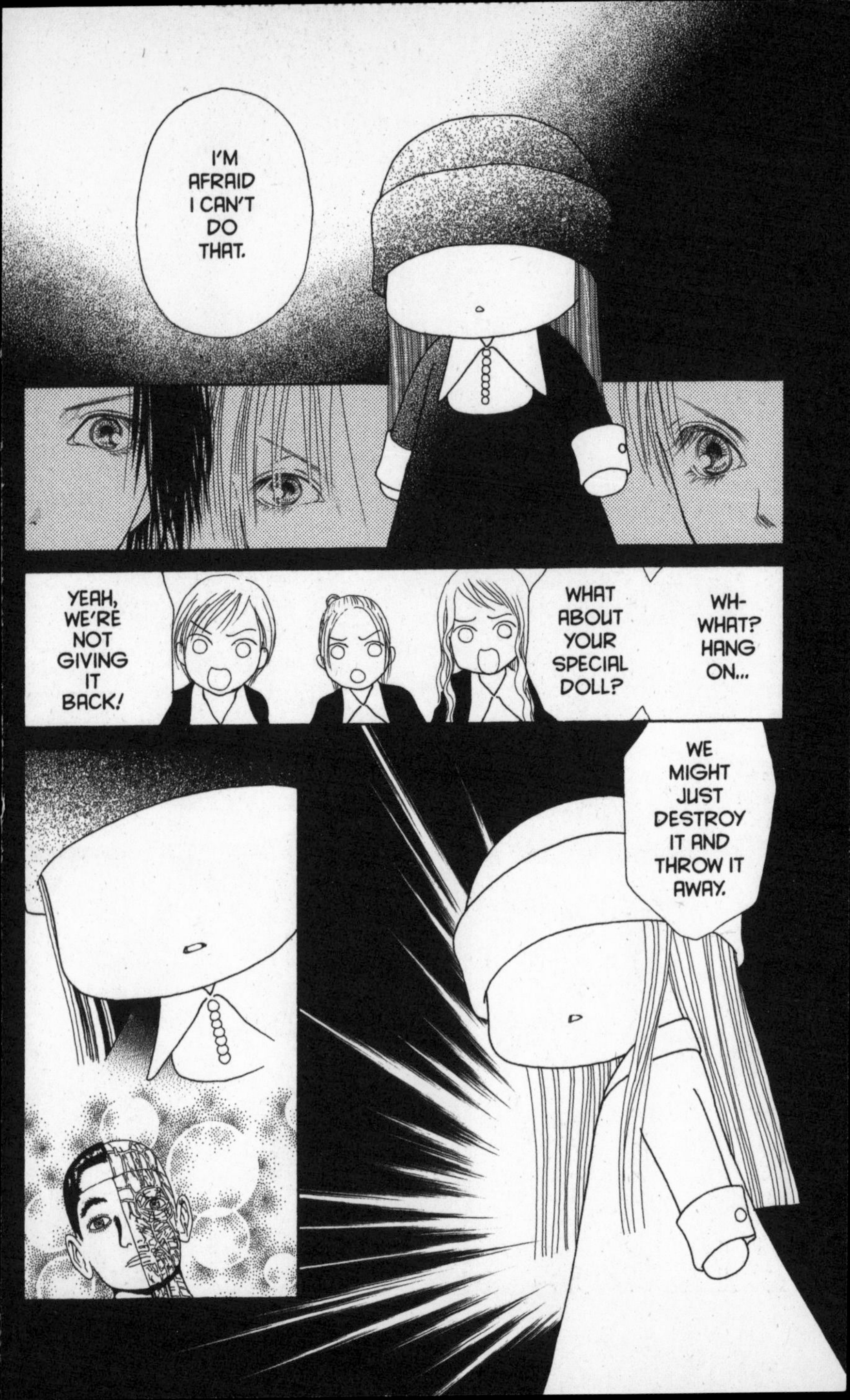
I'M AFRAID I CAN'T DO THAT.
WH- WHAT? HANG ON...
WHAT ABOUT YOUR SPECIAL DOLL?
YEAH, WE'RE NOT GIVING IT BACK!
WE MIGHT JUST DESTROY IT AND THROW IT AWAY.

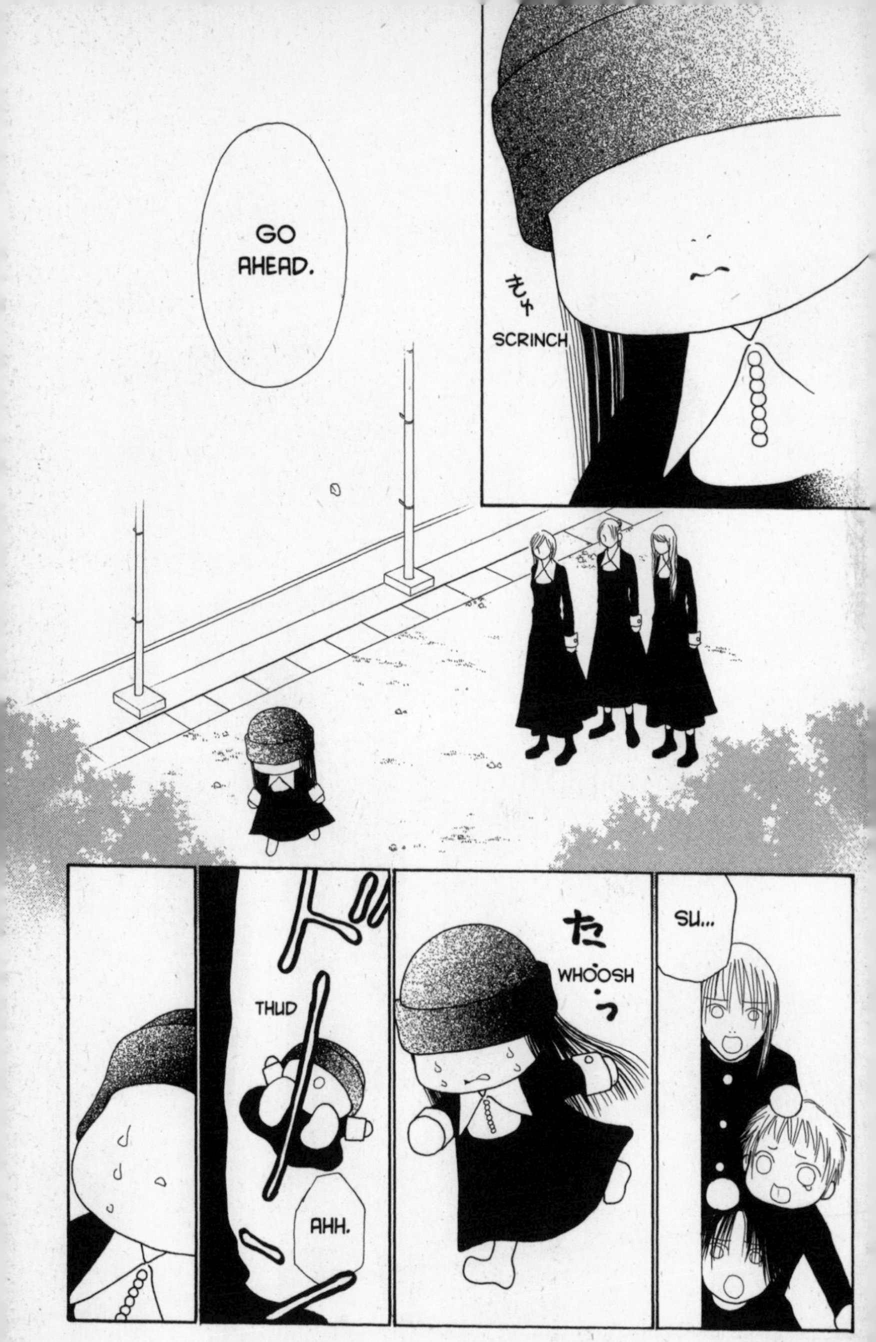
もゅ
SCRINCH
GO AHEAD.
SU...
たっ
WHOOSH
ド
THUD
AHH.

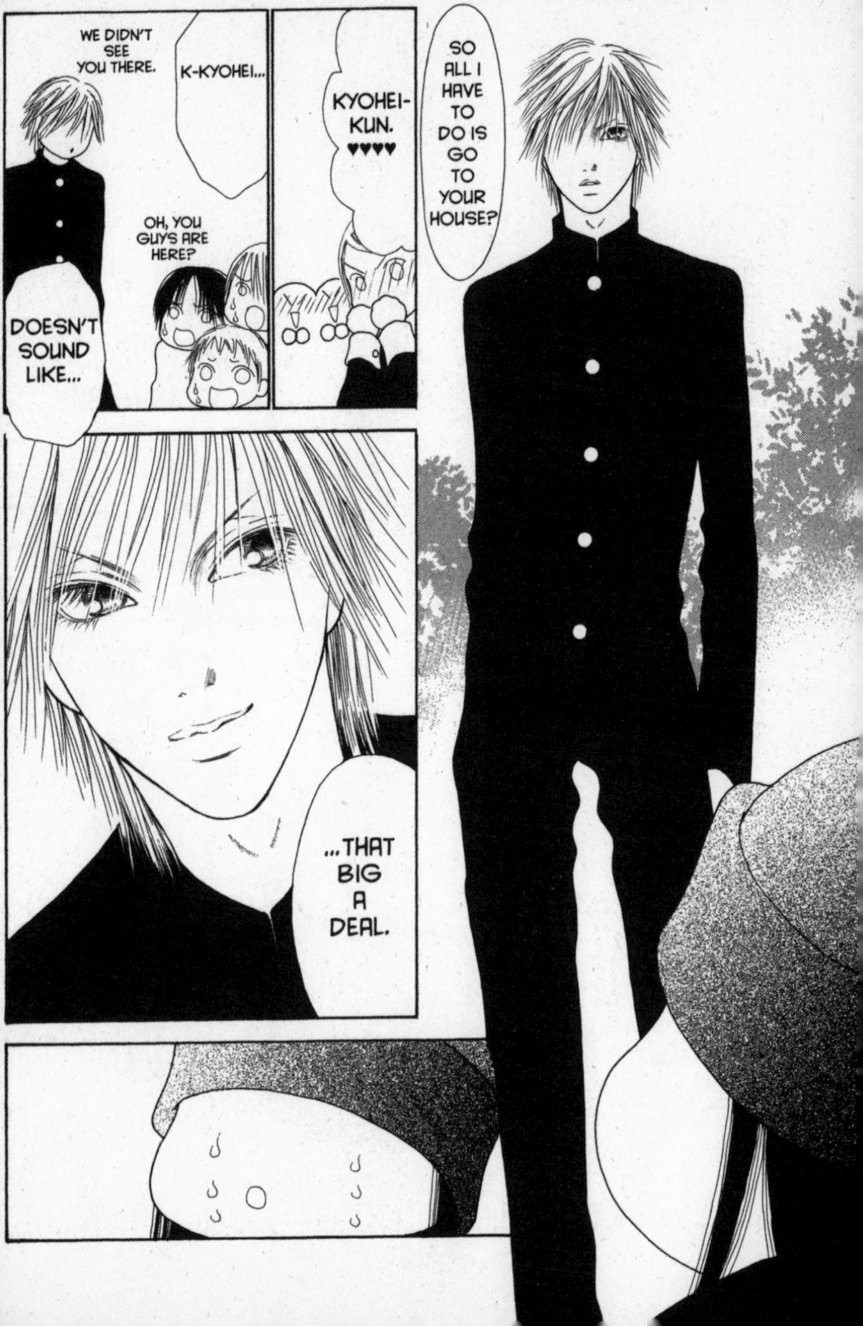
SO ALL I HAVE TO DO IS GO TO YOUR HOUSE?
KYOHEI-KUN. ♥♥♥♥
K-KYOHEI...
WE DIDN'T SEE YOU THERE.
OH, YOU GUYS ARE HERE?
DOESN'T SOUND LIKE...
...THAT BIG A DEAL.

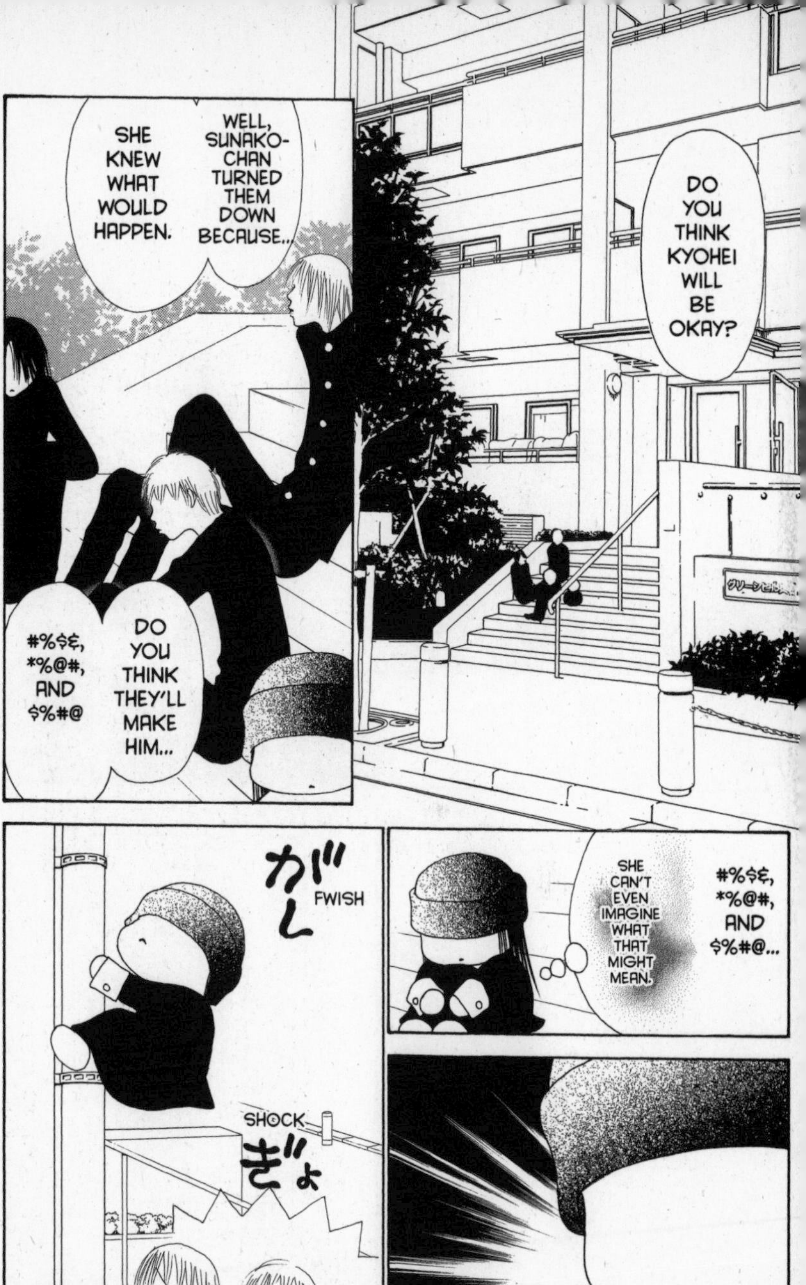
DO YOU THINK KYOHEI WILL BE OKAY?
WELL, SUNAKO-CHAN TURNED THEM DOWN BECAUSE...
SHE KNEW WHAT WOULD HAPPEN.
DO YOU THINK THEY'LL MAKE HIM...
#%$&, *%@#, AND $%#@
#%$&, *%@#, AND $%#@...
SHE CAN'T EVEN IMAGINE WHAT THAT MIGHT MEAN.
がし
FWISH
SHOCK
ぎょ

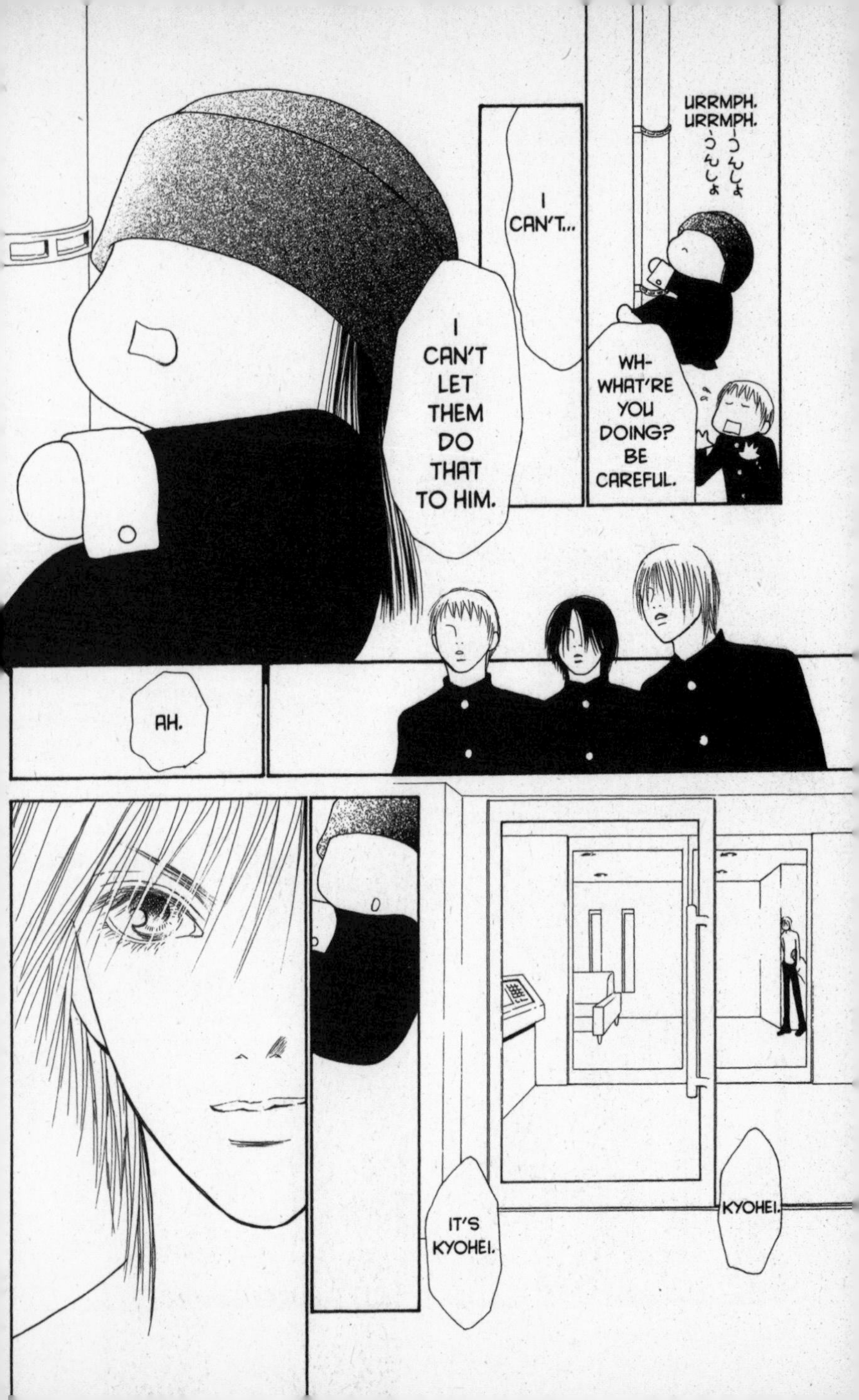
URRMPH. URRMPH.
うんしょ うんしょ
WH- WHAT'RE YOU DOING? BE CAREFUL.
I CAN'T...
I CAN'T LET THEM DO THAT TO HIM.
AH.
KYOHEI.
IT'S KYOHEI.

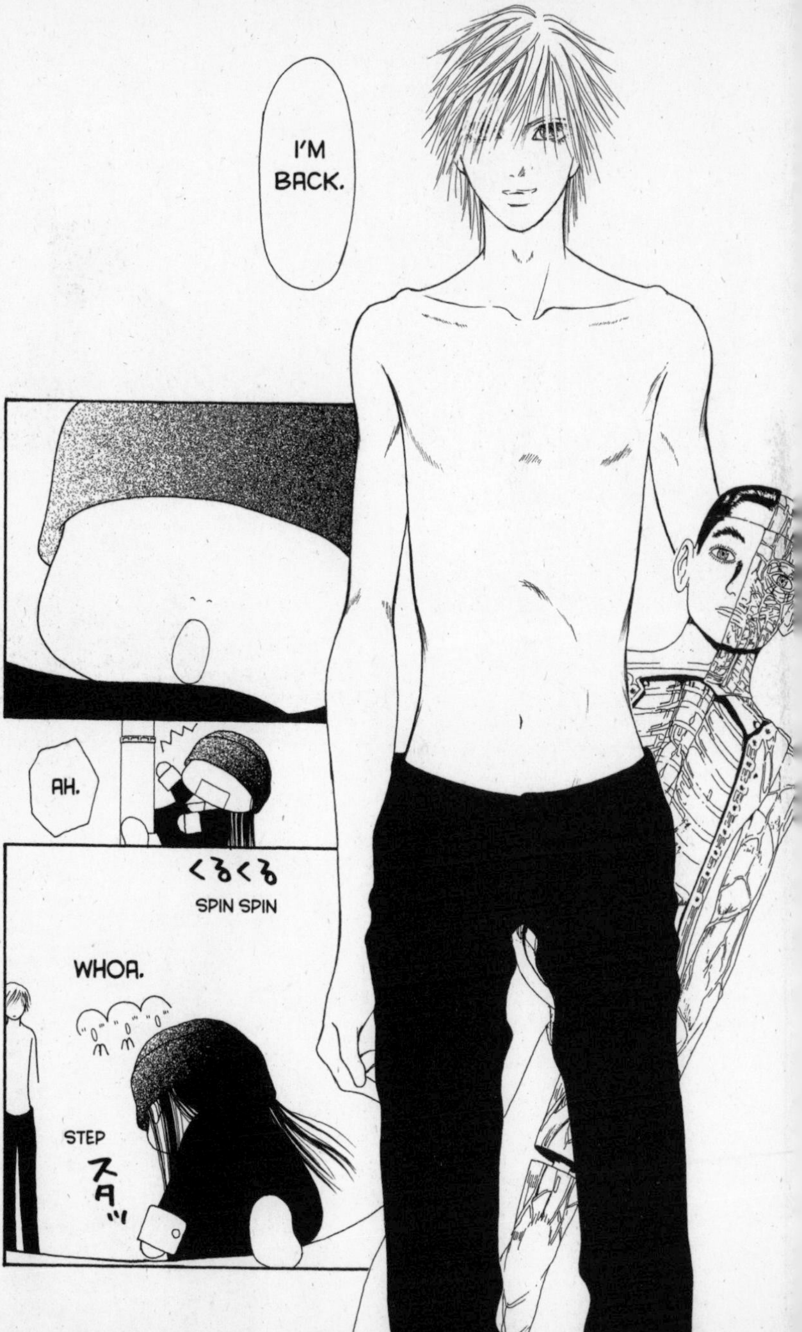
I'M BACK.
AH.
くるくる
SPIN SPIN
WHOA.
STEP
スタッ

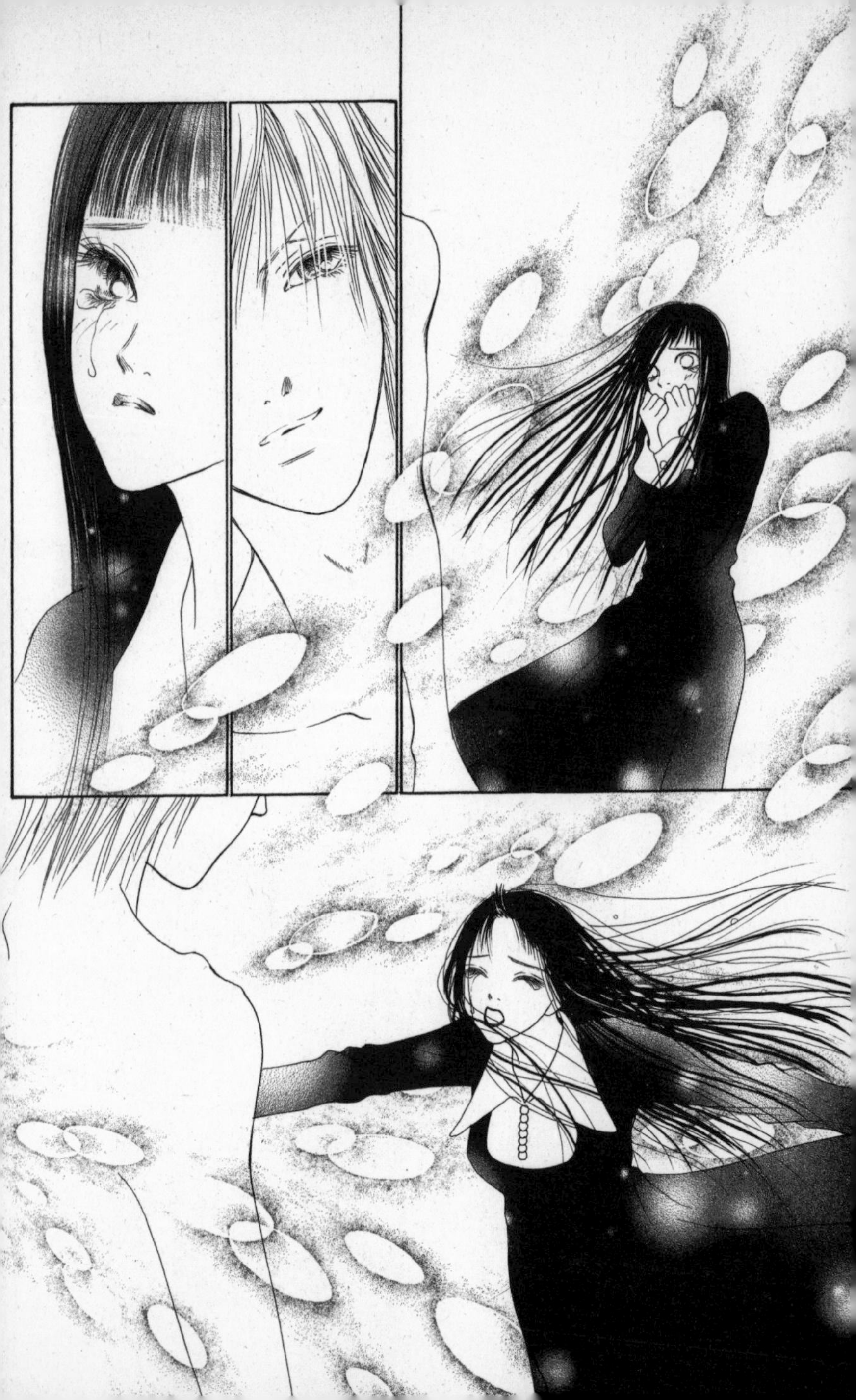

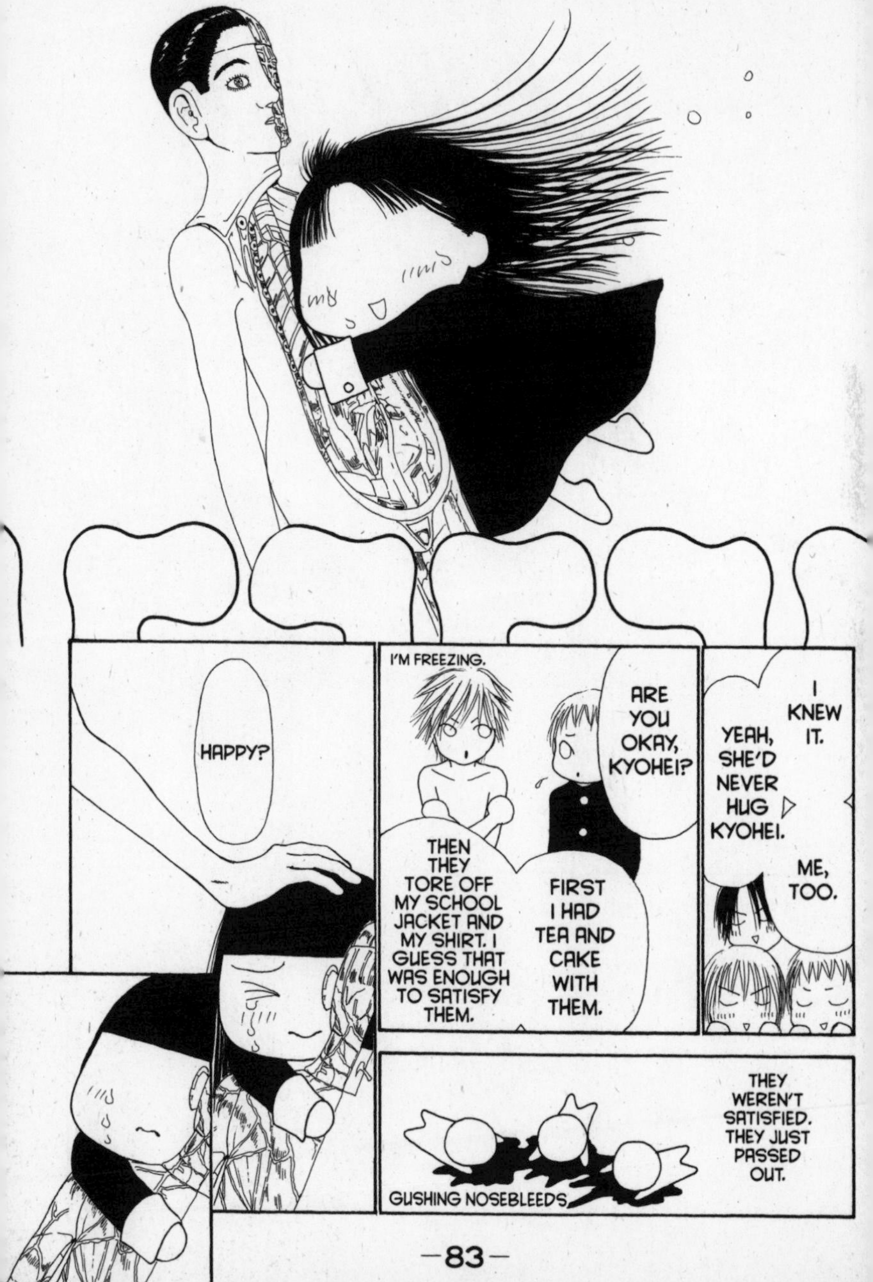
I KNEW IT.
YEAH, SHE'D NEVER HUG KYOHEI.
ME, TOO.
ARE YOU OKAY, KYOHEI?
I'M FREEZING.
FIRST I HAD TEA AND CAKE WITH THEM.
THEN THEY TORE OFF MY SCHOOL JACKET AND MY SHIRT. I GUESS THAT WAS ENOUGH TO SATISFY THEM.
THEY WEREN'T SATISFIED. THEY JUST PASSED OUT.
GUSHING NOSEBLEEDS
HAPPY?

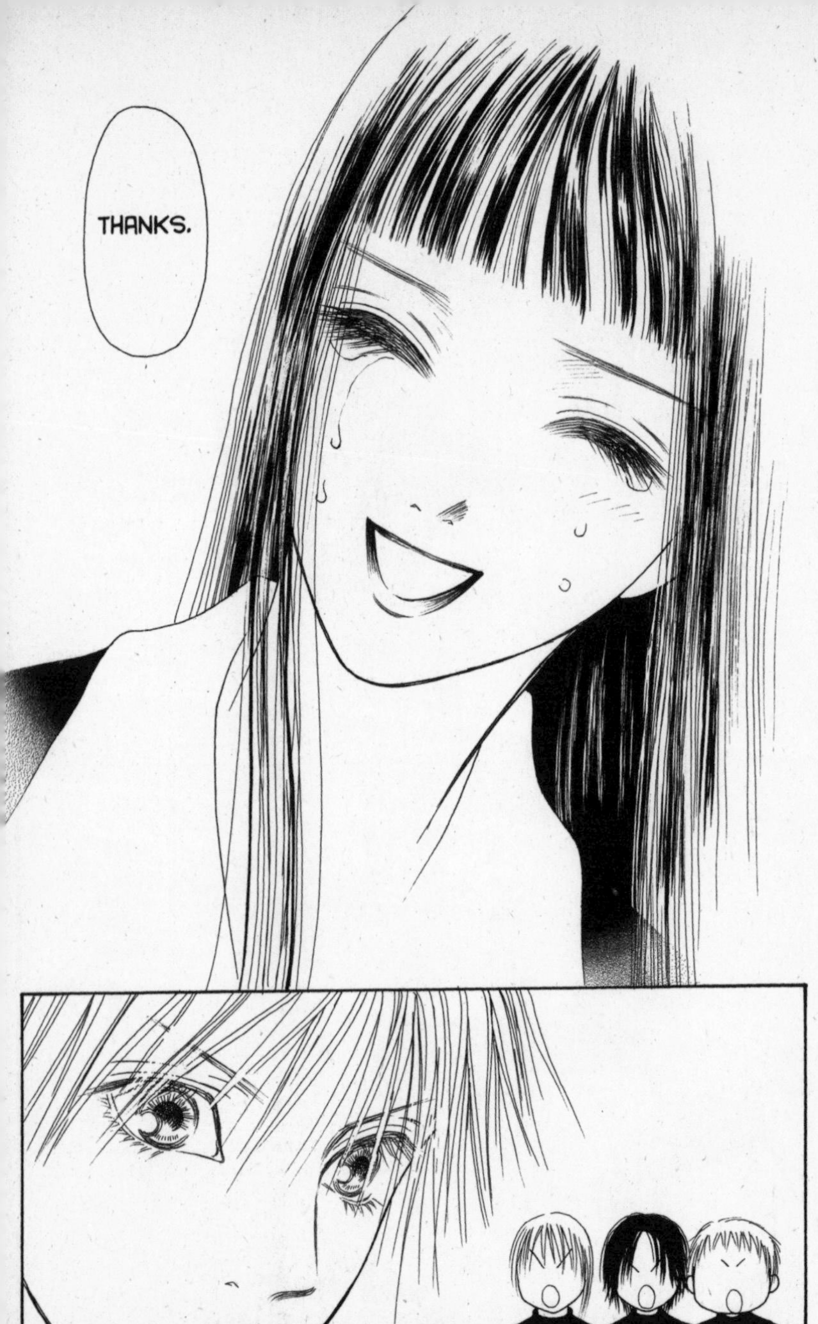
THANKS.

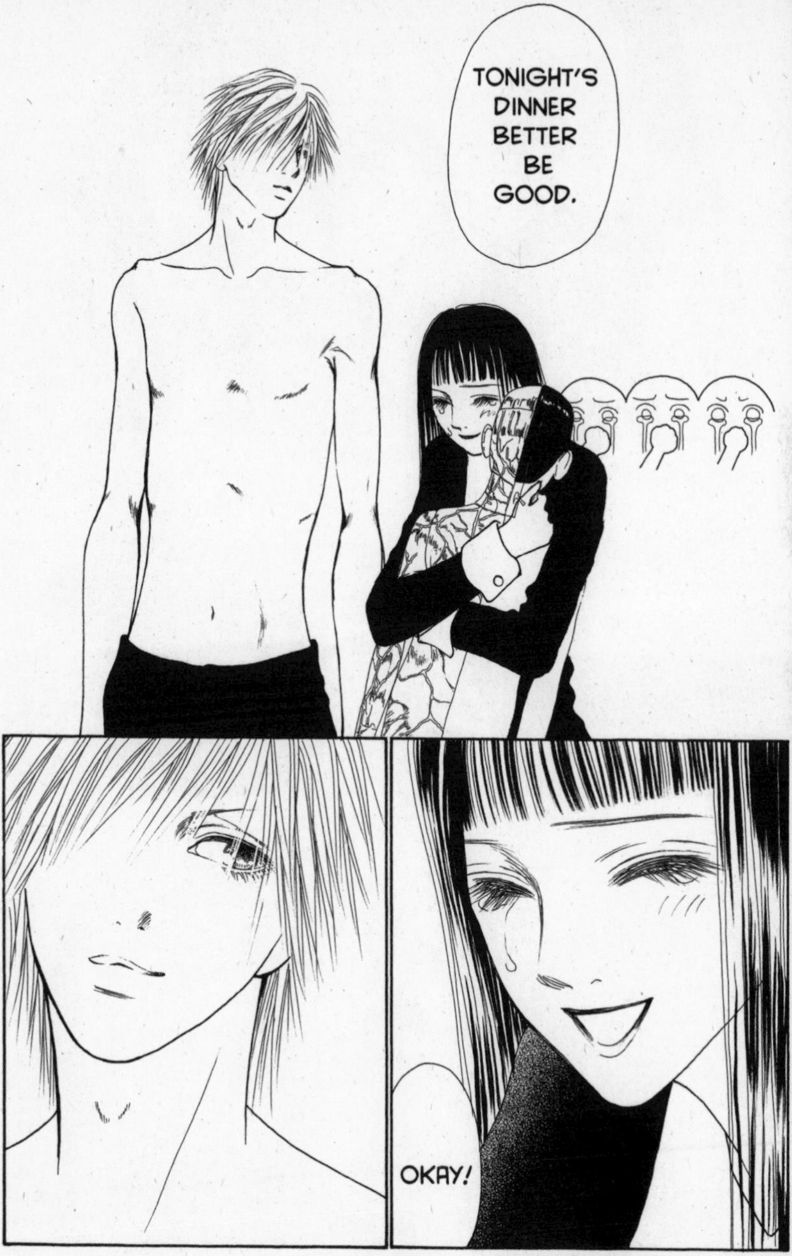
TONIGHT'S DINNER BETTER BE GOOD.
OKAY!

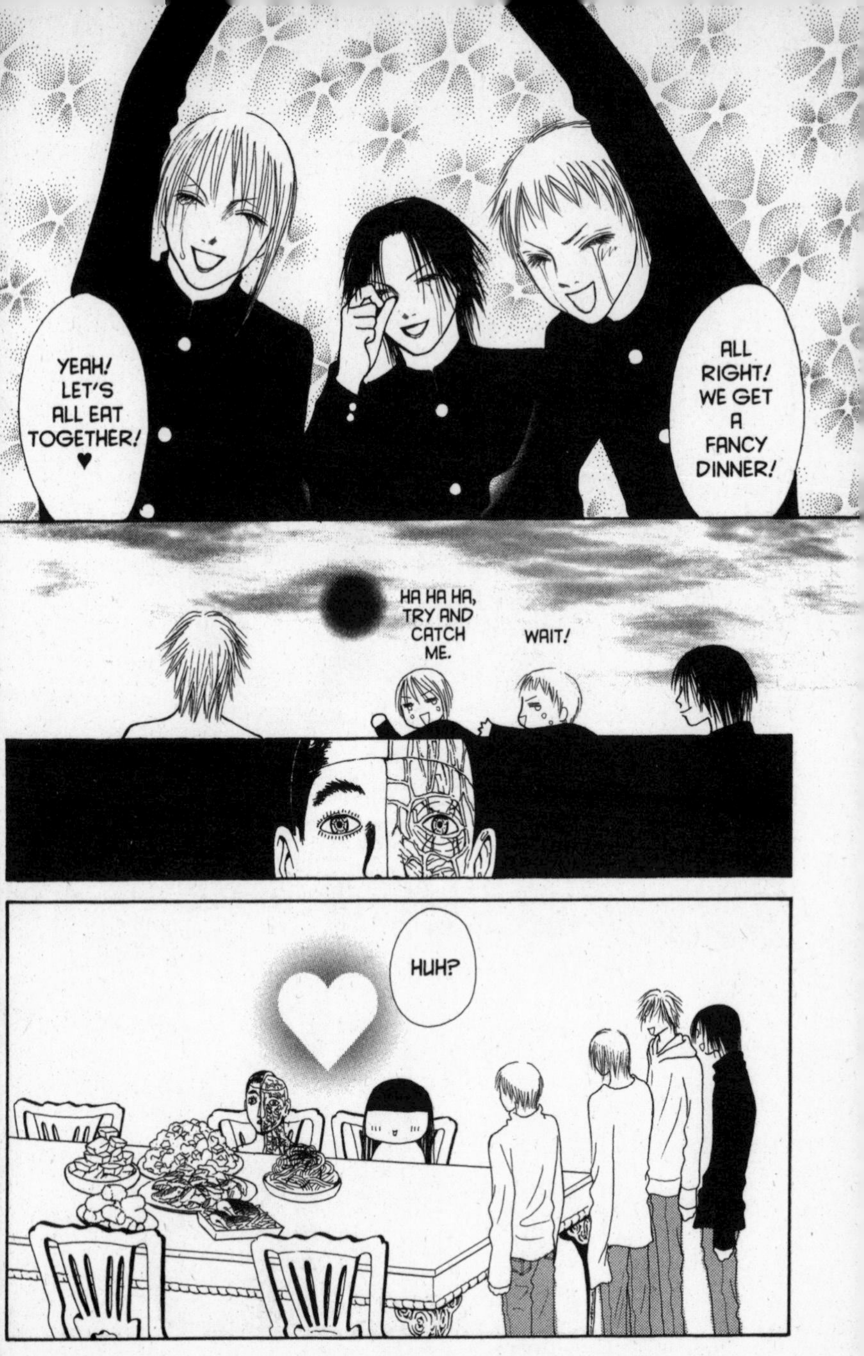
ALL RIGHT! WE GET A FANCY DINNER!
YEAH! LET'S ALL EAT TOGETHER! ♥
WAIT!
HA HA HA, TRY AND CATCH ME.
HUH?

CHAPTER 45 - SUNAKO THE CHAMPION

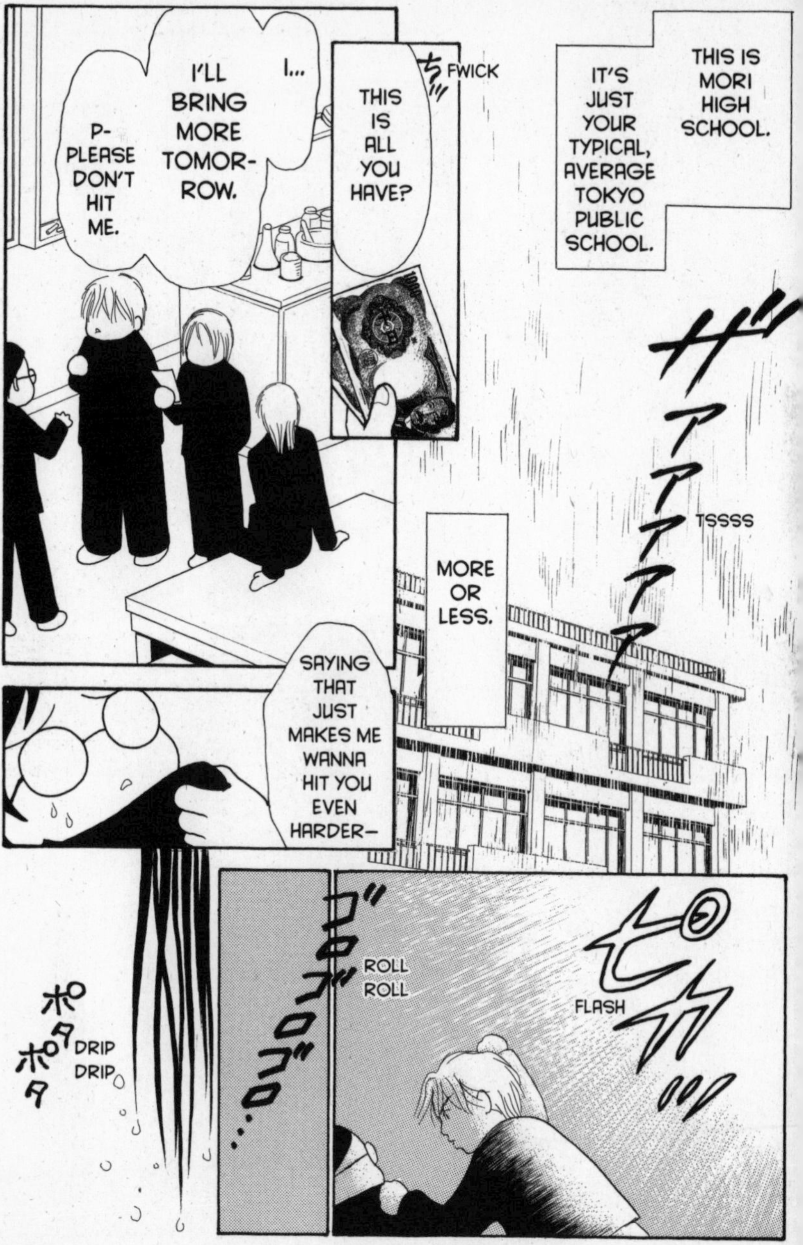
THIS IS MORI HIGH SCHOOL.
IT'S JUST YOUR TYPICAL, AVERAGE TOKYO PUBLIC SCHOOL.
ザァァァァァ
TSSSS
MORE OR LESS.
ち FWICK
THIS IS ALL YOU HAVE?
I...
I'LL BRING MORE TOMORROW.
P-PLEASE DON'T HIT ME.
SAYING THAT JUST MAKES ME WANNA HIT YOU EVEN HARDER—
ピカッ
FLASH
ゴロゴロ…
ROLL ROLL
ポタポタ
DRIP DRIP

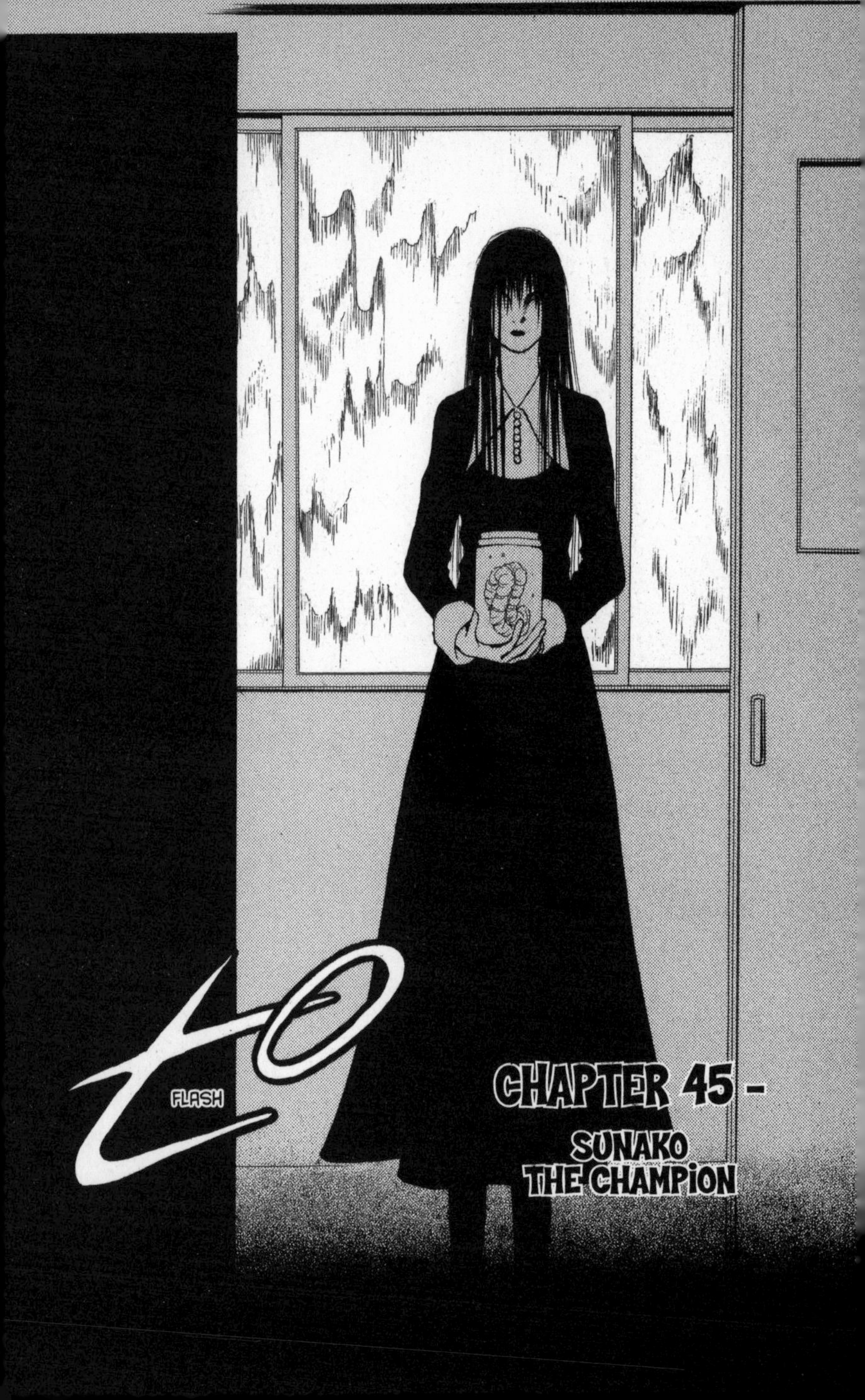
FLASH
CHAPTER 45 -
SUNAKO THE CHAMPION

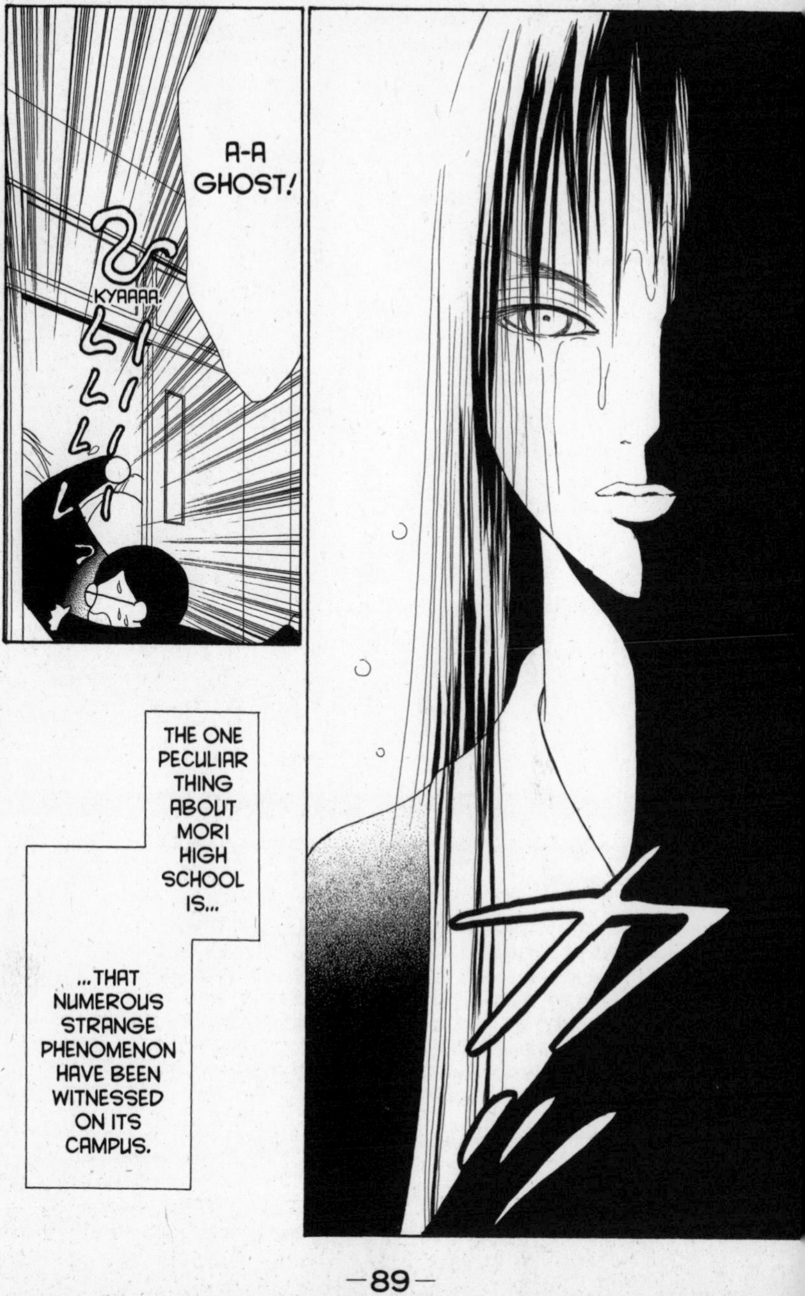
A-A GHOST!
KYAAAA.
THE ONE PECULIAR THING ABOUT MORI HIGH SCHOOL IS...
...THAT NUMEROUS STRANGE PHENOMENON HAVE BEEN WITNESSED ON ITS CAMPUS.

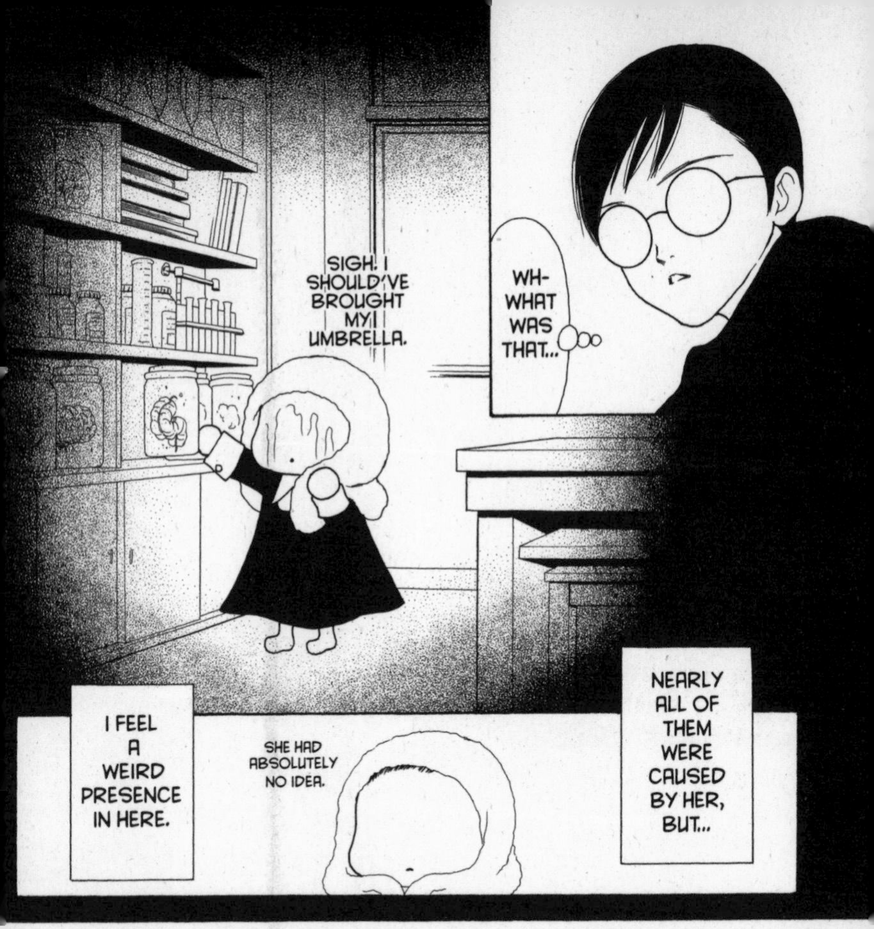
WH- WHAT WAS THAT...
SIGH. I SHOULD'VE BROUGHT MY UMBRELLA.
NEARLY ALL OF THEM WERE CAUSED BY HER, BUT...
SHE HAD ABSOLUTELY NO IDEA.
I FEEL A WEIRD PRESENCE IN HERE.

BEHIND THE SCENES

I DON'T EVEN WANNA REMEMBER THIS. SERIOUSLY. AFTER WHAT HAPPENED LAST TIME, I WAS REALLY SCARED ABOUT MAKING MY DEADLINES. I WORKED EVERY SINGLE DAY WITHOUT A BREAK. I TURNED DOWN EVERY INVITATION FROM FRIENDS WHO WANTED TO GO OUT. KIYOHARU HAD A CONCERT JUST BEFORE MY DEADLINE. ♥ BUT I JUST COULDN'T FINISH ON TIME. I CRIED EVERY DAY. I CRIED LIKE CRAZY WHEN I MET MY EDITOR. THAT HAD NEVER HAPPENED TO ME BEFORE.

I CRIED AS I WORKED EVEN THOUGH MY ASSISTANT WAS RIGHT NEXT TO ME.

I ENDED UP NOT GOING TO THE KIYOHARU CONCERT...

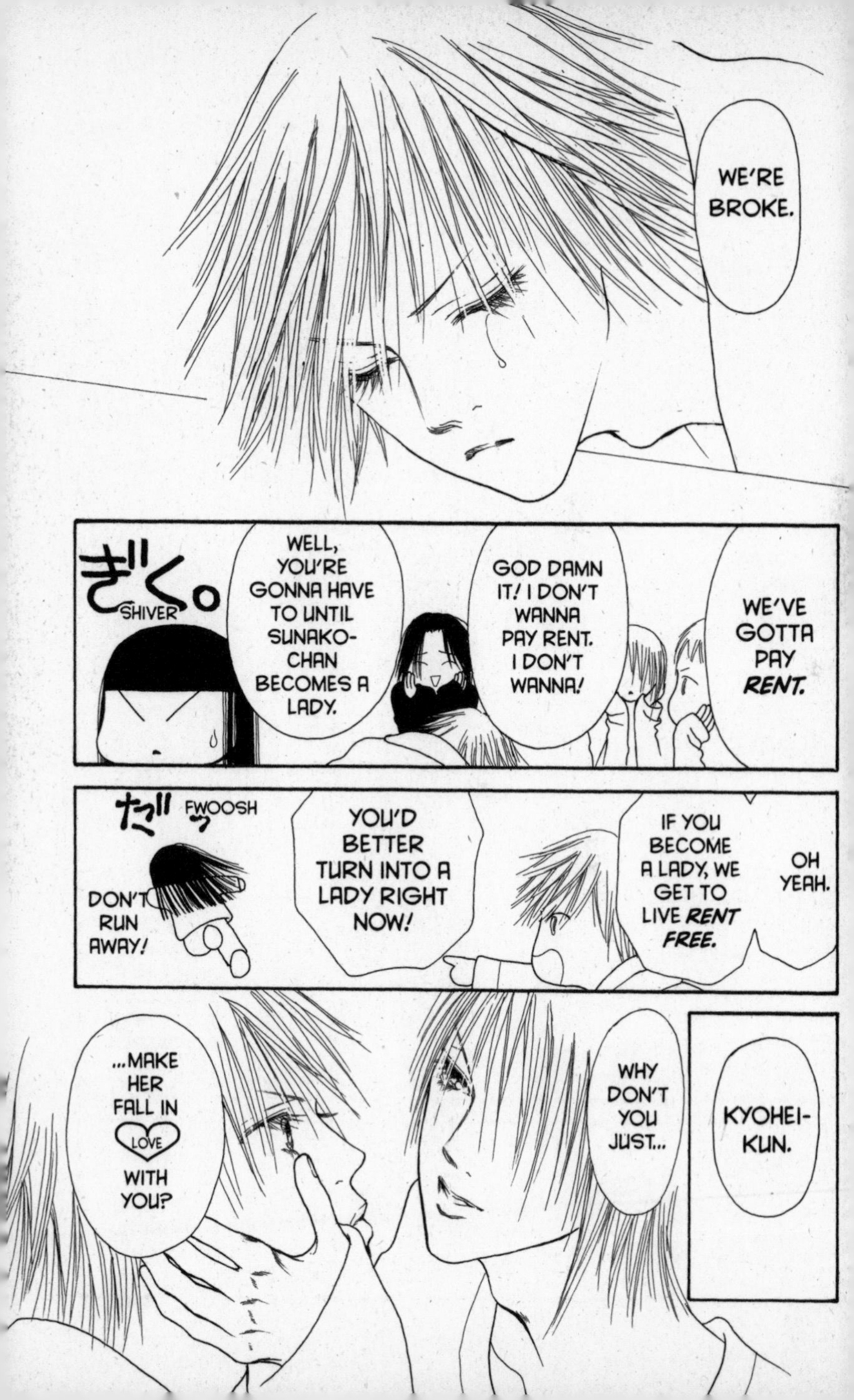
WE'RE BROKE.
WE'VE GOTTA PAY RENT.
GOD DAMN IT! I DON'T WANNA PAY RENT. I DON'T WANNA!
WELL, YOU'RE GONNA HAVE TO UNTIL SUNAKO-CHAN BECOMES A LADY.
ぎく。
SHIVER
OH YEAH.
IF YOU BECOME A LADY, WE GET TO LIVE RENT FREE.
YOU'D BETTER TURN INTO A LADY RIGHT NOW!
だッ
FWOOSH
DON'T RUN AWAY!
KYOHEI-KUN.
WHY DON'T YOU JUST...
...MAKE HER FALL IN LOVE WITH YOU?

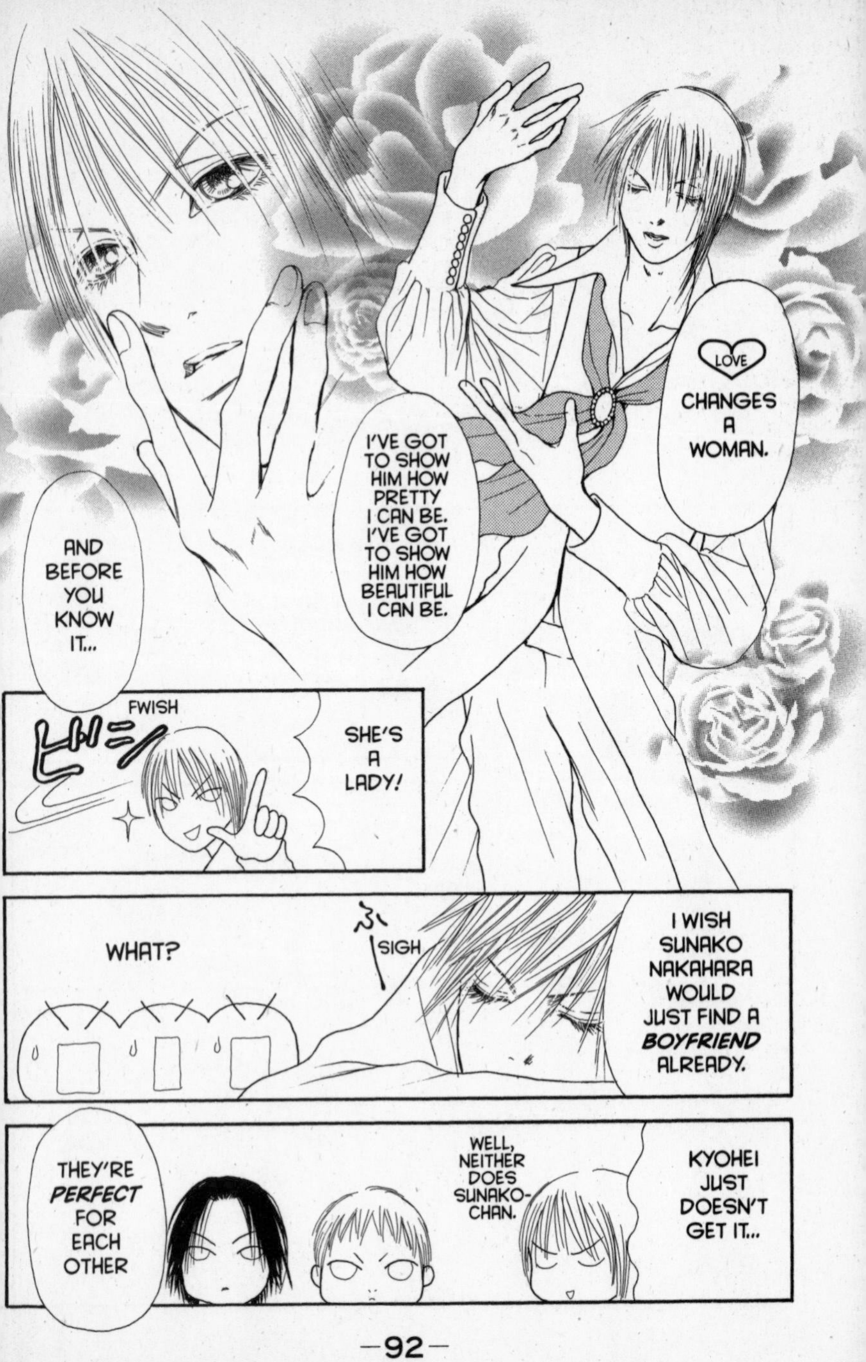
LOVE CHANGES A WOMAN.
I'VE GOT TO SHOW HIM HOW PRETTY I CAN BE. I'VE GOT TO SHOW HIM HOW BEAUTIFUL I CAN BE.
AND BEFORE YOU KNOW IT...
SHE'S A LADY!
FWISH
I WISH SUNAKO NAKAHARA WOULD JUST FIND A *BOYFRIEND* ALREADY.
SIGH
WHAT?
KYOHEI JUST DOESN'T GET IT...
WELL, NEITHER DOES SUNAKO-CHAN.
THEY'RE *PERFECT* FOR EACH OTHER

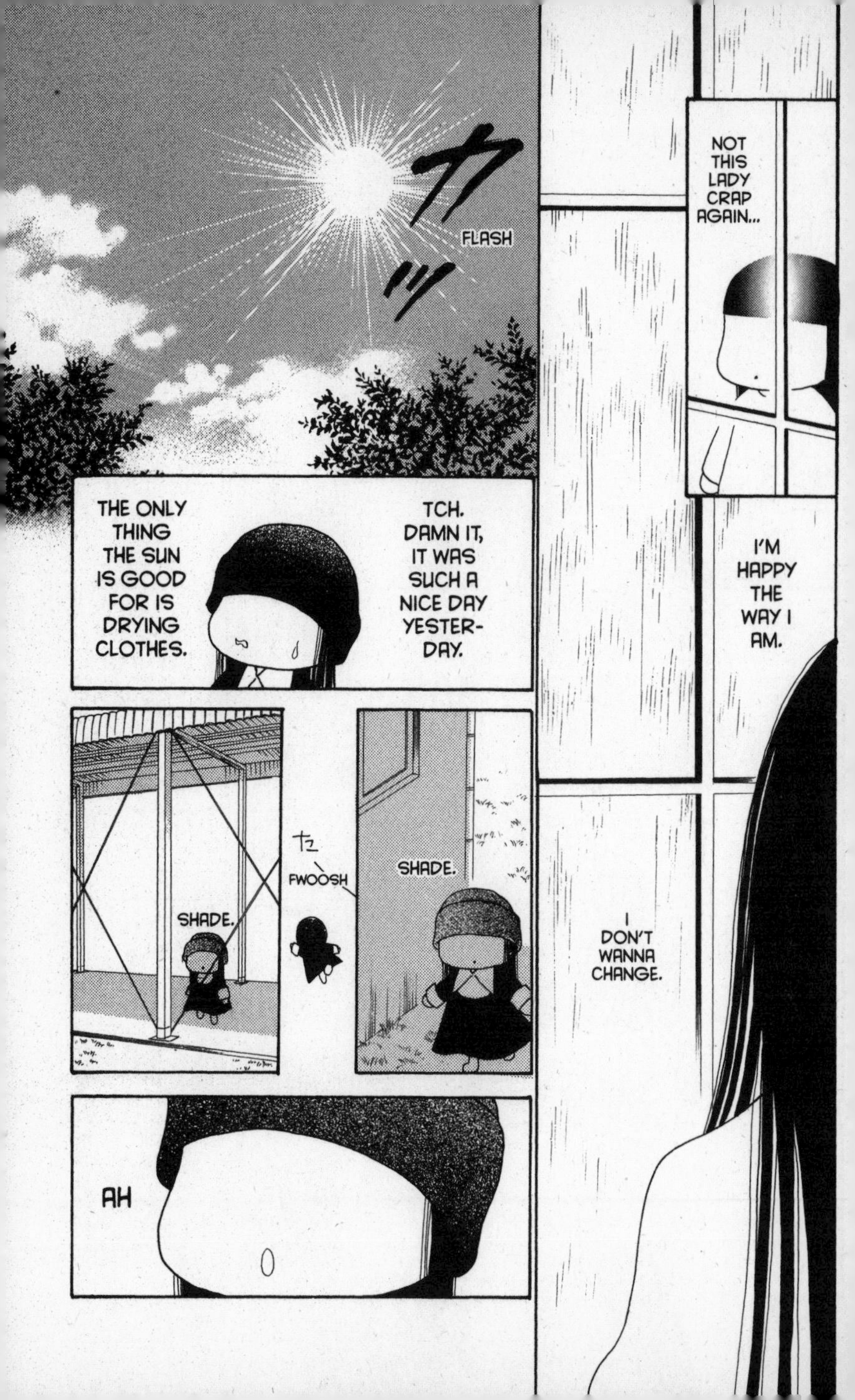
NOT THIS LADY CRAP AGAIN...
I'M HAPPY THE WAY I AM.
I DON'T WANNA CHANGE.
FLASH
TCH. DAMN IT, IT WAS SUCH A NICE DAY YESTER-DAY.
THE ONLY THING THE SUN IS GOOD FOR IS DRYING CLOTHES.
SHADE.
FWOOSH
SHADE.
AH

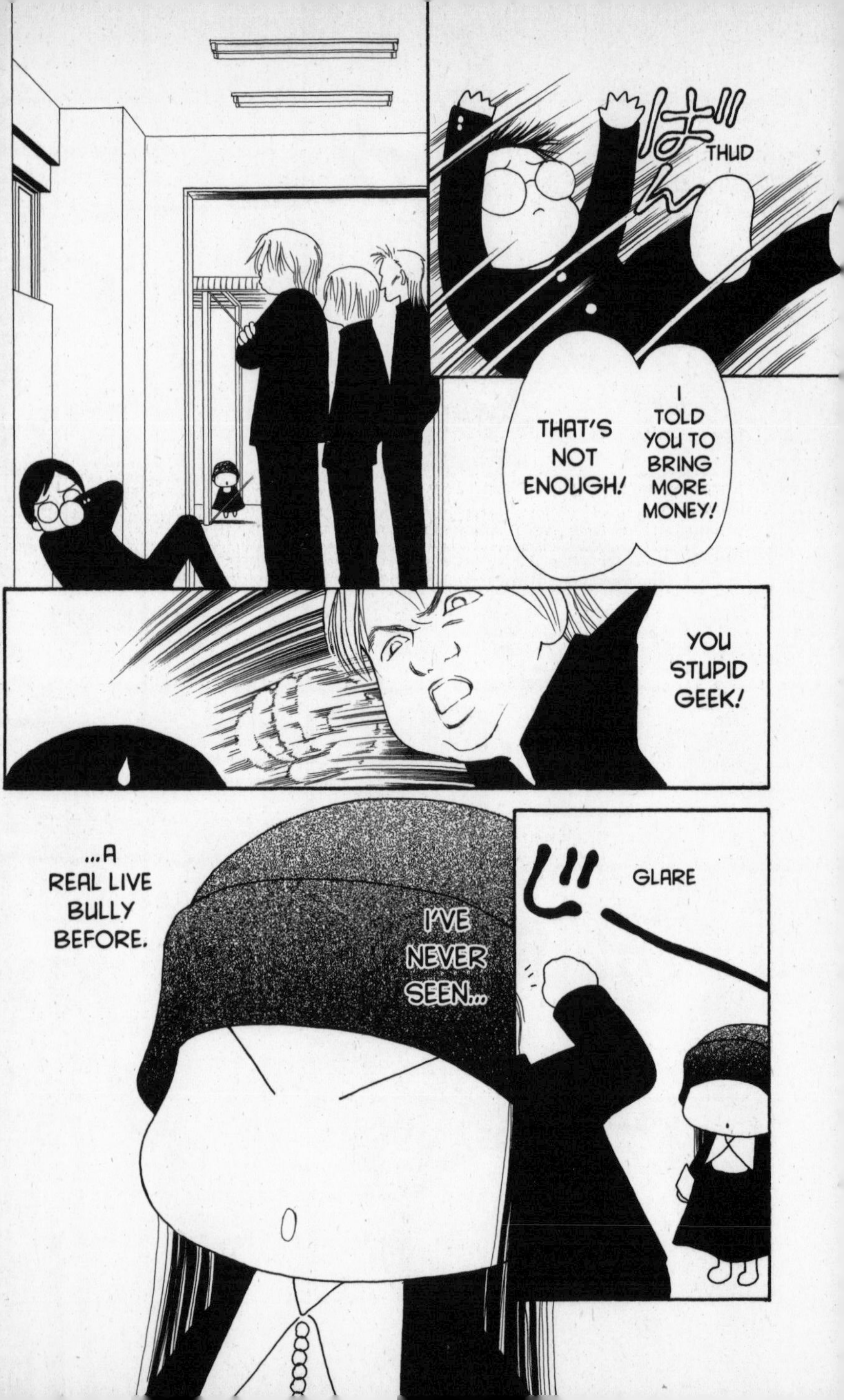
ばん
THUD
I TOLD YOU TO BRING MORE MONEY!
THAT'S NOT ENOUGH!
YOU STUPID GEEK!
じー
GLARE
I'VE NEVER SEEN...
...A REAL LIVE BULLY BEFORE.

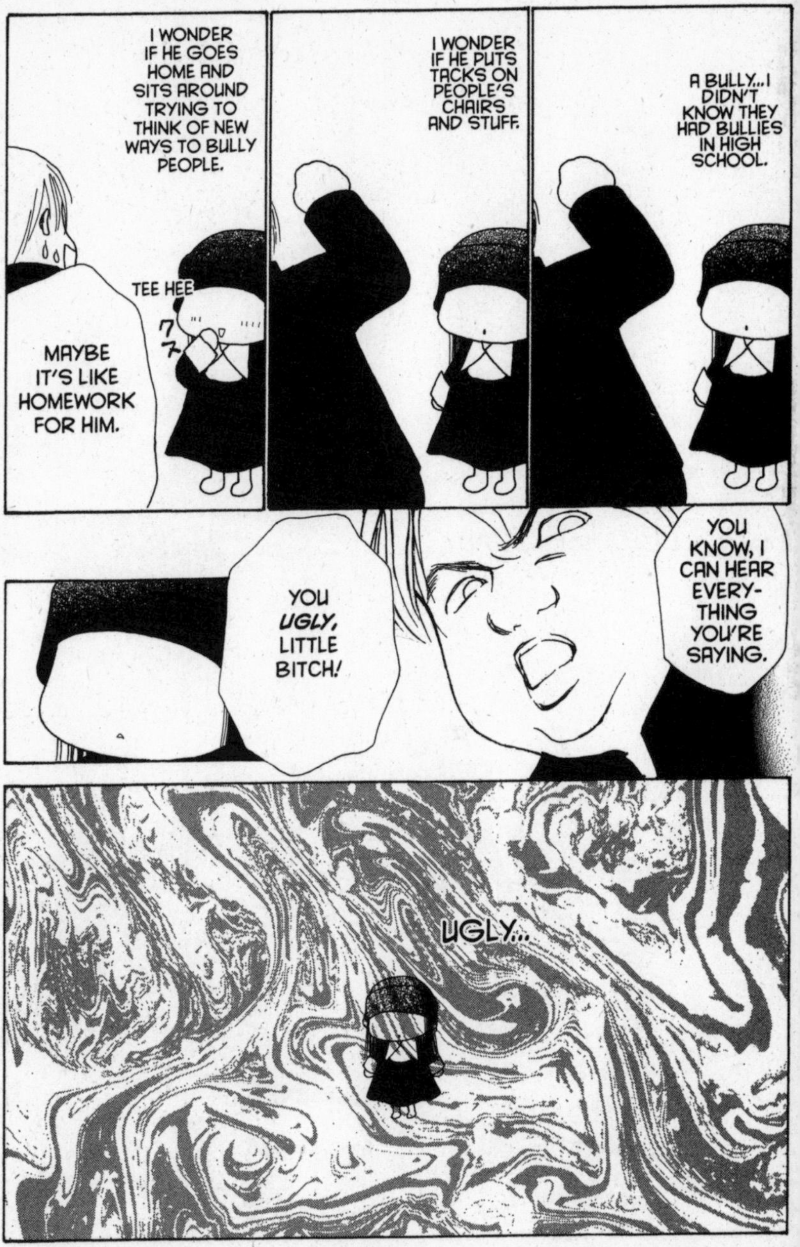
A BULLY...I DIDN'T KNOW THEY HAD BULLIES IN HIGH SCHOOL.
I WONDER IF HE PUTS TACKS ON PEOPLE'S CHAIRS AND STUFF.
I WONDER IF HE GOES HOME AND SITS AROUND TRYING TO THINK OF NEW WAYS TO BULLY PEOPLE.
TEE HEE
MAYBE IT'S LIKE HOMEWORK FOR HIM.
YOU KNOW, I CAN HEAR EVERY-THING YOU'RE SAYING.
YOU *UGLY,* LITTLE BITCH!
UGLY...

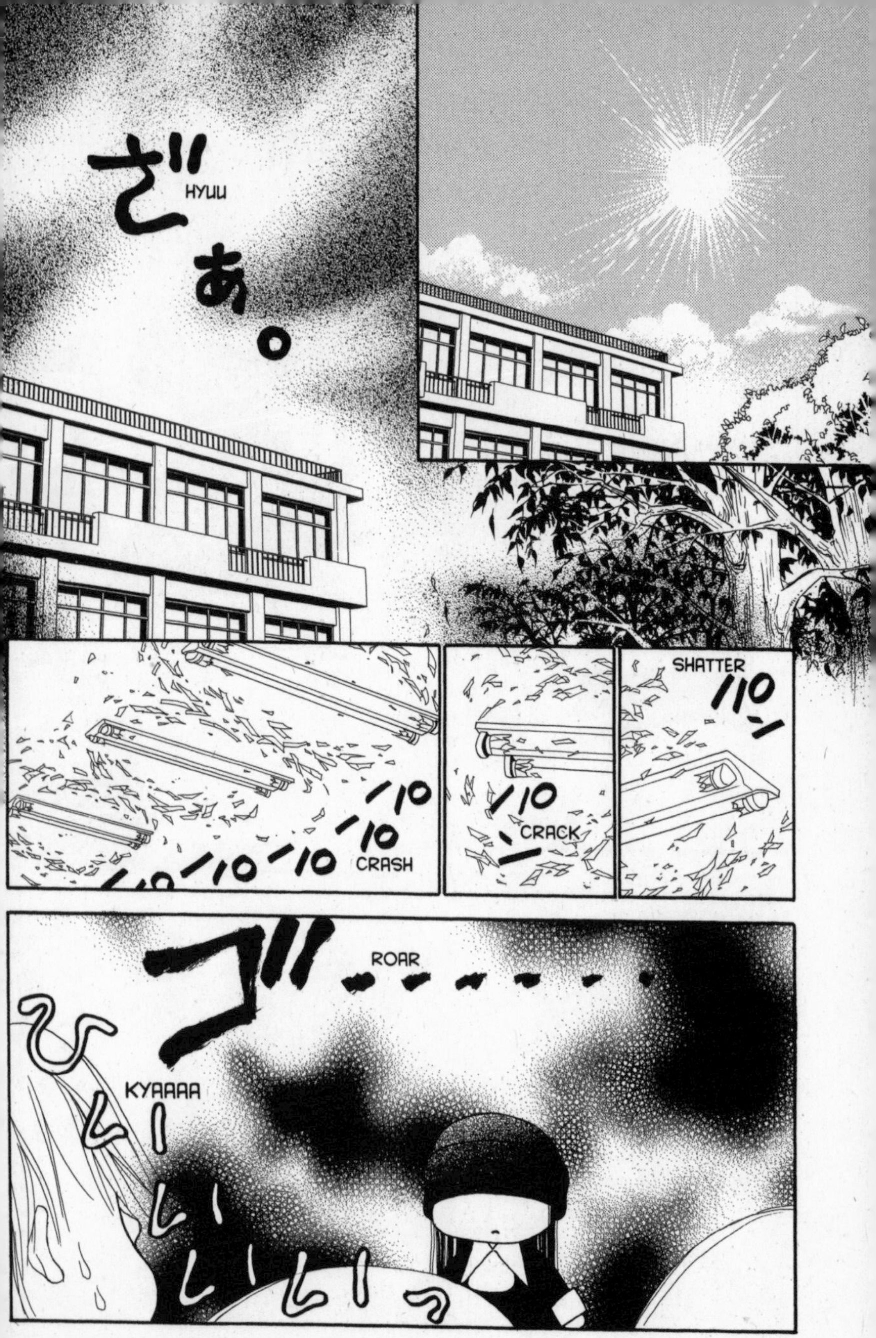
ざぁ。
HYUU
SHATTER
パン
CRACK
CRASH
ROAR
KYAAAA

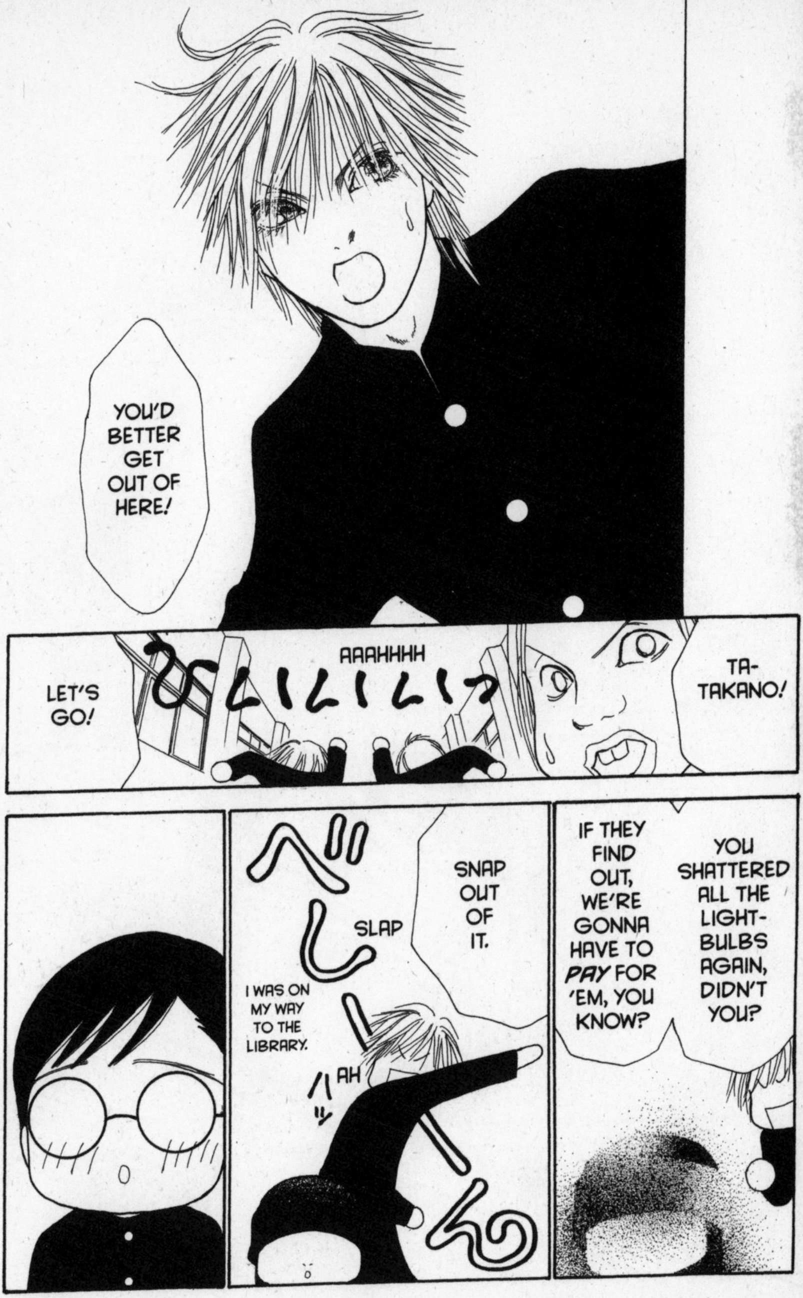
YOU'D BETTER GET OUT OF HERE!
TA-TAKANO!
AAAHHHH
LET'S GO!
YOU SHATTERED ALL THE LIGHT-BULBS AGAIN, DIDN'T YOU?
IF THEY FIND OUT, WE'RE GONNA HAVE TO *PAY* FOR 'EM, YOU KNOW?
SNAP OUT OF IT.
SLAP
I WAS ON MY WAY TO THE LIBRARY.
AH

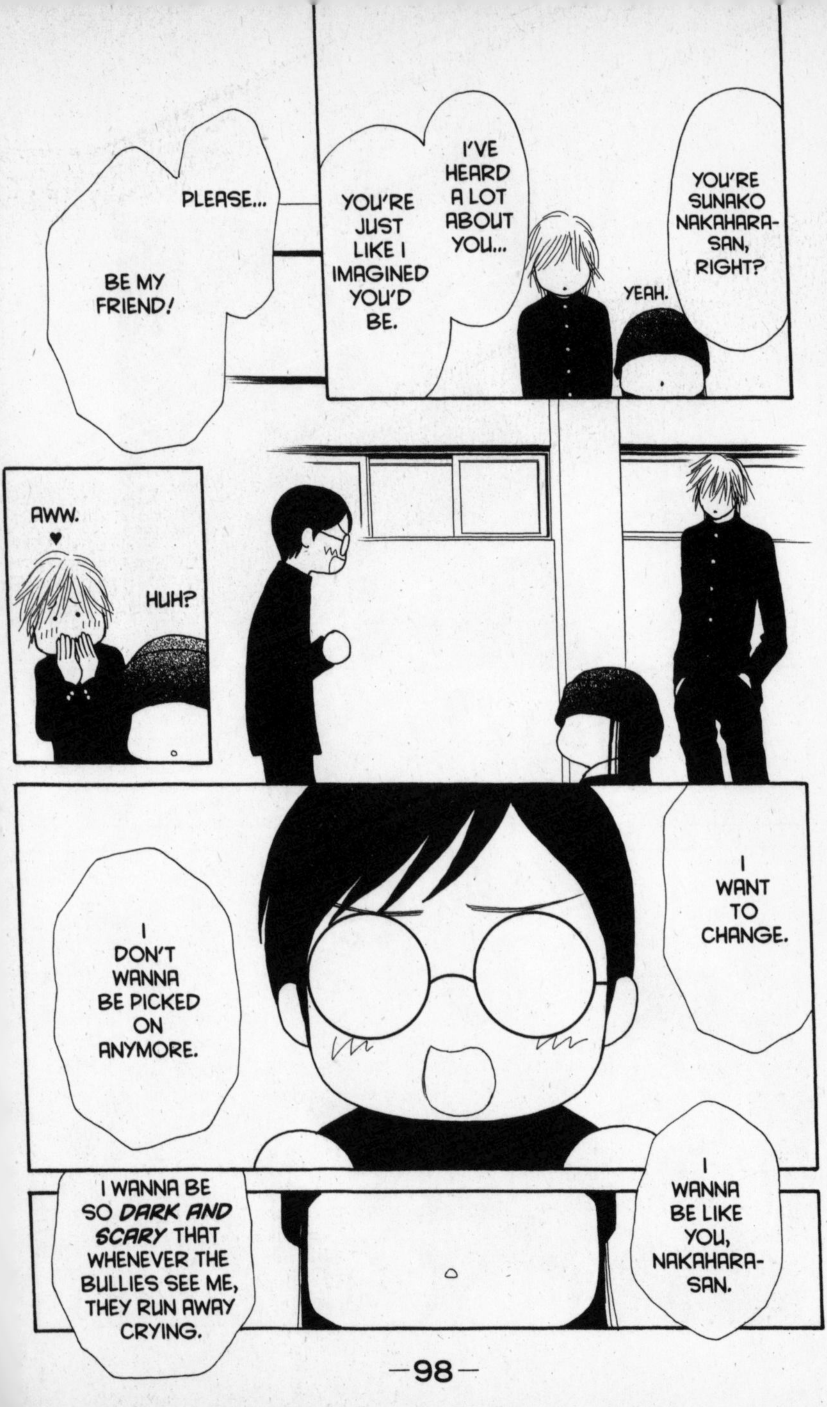
YOU'RE SUNAKO NAKAHARA-SAN, RIGHT?
YEAH.
I'VE HEARD A LOT ABOUT YOU...
YOU'RE JUST LIKE I IMAGINED YOU'D BE.
PLEASE... BE MY FRIEND!
AWW. ♥
HUH?
I WANT TO CHANGE.
I DON'T WANNA BE PICKED ON ANYMORE.
I WANNA BE LIKE YOU, NAKAHARA-SAN.
I WANNA BE SO *DARK AND SCARY* THAT WHENEVER THE BULLIES SEE ME, THEY RUN AWAY CRYING.

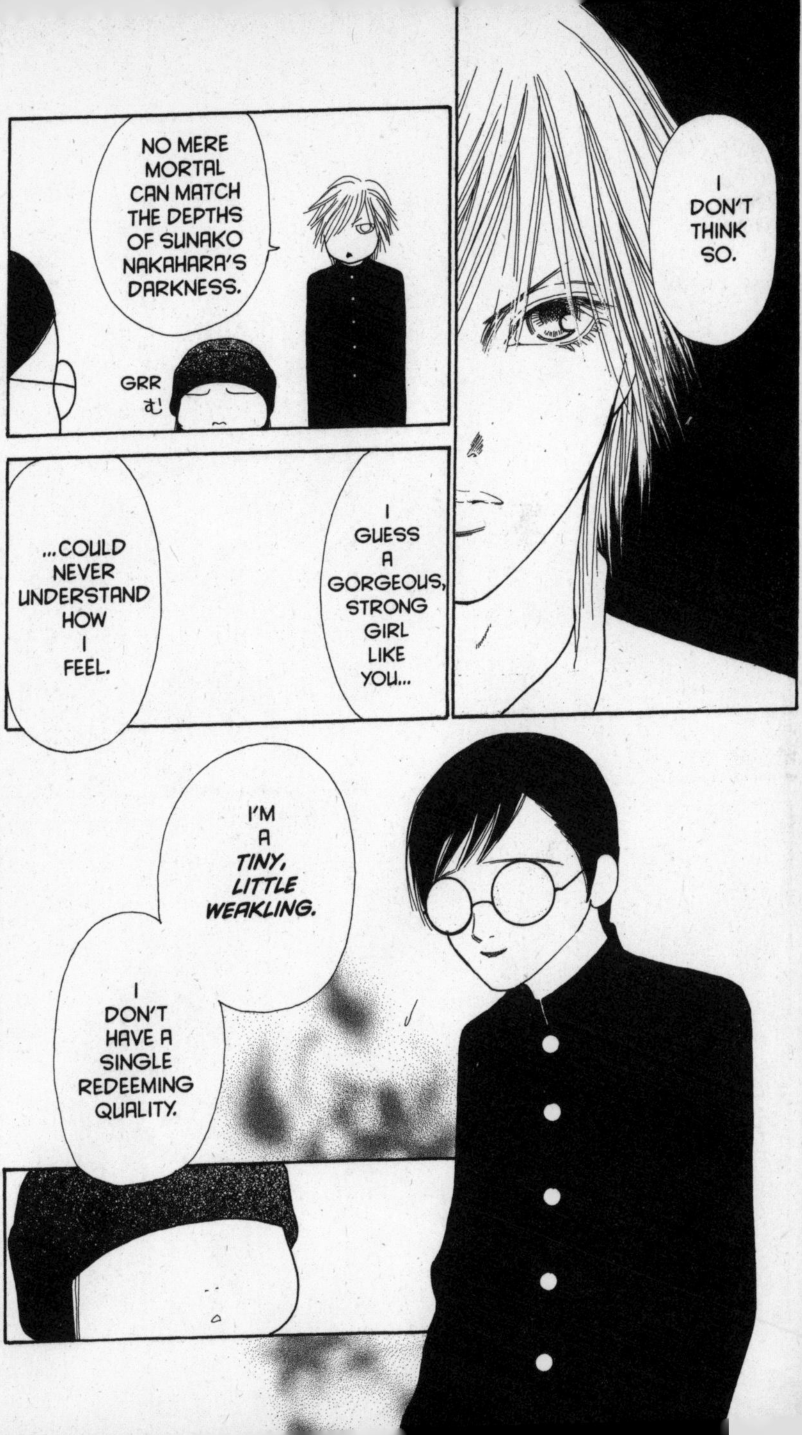
I DON'T THINK SO.
NO MERE MORTAL CAN MATCH THE DEPTHS OF SUNAKO NAKAHARA'S DARKNESS.
GRR むっ!
I GUESS A GORGEOUS, STRONG GIRL LIKE YOU...
...COULD NEVER UNDERSTAND HOW I FEEL.
I'M A *TINY, LITTLE WEAKLING.*
I DON'T HAVE A SINGLE REDEEMING QUALITY.

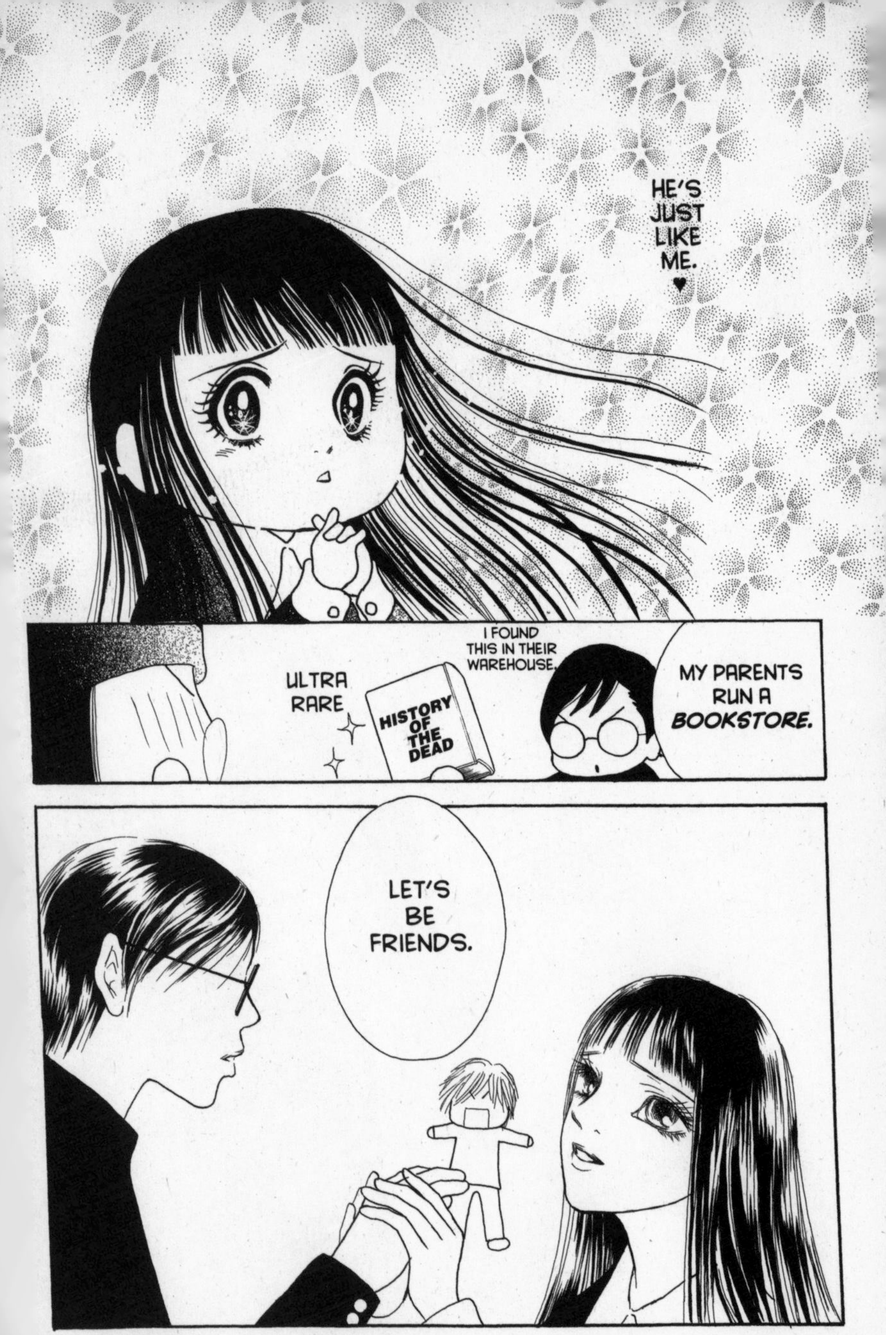
HE'S JUST LIKE ME. ♥
MY PARENTS RUN A *BOOKSTORE.*
I FOUND THIS IN THEIR WAREHOUSE.
HISTORY OF THE DEAD
ULTRA RARE
LET'S BE FRIENDS.

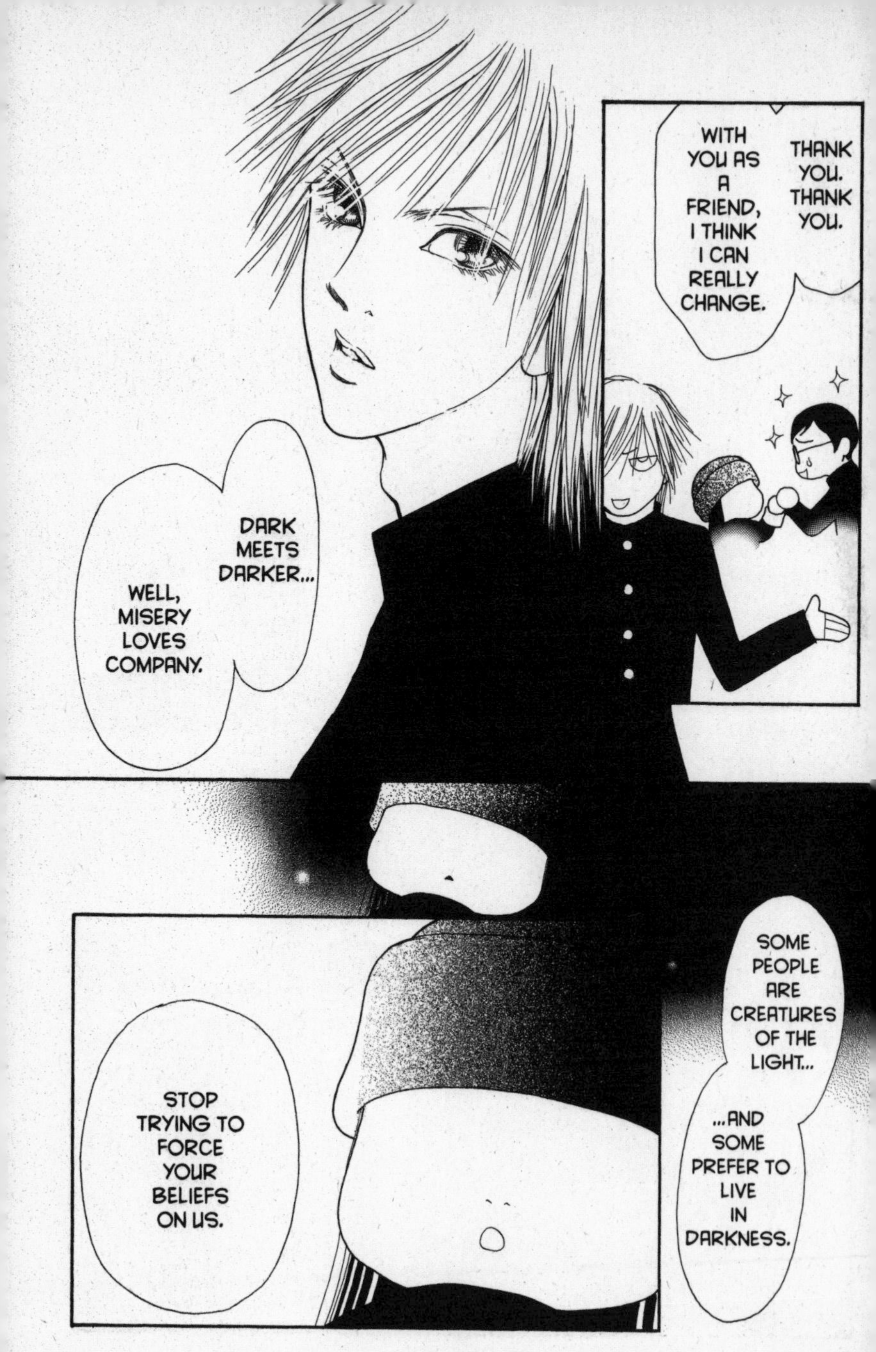
THANK YOU. THANK YOU.
WITH YOU AS A FRIEND, I THINK I CAN REALLY CHANGE.
DARK MEETS DARKER...
WELL, MISERY LOVES COMPANY.
SOME PEOPLE ARE CREATURES OF THE LIGHT...
...AND SOME PREFER TO LIVE IN DARKNESS.
STOP TRYING TO FORCE YOUR BELIEFS ON US.

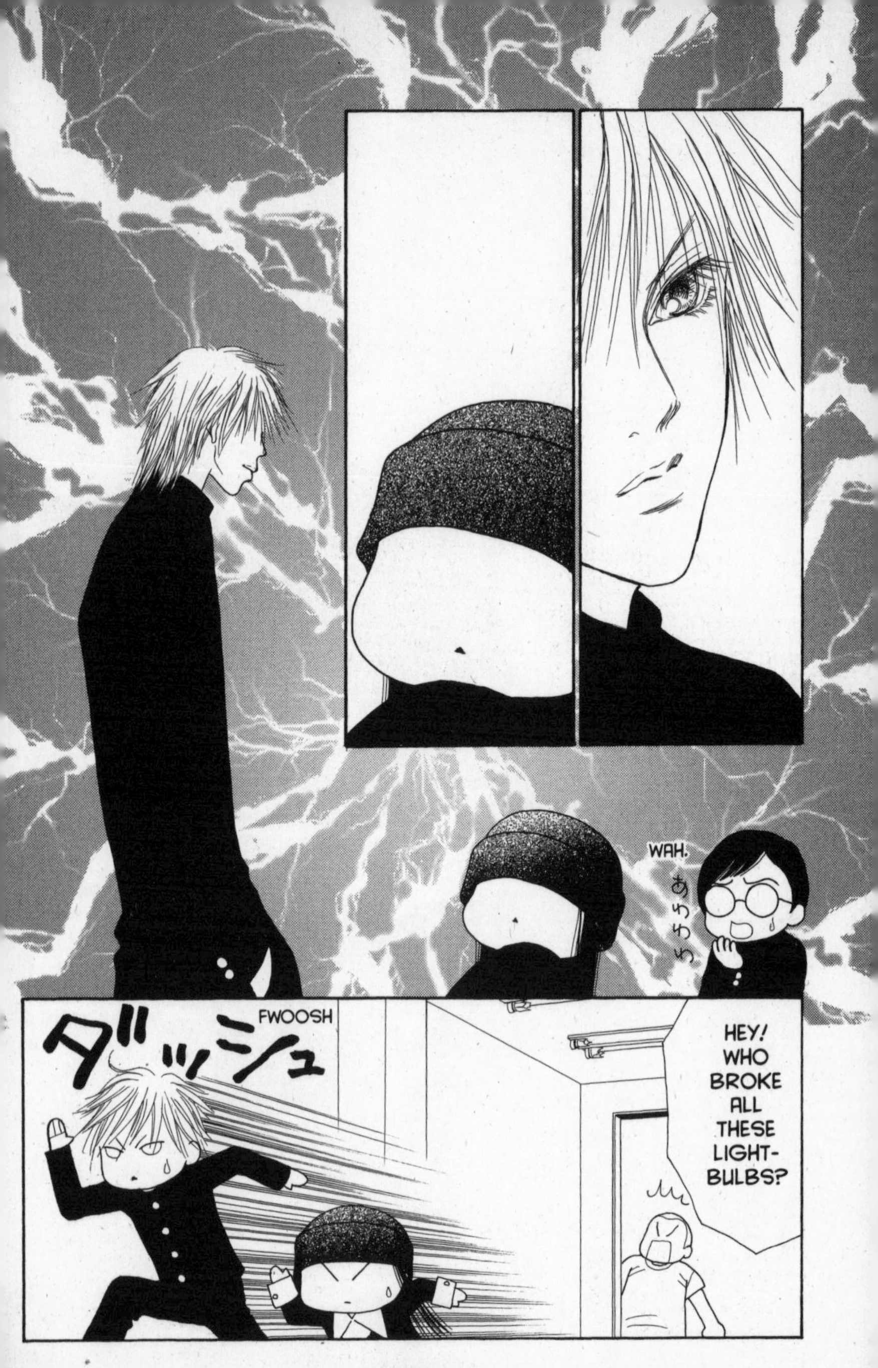
WAH.
あうううう
FWOOSH
ダッシュ
HEY! WHO BROKE ALL THESE LIGHT-BULBS?

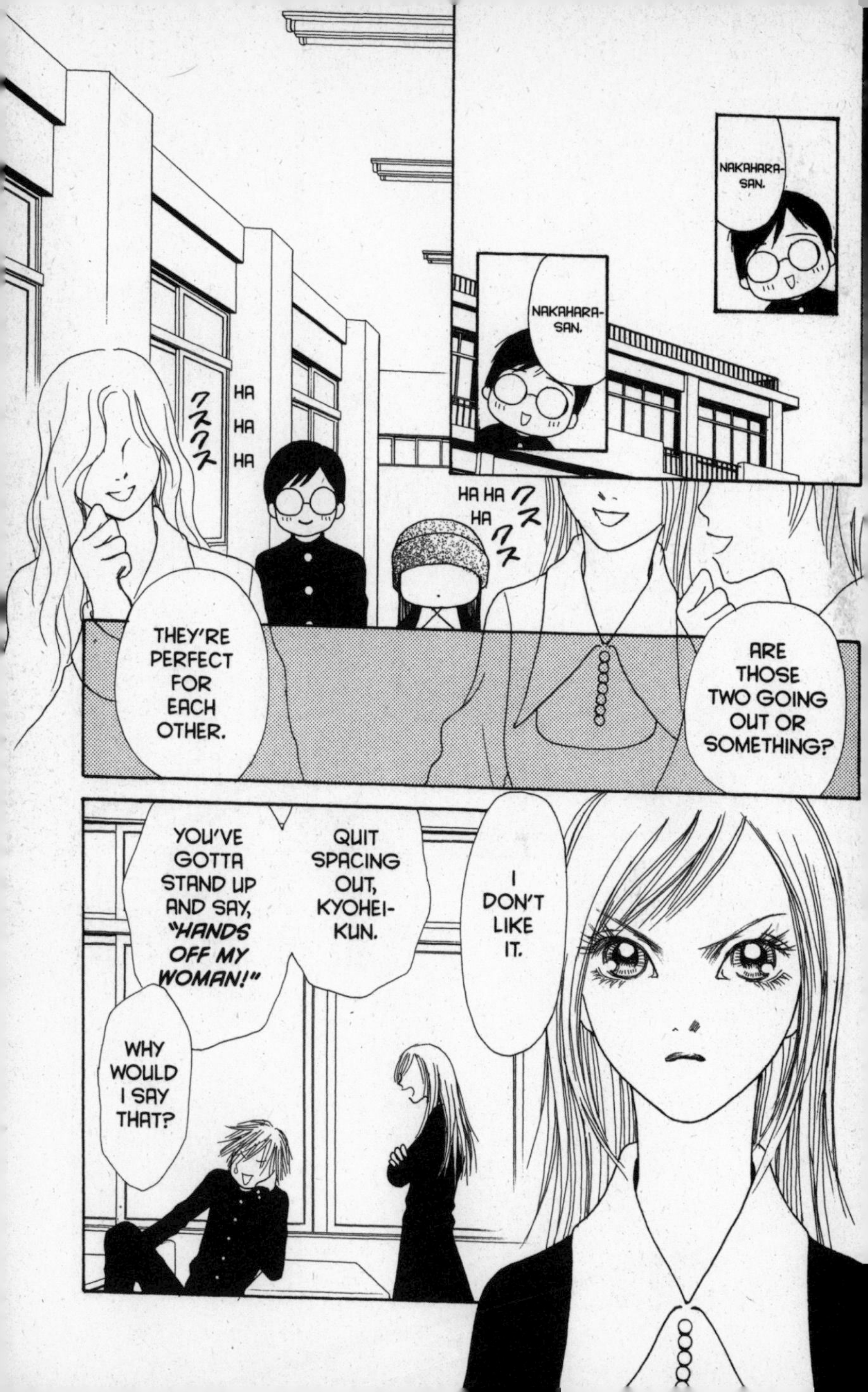
NAKAHARA-SAN.
NAKAHARA-SAN.
HA HA HA
クスクス
クスクス
HA HA HA
ARE THOSE TWO GOING OUT OR SOMETHING?
THEY'RE PERFECT FOR EACH OTHER.
I DON'T LIKE IT.
QUIT SPACING OUT, KYOHEI-KUN.
YOU'VE GOTTA STAND UP AND SAY, *"HANDS OFF MY WOMAN!"*
WHY WOULD I SAY THAT?

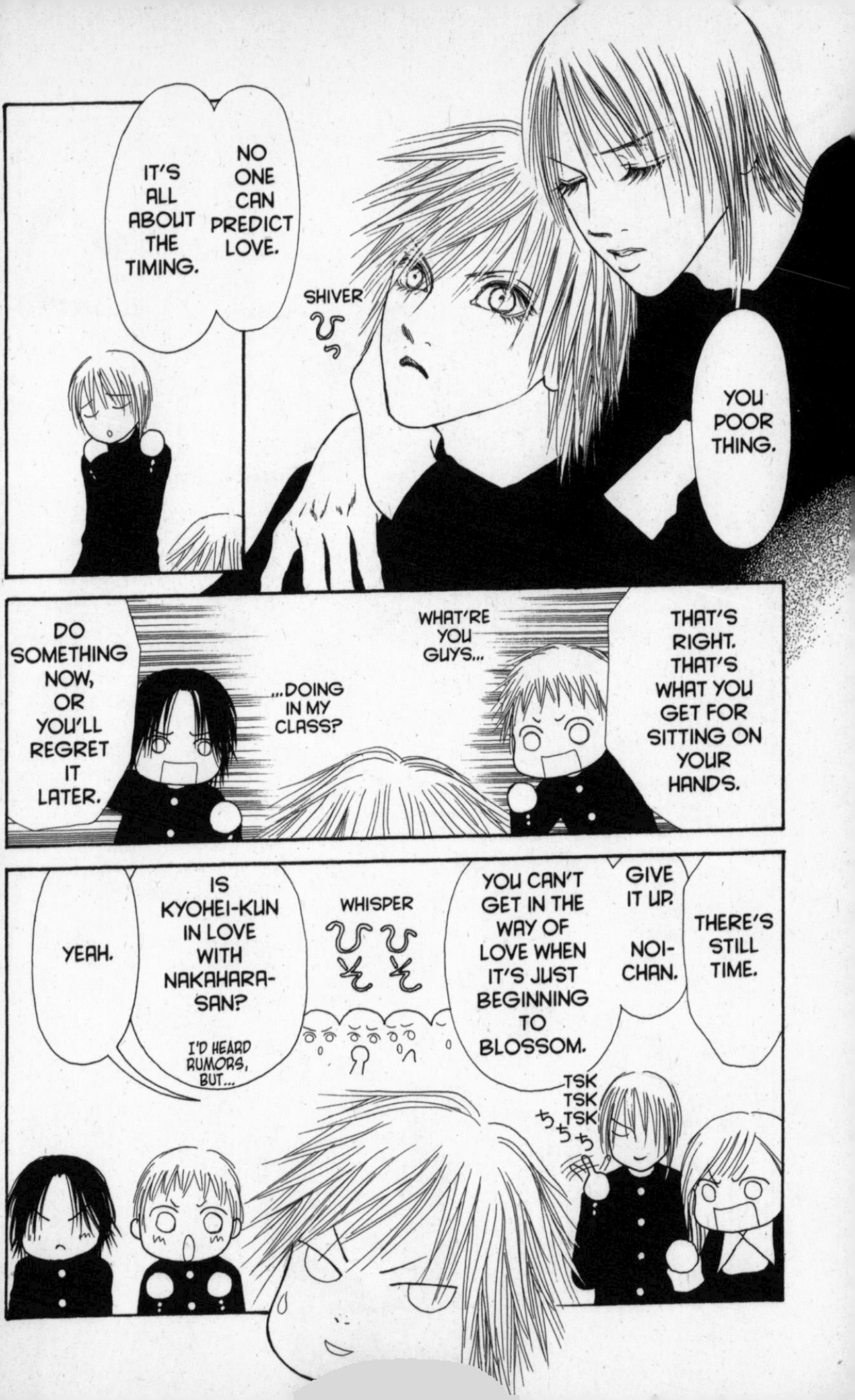
YOU POOR THING.
SHIVER
NO ONE CAN PREDICT LOVE.
IT'S ALL ABOUT THE TIMING.
THAT'S RIGHT. THAT'S WHAT YOU GET FOR SITTING ON YOUR HANDS.
WHAT'RE YOU GUYS...
...DOING IN MY CLASS?
DO SOMETHING NOW, OR YOU'LL REGRET IT LATER.
THERE'S STILL TIME.
GIVE IT UP. NOI-CHAN.
YOU CAN'T GET IN THE WAY OF LOVE WHEN IT'S JUST BEGINNING TO BLOSSOM.
TSK TSK TSK
WHISPER
IS KYOHEI-KUN IN LOVE WITH NAKAHARA-SAN?
I'D HEARD RUMORS, BUT...
YEAH.

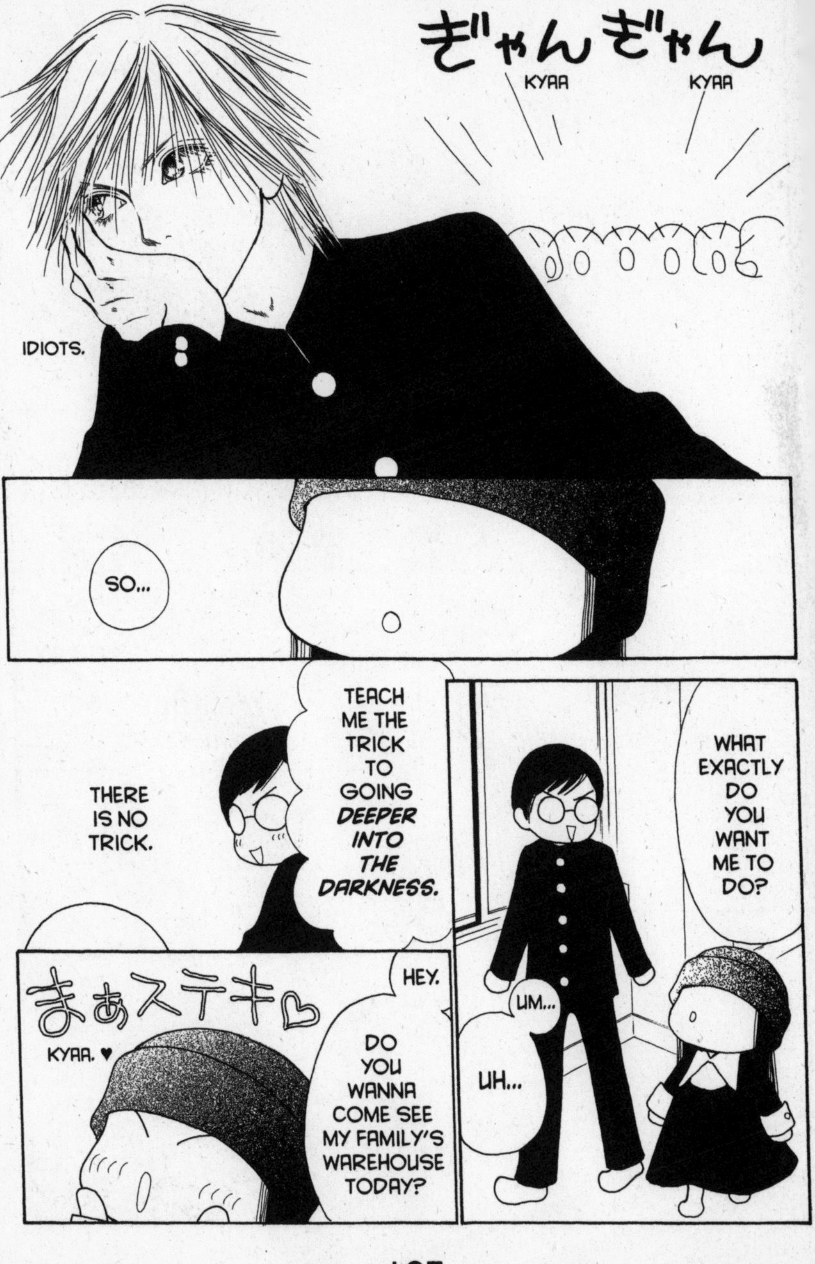
ぎゃんぎゃん
KYAA
KYAA
IDIOTS.
SO...
WHAT EXACTLY DO YOU WANT ME TO DO?
UM...
UH...
TEACH ME THE TRICK TO GOING *DEEPER INTO THE DARKNESS.*
THERE IS NO TRICK.
HEY.
DO YOU WANNA COME SEE MY FAMILY'S WAREHOUSE TODAY?
まぁステキ♡
KYAA. ♥

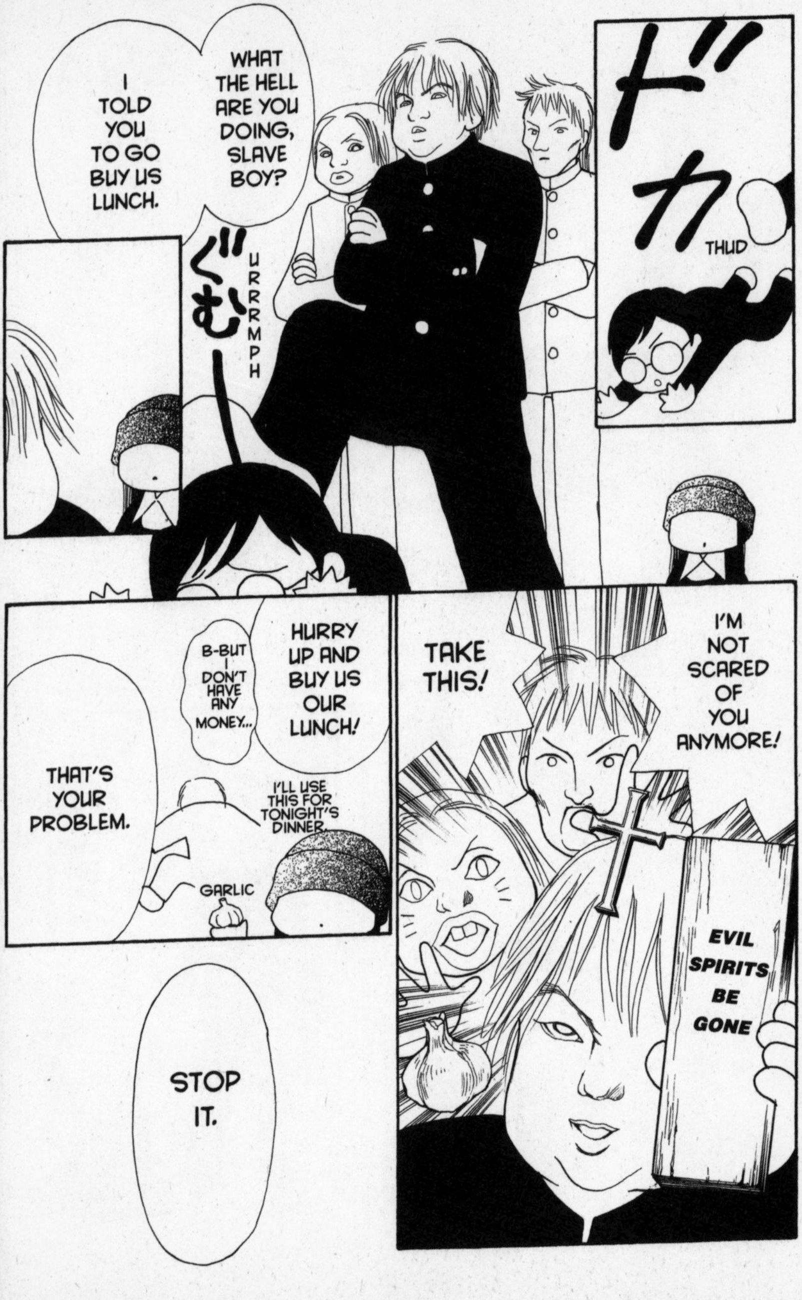
ドカ
THUD
WHAT THE HELL ARE YOU DOING, SLAVE BOY?
I TOLD YOU TO GO BUY US LUNCH.
ぐむ
URRRMPH
HURRY UP AND BUY US OUR LUNCH!
B-BUT I DON'T HAVE ANY MONEY...
THAT'S YOUR PROBLEM.
I'LL USE THIS FOR TONIGHT'S DINNER.
GARLIC
I'M NOT SCARED OF YOU ANYMORE!
TAKE THIS!
EVIL SPIRITS BE GONE
STOP IT.

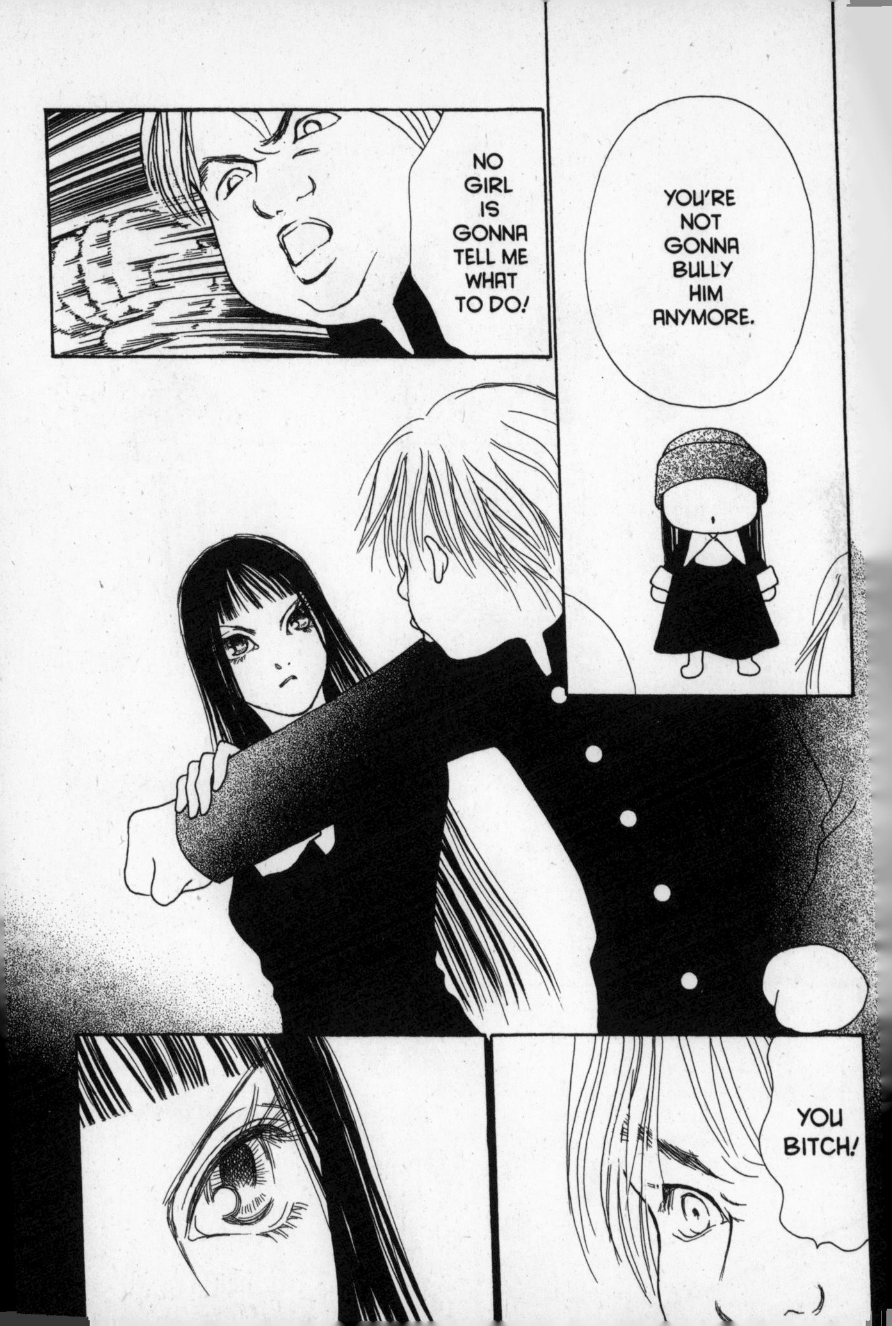
YOU'RE NOT GONNA BULLY HIM ANYMORE.
NO GIRL IS GONNA TELL ME WHAT TO DO!
YOU BITCH!

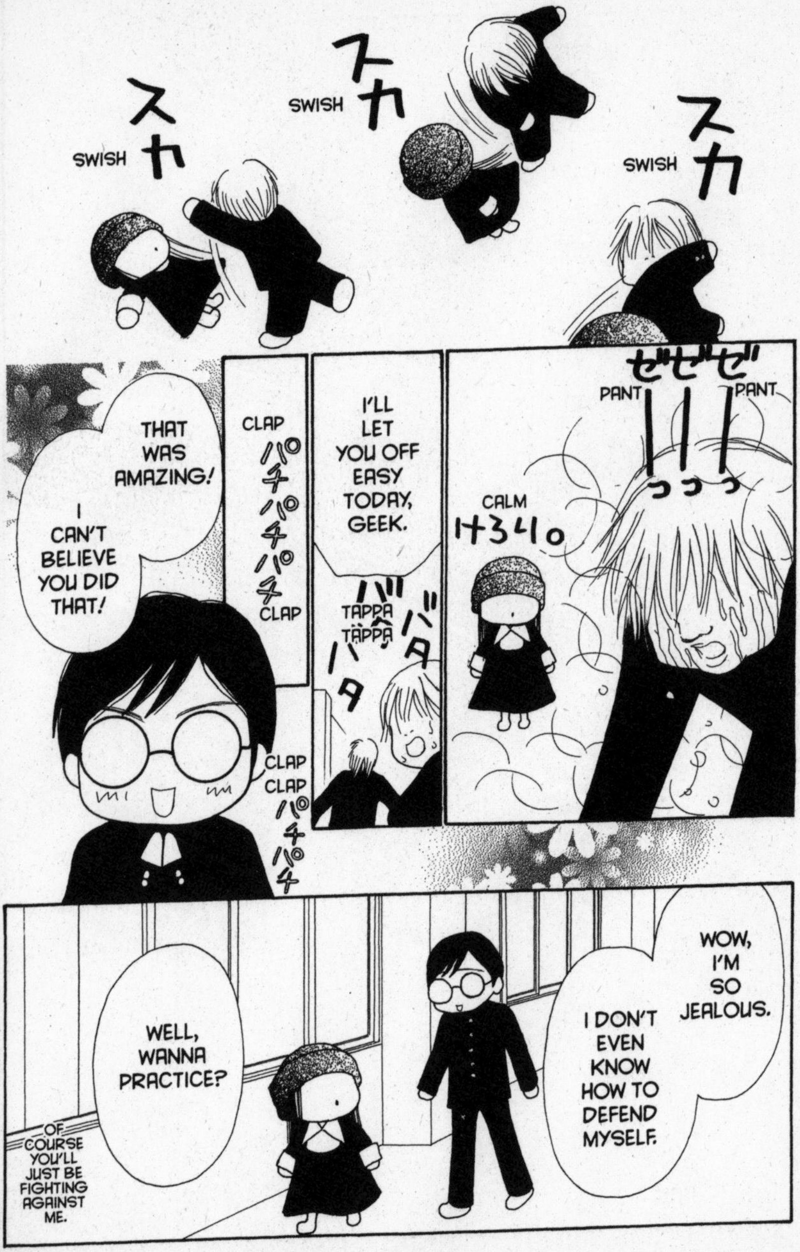
SWISH スカ
SWISH スカ
SWISH スカ
PANT ぜぜぜ PANT
っっっ
CALM けろん。
I'LL LET YOU OFF EASY TODAY, GEEK.
TAPPA TAPPA バタバタ
CLAP パチパチパチ CLAP
THAT WAS AMAZING!
I CAN'T BELIEVE YOU DID THAT!
CLAP CLAP パチパチ
WOW, I'M SO JEALOUS.
I DON'T EVEN KNOW HOW TO DEFEND MYSELF.
WELL, WANNA PRACTICE?
OF COURSE YOU'LL JUST BE FIGHTING AGAINST ME.

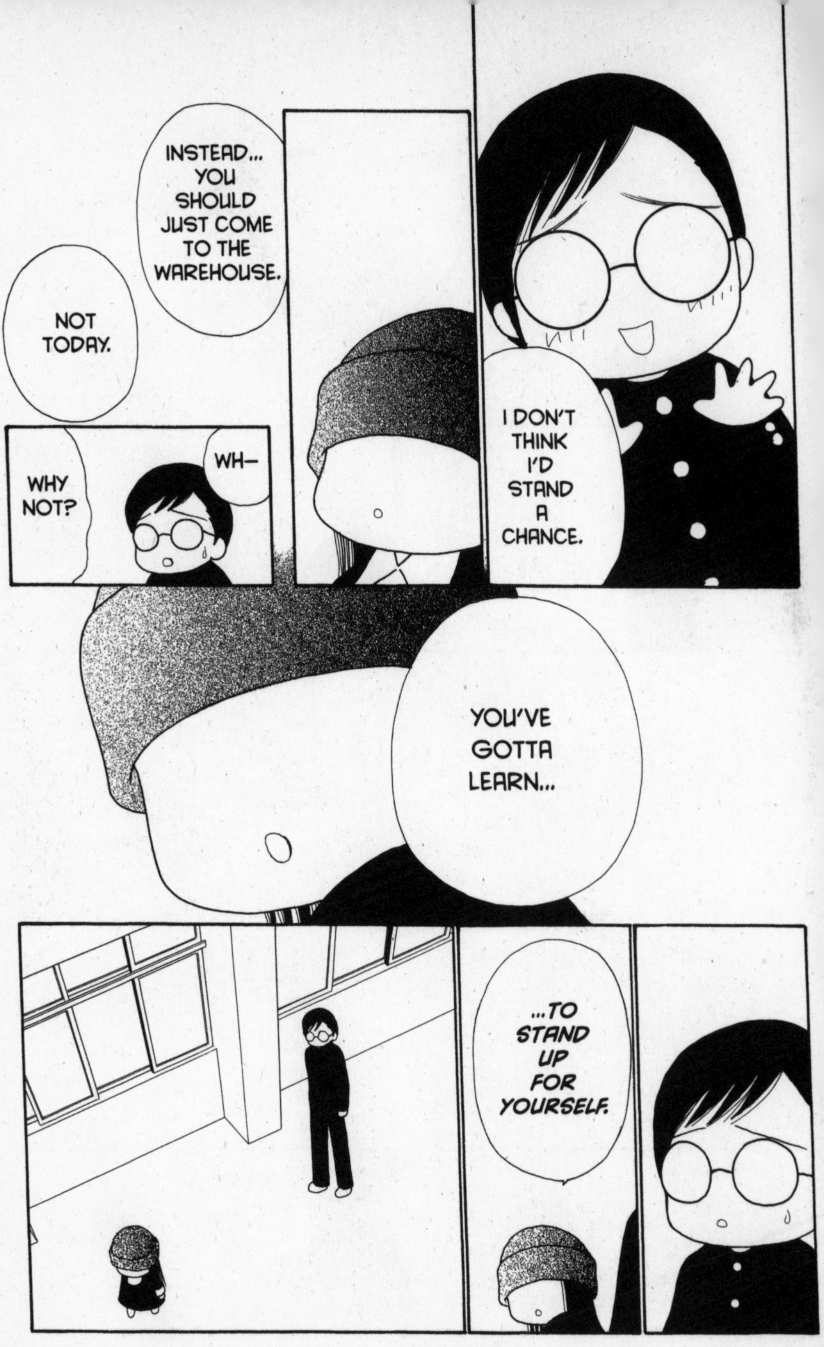
I DON'T THINK I'D STAND A CHANCE.
INSTEAD... YOU SHOULD JUST COME TO THE WAREHOUSE.
NOT TODAY.
WH-
WHY NOT?
YOU'VE GOTTA LEARN...
...TO STAND UP FOR YOURSELF.

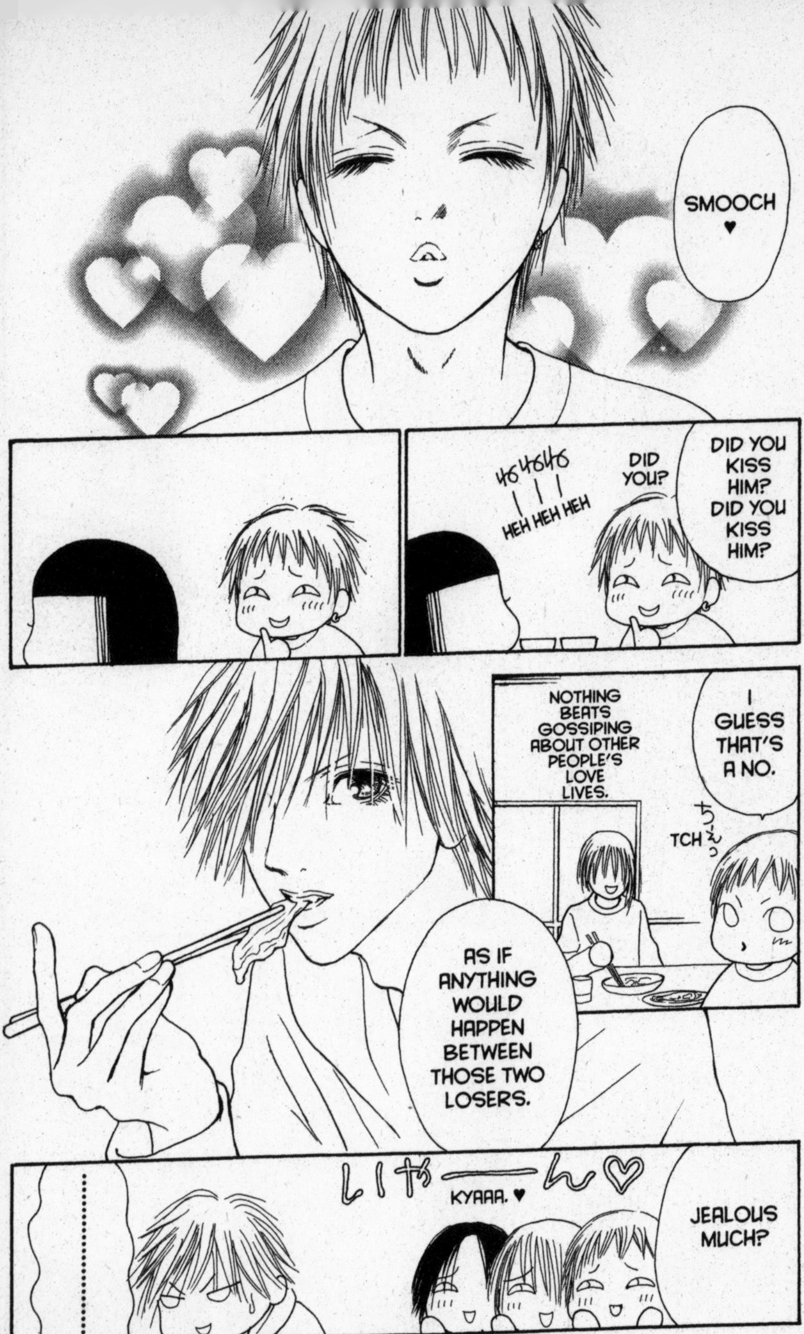
SMOOCH ♥
DID YOU KISS HIM? DID YOU KISS HIM?
DID YOU?
HEH HEH HEH
I GUESS THAT'S A NO.
NOTHING BEATS GOSSIPING ABOUT OTHER PEOPLE'S LOVE LIVES.
TCH
AS IF ANYTHING WOULD HAPPEN BETWEEN THOSE TWO LOSERS.
JEALOUS MUCH?
KYAAA. ♥
......

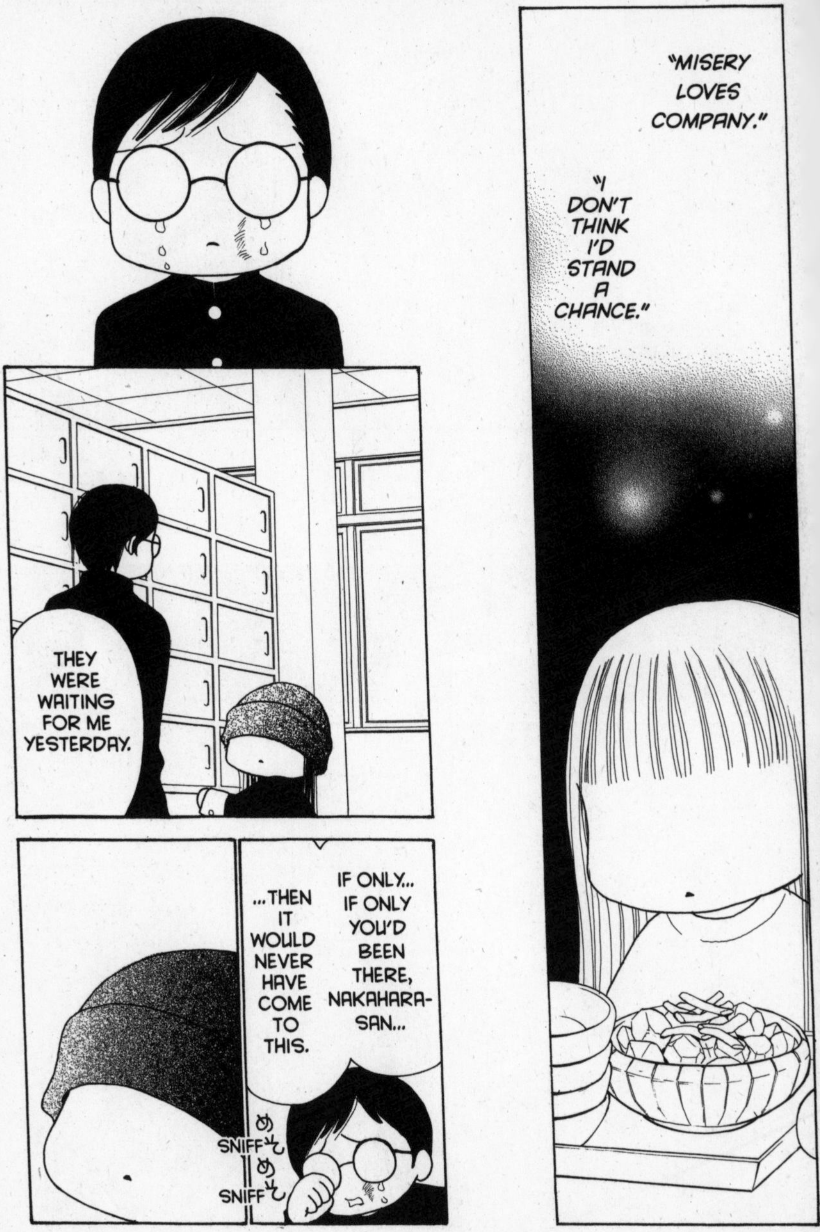
"MISERY LOVES COMPANY."
"I DON'T THINK I'D STAND A CHANCE."
THEY WERE WAITING FOR ME YESTERDAY.
IF ONLY... IF ONLY YOU'D BEEN THERE, NAKAHARA-SAN...
...THEN IT WOULD NEVER HAVE COME TO THIS.
SNIFF めそ
SNIFF めそ

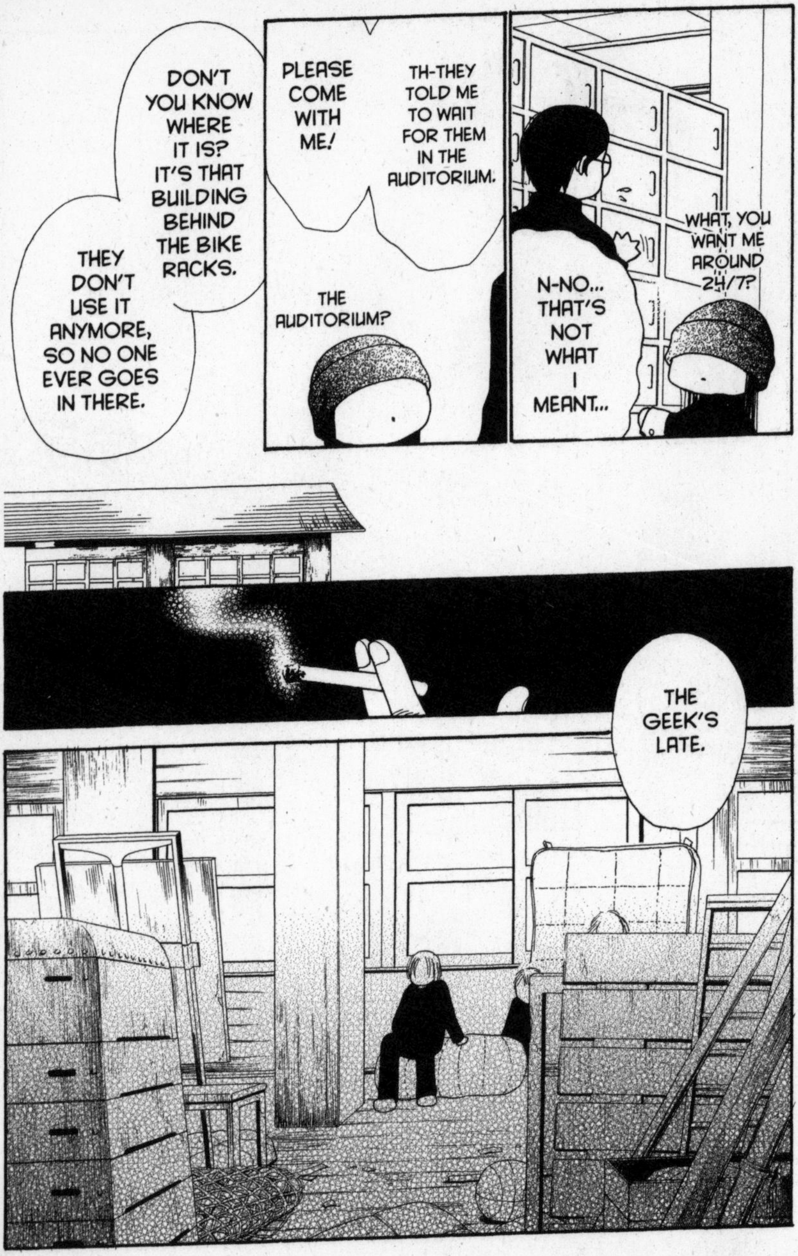
WHAT, YOU WANT ME AROUND 24/7?
N-NO... THAT'S NOT WHAT I MEANT...
TH-THEY TOLD ME TO WAIT FOR THEM IN THE AUDITORIUM.
PLEASE COME WITH ME!
THE AUDITORIUM?
DON'T YOU KNOW WHERE IT IS? IT'S THAT BUILDING BEHIND THE BIKE RACKS.
THEY DON'T USE IT ANYMORE, SO NO ONE EVER GOES IN THERE.
THE GEEK'S LATE.

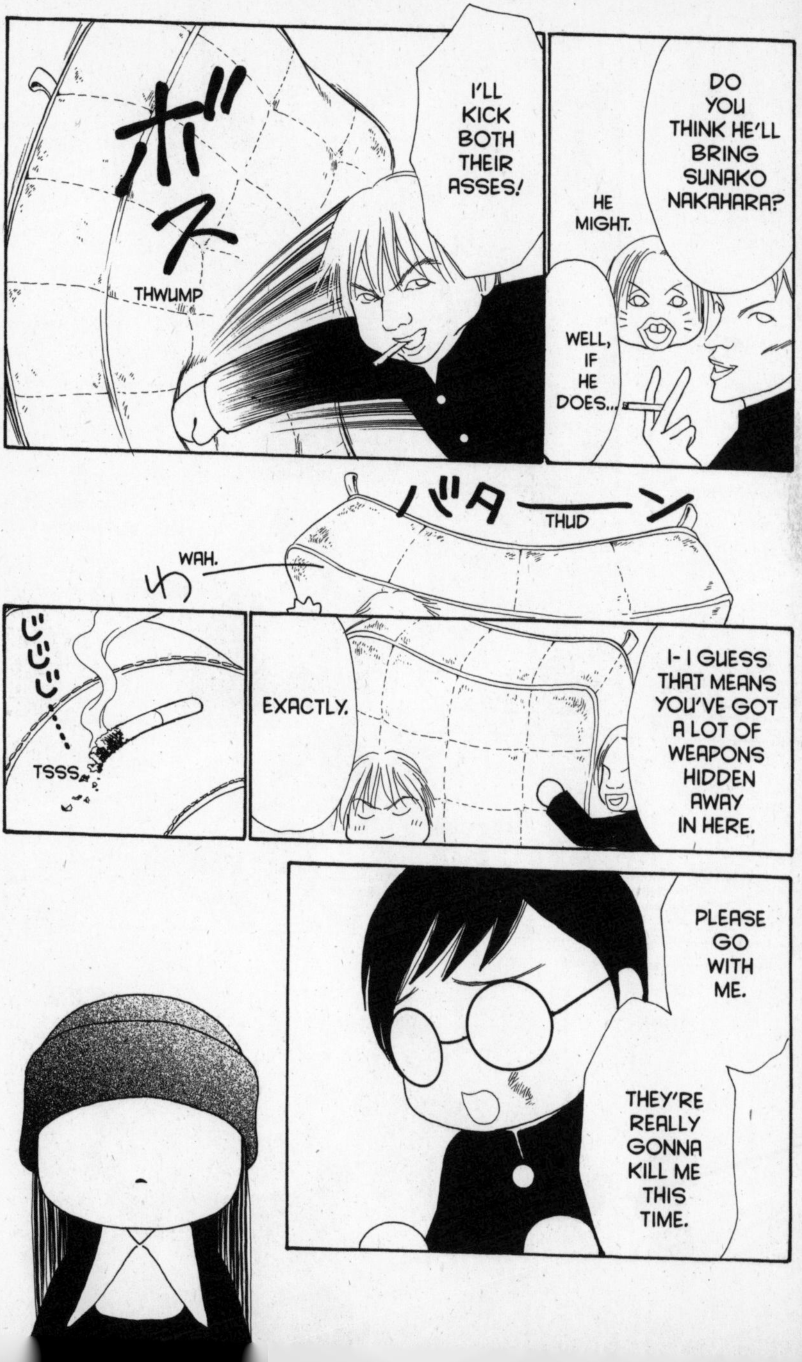
DO YOU THINK HE'LL BRING SUNAKO NAKAHARA?
HE MIGHT.
WELL, IF HE DOES...
I'LL KICK BOTH THEIR ASSES!
ボス
THWUMP
バターン
THUD
WAH.
I- I GUESS THAT MEANS YOU'VE GOT A LOT OF WEAPONS HIDDEN AWAY IN HERE.
EXACTLY.
じじじ
TSSS
PLEASE GO WITH ME.
THEY'RE REALLY GONNA KILL ME THIS TIME.

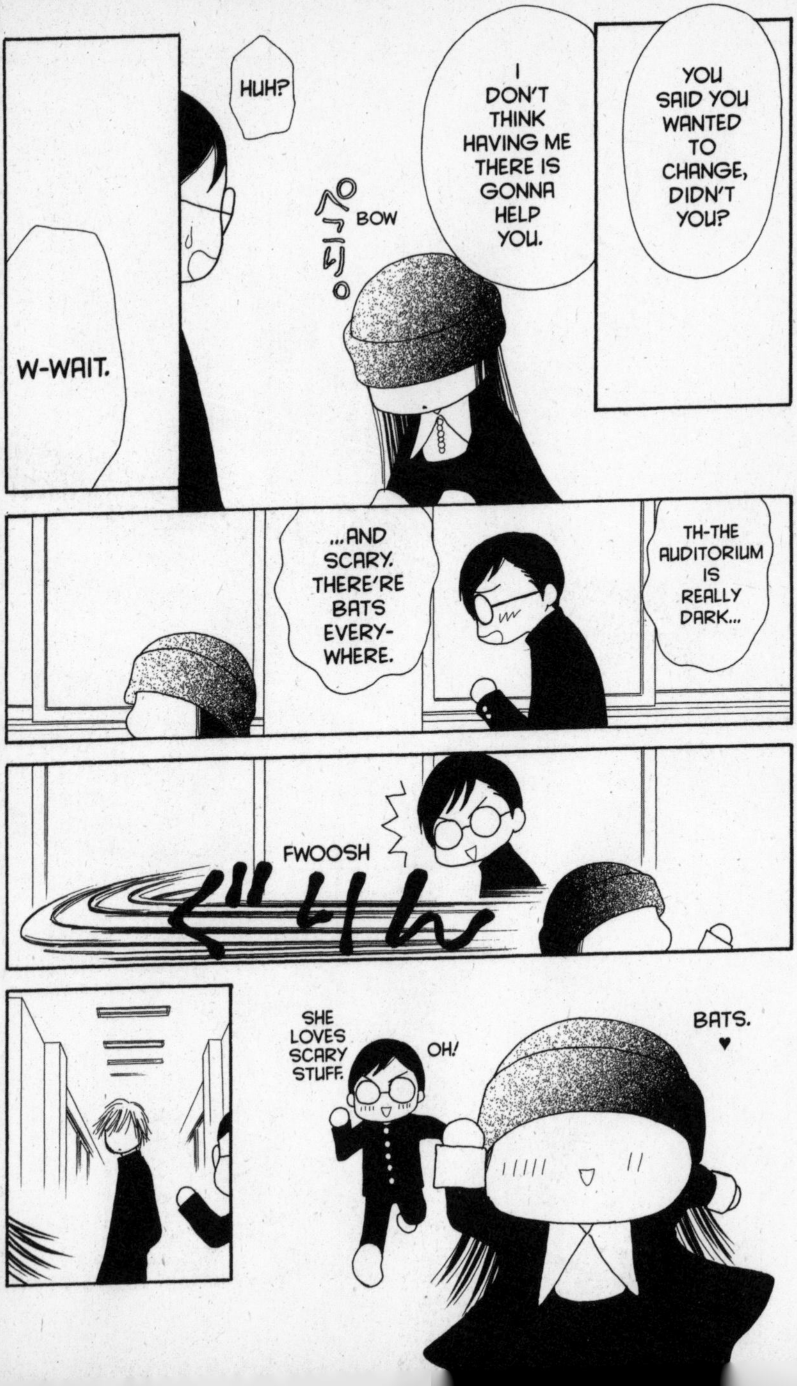

YOU SAID YOU WANTED TO CHANGE, DIDN'T YOU?
I DON'T THINK HAVING ME THERE IS GONNA HELP YOU.
ぺこり。
BOW
HUH?
W-WAIT.
TH-THE AUDITORIUM IS REALLY DARK...
...AND SCARY. THERE'RE BATS EVERYWHERE.
FWOOSH
BATS. ♥
OH!
SHE LOVES SCARY STUFF.

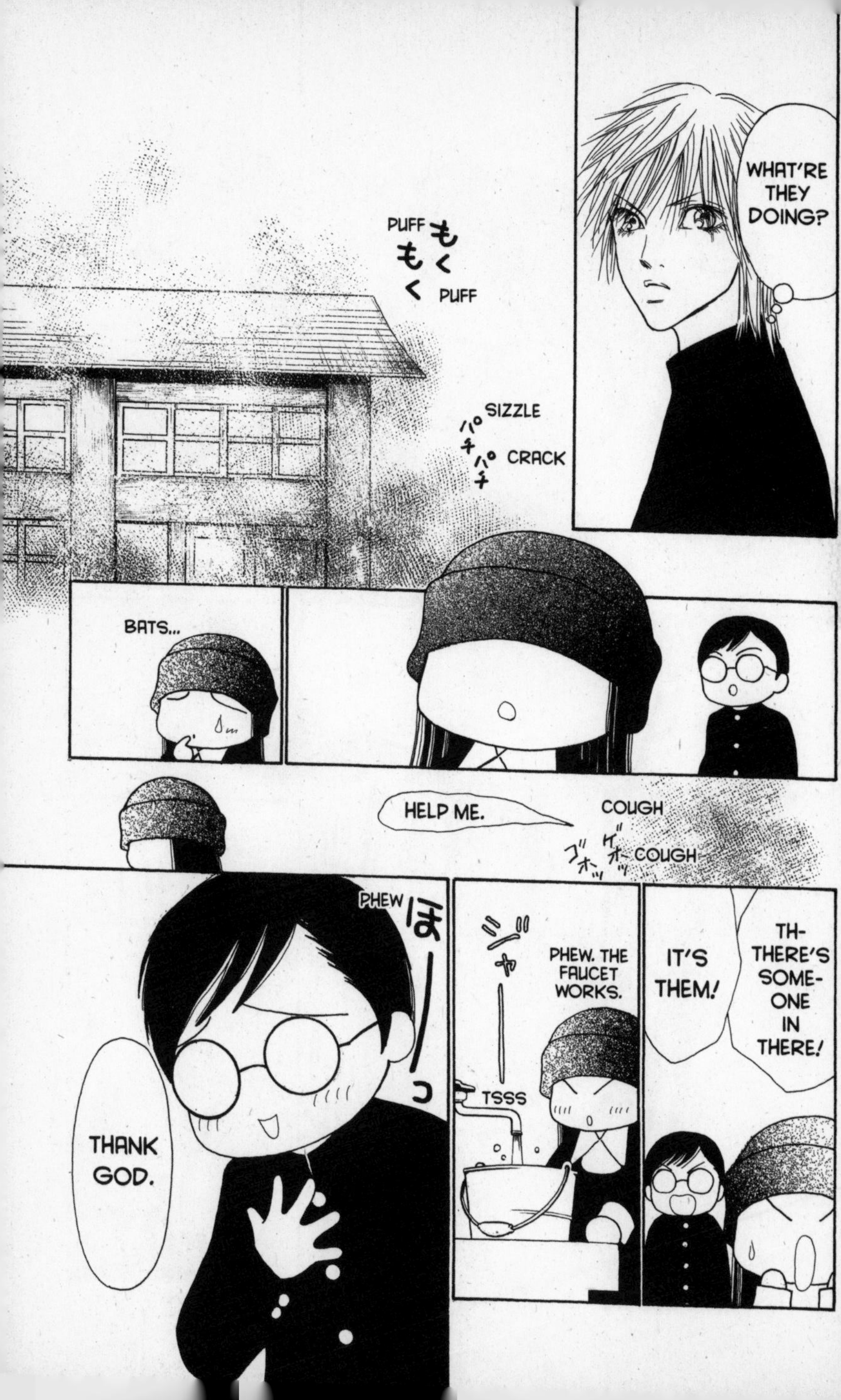
WHAT'RE THEY DOING?
PUFF もく
もく PUFF
SIZZLE パチ
パチ CRACK
BATS...
COUGH
COUGH
HELP ME.
TH-THERE'S SOME-ONE IN THERE!
IT'S THEM!
ジャー
PHEW. THE FAUCET WORKS.
TSSS
PHEW ほーっ
THANK GOD.

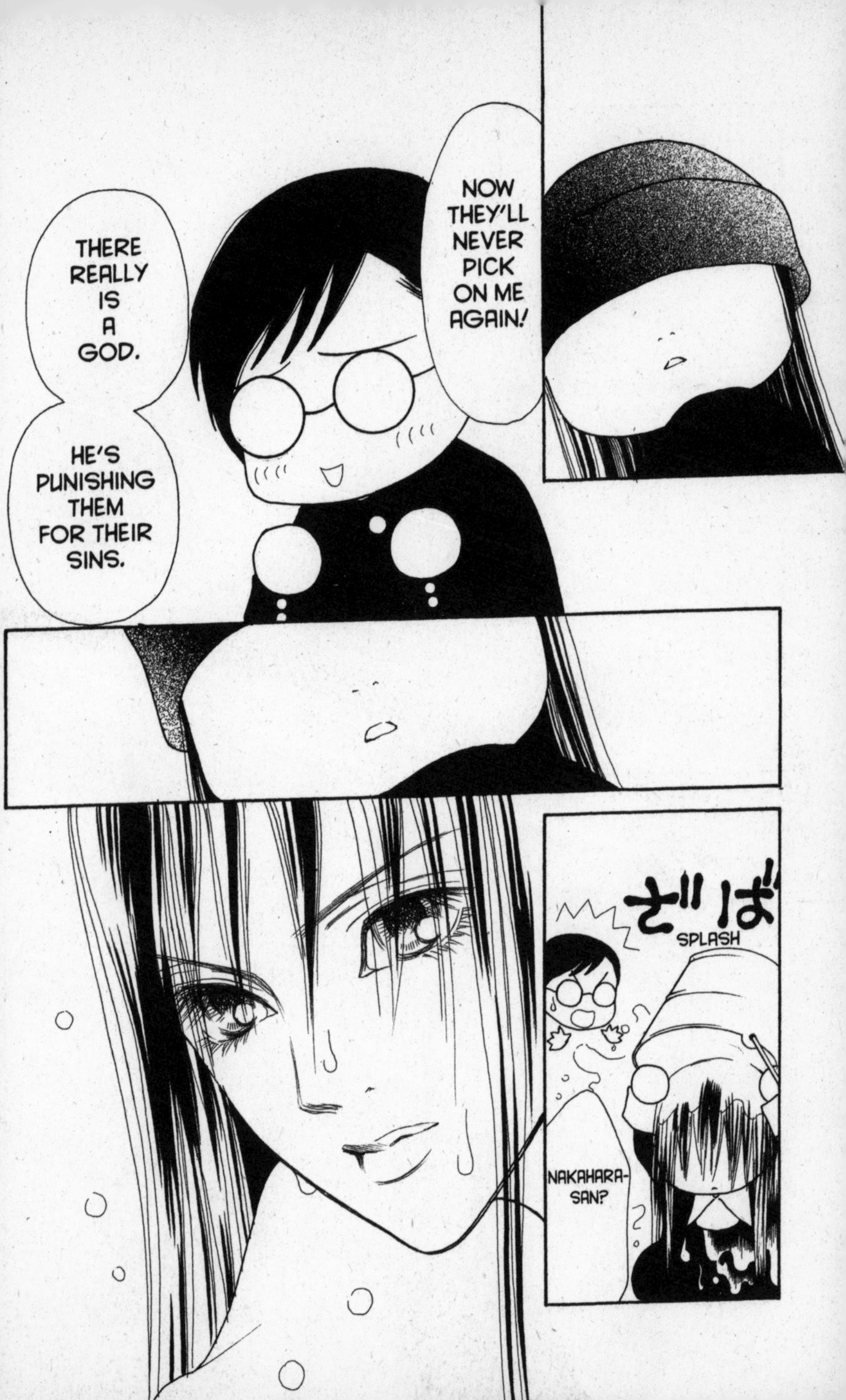
NOW THEY'LL NEVER PICK ON ME AGAIN!
THERE REALLY IS A GOD.
HE'S PUNISHING THEM FOR THEIR SINS.
ざば
SPLASH
NAKAHARA-SAN?

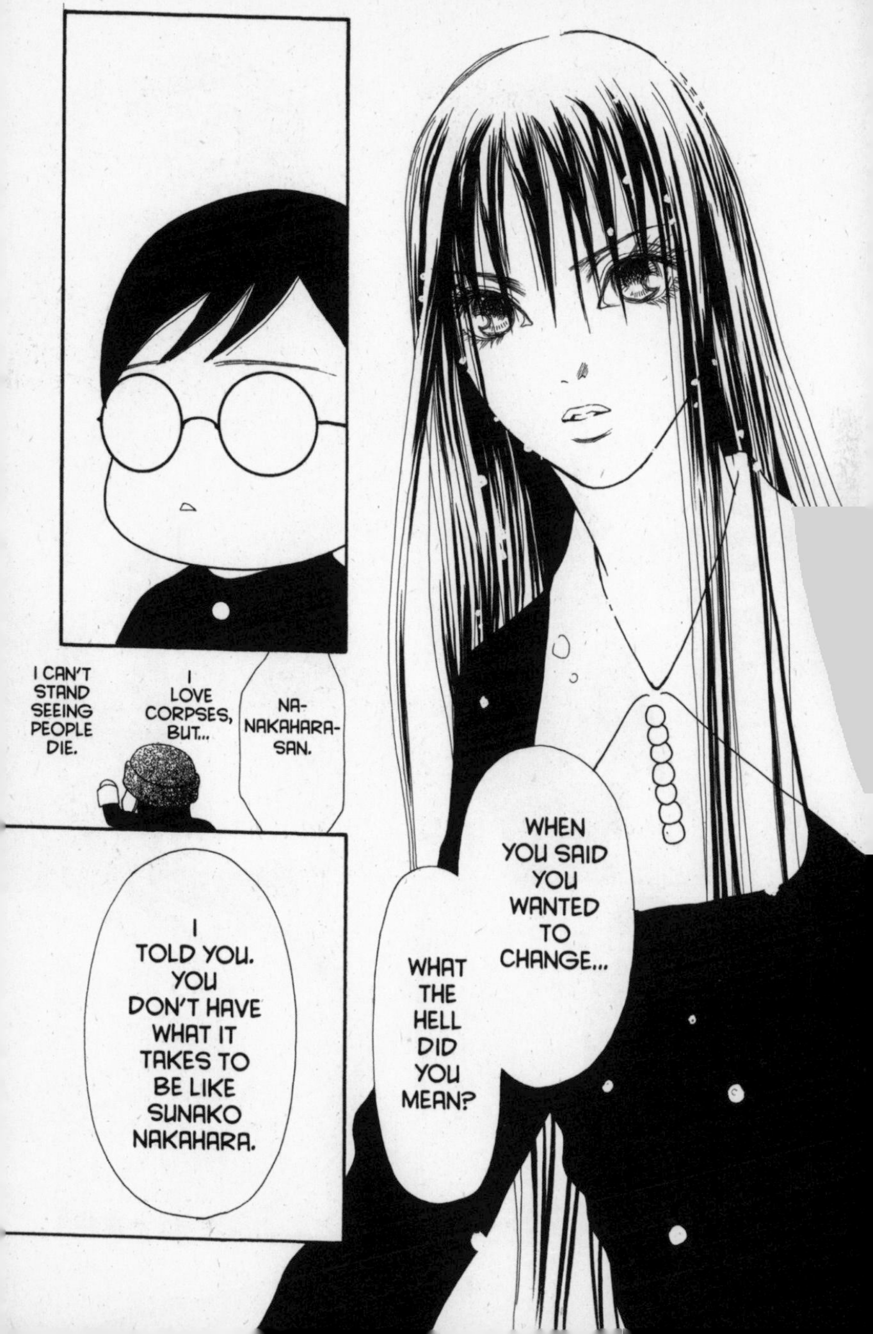
WHEN YOU SAID YOU WANTED TO CHANGE...
WHAT THE HELL DID YOU MEAN?
NA-NAKAHARA-SAN.
I LOVE CORPSES, BUT...
I CAN'T STAND SEEING PEOPLE DIE.
I TOLD YOU. YOU DON'T HAVE WHAT IT TAKES TO BE LIKE SUNAKO NAKAHARA.

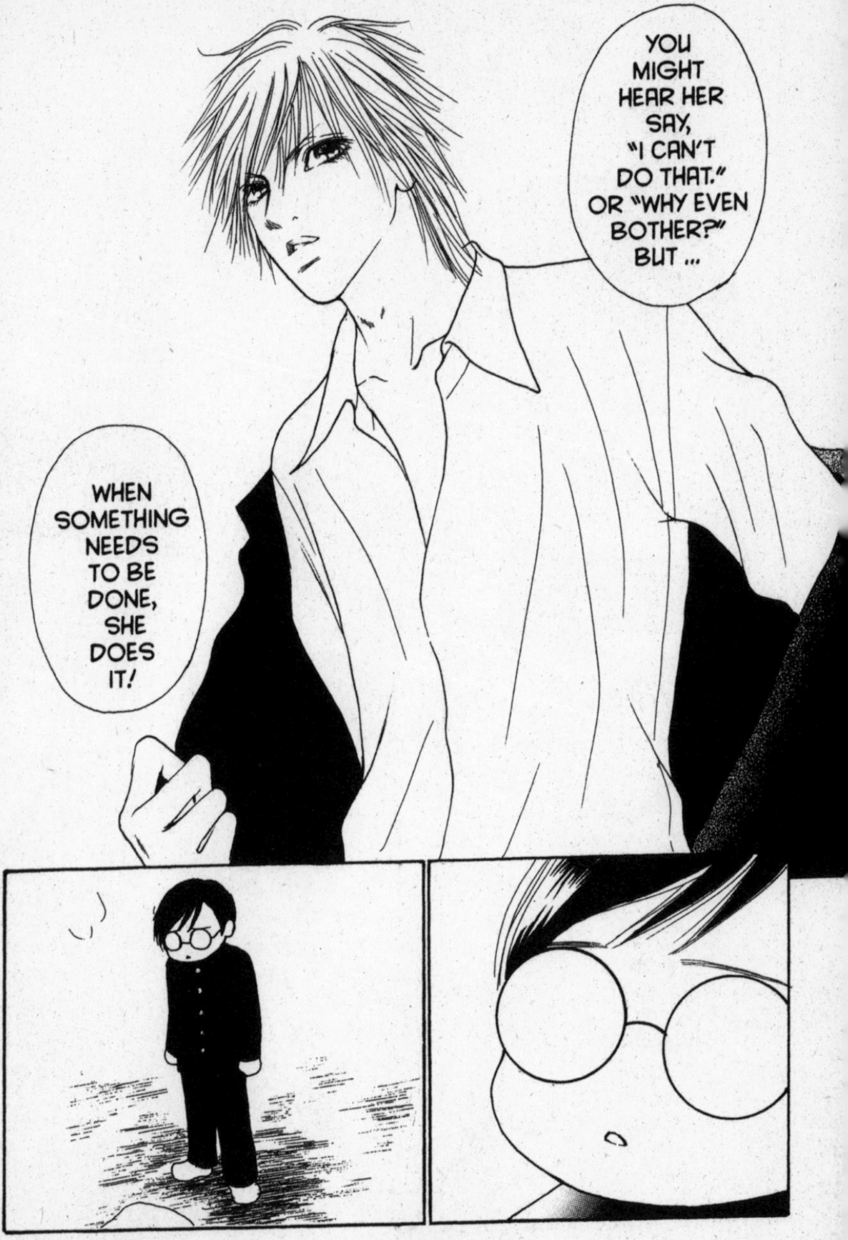
YOU MIGHT HEAR HER SAY, "I CAN'T DO THAT." OR "WHY EVEN BOTHER?" BUT ...
WHEN SOMETHING NEEDS TO BE DONE, SHE DOES IT!

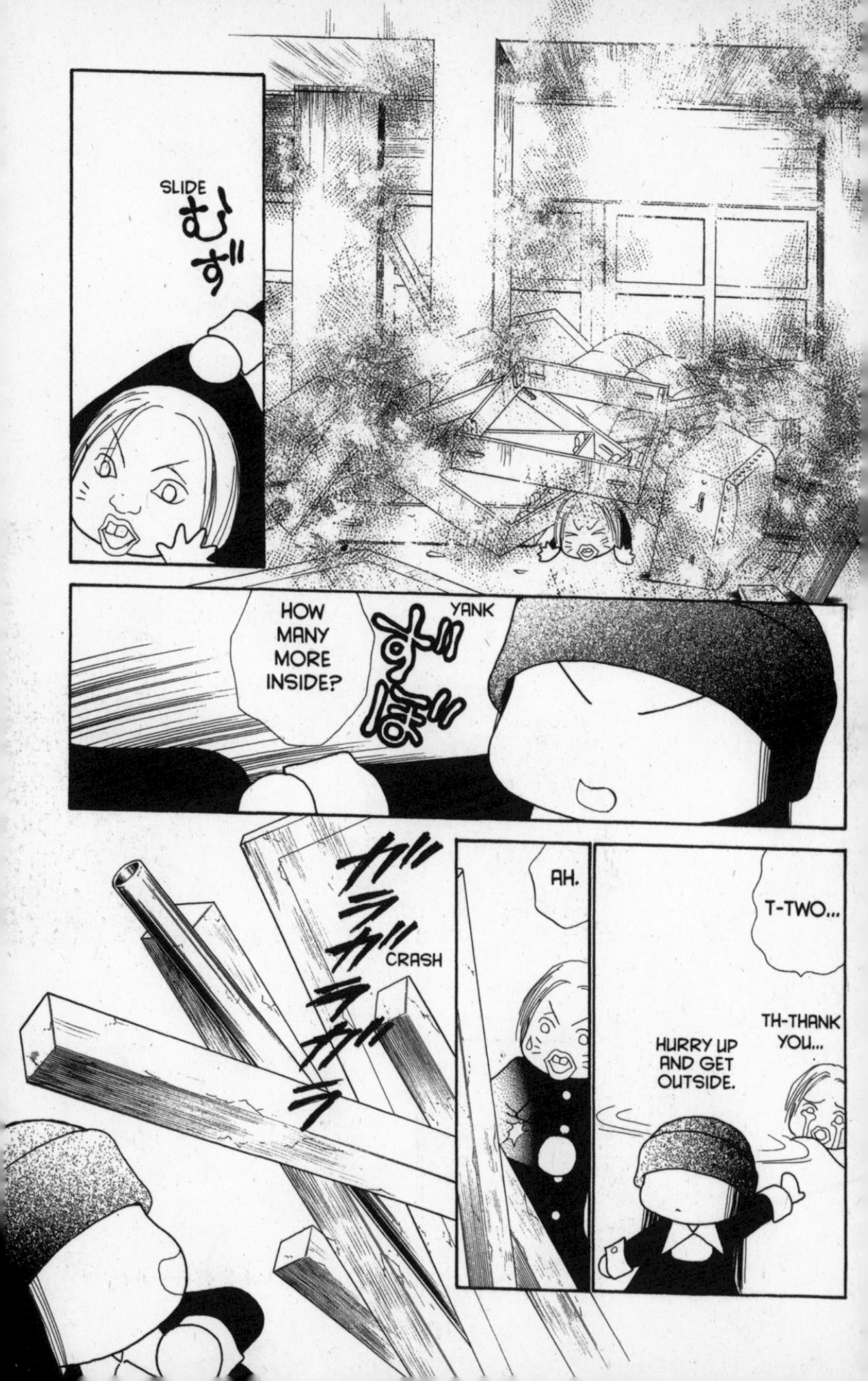
SLIDE
むず
YANK
HOW MANY MORE INSIDE?
T-TWO...
TH-THANK YOU...
HURRY UP AND GET OUTSIDE.
AH.
CRASH

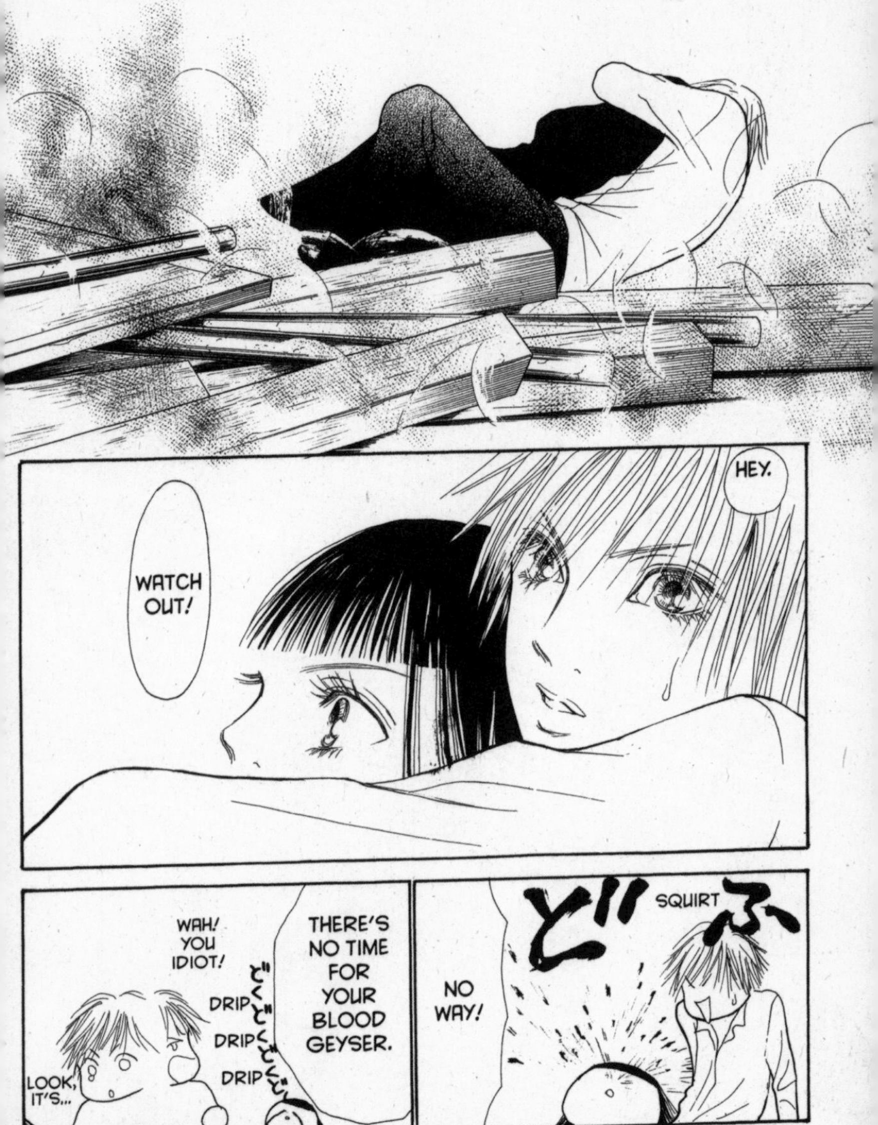
HEY.
WATCH OUT!
SQUIRT
NO WAY!
THERE'S NO TIME FOR YOUR BLOOD GEYSER.
WAH! YOU IDIOT!
DRIP
DRIP
DRIP
LOOK, IT'S...

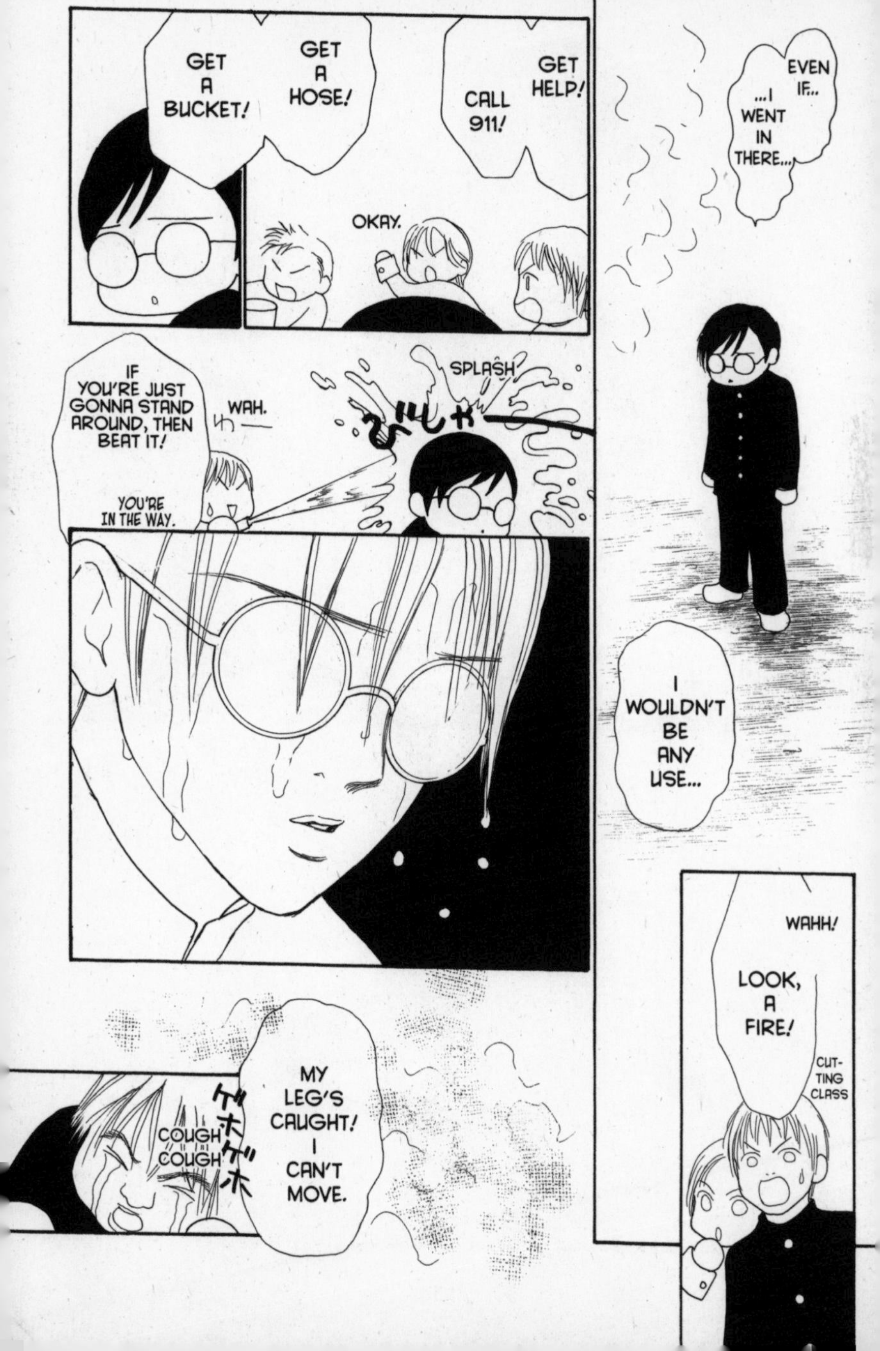
EVEN IF...
...I WENT IN THERE...
I WOULDN'T BE ANY USE...
WAHH!
LOOK, A FIRE!
CUT-TING CLASS
GET HELP!
CALL 911!
GET A HOSE!
GET A BUCKET!
OKAY.
SPLASH
びしゃ
IF YOU'RE JUST GONNA STAND AROUND, THEN BEAT IT!
WAH.
わー
YOU'RE IN THE WAY.
MY LEG'S CAUGHT! I CAN'T MOVE.
ゲホゲホ
COUGH COUGH

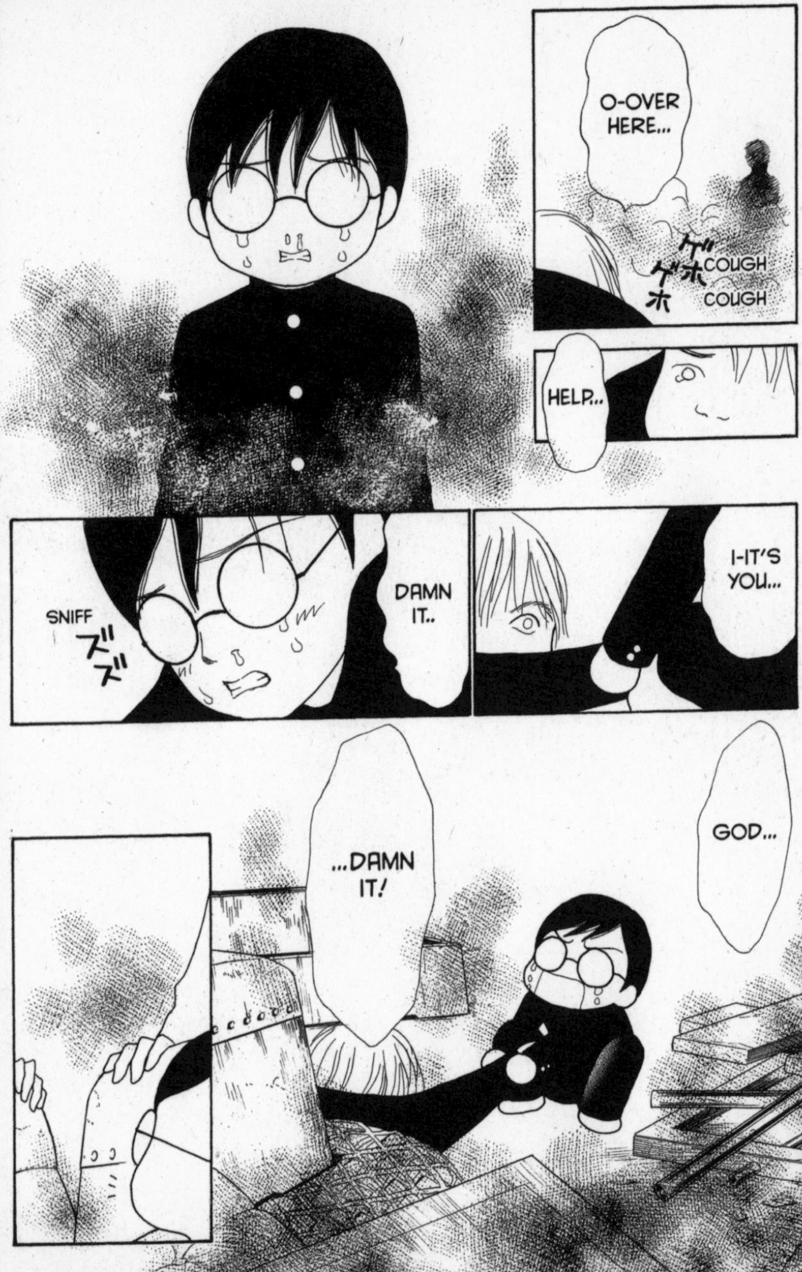
O-OVER HERE...
ゲホゲホ
COUGH COUGH
HELP...
I-IT'S YOU...
DAMN IT..
SNIFF
ズズ
GOD...
...DAMN IT!

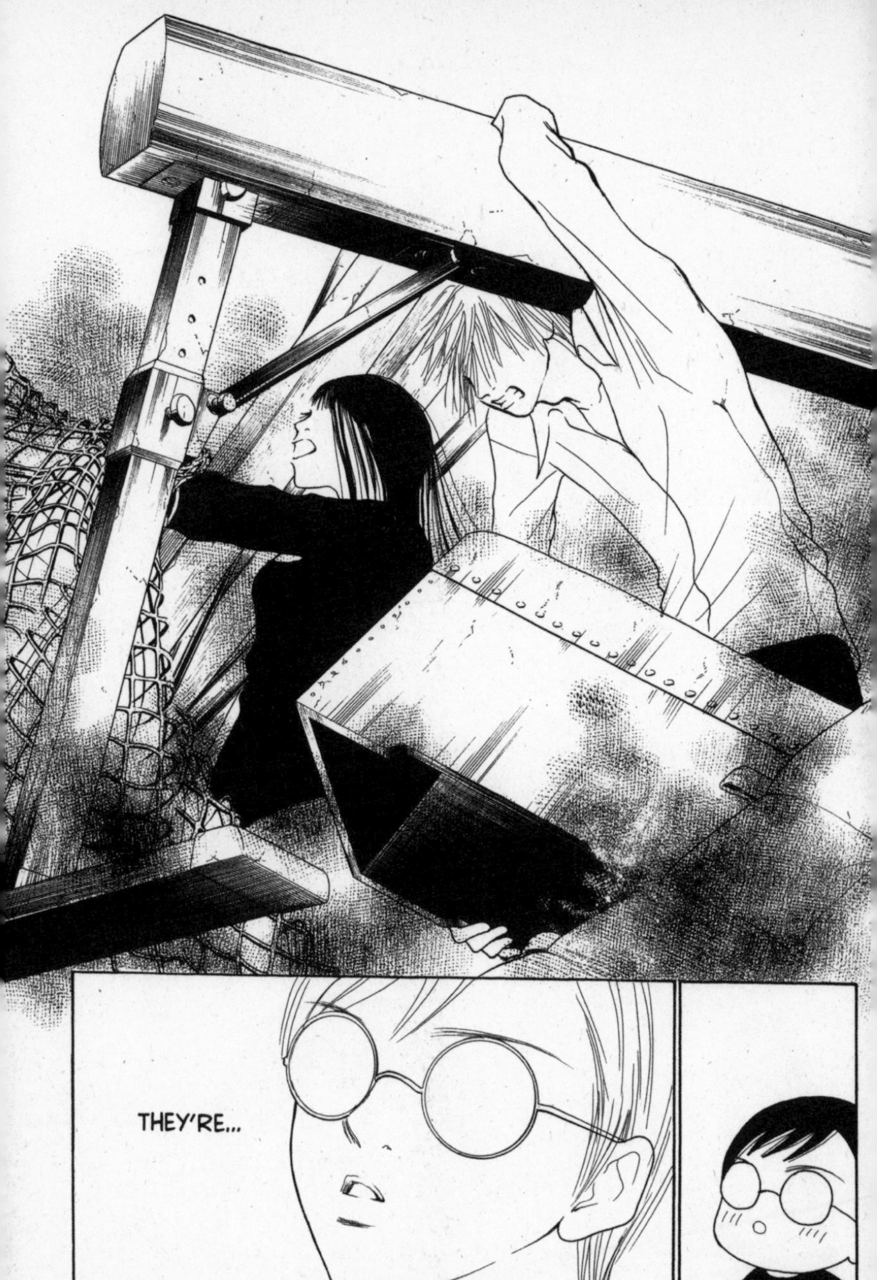
THEY'RE...

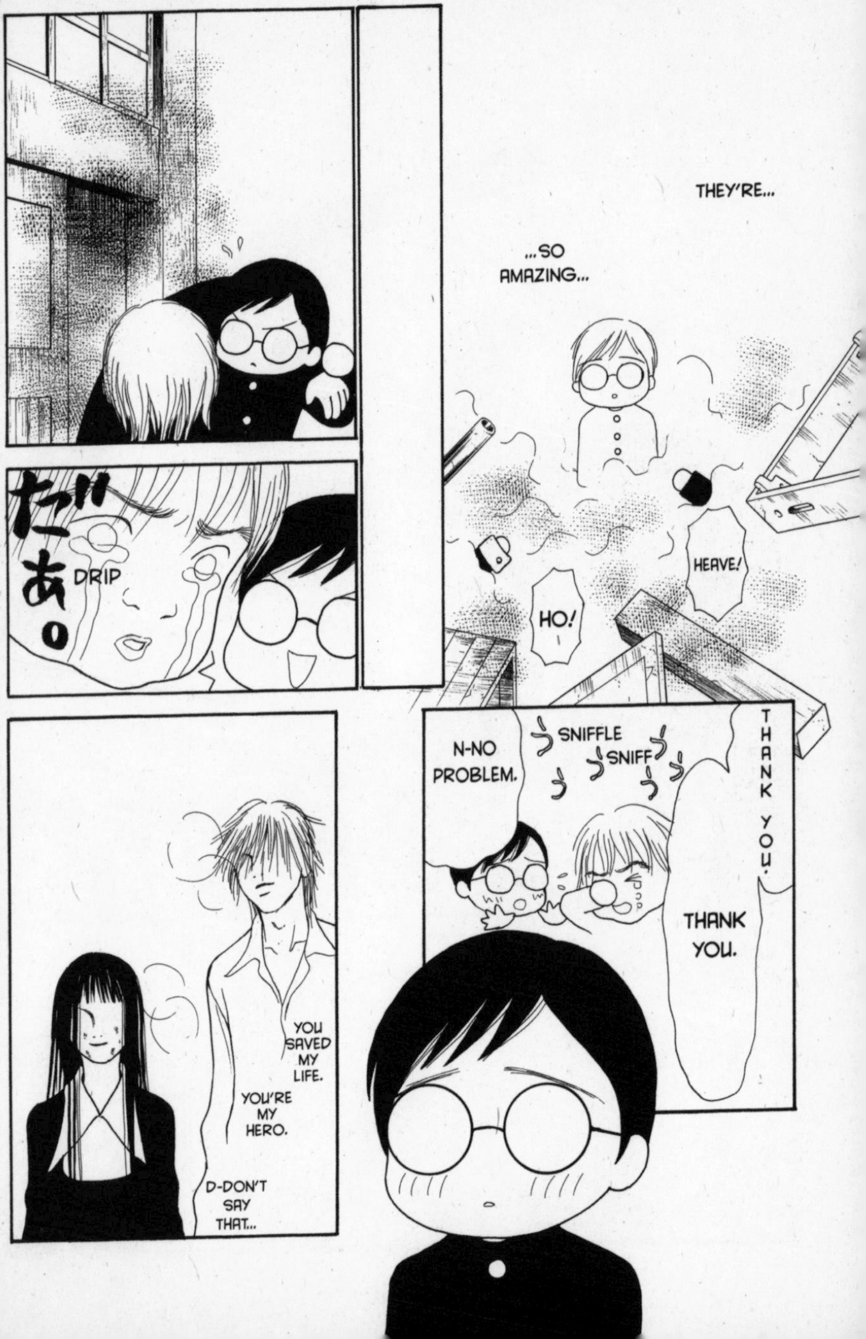

THEY'RE...
...SO AMAZING...
HEAVE!
HO!
だあ
DRIP
THANK YOU.
SNIFFLE
SNIFF
N-NO PROBLEM.
THANK YOU.
YOU SAVED MY LIFE.
YOU'RE MY HERO.
D-DON'T SAY THAT...

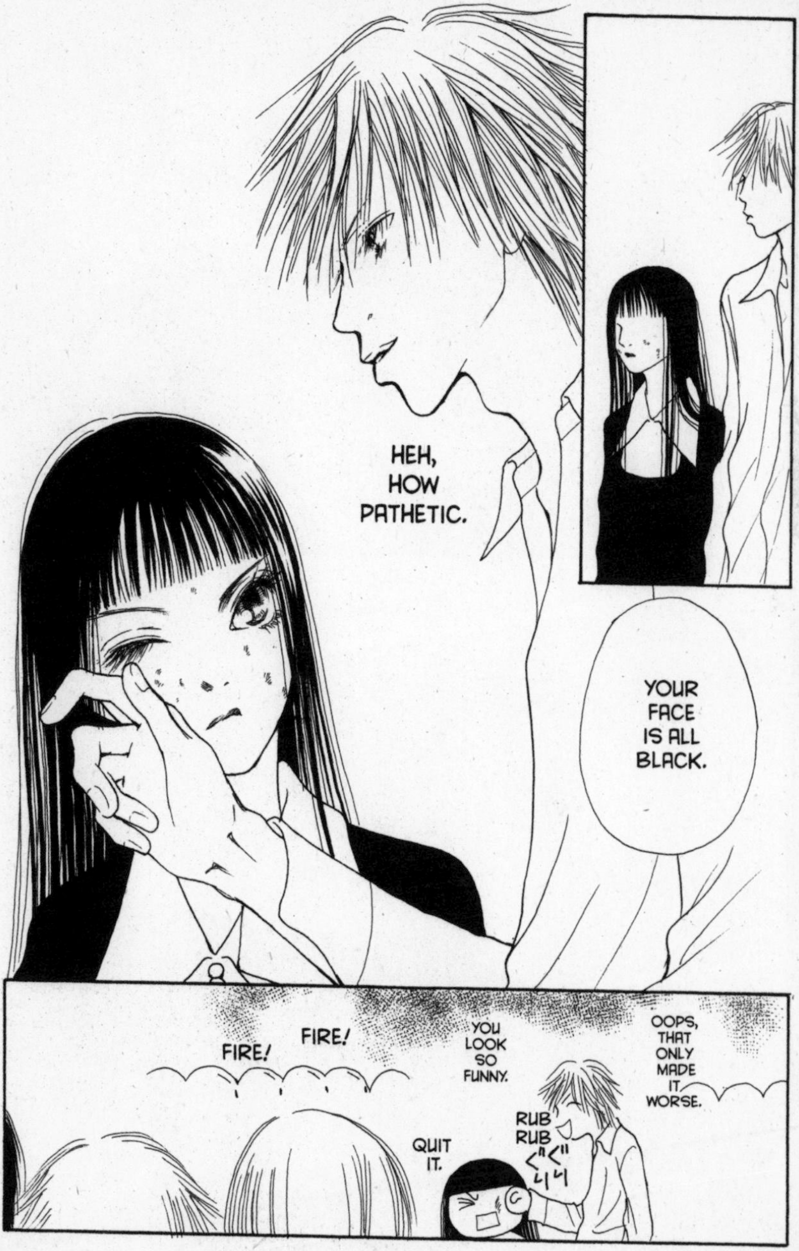
HEH, HOW PATHETIC.
YOUR FACE IS ALL BLACK.
OOPS, THAT ONLY MADE IT WORSE.
YOU LOOK SO FUNNY.
FIRE!
FIRE!
RUB RUB
QUIT IT.

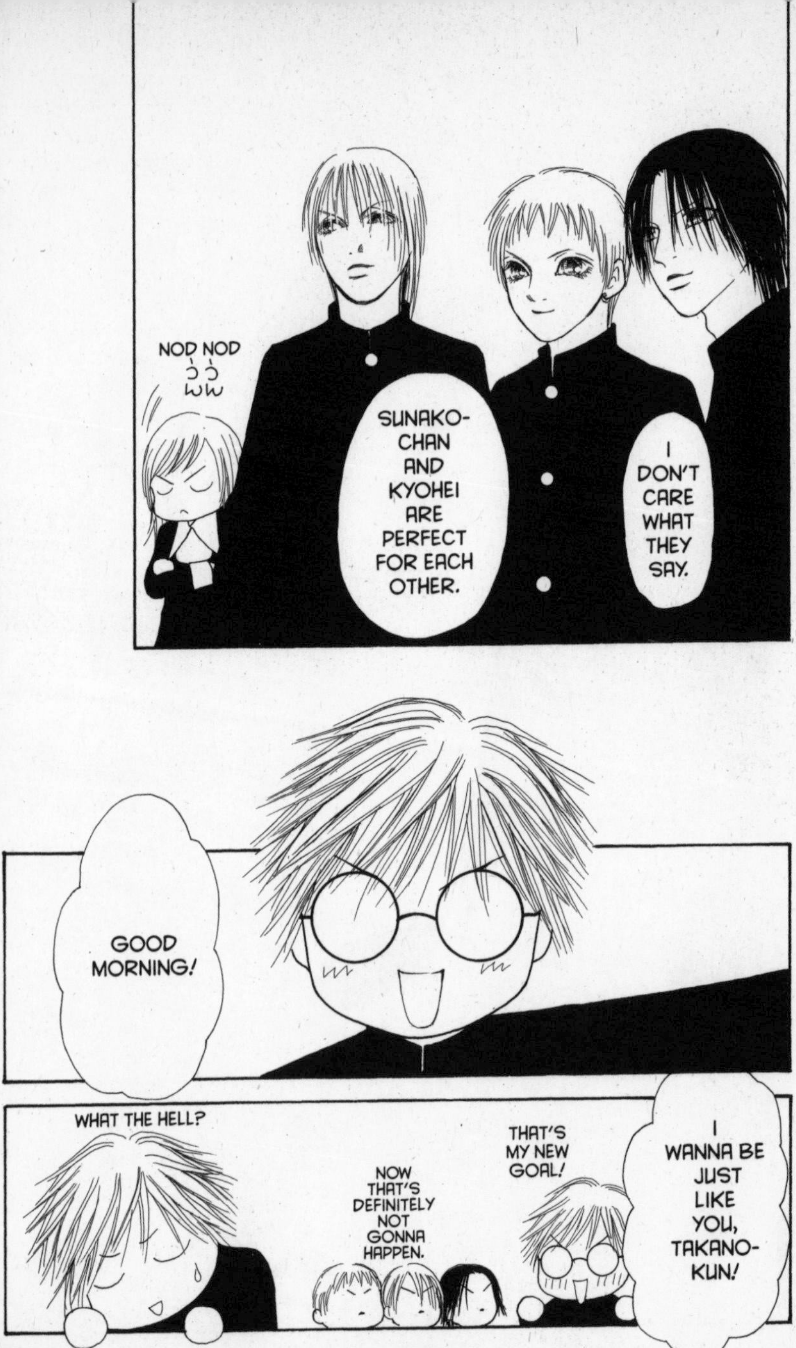
I DON'T CARE WHAT THEY SAY.
SUNAKO-CHAN AND KYOHEI ARE PERFECT FOR EACH OTHER.
NOD NOD
GOOD MORNING!
I WANNA BE JUST LIKE YOU, TAKANO-KUN!
THAT'S MY NEW GOAL!
NOW THAT'S DEFINITELY NOT GONNA HAPPEN.
WHAT THE HELL?

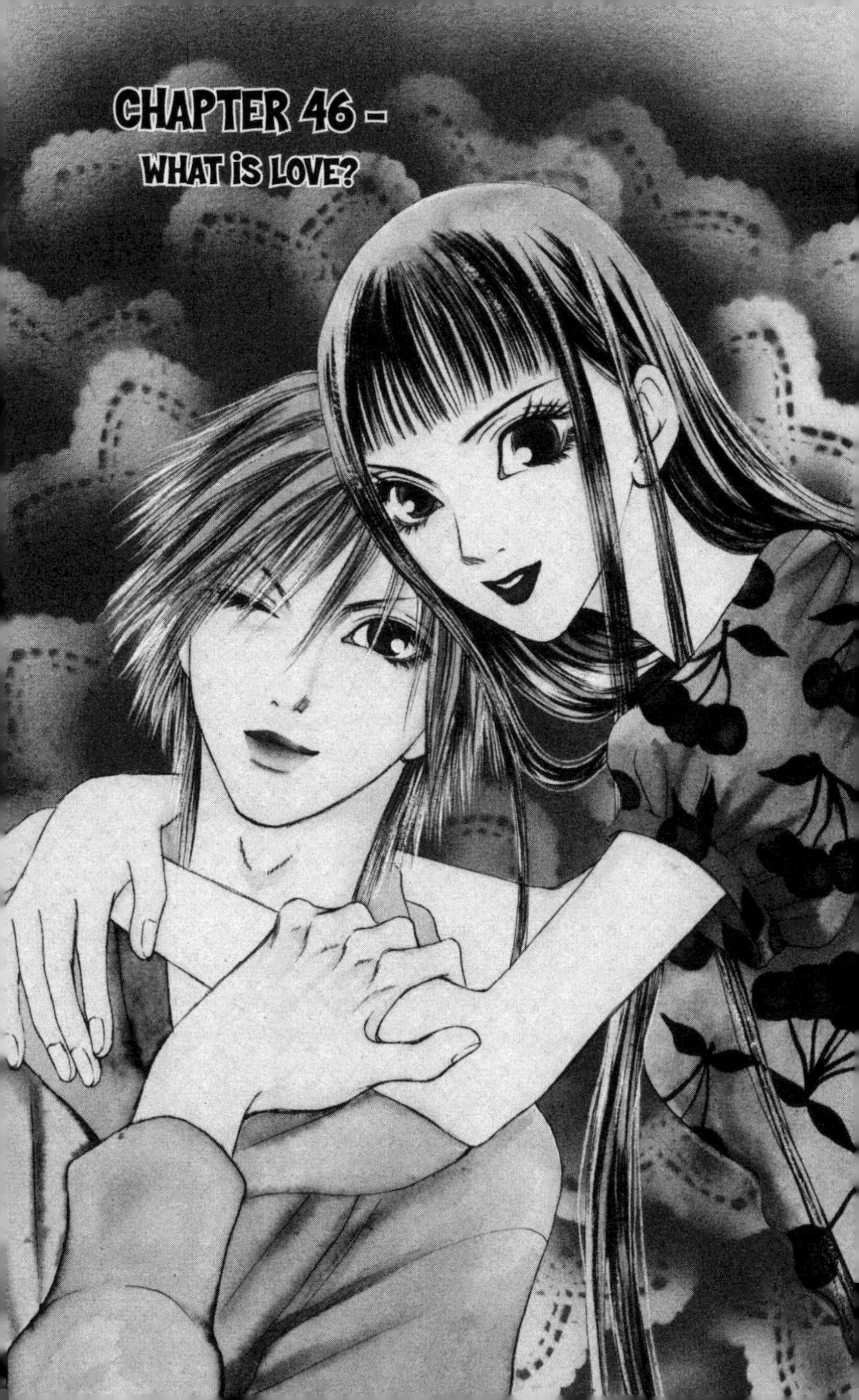
CHAPTER 46 -
WHAT IS LOVE?

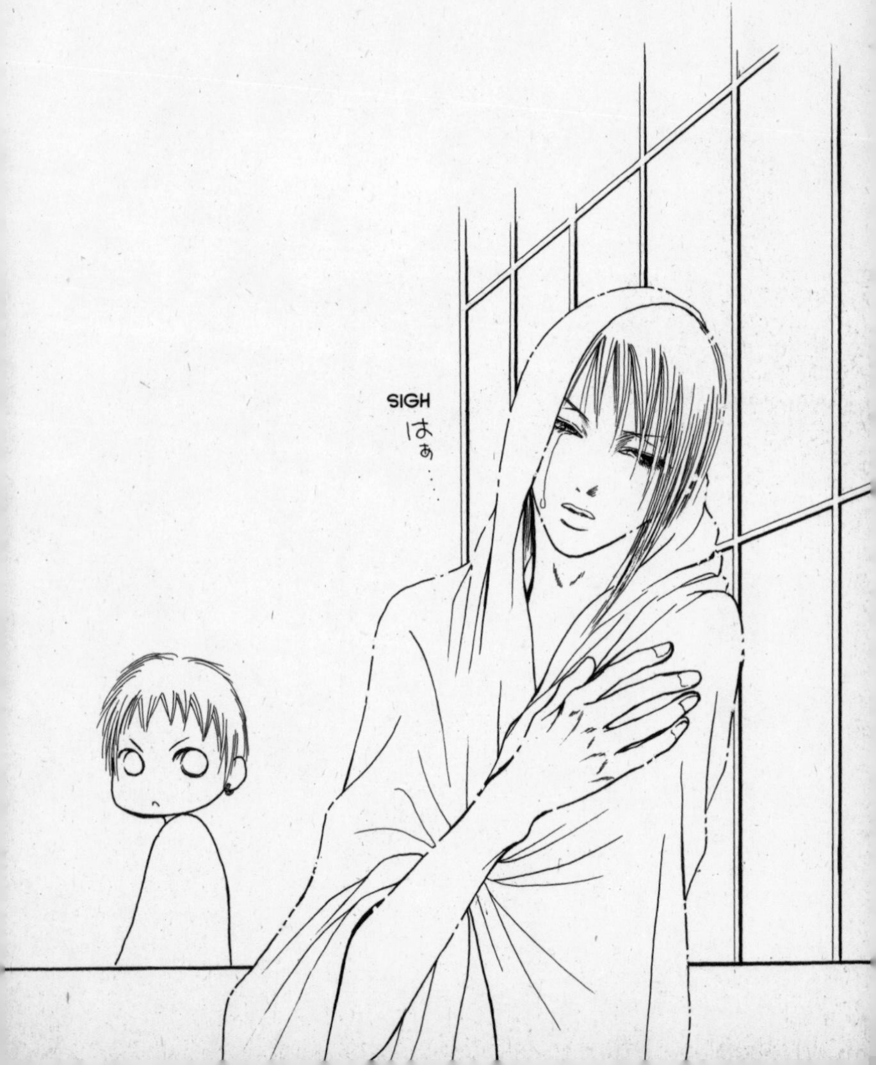
SIGH
はぁ…

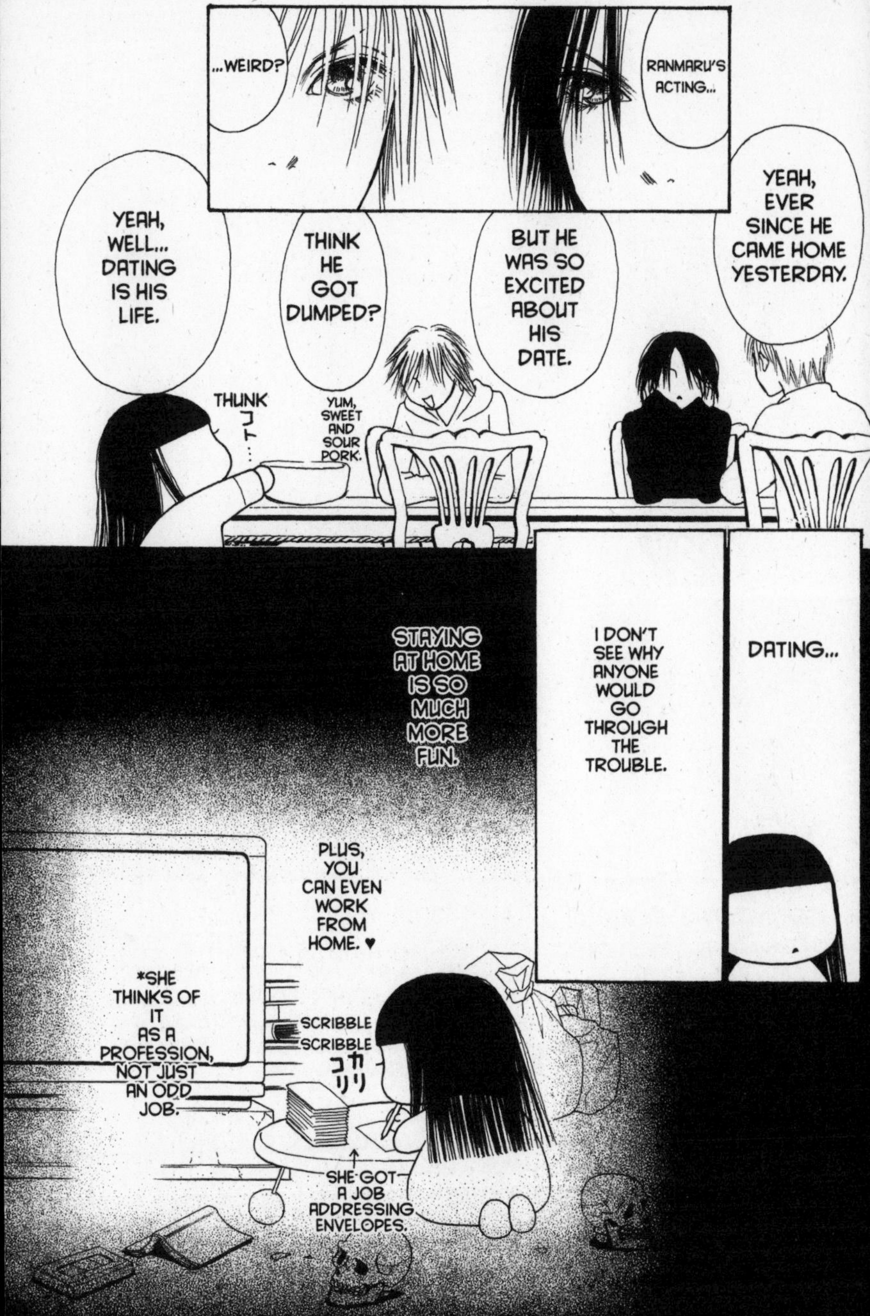
RANMARU'S ACTING...
...WEIRD?
YEAH, EVER SINCE HE CAME HOME YESTERDAY.
BUT HE WAS SO EXCITED ABOUT HIS DATE.
THINK HE GOT DUMPED?
YUM, SWEET AND SOUR PORK.
YEAH, WELL... DATING IS HIS LIFE.
THUNK
コト…
DATING...
I DON'T SEE WHY ANYONE WOULD GO THROUGH THE TROUBLE.
STAYING AT HOME IS SO MUCH MORE FUN.
PLUS, YOU CAN EVEN WORK FROM HOME. ♥
SCRIBBLE SCRIBBLE
カリコリ
*SHE THINKS OF IT AS A PROFESSION, NOT JUST AN ODD JOB.
SHE GOT A JOB ADDRESSING ENVELOPES.

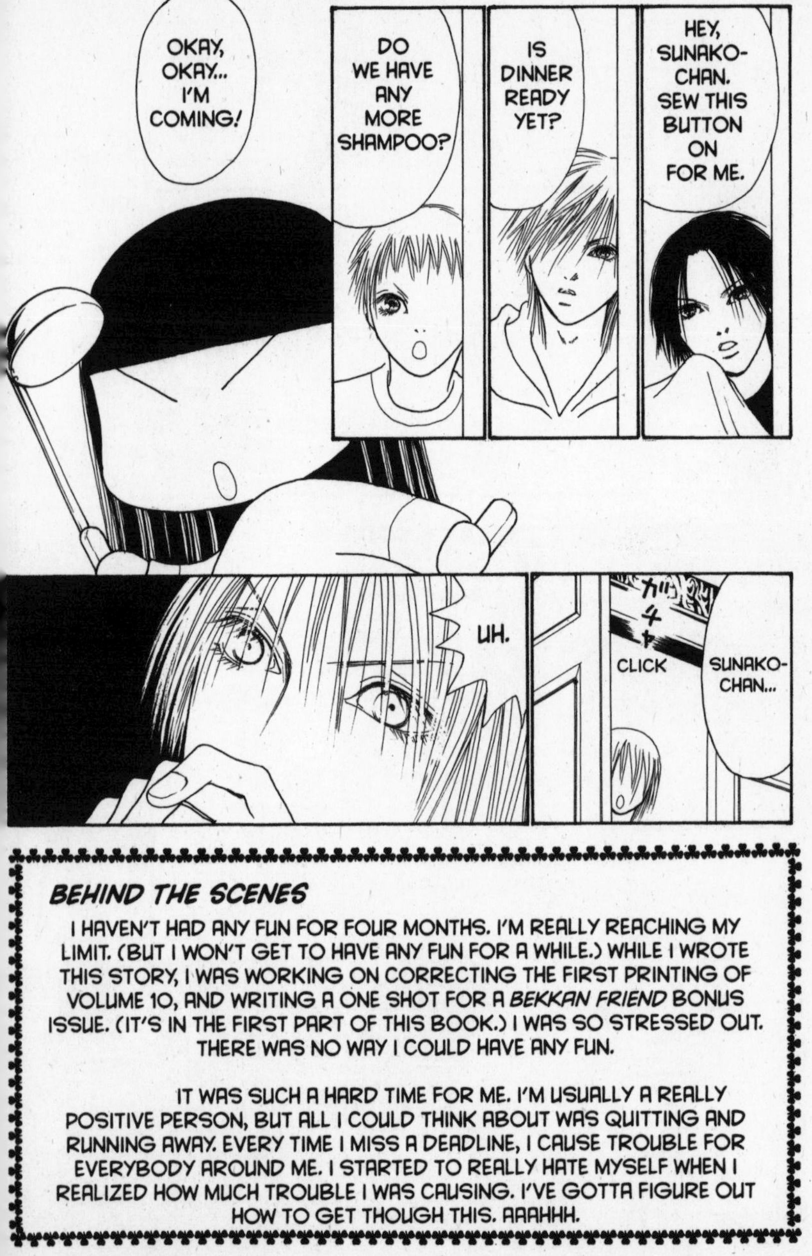
HEY, SUNAKO-CHAN. SEW THIS BUTTON ON FOR ME.
IS DINNER READY YET?
DO WE HAVE ANY MORE SHAMPOO?
OKAY, OKAY... I'M COMING!
SUNAKO-CHAN...
CLICK
UH.

BEHIND THE SCENES

I HAVEN'T HAD ANY FUN FOR FOUR MONTHS. I'M REALLY REACHING MY LIMIT. (BUT I WON'T GET TO HAVE ANY FUN FOR A WHILE.) WHILE I WROTE THIS STORY, I WAS WORKING ON CORRECTING THE FIRST PRINTING OF VOLUME 10, AND WRITING A ONE SHOT FOR A *BEKKAN FRIEND* BONUS ISSUE. (IT'S IN THE FIRST PART OF THIS BOOK.) I WAS SO STRESSED OUT. THERE WAS NO WAY I COULD HAVE ANY FUN.

IT WAS SUCH A HARD TIME FOR ME. I'M USUALLY A REALLY POSITIVE PERSON, BUT ALL I COULD THINK ABOUT WAS QUITTING AND RUNNING AWAY. EVERY TIME I MISS A DEADLINE, I CAUSE TROUBLE FOR EVERYBODY AROUND ME. I STARTED TO REALLY HATE MYSELF WHEN I REALIZED HOW MUCH TROUBLE I WAS CAUSING. I'VE GOTTA FIGURE OUT HOW TO GET THOUGH THIS. AAAHHH.

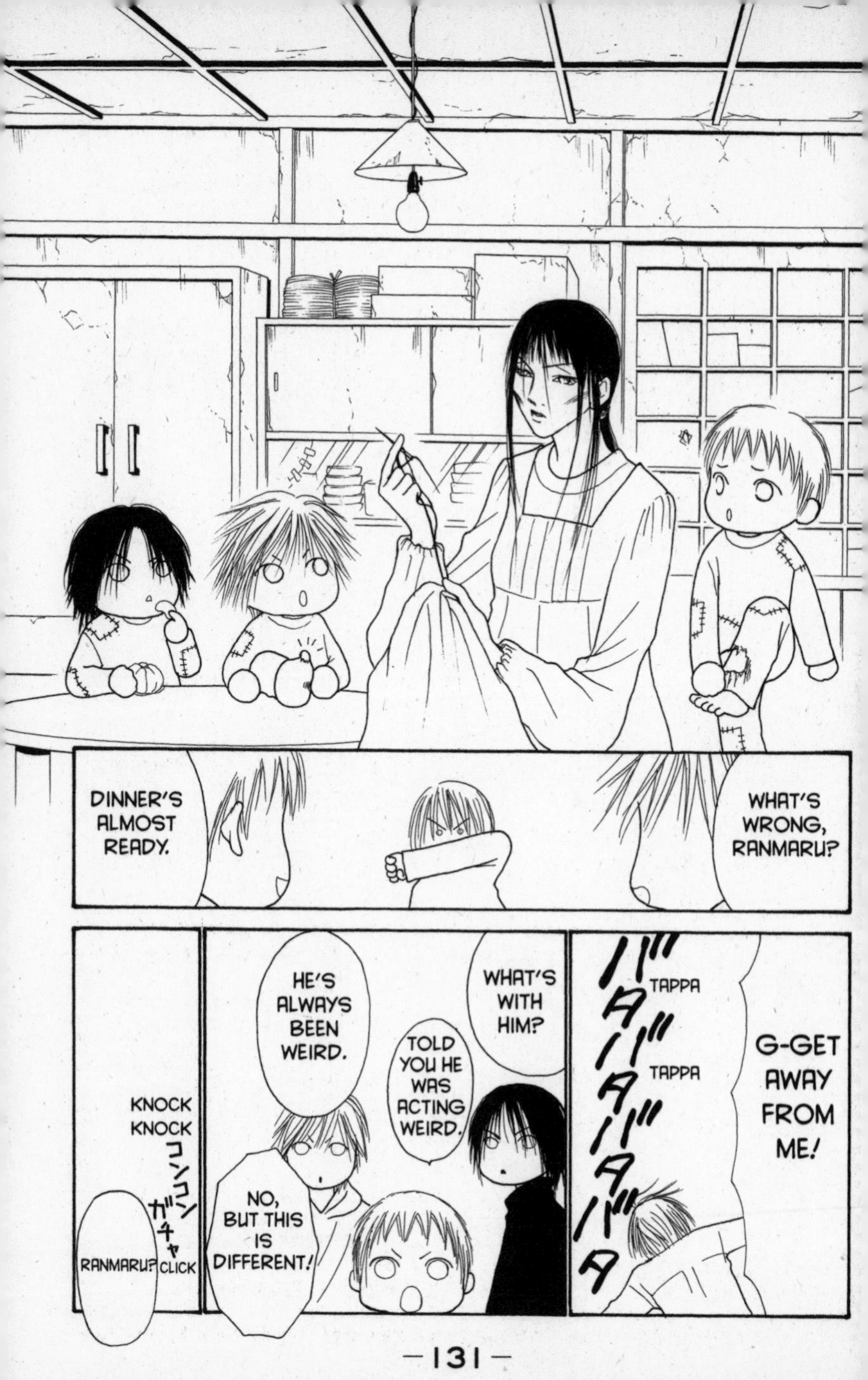
WHAT'S WRONG, RANMARU?
DINNER'S ALMOST READY.
G-GET AWAY FROM ME!
バタバタバタバタ
TAPPA TAPPA
WHAT'S WITH HIM?
TOLD YOU HE WAS ACTING WEIRD.
HE'S ALWAYS BEEN WEIRD.
NO, BUT THIS IS DIFFERENT!
コンコン
KNOCK KNOCK
ガチャ
CLICK
RANMARU?

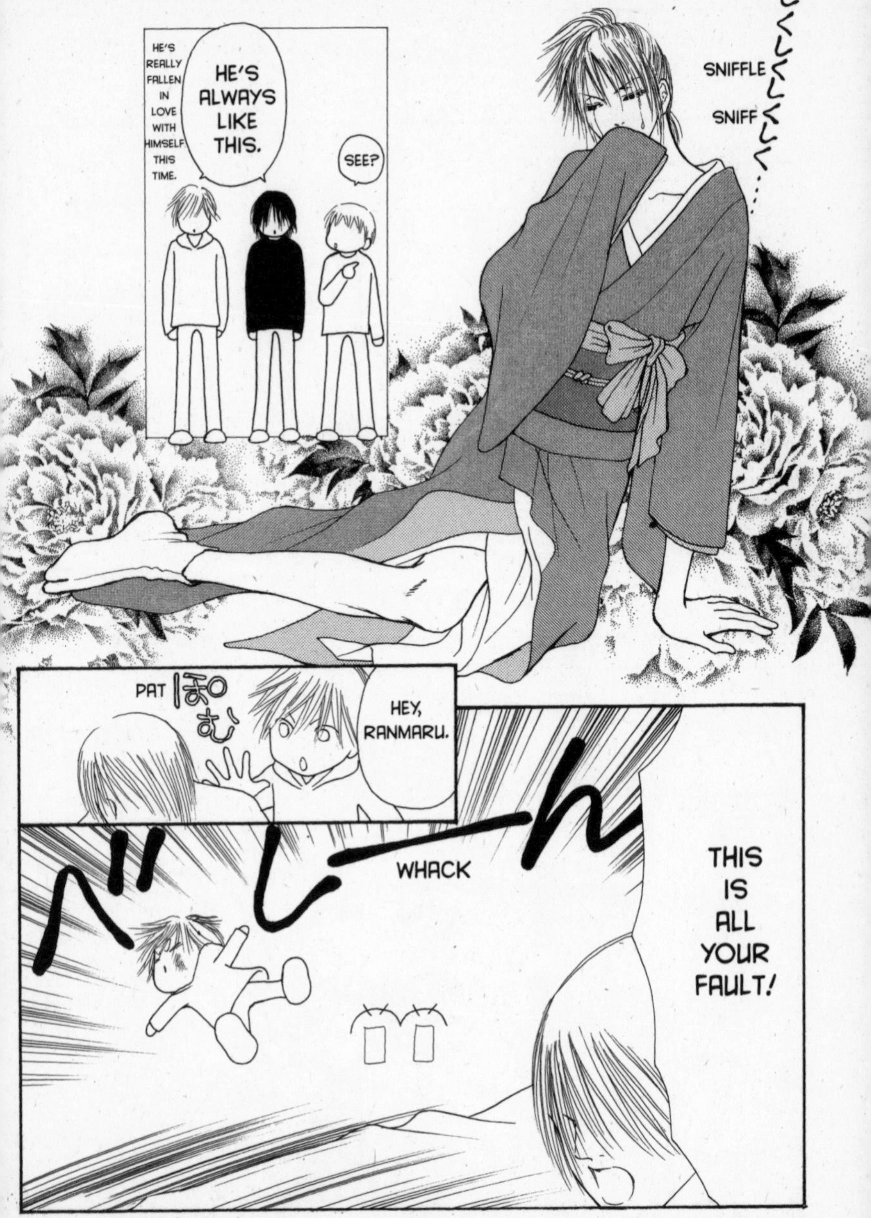
しくしくしくしく…
SNIFFLE
SNIFF
SEE?
HE'S ALWAYS LIKE THIS.
HE'S REALLY FALLEN IN LOVE WITH HIMSELF THIS TIME.
HEY, RANMARU.
ぽむ
PAT
THIS IS ALL YOUR FAULT!
べしーん
WHACK

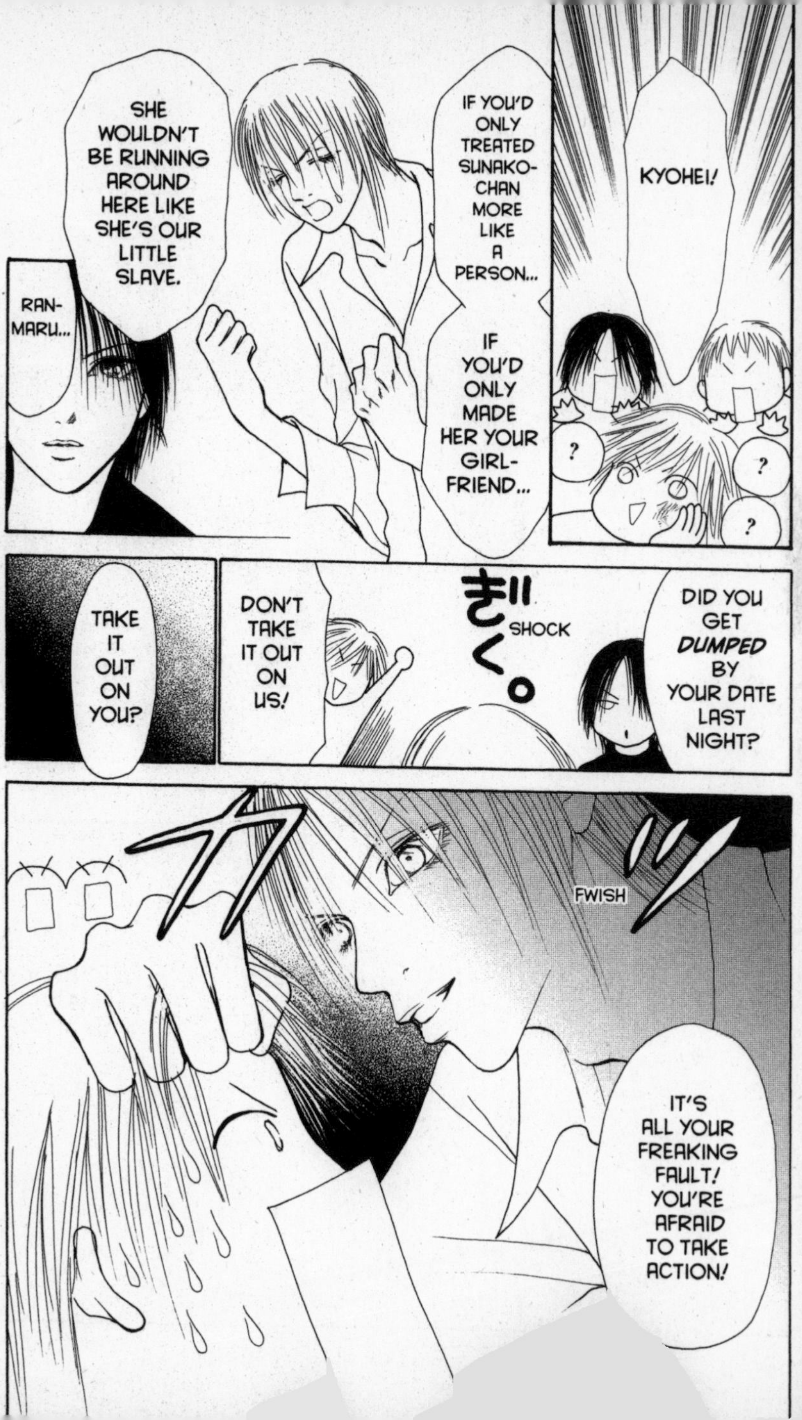
KYOHEI!
IF YOU'D ONLY TREATED SUNAKO-CHAN MORE LIKE A PERSON...
IF YOU'D ONLY MADE HER YOUR GIRL-FRIEND...
SHE WOULDN'T BE RUNNING AROUND HERE LIKE SHE'S OUR LITTLE SLAVE.
RAN-MARU...
DID YOU GET *DUMPED* BY YOUR DATE LAST NIGHT?
ぎく。
SHOCK
DON'T TAKE IT OUT ON US!
TAKE IT OUT ON YOU?
FWISH
IT'S ALL YOUR FREAKING FAULT! YOU'RE AFRAID TO TAKE ACTION!

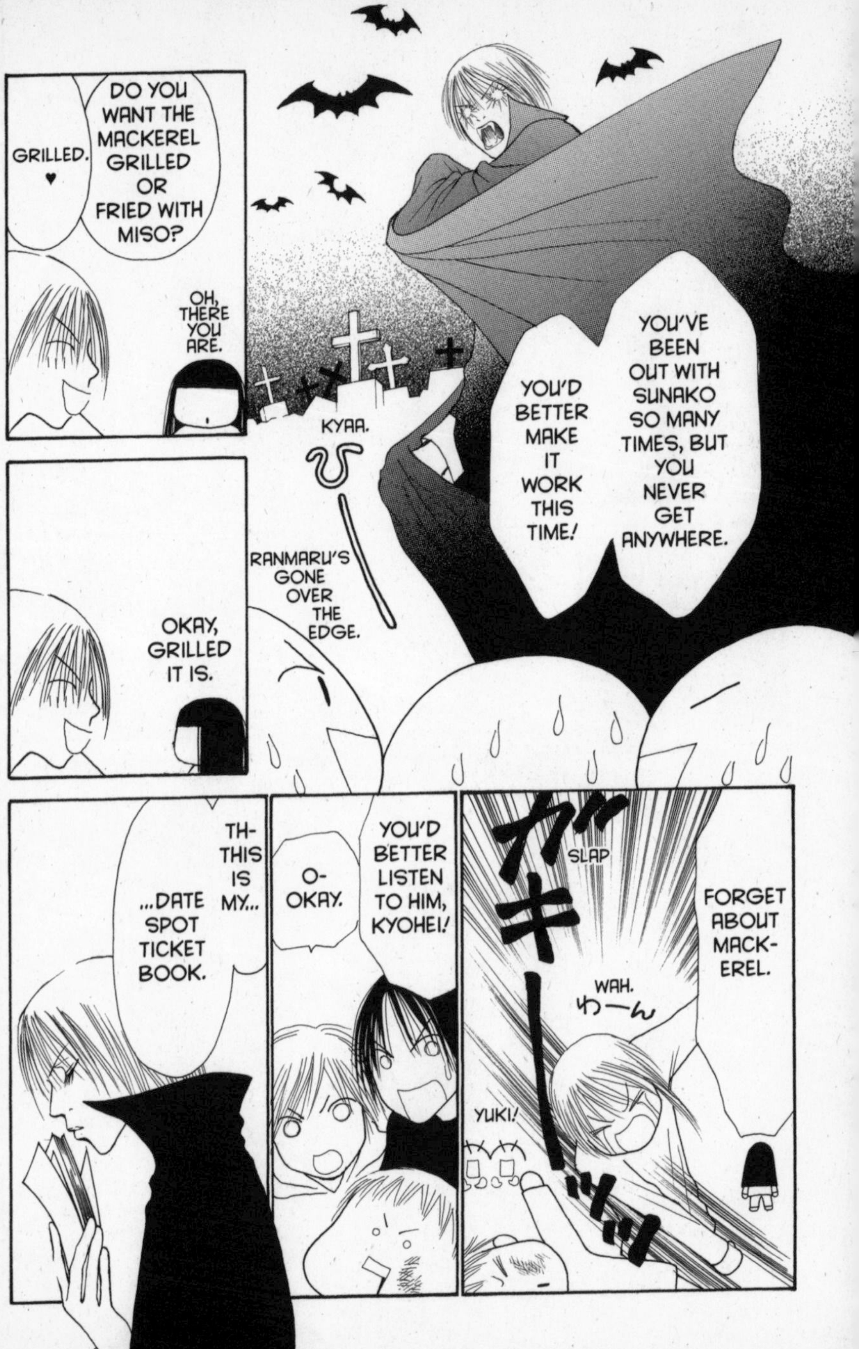
YOU'VE BEEN OUT WITH SUNAKO SO MANY TIMES, BUT YOU NEVER GET ANYWHERE.
YOU'D BETTER MAKE IT WORK THIS TIME!
KYAA.
RANMARU'S GONE OVER THE EDGE.
DO YOU WANT THE MACKEREL GRILLED OR FRIED WITH MISO?
GRILLED. ♥
OH, THERE YOU ARE.
OKAY, GRILLED IT IS.
FORGET ABOUT MACK-EREL.
SLAP
WAH.
わーん
YUKI!
YOU'D BETTER LISTEN TO HIM, KYOHEI!
O-OKAY.
TH-THIS IS MY...
...DATE SPOT TICKET BOOK.

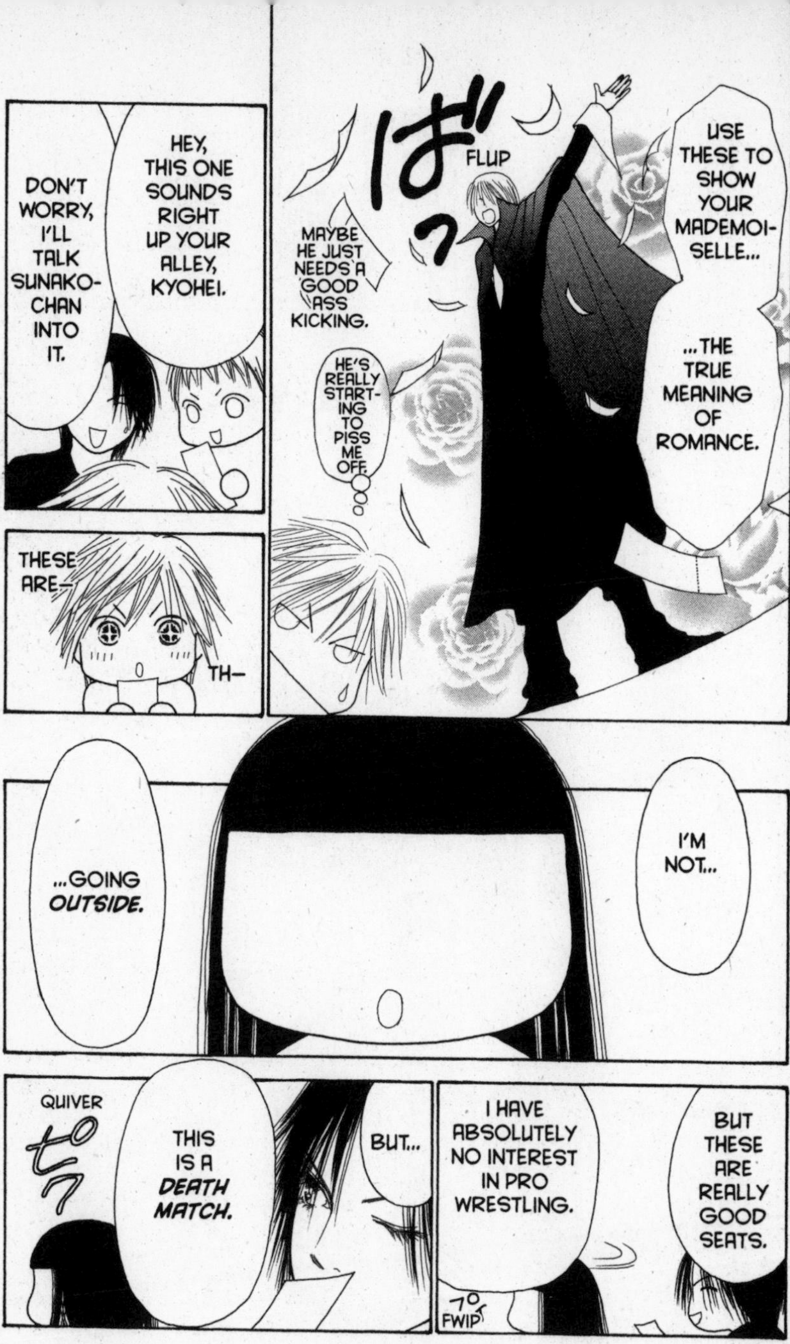
USE THESE TO SHOW YOUR MADEMOISELLE...
...THE TRUE MEANING OF ROMANCE.
ばっ
FLUP
MAYBE HE JUST NEEDS A GOOD ASS KICKING.
HE'S REALLY STARTING TO PISS ME OFF.
HEY, THIS ONE SOUNDS RIGHT UP YOUR ALLEY, KYOHEI.
DON'T WORRY, I'LL TALK SUNAKO-CHAN INTO IT.
THESE ARE—
TH—
I'M NOT...
...GOING OUTSIDE.
BUT THESE ARE REALLY GOOD SEATS.
I HAVE ABSOLUTELY NO INTEREST IN PRO WRESTLING.
FWIP
BUT...
THIS IS A DEATH MATCH.
QUIVER

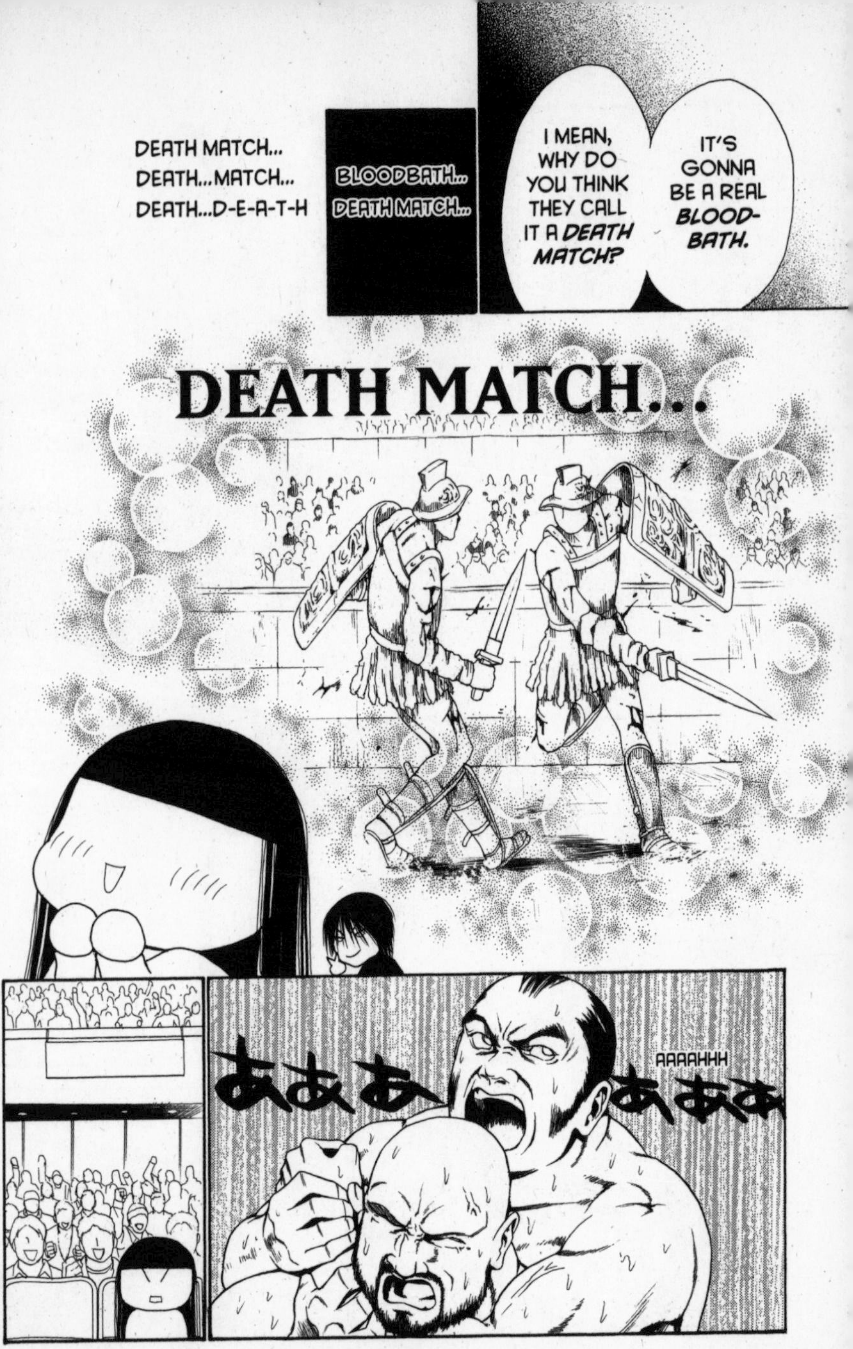
IT'S GONNA BE A REAL BLOOD-BATH.
I MEAN, WHY DO YOU THINK THEY CALL IT A DEATH MATCH?
BLOODBATH... DEATH MATCH...
DEATH MATCH... DEATH...MATCH... DEATH...D-E-A-T-H
DEATH MATCH...
あああ
AAAAHHH
あああ

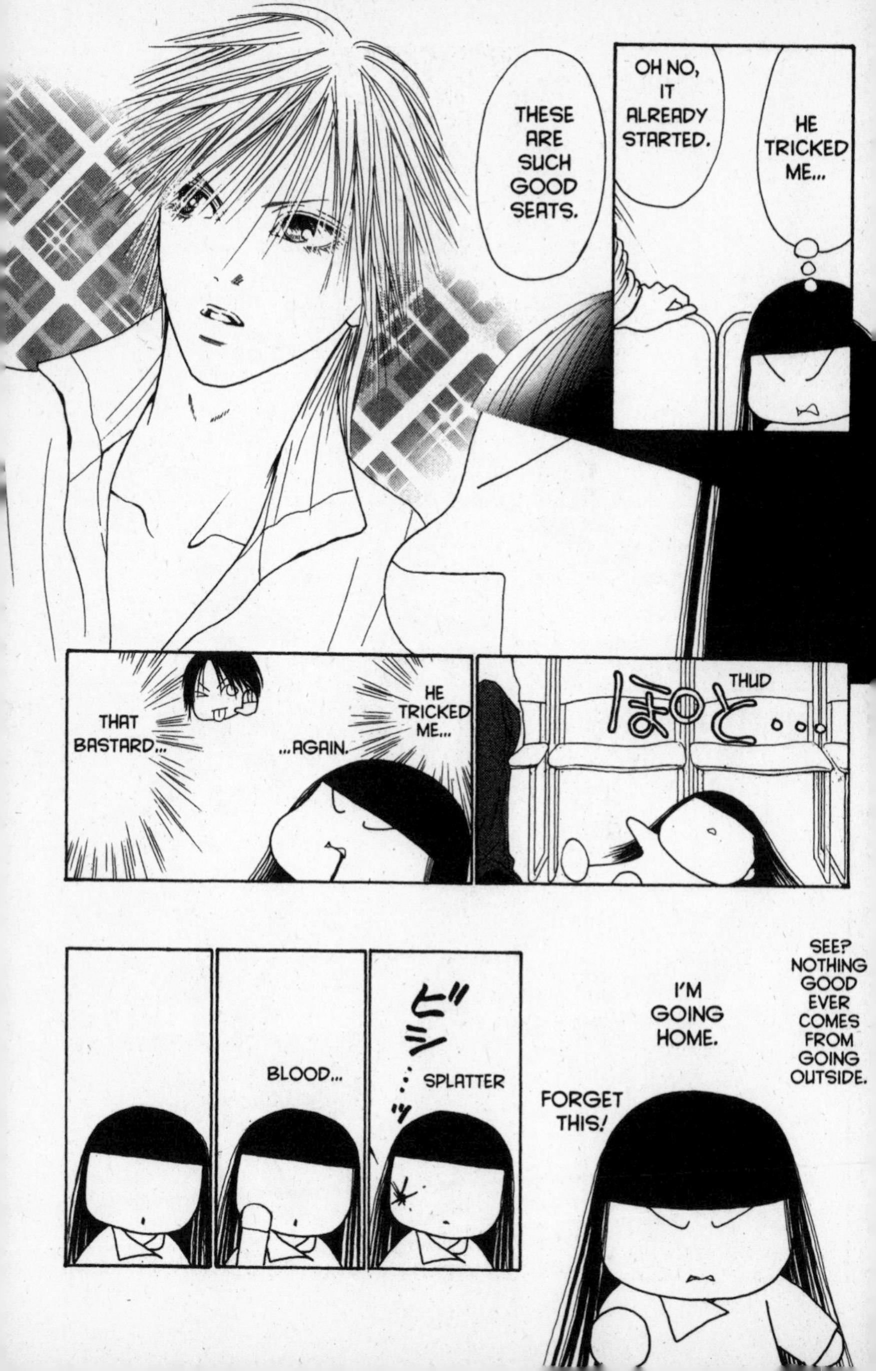
HE TRICKED ME...
OH NO, IT ALREADY STARTED.
THESE ARE SUCH GOOD SEATS.
ぽと...
THUD
HE TRICKED ME...
...AGAIN.
THAT BASTARD...
SEE? NOTHING GOOD EVER COMES FROM GOING OUTSIDE.
I'M GOING HOME.
FORGET THIS!
ビシ
SPLATTER
BLOOD...

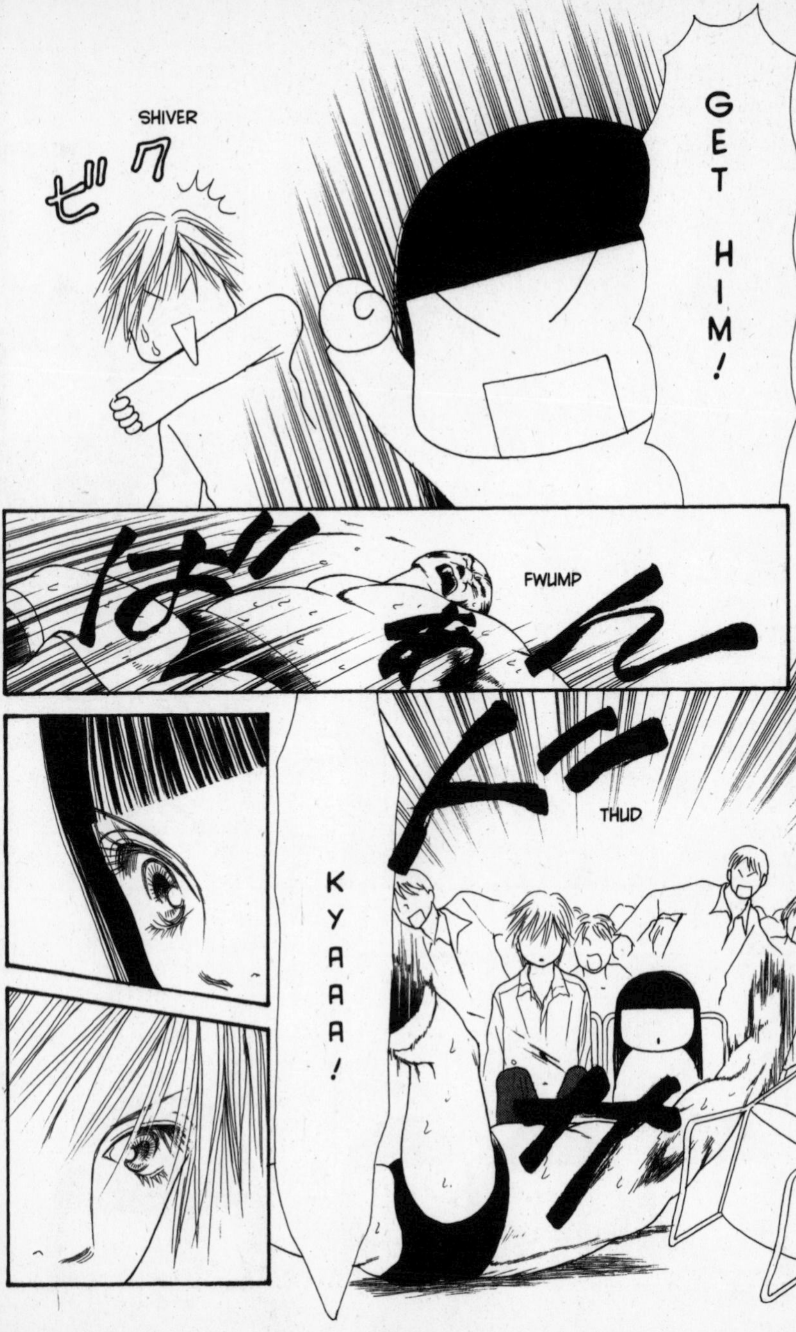
GET HIM!
SHIVER
FWUMP
THUD
KYAAAA!

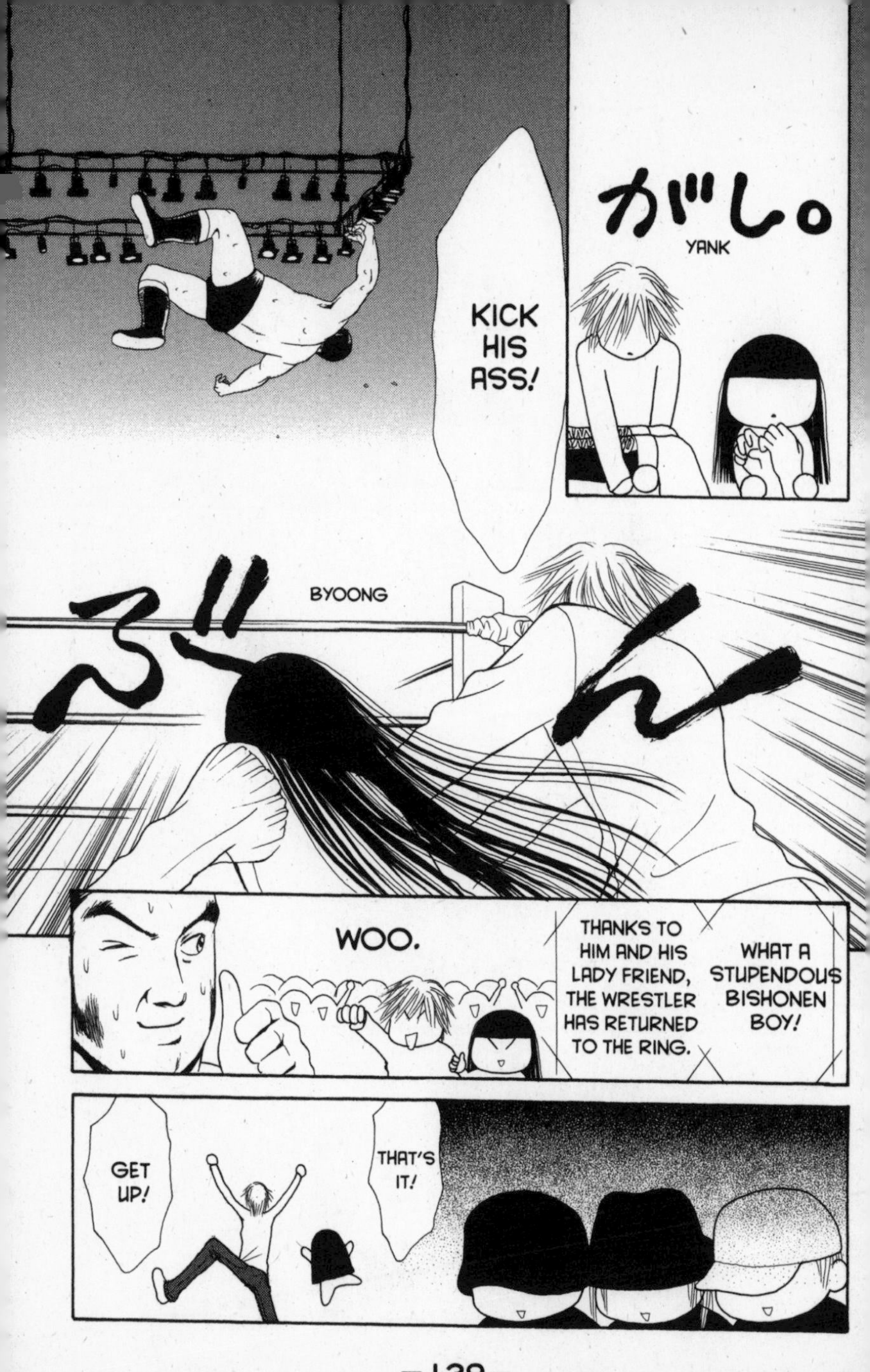

がし。
YANK
KICK HIS ASS!
ぶん
BYOONG
WHAT A STUPENDOUS BISHONEN BOY!
THANKS TO HIM AND HIS LADY FRIEND, THE WRESTLER HAS RETURNED TO THE RING.
WOO.
THAT'S IT!
GET UP!

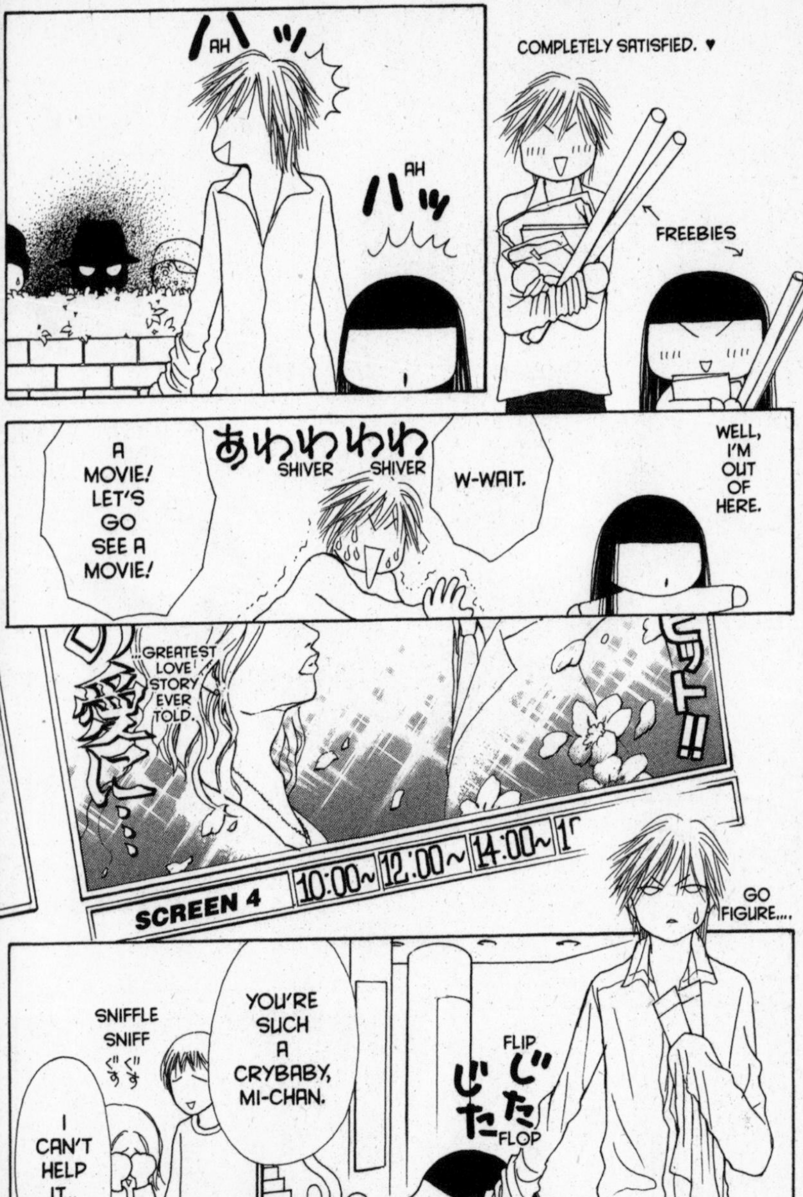
COMPLETELY SATISFIED. ♥
FREEBIES
ハッ AH
ハッ AH
WELL, I'M OUT OF HERE.
W-WAIT.
あわわわわ SHIVER SHIVER
A MOVIE! LET'S GO SEE A MOVIE!
GO FIGURE....
ヒット!!
...GREATEST LOVE STORY EVER TOLD.
愛に...
10:00~ 12:00~ 14:00~
SCREEN 4
じたじた FLIP FLOP
YOU'RE SUCH A CRYBABY, MI-CHAN.
SNIFFLE SNIFF ぐすぐす
I CAN'T HELP IT...

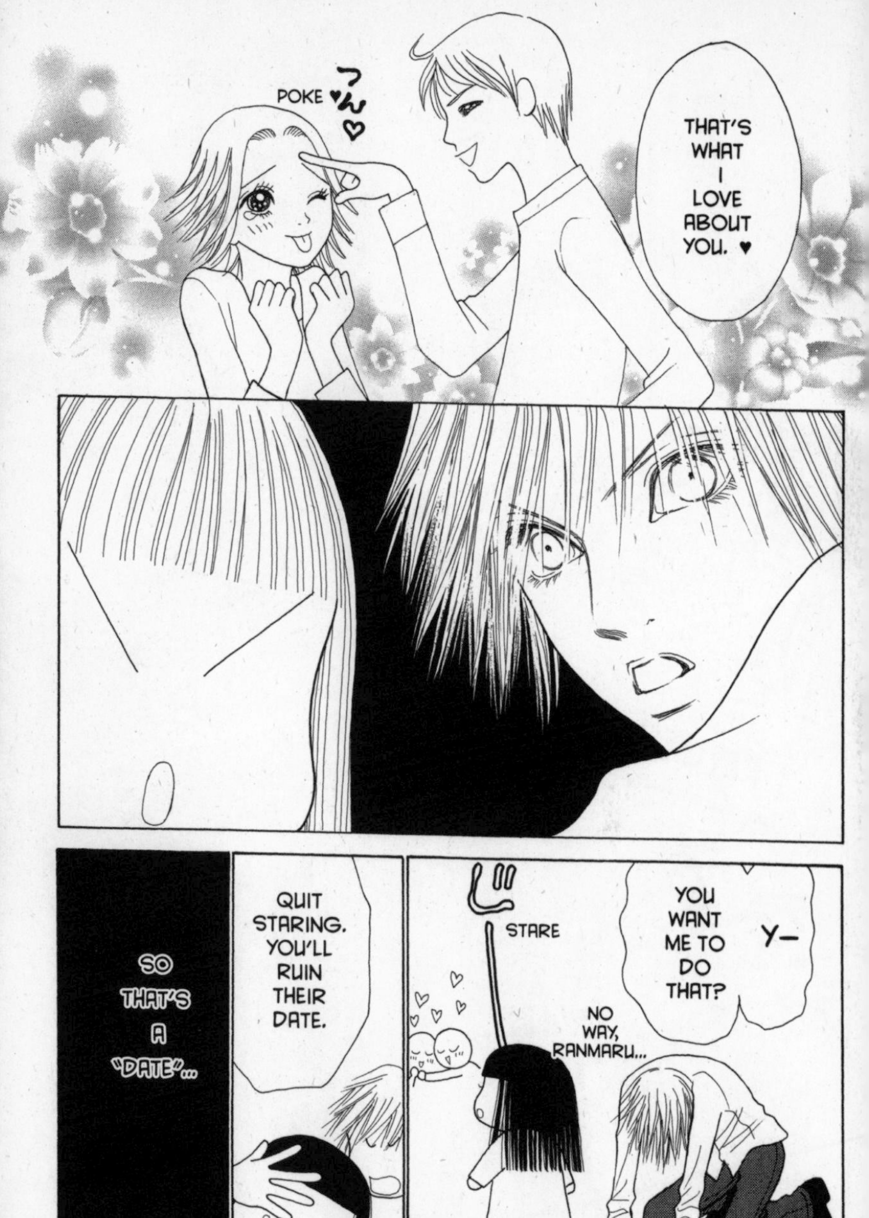
THAT'S WHAT I LOVE ABOUT YOU. ♥
POKE ♥ つん♡
Y—
YOU WANT ME TO DO THAT?
じ
STARE
NO WAY, RANMARU...
QUIT STARING. YOU'LL RUIN THEIR DATE.
SO THAT'S A "DATE"...

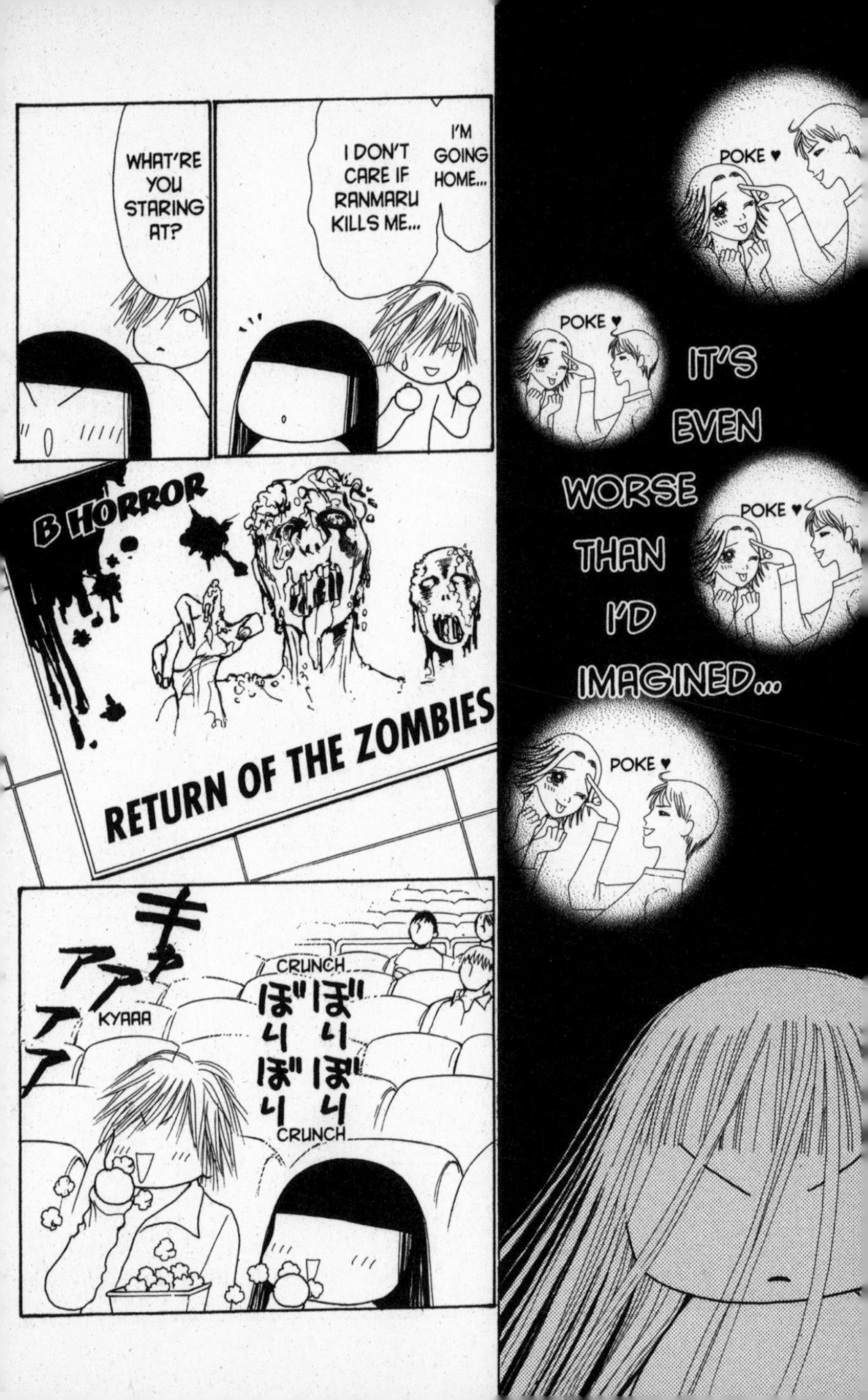
POKE ♥
POKE ♥
IT'S EVEN WORSE THAN I'D IMAGINED...
POKE ♥
POKE ♥
I'M GOING HOME...
I DON'T CARE IF RANMARU KILLS ME...
WHAT'RE YOU STARING AT?
B HORROR
RETURN OF THE ZOMBIES
CRUNCH
ぼりぼり
ぼりぼり
CRUNCH
キャアアアア
KYAAA

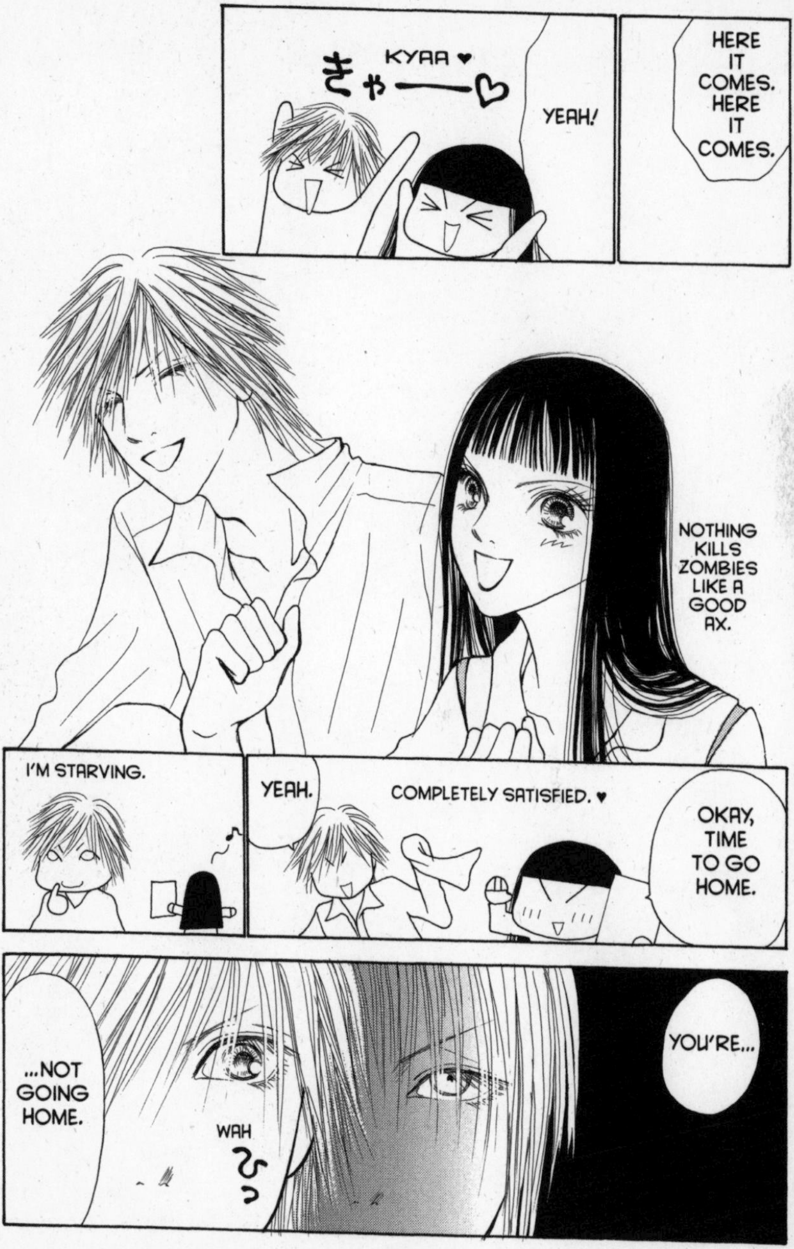
HERE IT COMES. HERE IT COMES.
YEAH!
KYAA ♥
きゃー♡
NOTHING KILLS ZOMBIES LIKE A GOOD AX.
OKAY, TIME TO GO HOME.
COMPLETELY SATISFIED. ♥
YEAH.
I'M STARVING.
YOU'RE...
WAH
ひっ
...NOT GOING HOME.

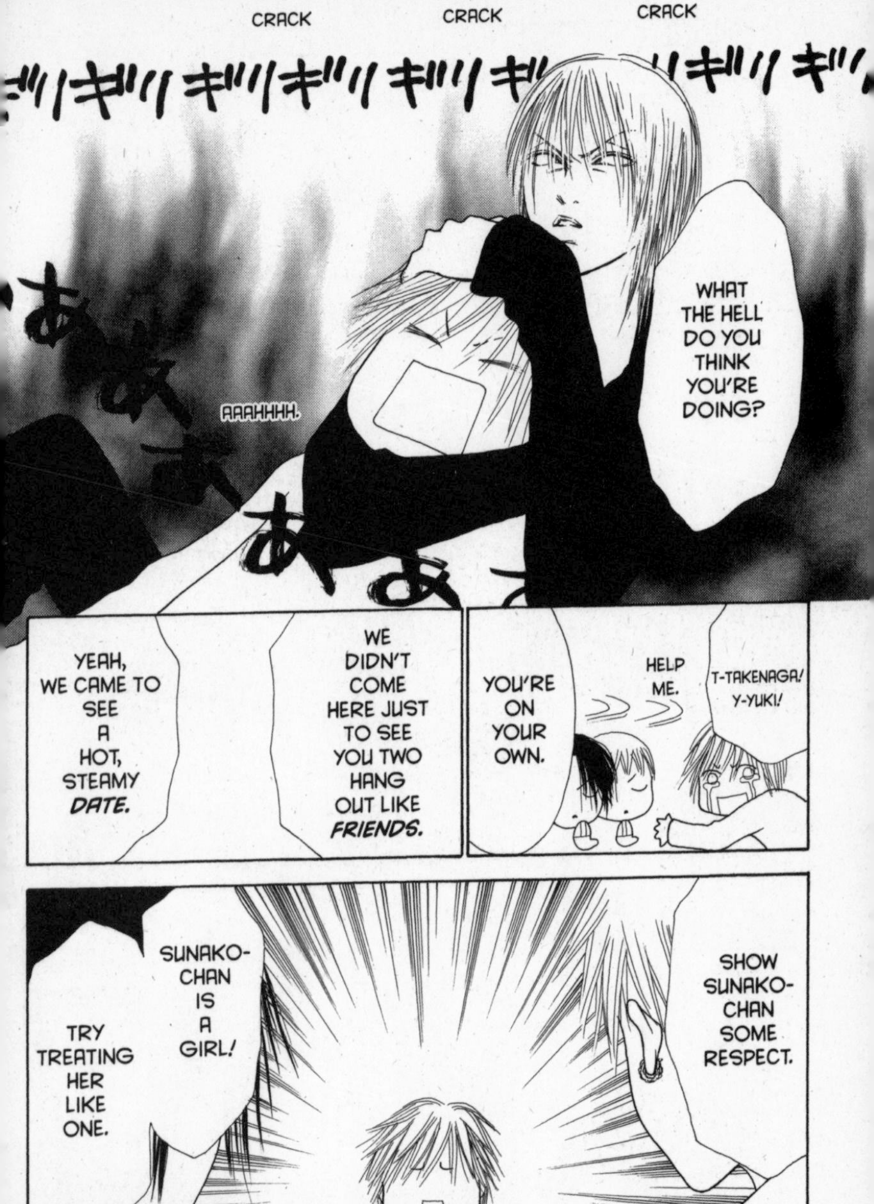
CRACK
CRACK
CRACK
WHAT THE HELL DO YOU THINK YOU'RE DOING?
AAAHHHH.
T-TAKENAGA! Y-YUKI!
HELP ME.
YOU'RE ON YOUR OWN.
WE DIDN'T COME HERE JUST TO SEE YOU TWO HANG OUT LIKE FRIENDS.
YEAH, WE CAME TO SEE A HOT, STEAMY DATE.
SHOW SUNAKO-CHAN SOME RESPECT.
SUNAKO-CHAN IS A GIRL!
TRY TREATING HER LIKE ONE.

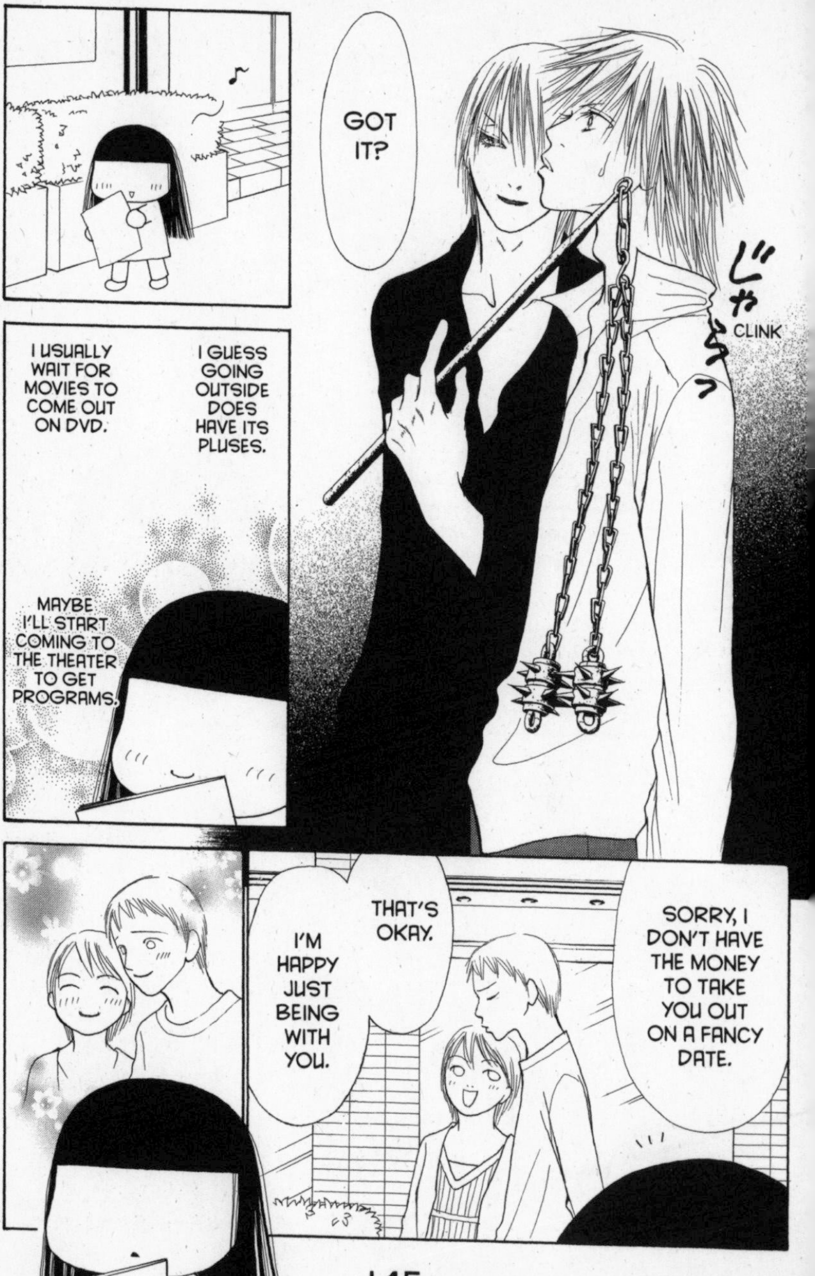
GOT IT?
じゃらっ
CLINK
I USUALLY WAIT FOR MOVIES TO COME OUT ON DVD.
I GUESS GOING OUTSIDE DOES HAVE ITS PLUSES.
MAYBE I'LL START COMING TO THE THEATER TO GET PROGRAMS.
SORRY, I DON'T HAVE THE MONEY TO TAKE YOU OUT ON A FANCY DATE.
THAT'S OKAY.
I'M HAPPY JUST BEING WITH YOU.

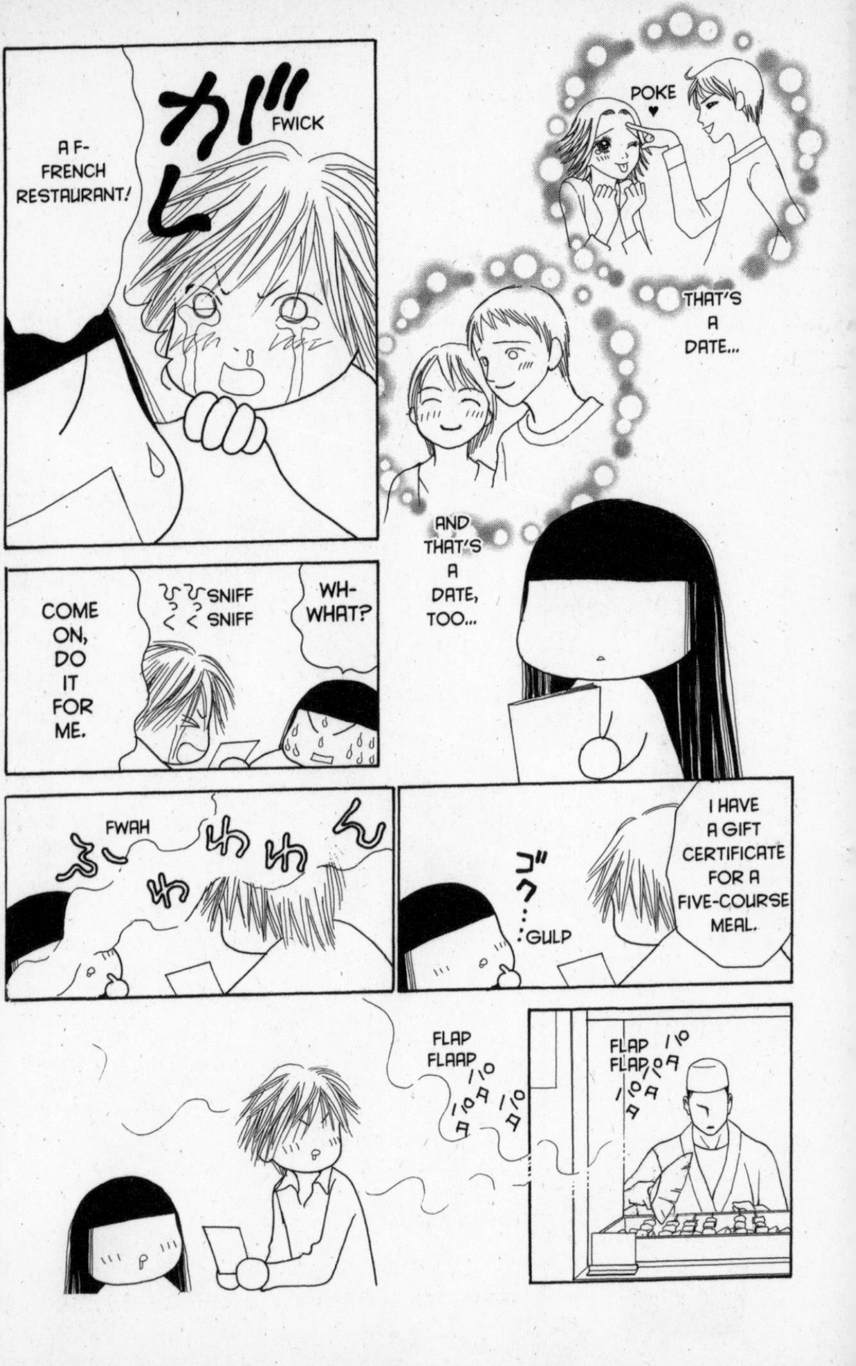

POKE ♥
THAT'S A DATE...
AND THAT'S A DATE, TOO...
がし
FWICK
A F-FRENCH RESTAURANT!
WH-WHAT?
SNIFF SNIFF
COME ON, DO IT FOR ME.
I HAVE A GIFT CERTIFICATE FOR A FIVE-COURSE MEAL.
ゴク...
GULP
FWAH
FLAP FLAP
FLAP FLAAP

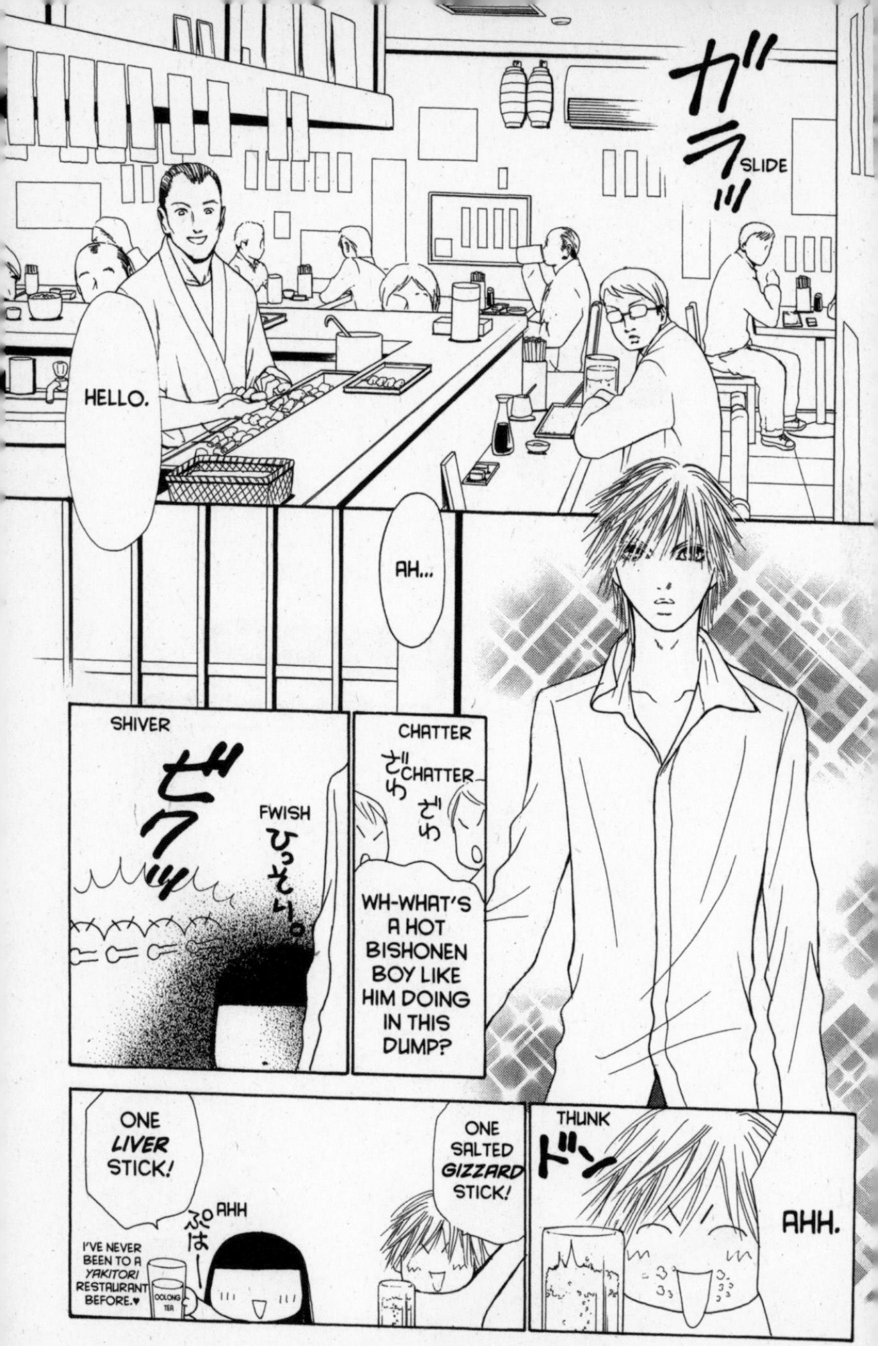
ガラッ
SLIDE
HELLO.
AH...
CHATTER
ざわ CHATTER
ざわ
WH-WHAT'S A HOT BISHONEN BOY LIKE HIM DOING IN THIS DUMP?
SHIVER
ゾクッ
FWISH
ひっそり。
THUNK
ドン
AHH.
ONE SALTED GIZZARD STICK!
ONE LIVER STICK!
ぷはー
AHH
I'VE NEVER BEEN TO A YAKITORI RESTAURANT BEFORE.♥
OOLONG TEA

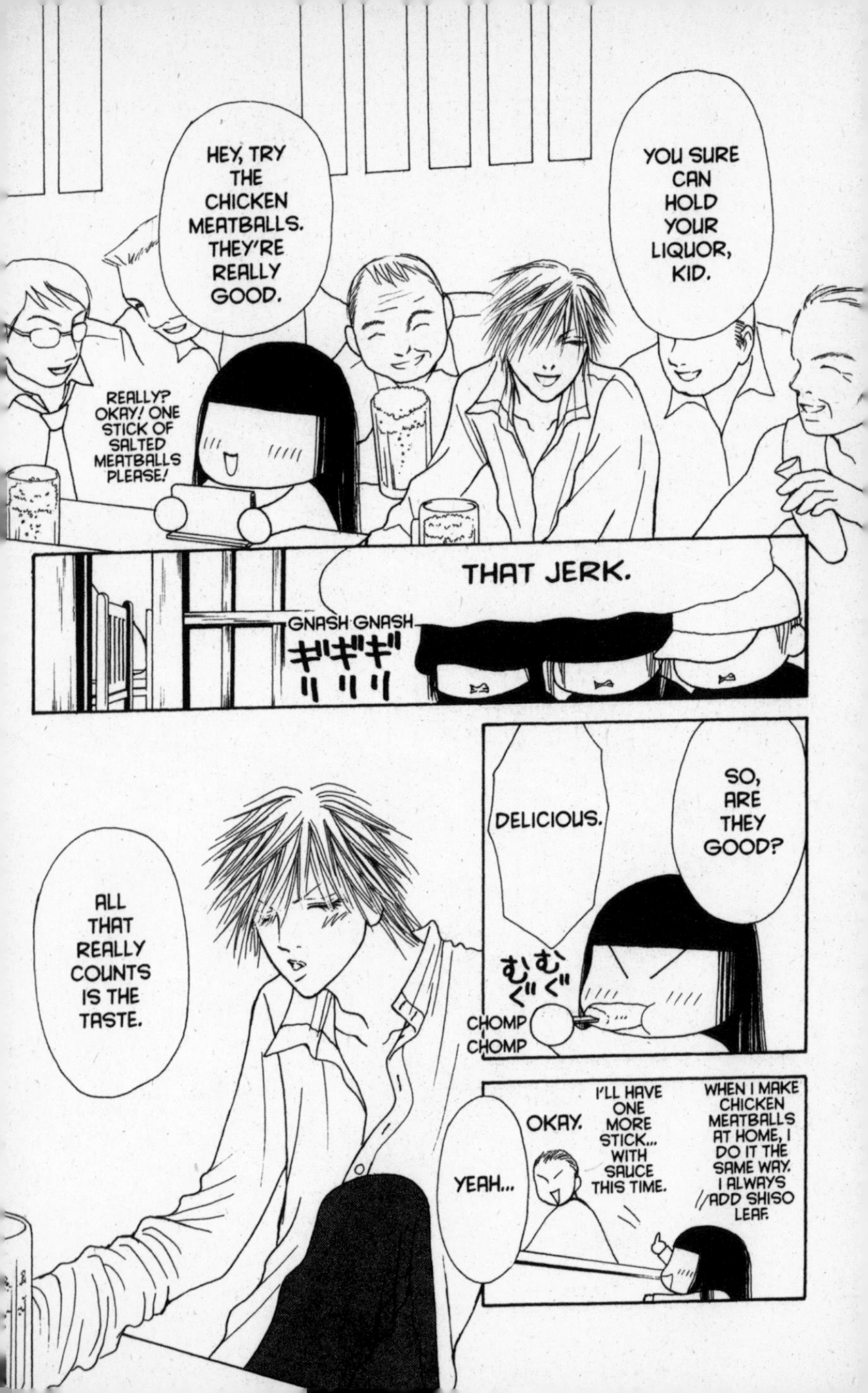
YOU SURE CAN HOLD YOUR LIQUOR, KID.
HEY, TRY THE CHICKEN MEATBALLS. THEY'RE REALLY GOOD.
REALLY? OKAY! ONE STICK OF SALTED MEATBALLS PLEASE!
THAT JERK.
GNASH GNASH
ギリギリギリ
SO, ARE THEY GOOD?
DELICIOUS.
むぐむぐ
CHOMP CHOMP
WHEN I MAKE CHICKEN MEATBALLS AT HOME, I DO IT THE SAME WAY. I ALWAYS ADD SHISO LEAF.
I'LL HAVE ONE MORE STICK... WITH SAUCE THIS TIME.
OKAY.
YEAH...
ALL THAT REALLY COUNTS IS THE TASTE.

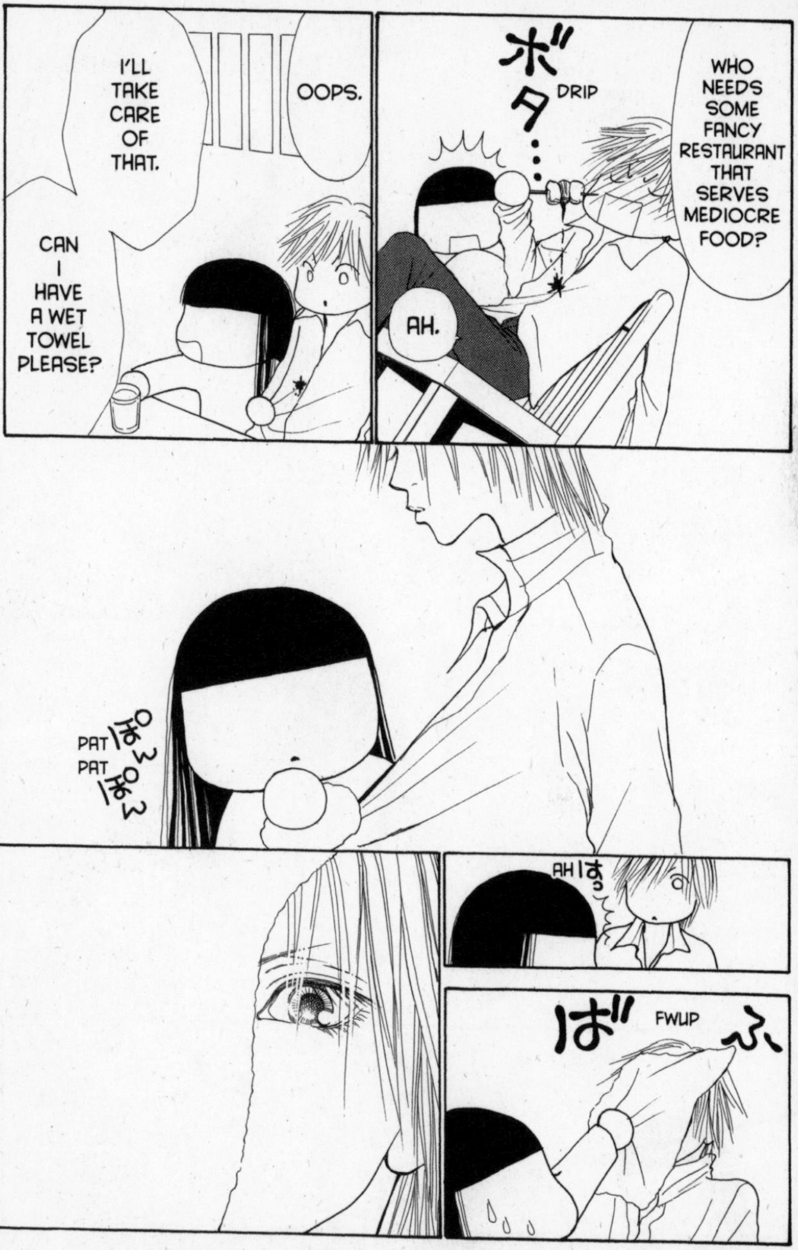
WHO NEEDS SOME FANCY RESTAURANT THAT SERVES MEDIOCRE FOOD?
ボタ…
DRIP
AH.
OOPS.
I'LL TAKE CARE OF THAT.
CAN I HAVE A WET TOWEL PLEASE?
ぽんぽん
PAT PAT
はっ
AH
ばふ
FWUP

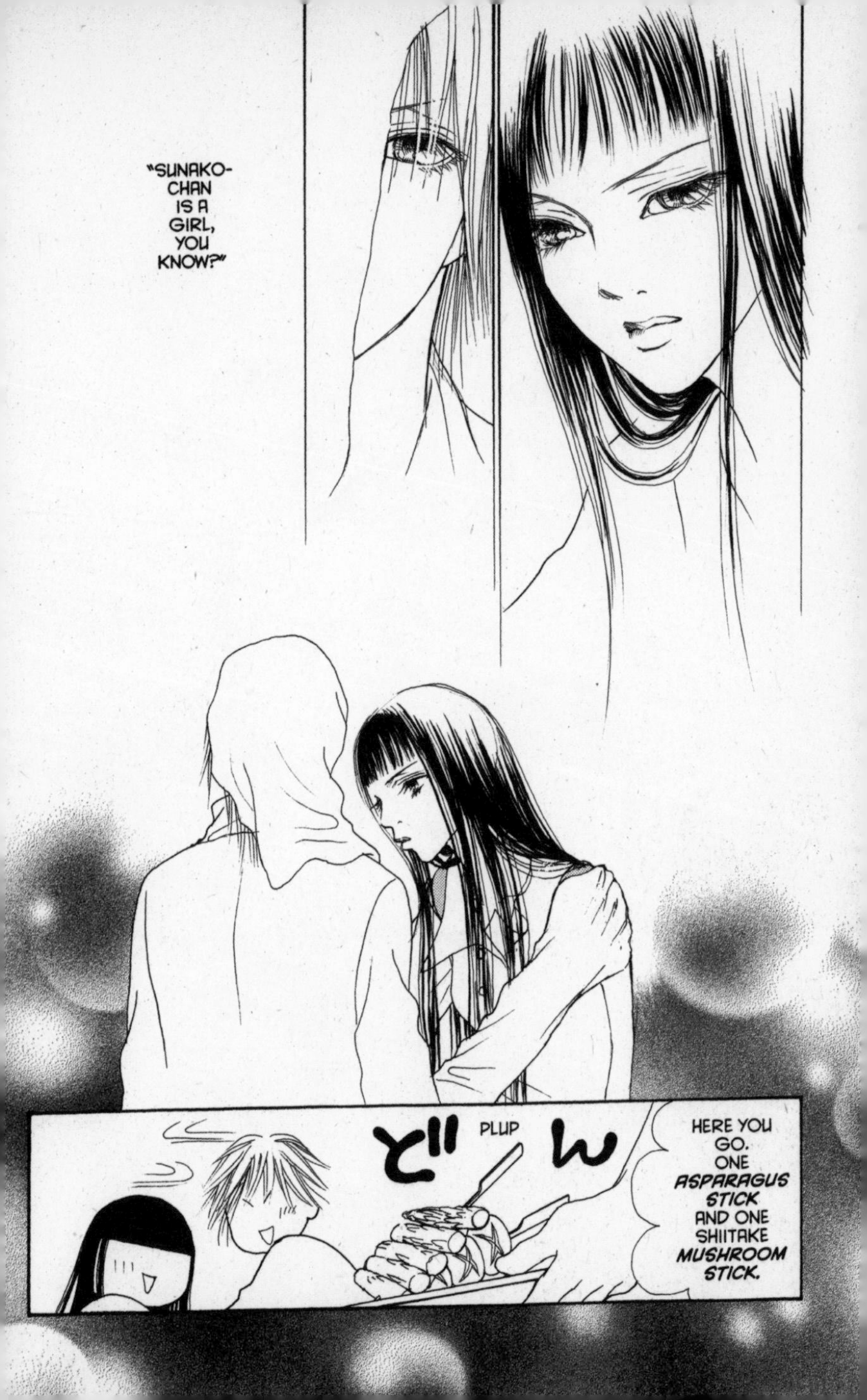
"SUNAKO-CHAN IS A GIRL, YOU KNOW?"
HERE YOU GO. ONE ASPARAGUS STICK AND ONE SHIITAKE MUSHROOM STICK.
どん
PLUP
!!!

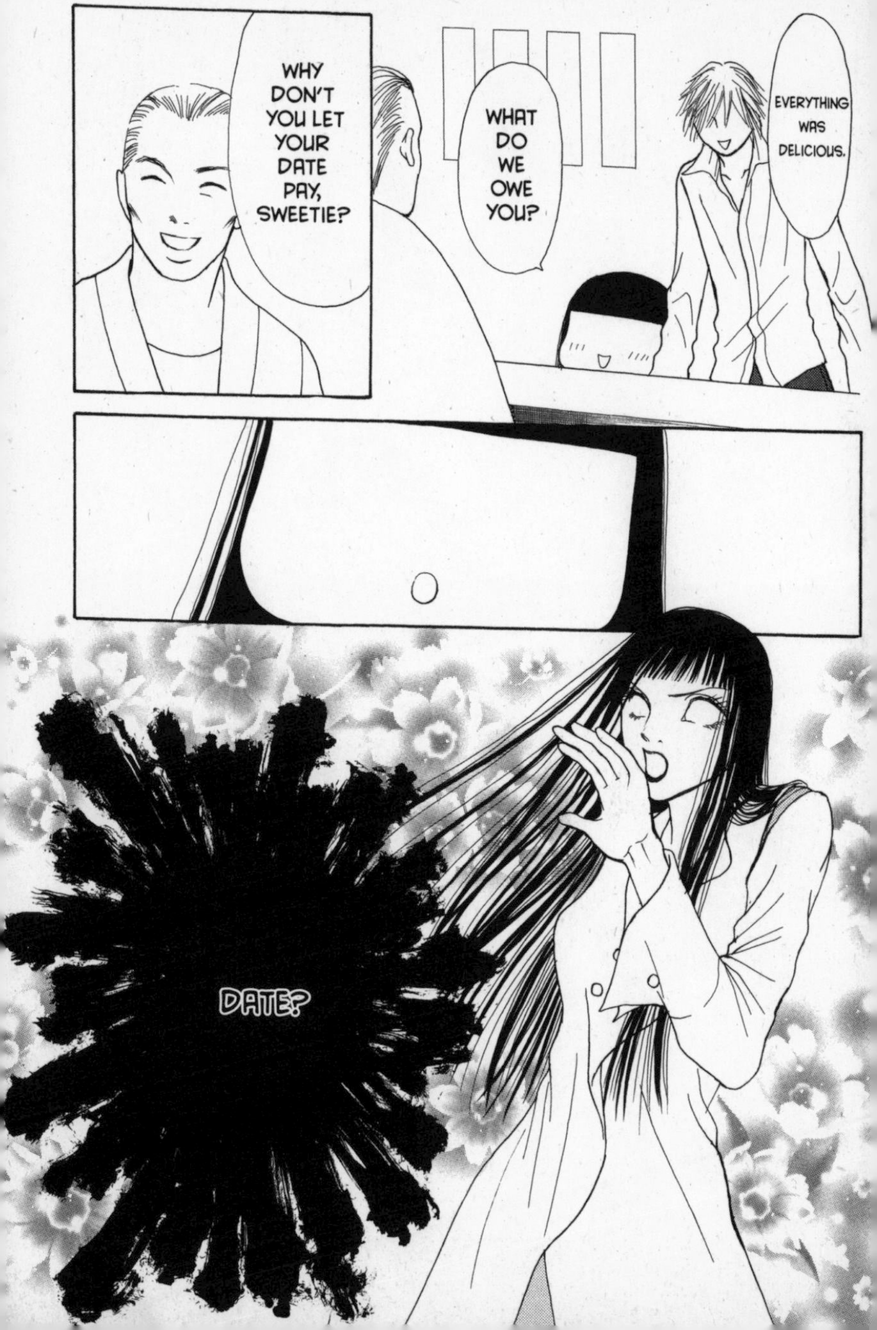
EVERYTHING WAS DELICIOUS.
WHAT DO WE OWE YOU?
WHY DON'T YOU LET YOUR DATE PAY, SWEETIE?
DATE?

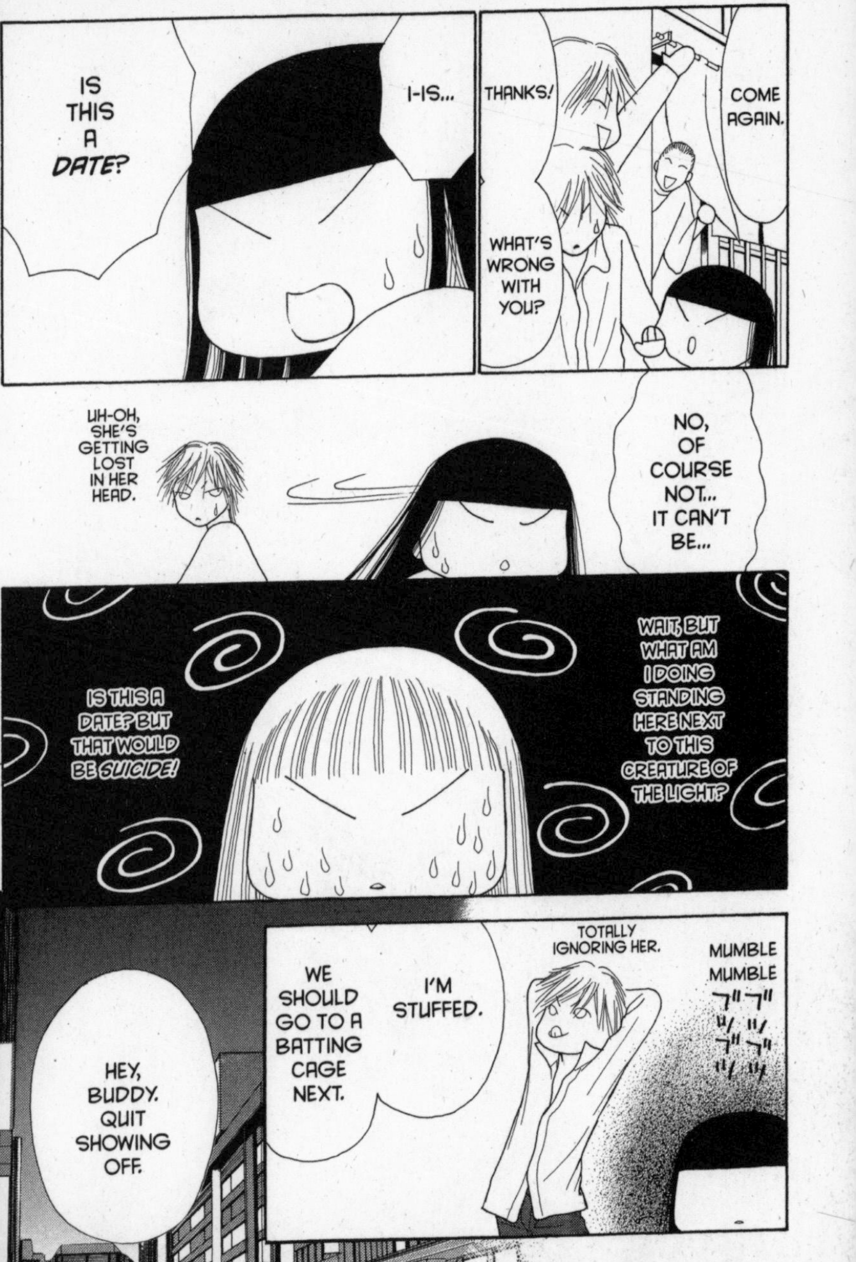
COME AGAIN.
THANKS!
WHAT'S WRONG WITH YOU?
I-IS...
IS THIS A *DATE?*
NO, OF COURSE NOT... IT CAN'T BE...
UH-OH, SHE'S GETTING LOST IN HER HEAD.
WAIT, BUT WHAT AM I DOING STANDING HERE NEXT TO THIS CREATURE OF THE LIGHT?
IS THIS A DATE? BUT THAT WOULD BE *SUICIDE!*
MUMBLE MUMBLE
ブツブツ
ブツブツ
TOTALLY IGNORING HER.
I'M STUFFED.
WE SHOULD GO TO A BATTING CAGE NEXT.
HEY, BUDDY. QUIT SHOWING OFF.

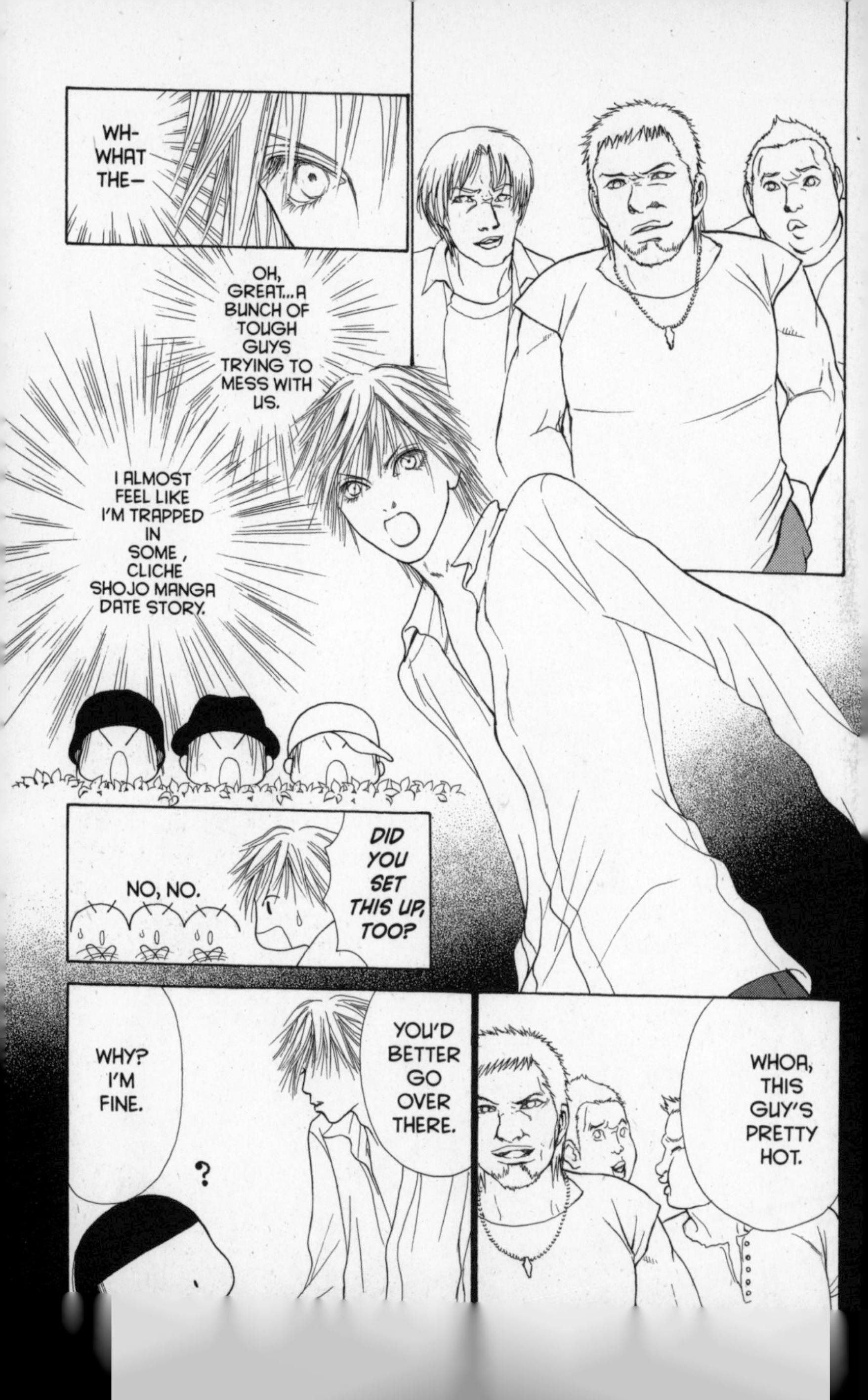
WH- WHAT THE—
OH, GREAT...A BUNCH OF TOUGH GUYS TRYING TO MESS WITH US.
I ALMOST FEEL LIKE I'M TRAPPED IN SOME CLICHE SHOJO MANGA DATE STORY.
DID YOU SET THIS UP, TOO?
NO, NO.
WHOA, THIS GUY'S PRETTY HOT.
YOU'D BETTER GO OVER THERE.
WHY? I'M FINE.
?

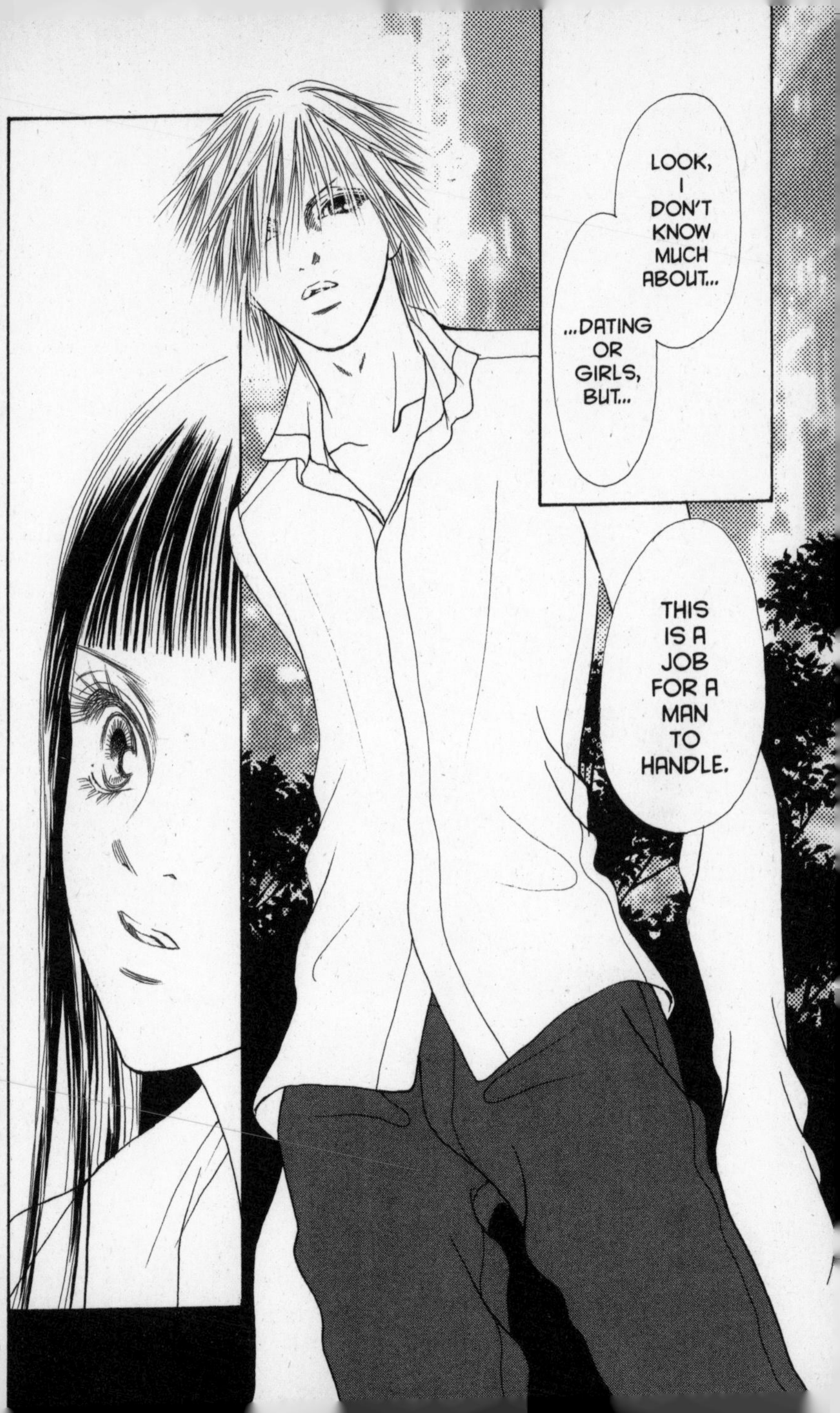
LOOK, I DON'T KNOW MUCH ABOUT...
...DATING OR GIRLS, BUT...
THIS IS A JOB FOR A MAN TO HANDLE.

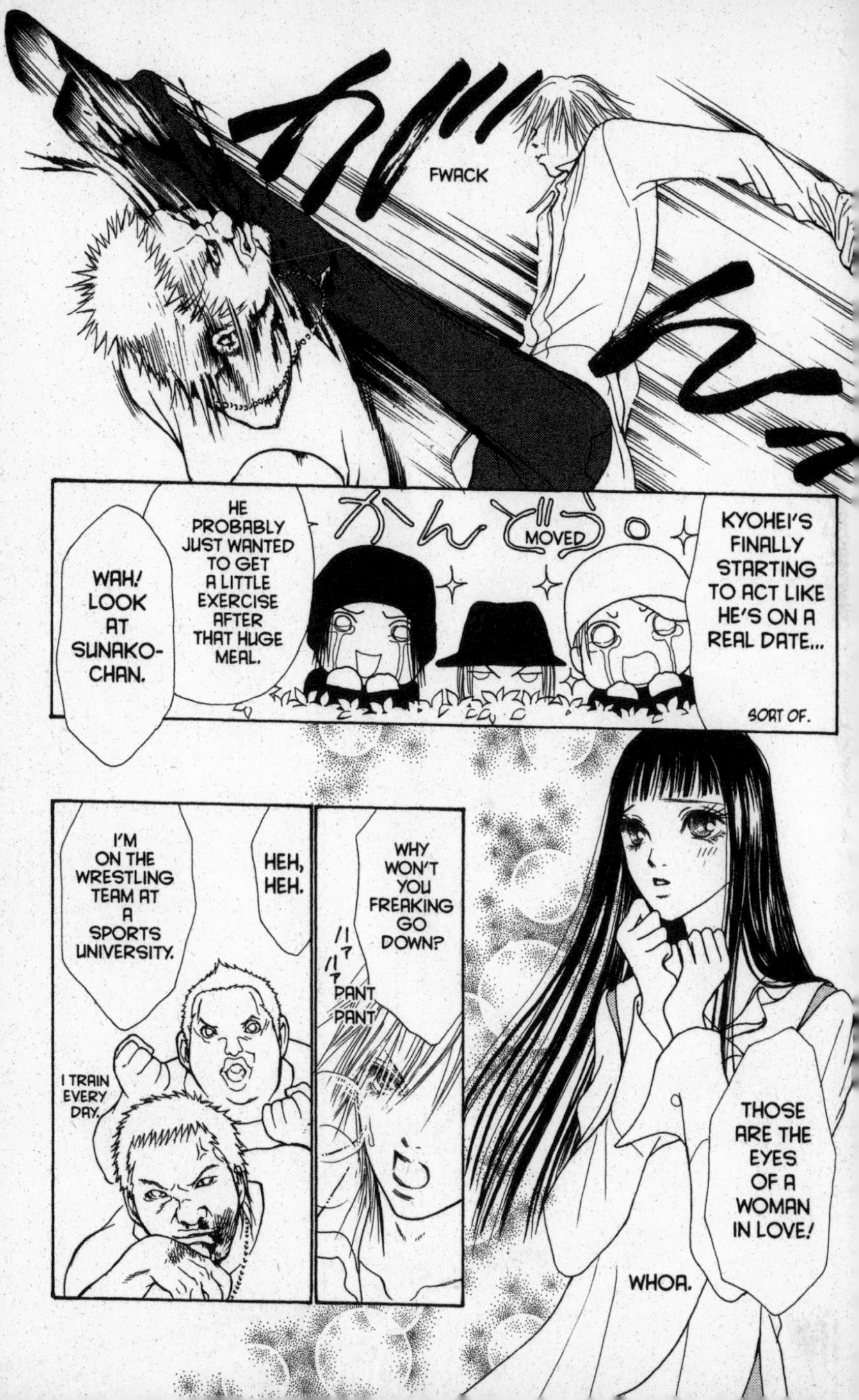
FWACK
KYOHEI'S FINALLY STARTING TO ACT LIKE HE'S ON A REAL DATE...
SORT OF.
かんどう。
MOVED
HE PROBABLY JUST WANTED TO GET A LITTLE EXERCISE AFTER THAT HUGE MEAL.
WAH! LOOK AT SUNAKO-CHAN.
THOSE ARE THE EYES OF A WOMAN IN LOVE!
WHOA.
WHY WON'T YOU FREAKING GO DOWN?
ハァ ハァ
PANT PANT
HEH, HEH.
I'M ON THE WRESTLING TEAM AT A SPORTS UNIVERSITY.
I TRAIN EVERY DAY.

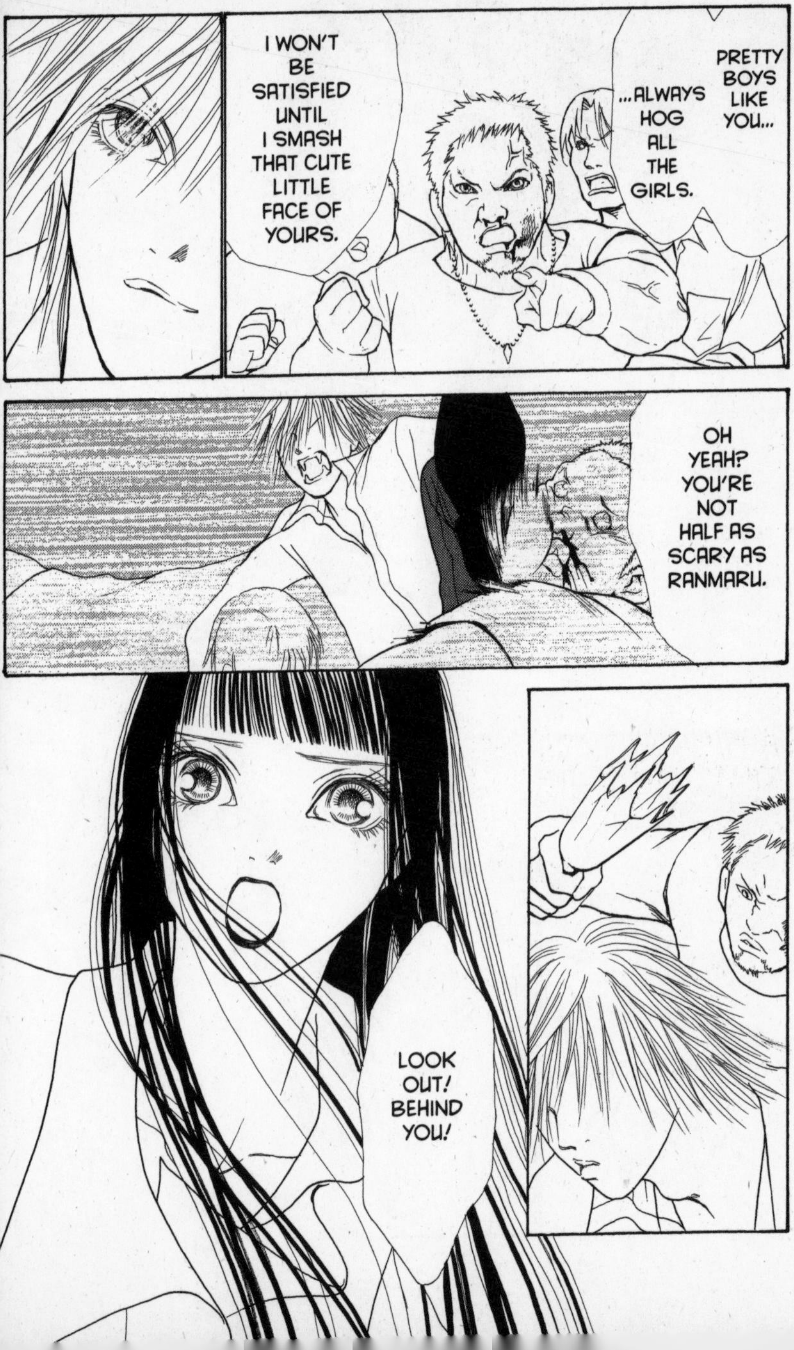
PRETTY BOYS LIKE YOU...
...ALWAYS HOG ALL THE GIRLS.
I WON'T BE SATISFIED UNTIL I SMASH THAT CUTE LITTLE FACE OF YOURS.
OH YEAH? YOU'RE NOT HALF AS SCARY AS RANMARU.
LOOK OUT! BEHIND YOU!

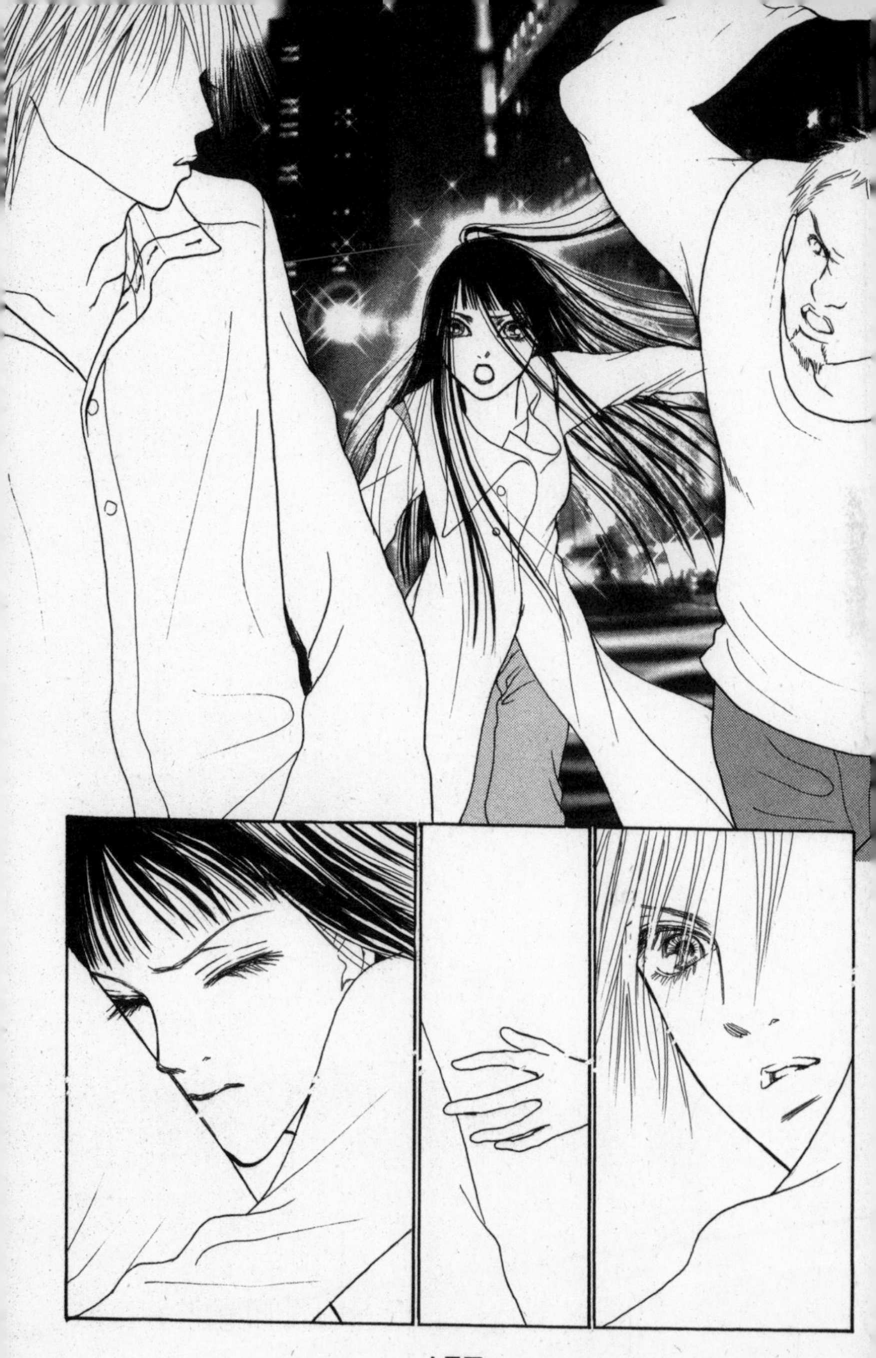

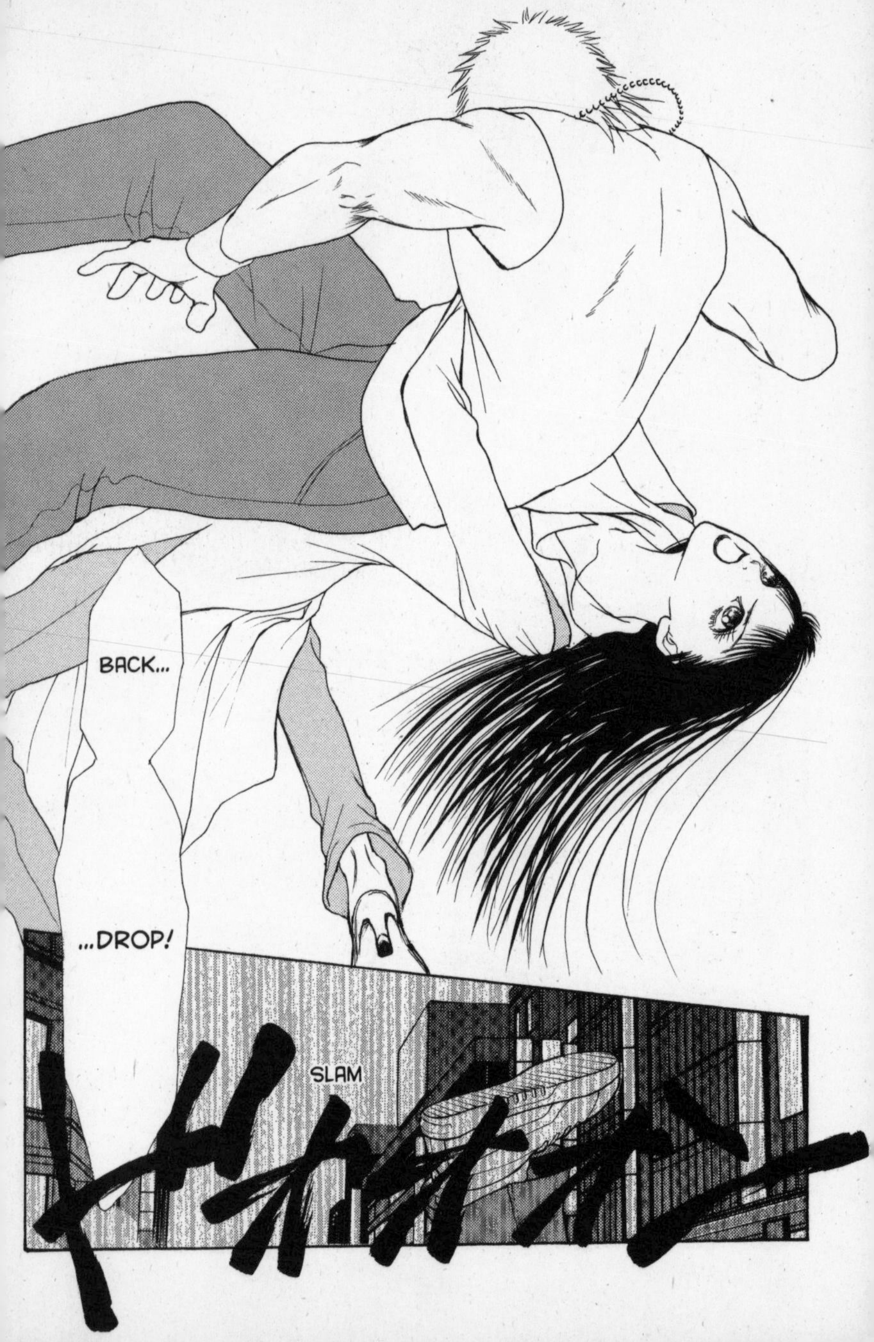
BACK...
...DROP!
SLAM

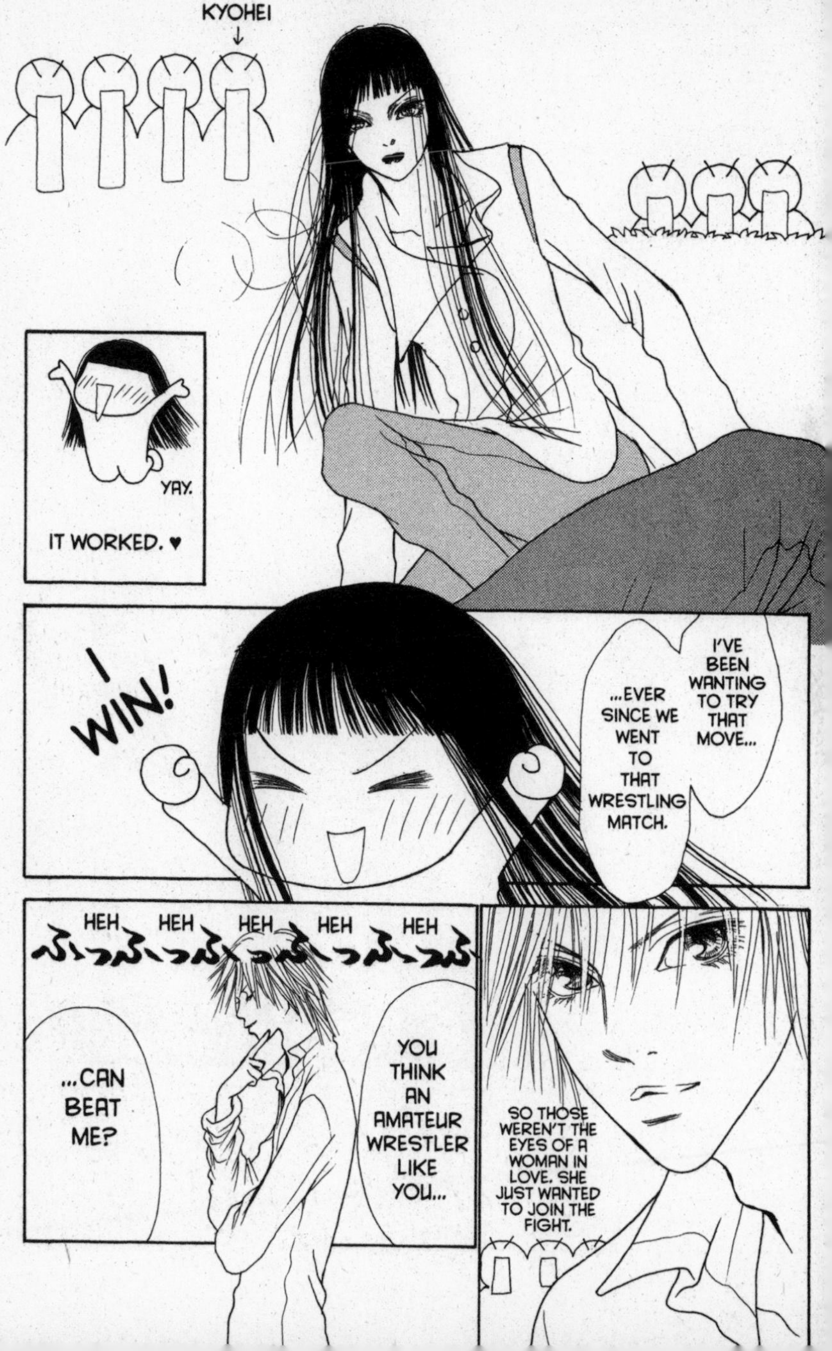
KYOHEI
YAY.
IT WORKED. ♥
I'VE BEEN WANTING TO TRY THAT MOVE...
...EVER SINCE WE WENT TO THAT WRESTLING MATCH.
I WIN!
SO THOSE WEREN'T THE EYES OF A WOMAN IN LOVE. SHE JUST WANTED TO JOIN THE FIGHT.
HEH HEH HEH HEH HEH
ふっふっふっふっふっふ
YOU THINK AN AMATEUR WRESTLER LIKE YOU...
...CAN BEAT ME?

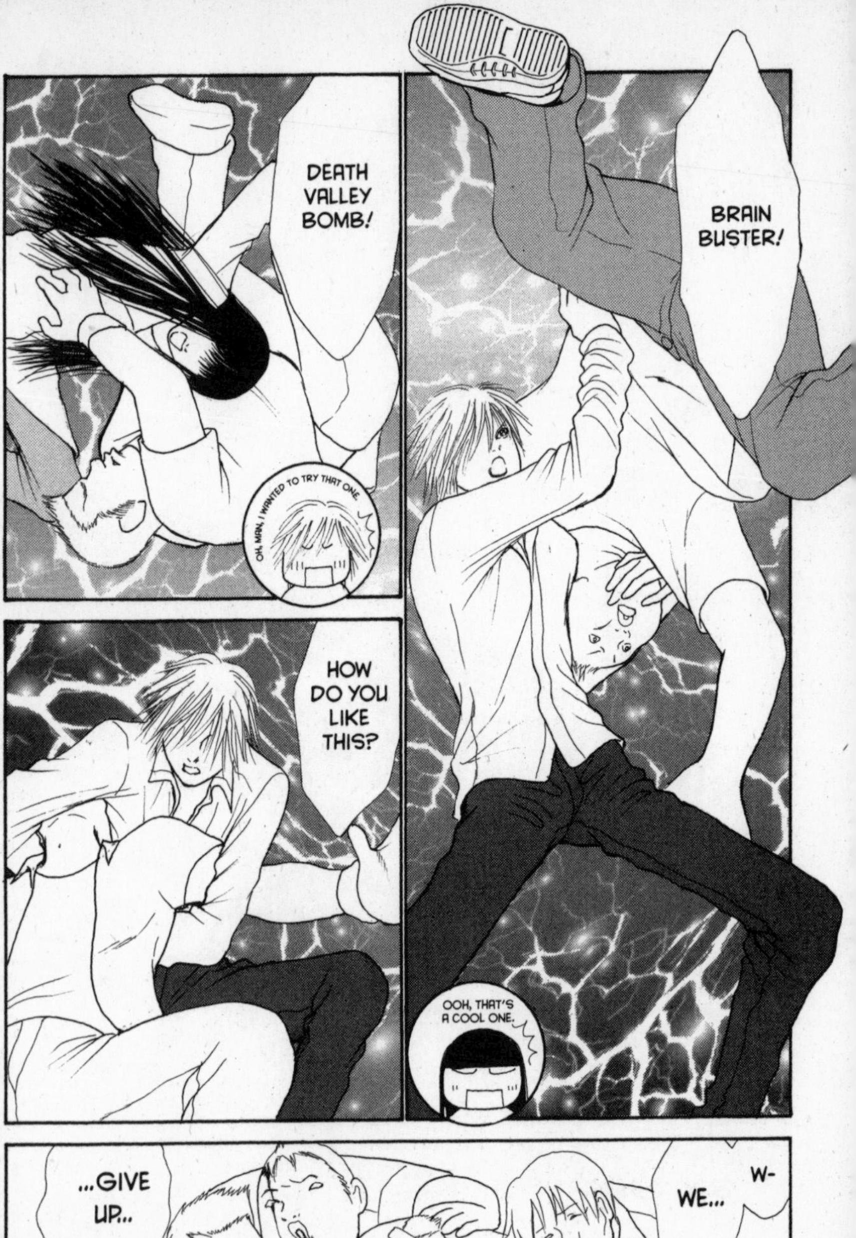
BRAIN BUSTER!
OOH, THAT'S A COOL ONE.
DEATH VALLEY BOMB!
OH, MAN, I WANTED TO TRY THAT ONE.
HOW DO YOU LIKE THIS?
W-
WE...
...GIVE UP...

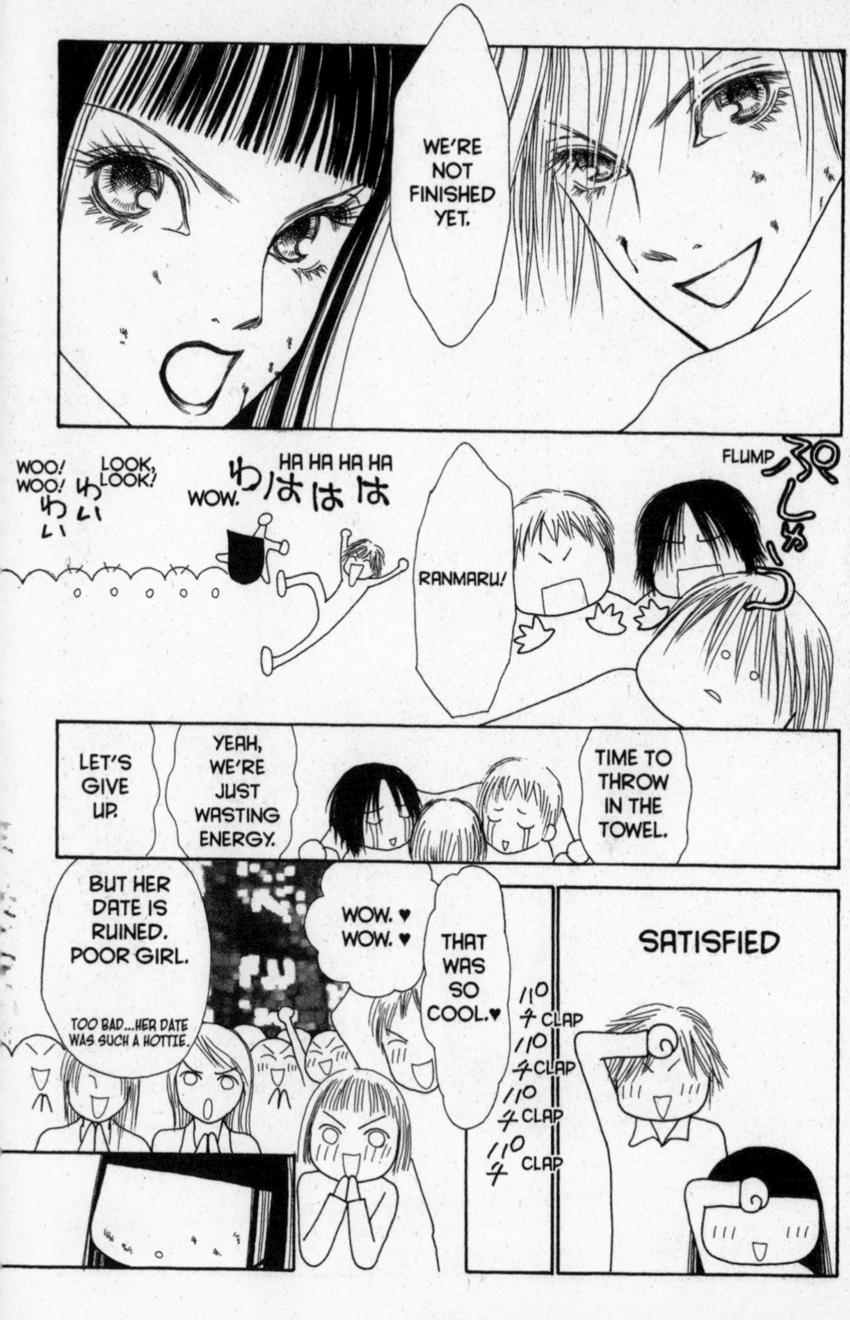

WE'RE NOT FINISHED YET.
FLUMP
RANMARU!
HA HA HA HA
わははは
WOW.
LOOK, LOOK!
わい
WOO! WOO!
わい
TIME TO THROW IN THE TOWEL.
YEAH, WE'RE JUST WASTING ENERGY.
LET'S GIVE UP.
SATISFIED
CLAP
CLAP
CLAP
CLAP
THAT WAS SO COOL.♥
WOW.♥ WOW.♥
BUT HER DATE IS RUINED. POOR GIRL.
TOO BAD...HER DATE WAS SUCH A HOTTIE.

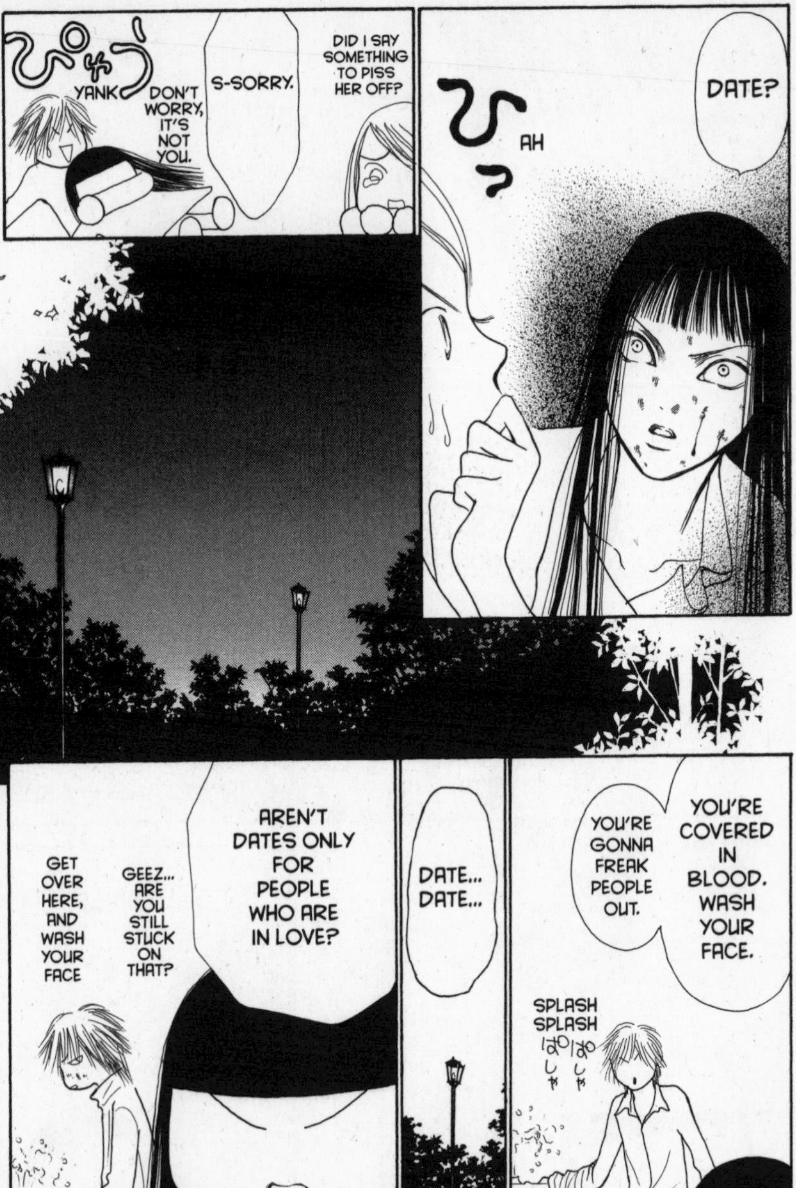
DATE?
AH
ひっ
DID I SAY SOMETHING TO PISS HER OFF?
S-SORRY.
DON'T WORRY, IT'S NOT YOU.
YANK
YOU'RE COVERED IN BLOOD. WASH YOUR FACE.
YOU'RE GONNA FREAK PEOPLE OUT.
SPLASH SPLASH
ぱしゃ ぱしゃ
DATE... DATE...
AREN'T DATES ONLY FOR PEOPLE WHO ARE IN LOVE?
GEEZ... ARE YOU STILL STUCK ON THAT?
GET OVER HERE, AND WASH YOUR FACE

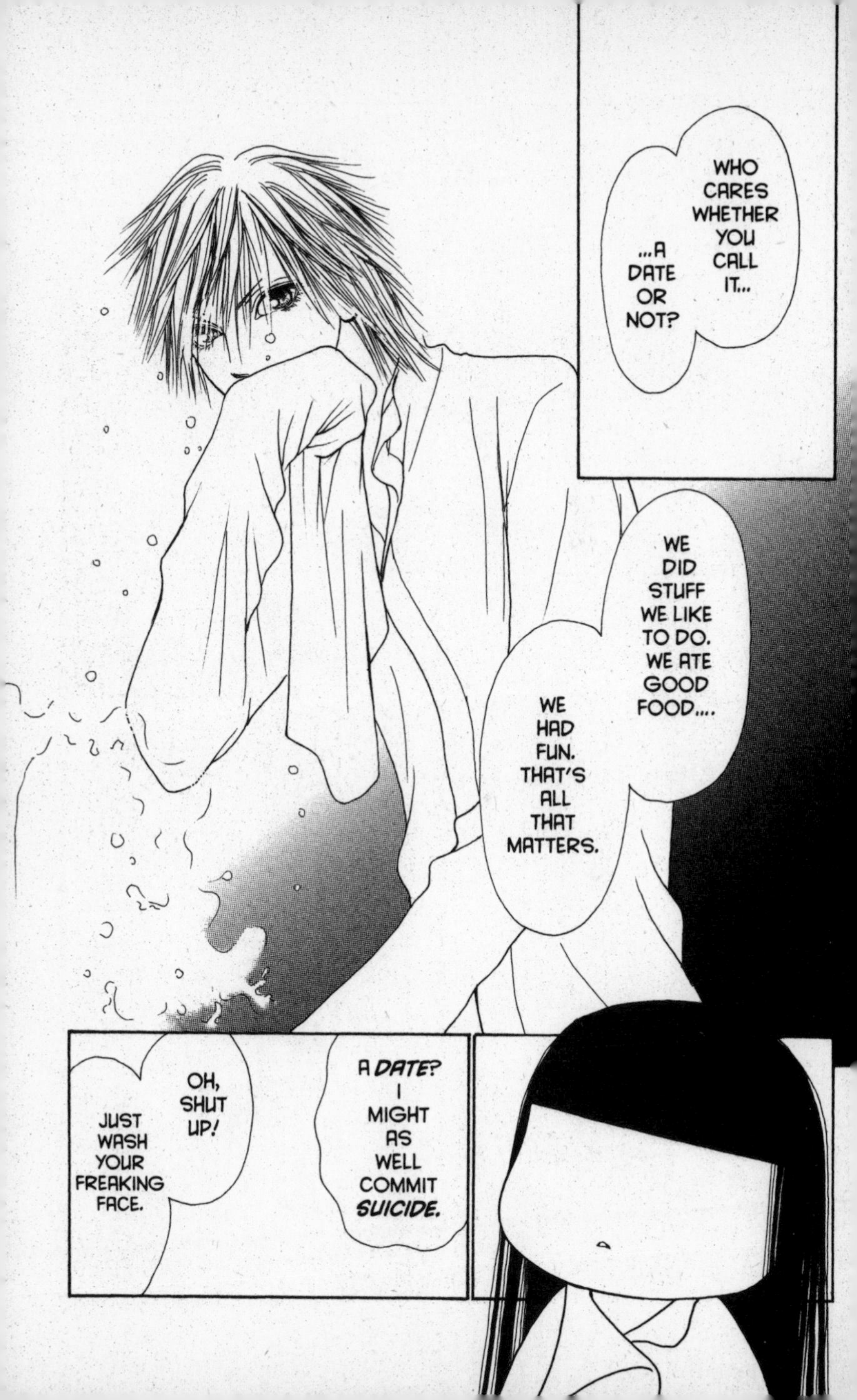
WHO CARES WHETHER YOU CALL IT...
...A DATE OR NOT?
WE DID STUFF WE LIKE TO DO. WE ATE GOOD FOOD....
WE HAD FUN. THAT'S ALL THAT MATTERS.
A *DATE*? I MIGHT AS WELL COMMIT ***SUICIDE***.
OH, SHUT UP!
JUST WASH YOUR FREAKING FACE.

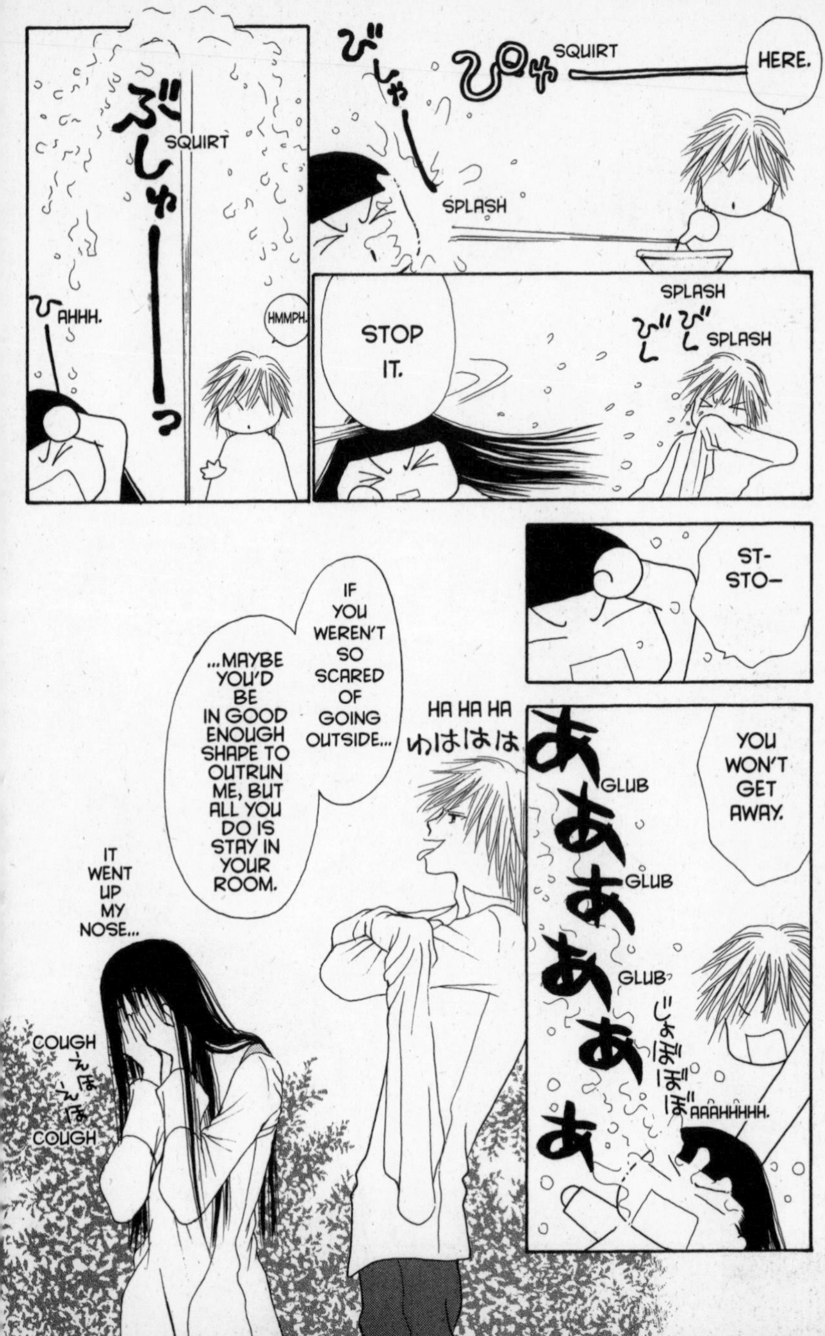
HERE.
ぴゅ SQUIRT
びしゃー
SPLASH
STOP IT.
SPLASH
SPLASH
ぶしゃーっ
SQUIRT
HMMPH.
AHHH.
ST- STO–
YOU WON'T GET AWAY.
あああああ
GLUB
GLUB
GLUB
じょぼぼぼ
AAAHHHHH.
HA HA HA
わははは
IF YOU WEREN'T SO SCARED OF GOING OUTSIDE...
...MAYBE YOU'D BE IN GOOD ENOUGH SHAPE TO OUTRUN ME, BUT ALL YOU DO IS STAY IN YOUR ROOM.
IT WENT UP MY NOSE...
COUGH
えほ えほ
COUGH

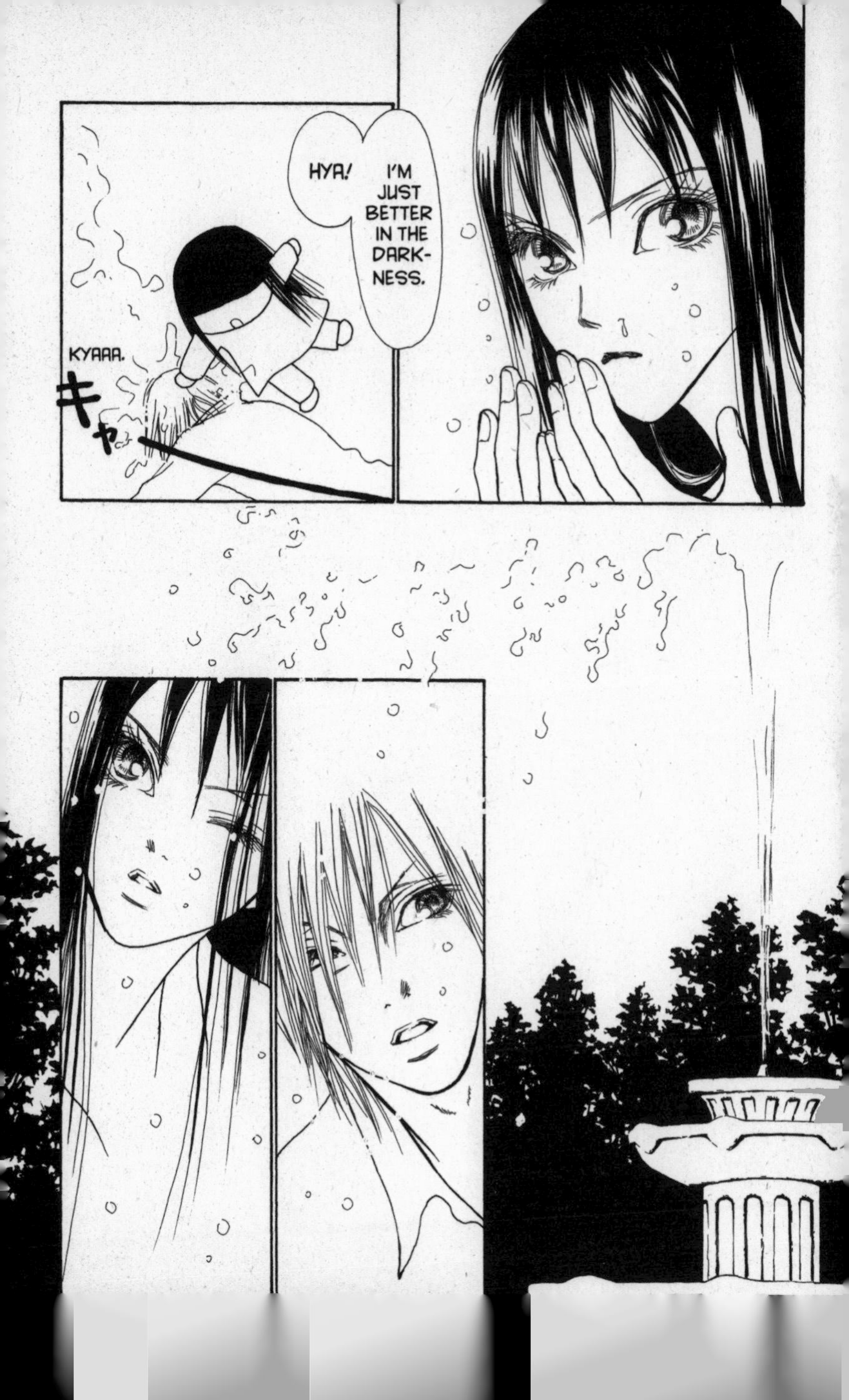
HYA! I'M JUST BETTER IN THE DARKNESS.
KYAAA.
キャ

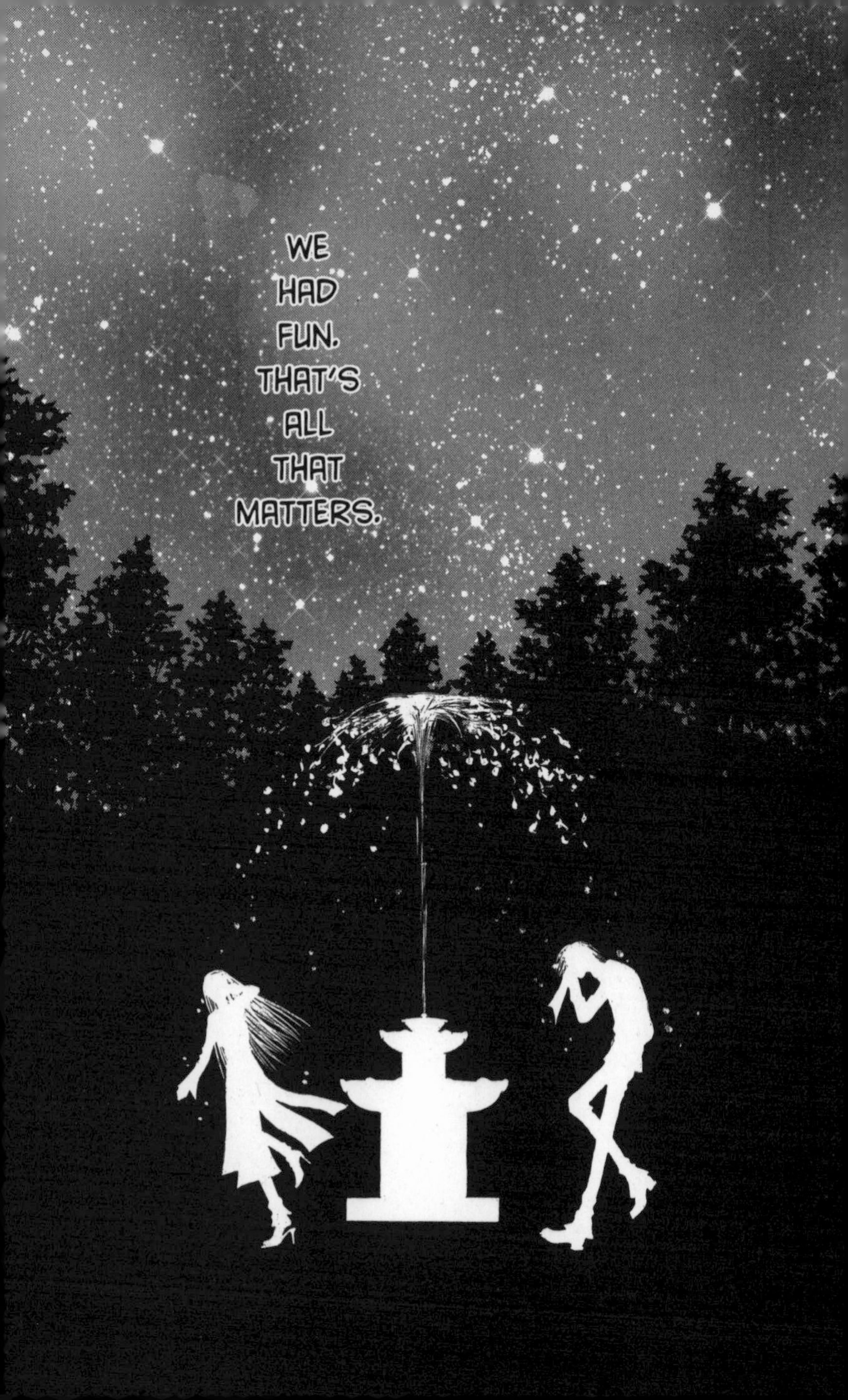
WE HAD FUN. THAT'S ALL THAT MATTERS.

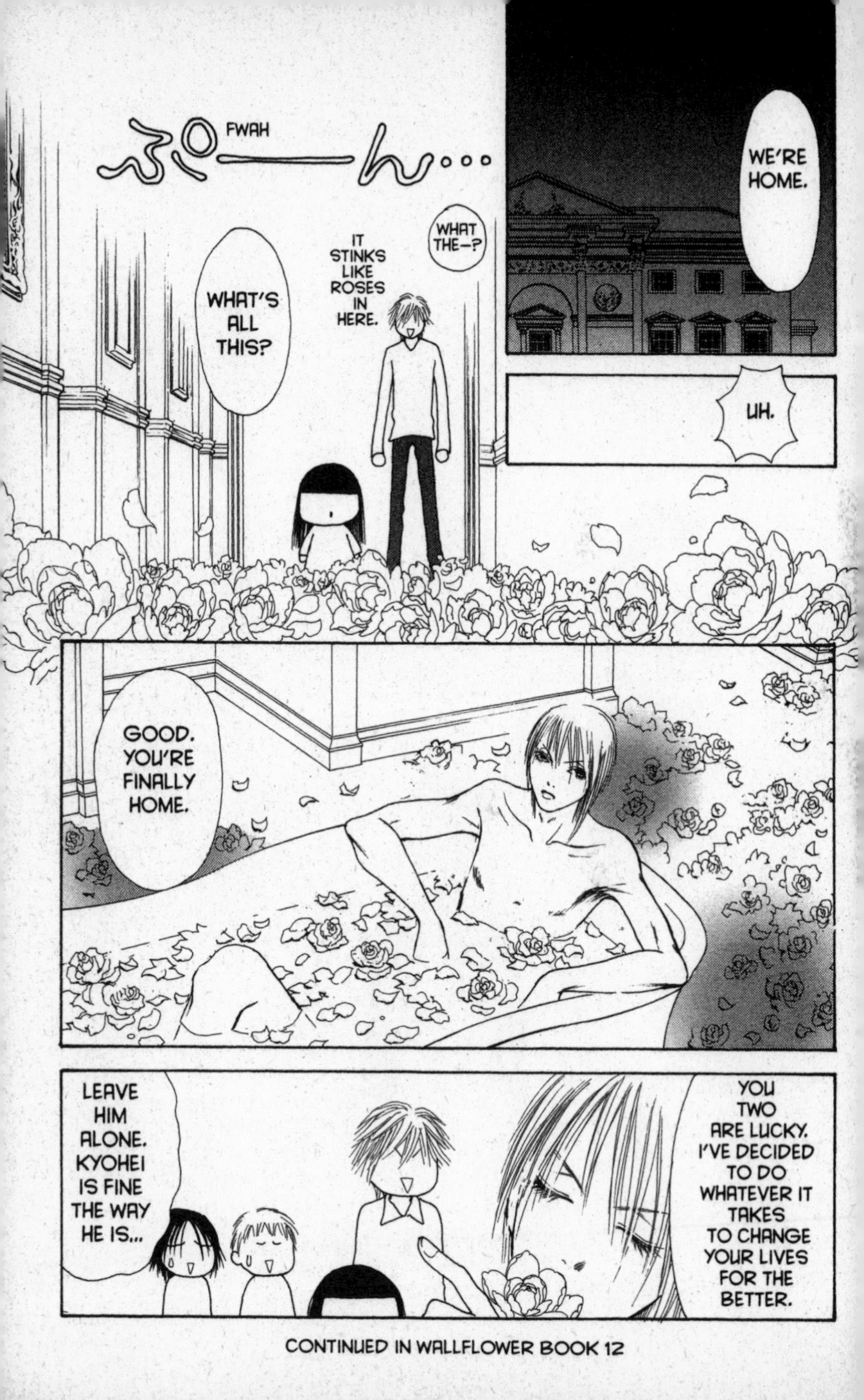

WE'RE HOME.
UH.
FWAH
WHAT THE–?
IT STINKS LIKE ROSES IN HERE.
WHAT'S ALL THIS?
GOOD. YOU'RE FINALLY HOME.
YOU TWO ARE LUCKY. I'VE DECIDED TO DO WHATEVER IT TAKES TO CHANGE YOUR LIVES FOR THE BETTER.
LEAVE HIM ALONE. KYOHEI IS FINE THE WAY HE IS...

CONTINUED IN WALLFLOWER BOOK 12

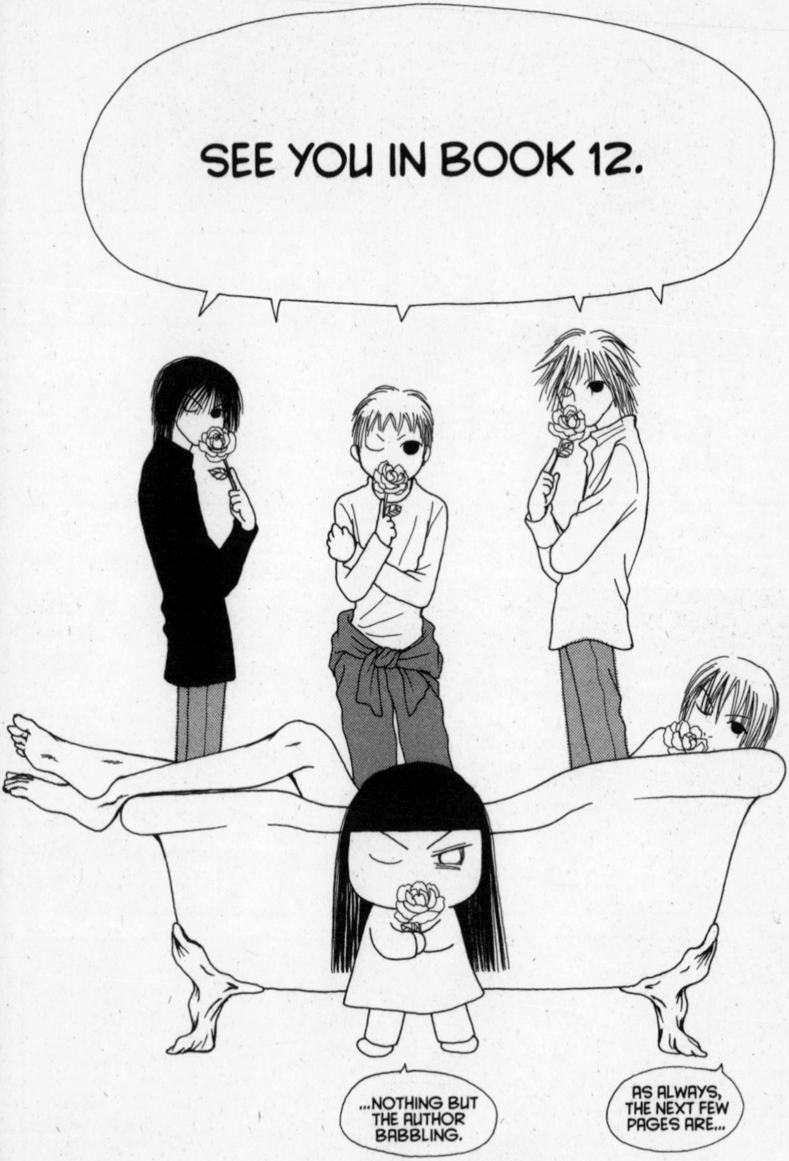
SEE YOU IN BOOK 12.
AS ALWAYS, THE NEXT FEW PAGES ARE...
...NOTHING BUT THE AUTHOR BABBLING.

I'M TENNOSUKE HAYAKAWA.

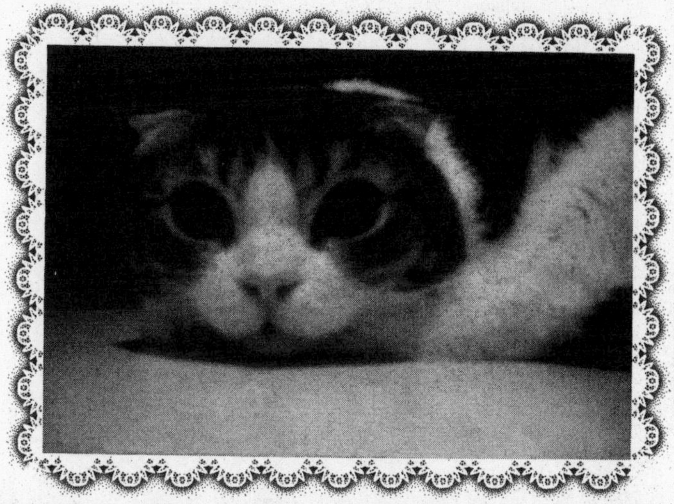
IT'S BEEN ONE YEAR SINCE TEN CAME INTO MY LIFE.
HE USED TO FIT IN THE PALM OF MY HAND, BUT HE'S GOTTEN SO BIG.
HE'S SO CUTE! I LOVE HIM. ♥
HE'S LIKE A SPOILED LITTLE PRINCE.

MY DRAWINGS OF HIM ARE ALWAYS REALLY BAD, SO IT'S TIME FOR A FULL-ON PHOTO SHOOT!

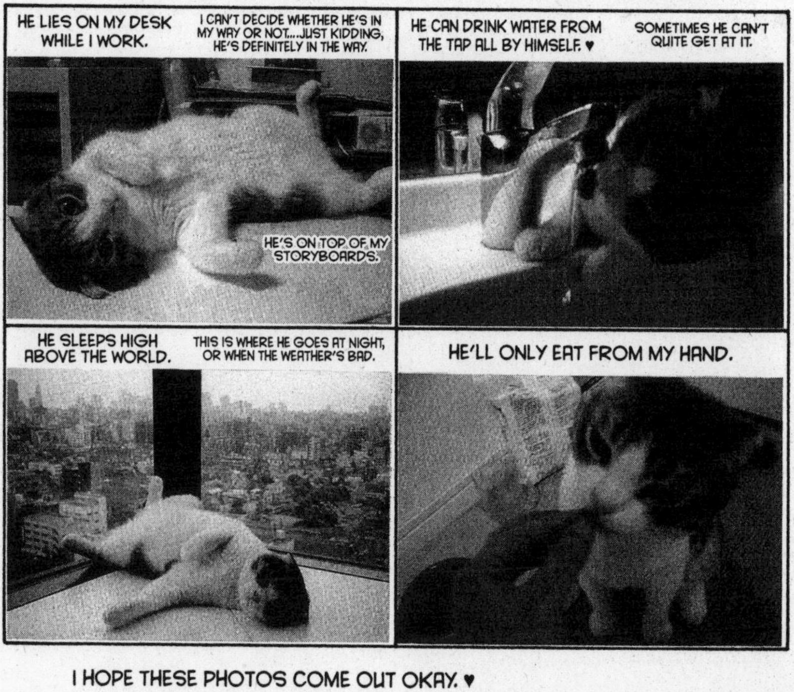
SOMETIMES HE CAN'T QUITE GET AT IT.
HE CAN DRINK WATER FROM THE TAP ALL BY HIMSELF. ♥
I CAN'T DECIDE WHETHER HE'S IN MY WAY OR NOT....JUST KIDDING, HE'S DEFINITELY IN THE WAY.
HE LIES ON MY DESK WHILE I WORK.
HE'S ON TOP OF MY STORYBOARDS.
HE'LL ONLY EAT FROM MY HAND.
THIS IS WHERE HE GOES AT NIGHT, OR WHEN THE WEATHER'S BAD.
HE SLEEPS HIGH ABOVE THE WORLD.

I HOPE THESE PHOTOS COME OUT OKAY. ♥

I HAD SUCH A BUSY SCHEDULE...
IT'D BEEN NINE MONTHS SINCE I'D SEEN

THE LOVE OF MY LIFE.

THAT'S IMPOSSIBLE! NO WONDER I THOUGHT I'D DIE FROM OVERWORK!
I WAS SO NERVOUS IT REMINDED ME OF THE FIRST TIME I WENT TO A KIYOHARU CONCERT.

I WENT TO SEE...

KIYOHARU TOKYO MONTHLY ACT VOL. 1
~The first show at the 3 floors~
SHIBUYA O EAST

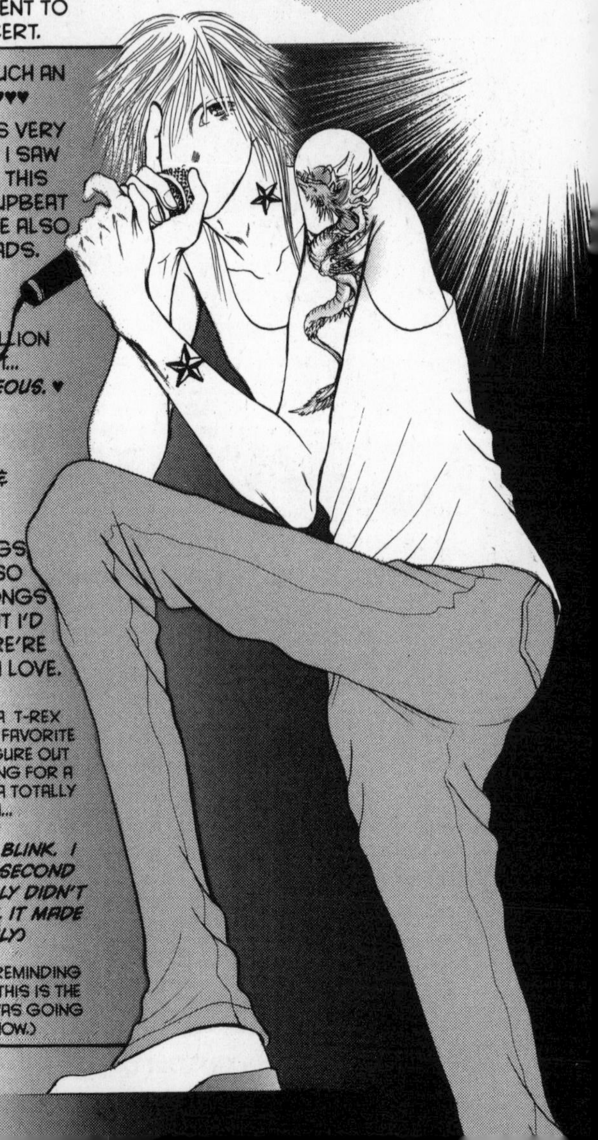

OH MY GOD! IT WAS SUCH AN ***AWESOME*** SHOW. ♥♥♥

HIS PERFORMANCE WAS VERY SUBDUED ♥ LAST TIME I SAW HIM IN CONCERT, BUT THIS TIME HE PLAYED SOME UPBEAT DANCE SONGS, TOO. HE ALSO PLAYED SOME BALLADS.

I'VE SAID IT OVER A MILLION TIMES ALREADY, BUT... ***KIYOHARU IS SO GORGEOUS.*** ♥

I WAS REALLY HAPPY BECAUSE HE PLAYED LOTS OF KUROYUME & SADS SONGS.

I LOVE HIS NEW SONGS BUT AS A FAN, IT'S SO EXCITING TO HEAR SONGS THAT I NEVER THOUGHT I'D HEAR LIVE AGAIN. THERE'RE SOOOO MANY SONGS I LOVE.

HE EVEN DID A COVER OF A T-REX SONG. THEY'RE ONE OF MY FAVORITE BANDS. ♥ ...I COULDN'T FIGURE OUT WHICH SONG HE WAS PLAYING FOR A WHILE, BECAUSE HE PLAYED A TOTALLY DIFFERENT VERSION...

I ***WISH I NEVER HAD TO BLINK. I DIDN'T WANNA MISS A SECOND OF THE SHOW. I ACTUALLY DIDN'T BLINK. HE WAS SO COOL IT MADE ME CRY. (SERIOUSLY)***

FOR SOME REASON, I KEPT REMINDING MYSELF, "THIS IS KIYOHARU. THIS IS THE REAL KIYOHARU." (I THINK I WAS GOING CRAZY DURING THE SHOW.)

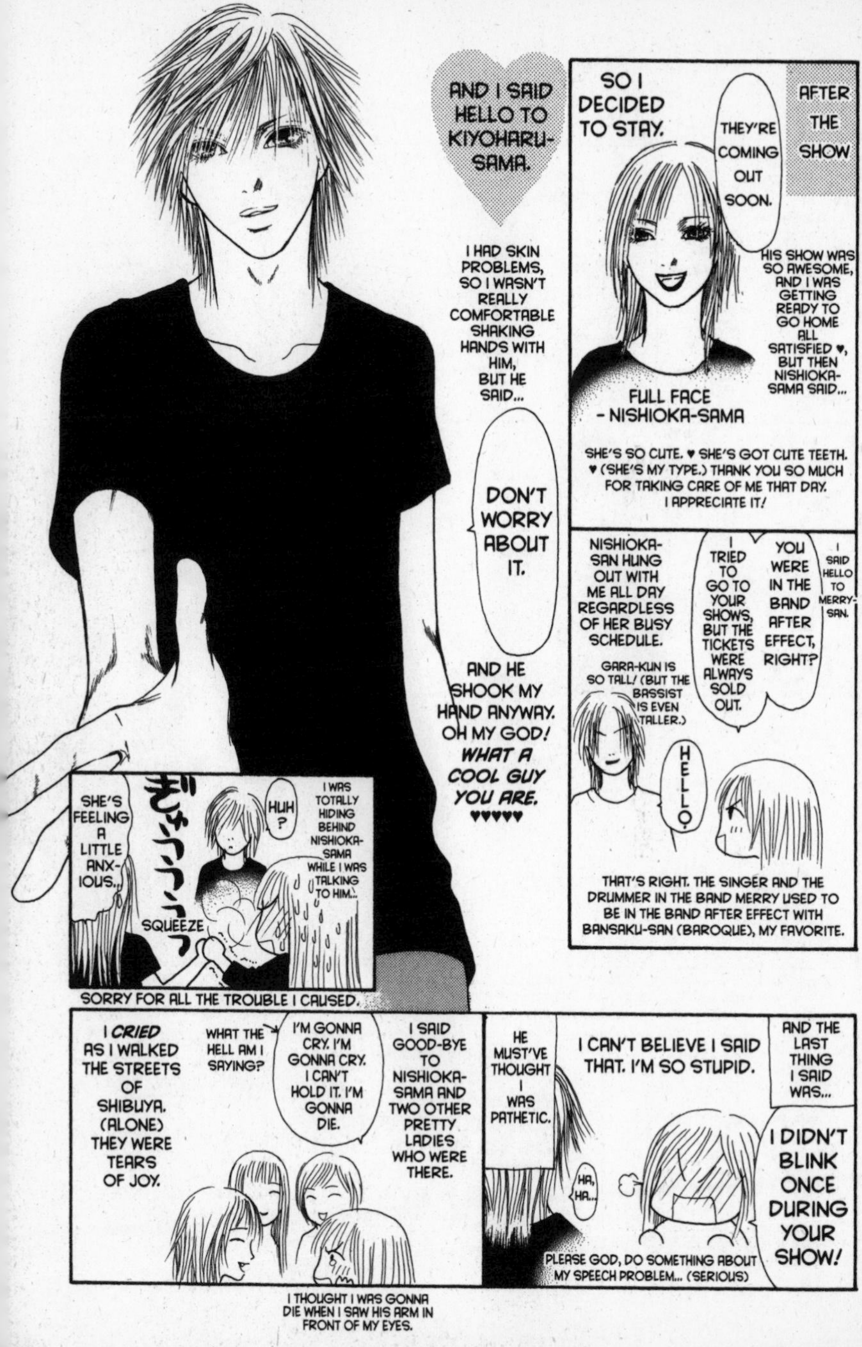
AFTER THE SHOW
HIS SHOW WAS SO AWESOME, AND I WAS GETTING READY TO GO HOME ALL SATISFIED ♥, BUT THEN NISHIOKA-SAMA SAID...
THEY'RE COMING OUT SOON.
SO I DECIDED TO STAY.
FULL FACE - NISHIOKA-SAMA
SHE'S SO CUTE. ♥ SHE'S GOT CUTE TEETH. ♥ (SHE'S MY TYPE.) THANK YOU SO MUCH FOR TAKING CARE OF ME THAT DAY. I APPRECIATE IT!
I SAID HELLO TO MERRY-SAN.
YOU WERE IN THE BAND AFTER EFFECT, RIGHT?
I TRIED TO GO TO YOUR SHOWS, BUT THE TICKETS WERE ALWAYS SOLD OUT.
NISHIOKA-SAN HUNG OUT WITH ME ALL DAY REGARDLESS OF HER BUSY SCHEDULE.
GARA-KUN IS SO TALL! (BUT THE BASSIST IS EVEN TALLER.)
HELLO.
THAT'S RIGHT. THE SINGER AND THE DRUMMER IN THE BAND MERRY USED TO BE IN THE BAND AFTER EFFECT WITH BANSAKU-SAN (BAROQUE), MY FAVORITE.
AND I SAID HELLO TO KIYOHARU-SAMA.
I HAD SKIN PROBLEMS, SO I WASN'T REALLY COMFORTABLE SHAKING HANDS WITH HIM, BUT HE SAID...
DON'T WORRY ABOUT IT.
AND HE SHOOK MY HAND ANYWAY. OH MY GOD! WHAT A COOL GUY YOU ARE. ♥♥♥♥♥
I WAS TOTALLY HIDING BEHIND NISHIOKA-SAMA WHILE I WAS TALKING TO HIM...
HUH?
ぎゅううう
SQUEEZE
SHE'S FEELING A LITTLE ANXIOUS...
SORRY FOR ALL THE TROUBLE I CAUSED.
AND THE LAST THING I SAID WAS...
I CAN'T BELIEVE I SAID THAT. I'M SO STUPID.
I DIDN'T BLINK ONCE DURING YOUR SHOW!
HE MUST'VE THOUGHT I WAS PATHETIC.
HA, HA...
PLEASE GOD, DO SOMETHING ABOUT MY SPEECH PROBLEM... (SERIOUS)
I SAID GOOD-BYE TO NISHIOKA-SAMA AND TWO OTHER PRETTY LADIES WHO WERE THERE.
I'M GONNA CRY. I'M GONNA CRY. I CAN'T HOLD IT. I'M GONNA DIE.
WHAT THE HELL AM I SAYING?
I CRIED AS I WALKED THE STREETS OF SHIBUYA. (ALONE) THEY WERE TEARS OF JOY.
I THOUGHT I WAS GONNA DIE WHEN I SAW HIS ARM IN FRONT OF MY EYES.

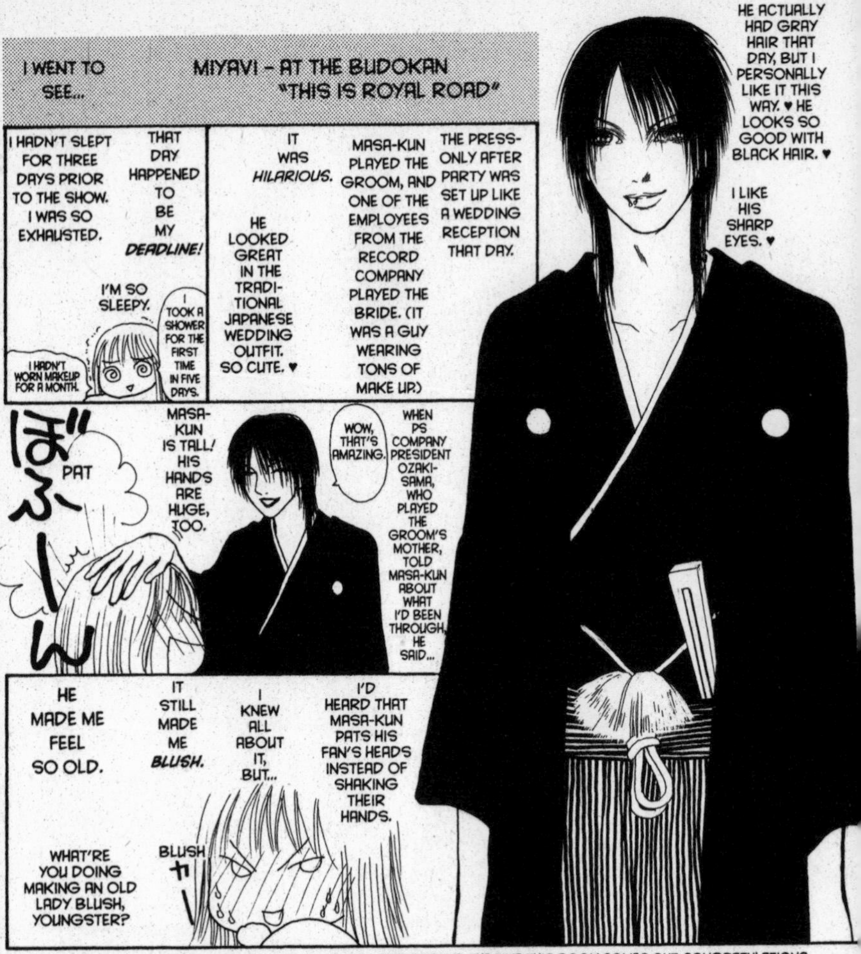
HE ACTUALLY HAD GRAY HAIR THAT DAY, BUT I PERSONALLY LIKE IT THIS WAY. ♥ HE LOOKS SO GOOD WITH BLACK HAIR. ♥
I LIKE HIS SHARP EYES. ♥
I WENT TO SEE...
MIYAVI – AT THE BUDOKAN "THIS IS ROYAL ROAD"
THE PRESS-ONLY AFTER PARTY WAS SET UP LIKE A WEDDING RECEPTION THAT DAY.
MASA-KUN PLAYED THE GROOM, AND ONE OF THE EMPLOYEES FROM THE RECORD COMPANY PLAYED THE BRIDE. (IT WAS A GUY WEARING TONS OF MAKE UP.)
IT WAS *HILARIOUS.*
HE LOOKED GREAT IN THE TRADITIONAL JAPANESE WEDDING OUTFIT. SO CUTE. ♥
THAT DAY HAPPENED TO BE MY *DEADLINE!*
I HADN'T SLEPT FOR THREE DAYS PRIOR TO THE SHOW. I WAS SO EXHAUSTED.
I'M SO SLEEPY.
I TOOK A SHOWER FOR THE FIRST TIME IN FIVE DAYS.
I HADN'T WORN MAKEUP FOR A MONTH.
WHEN PS COMPANY PRESIDENT OZAKI-SAMA, WHO PLAYED THE GROOM'S MOTHER, TOLD MASA-KUN ABOUT WHAT I'D BEEN THROUGH, HE SAID...
WOW, THAT'S AMAZING.
MASA-KUN IS TALL! HIS HANDS ARE HUGE, TOO.
PAT
ぼふーん
I'D HEARD THAT MASA-KUN PATS HIS FAN'S HEADS INSTEAD OF SHAKING THEIR HANDS.
I KNEW ALL ABOUT IT, BUT...
IT STILL MADE ME *BLUSH.*
HE MADE ME FEEL SO OLD.
BLUSH
WHAT'RE YOU DOING MAKING AN OLD LADY BLUSH, YOUNGSTER?

HE WILL BE RELEASING A RECORD THROUGH A MAJOR LABEL AROUND THE TIME THIS BOOK COMES OUT. CONGRATULATIONS. I WISH YOU THE BEST, MASA-KUN! MASA-KUN'S SONGS ARE AWESOME. ♥ I LOVE HIS DEEP, HUSKY VOICE. ♥ I LIKE "FUMINSHO NO NEMURIHIME (INSOMNIAC SLEEPING BEAUTY)" AND "COO QUACK CLUCK". ♥

GIFT

THE DRUMMER HIRO-KUN IS KIND OF LIKE MY FRIEND KAI-CHAN'S LITTLE BROTHER. SO I GUESS THAT MEANS HE'S MY LITTLE BROTHER, TOO (OR COULD HE BE MY SON?) HIRO-KUN IS SUCH A GOOD BOY. ♥ IF YOU SEE HIM, PLEASE GIVE HIM MY LOVE. ♥

I'VE BEEN GOING TO BOXING MATCHES LATELY. THE PROFESSIONAL BOXER OGURA IS A REALLY GREAT GUY. HE'S SO COOL WHEN HE'S FIGHTING. I'M A SATORU SUZUKI FAN. ♥

YOU MIGHT BE WONDERING WHY I'M NOT WRITING ANYTHING ABOUT BAROQUE.

THAT'S BECAUSE I DON'T WANNA THINK ABOUT THEM. IT MAKES ME SAD WHENEVER I THINK ABOUT THEM. I'VE BEEN CRYING EVER SINCE I SAW THEIR FINAL SHOW.

THANK YOU FOR BUYING KODANSHA COMICS. ♥

I DIDN'T GET TO THANK YOU GUYS EARLIER BECAUSE OF ALL THE EXTRA BONUS PAGES. SORRY ABOUT THAT.

I'M SO SORRY I WROTE SO MUCH NEGATIVE STUFF ON THE "BEHIND THE SCENES" PAGES. NOW I HAVE TIME TO GO OUT, SO I'M FEELING MUCH BETTER. I'M DOING OKAY.

I THOUGHT I'D GO CRAZY WHEN I WAS WORKING EVERY DAY WITHOUT A BREAK, BUT YOUR LETTERS KEPT ME GOING. THANK YOU SOOOOOO MUCH. I CAN NEVER THANK YOU ALL ENOUGH.

THERE ARE PEOPLE WHO TELL ME, "YOUR MANGA REALLY CHEERS ME UP." YOU GUYS ARE THE ONES WHO CHEER ME UP. (YOU GUYS ARE SO SWEET.)

I APOLOGIZE TO THOSE OF YOU WHO KEEP SAYING, "I HAVE NO IDEA WHO YOU'RE TALKING ABOUT IN YOUR BONUS PAGES." I OFTEN USE THE BONUS PAGES TO SHOW MY APPRECIATION TOWARDS PEOPLE WHO'VE TAKEN CARE OF ME (VERY WELL). OH, YEAH, AND I GUESS I WRITE ABOUT MY FRIENDS A LOT, TOO. I DIDN'T WRITE TOO MUCH ABOUT MY FRIENDS THIS TIME.

THANKS FOR DEALING WITH MY DEEP LOVE FOR TEN. BLUSH. I JUST CAN'T HELP IT. I LOVE TEN SO MUCH. THANKS FOR SENDING ME PHOTOS OF YOUR PETS. ♥ IT'S SO NICE TO SEE THEM. ♥

THANK YOU TO ALL OF YOU WHO SENT ME PRESENTS. I TREASURE THEM. ♥

I KNOW I'VE SAID THIS BEFORE, BUT REALLY, I'M GRATEFUL JUST TO RECEIVE LETTERS FROM YOU. PLEASE STOP SAYING, "SORRY FOR SENDING YOU A LETTER WITHOUT A GIFT." I'M SO HAPPY TO RECEIVE YOUR LETTERS!

HERE'S WHAT'S GOING ON IN MY LIFE NOW. I'M ON A SERIOUS DIET. MY WHOLE BODY IS SWOLLEN, AND IT LOOKS PRETTY BAD. IT'S SO HARD TO LOSE WEIGHT...I HOPE I HAVE A SUCCESS STORY FOR YOU IN BOOK 12! IF ANYBODY KNOWS A *SIMPLE* WAY TO LOSE WEIGHT, PLEASE LET ME KNOW. ⟵ MAYBE THIS SHOWS THAT I DON'T HAVE ENOUGH MOTIVATION.

THANK YOU SO MUCH FOR READING THIS WHOLE THING. SEE YOU IN BOOK 12. ♥

SPECIAL THANKS

HANA-CHAN
YOSHII
KIMURA-SAN
NAKAZAWA-SAN
HITOSHI HAYAKAWA
(BROTHER)

MINE-SAMA
INO-SAMA
SHIOZAWA-SAMA

EVERYBODY FROM THE EDITING DEPARTMENT
EVERYBODY WHO SENT ME LETTERS
EVERYBODY WHO'S READING THIS RIGHT NOW

About the Creator

Tomoko Hayakawa was born on March 4.

Since her debut as a manga creator, Tomoko Hayakawa has worked on many shojo titles with the theme of romantic love—only to realize that she could write about other subjects as well. She decided to pack her newest story with the things she likes most, which led to her current, enormously popular series, *The Wallflower*.

Her favorite things are: Tim Burton's *The Nightmare Before Christmas*, Jean-Paul Gaultier, and samurai dramas on TV. Her hobbies are collecting items with skull designs and watching *bishonen* (beautiful boys). Her dream is to build a mansion like the one the Addams family lives in. Her favorite pastime is to lie around at home with her cat, Ten (whose full name is Tennosuke).

Her zodiac sign is Pisces, and her blood group is AB.

Translation Notes

Japanese is a tricky language for most Westerners, and translation is often more an art than science. For your edification and reading pleasure, here are notes on some of the places where we could have gone in a different direction in our translation of the work, or where a Japanese cultural reference is used.

Sangetan soup, page 38

Sangetan soup is a Korean soup made with chicken, rice, ginseng, nutmeg, and garlic. It's reputed to have energy-rejuvenating properties.

Cho-san, page 50

The author is probably referring to the famous comedian Chousuke Ikariya, who died in 2004, around the time this story first appeared in Japan. The guys are supposed to be watching Cho-san do one of his famous bits on TV.

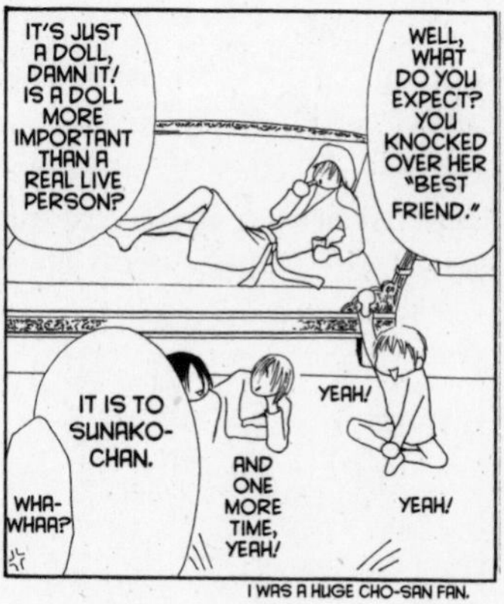
WELL, WHAT DO YOU EXPECT? YOU KNOCKED OVER HER "BEST FRIEND."
IT'S JUST A DOLL, DAMN IT! IS A DOLL MORE IMPORTANT THAN A REAL LIVE PERSON?
YEAH!
YEAH!
AND ONE MORE TIME, YEAH!
IT IS TO SUNAKO-CHAN.
WHA-WHAA?

I WAS A HUGE CHO-SAN FAN.

Hiroshi-kun gets some sun, page 54

SUNAKO-CHAN IS OUT IN THE SUN.
I GUESS SHE'S LETTING HIROSHI-KUN GET SOME SUN.
IT'S THAT TIME OF THE YEAR AGAIN...

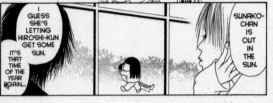

In Japan, on sunny days, people hang their futons and comforters outside. It's supposed to dry out the futon and kill any dust mites that might be inhabiting it. Here, the guys are suggesting that Sunako is hanging Hiroshi out to dry just as she would a futon.

Can of coffee and peanut and cracker snacks, page 54

Canned coffee beverages are extraordinarily popular in Japan, and there are numerous brands. Many American stars have done Japanese canned coffee commercials. The "peanut and cracker snacks" Yuki refers to are a delicious snack called *kakipii,* a mix of peanuts and tiny rice crackers.

GET ME AN ICE CREAM.
I WANT A CAN OF COFFEE.
CHING
CHING
GET ME SOME PEANUT AND CRACKER SNACKS.

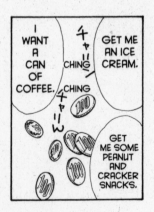

Hachiouji, page 61

Hachiouji is a suburb on the outskirts of Tokyo.

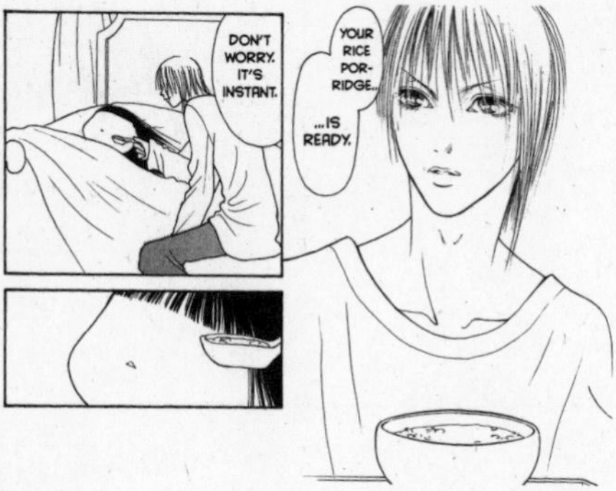

YOUR RICE POR-RIDGE...
...IS READY.
DON'T WORRY. IT'S INSTANT.

Instant rice porridge, page 62

Rice porridge, called *okayu* in Japanese, is commonly fed to sick people. It's sort of a Japanese version of chicken soup.

Addressing envelopes, page 129

Sunako got a job addressing envelopes. This used to be a common "work from home" job in Japan.

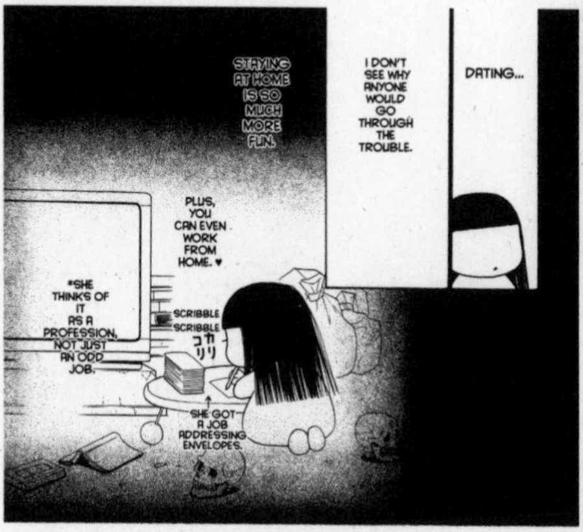

DATING...
I DON'T SEE WHY ANYONE WOULD GO THROUGH THE TROUBLE.
STAYING AT HOME IS SO MUCH MORE FUN.
PLUS, YOU CAN EVEN WORK FROM HOME. ♥
*SHE THINKS OF IT AS A PROFESSION, NOT JUST AN ODD JOB.
SCRIBBLE SCRIBBLE
SHE GOT A JOB ADDRESSING ENVELOPES.

Movie theater programs, page 145

Japanese movie theaters often sell programs for each movie they feature. The programs contain background information on the film and photos.

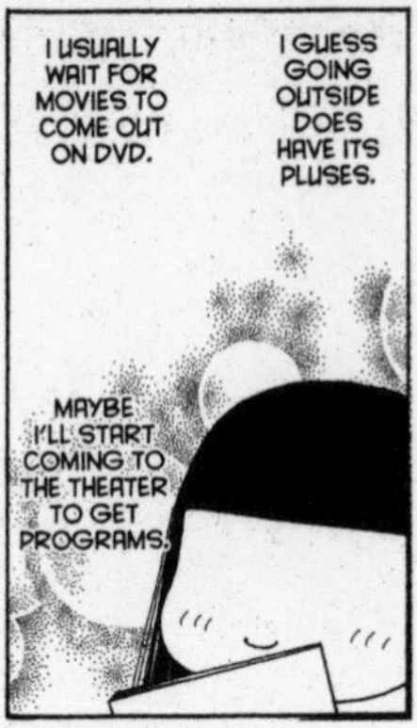
I GUESS GOING OUTSIDE DOES HAVE ITS PLUSES.
I USUALLY WAIT FOR MOVIES TO COME OUT ON DVD.
MAYBE I'LL START COMING TO THE THEATER TO GET PROGRAMS.

Yakitori, page 147

Sunako and Kyohei are at a *yakitori* restaurant. *Yakitori* literally means "grilled chicken." *Yakitori* restaurants can be found all over Japan.

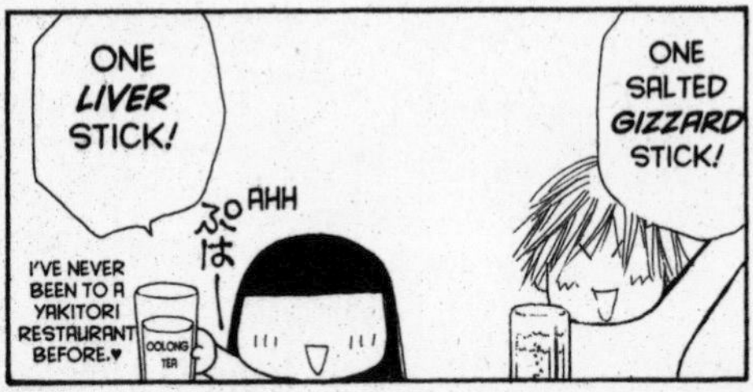
ONE SALTED *GIZZARD* STICK!
ONE *LIVER* STICK!
ぷはー AHH
I'VE NEVER BEEN TO A YAKITORI RESTAURANT BEFORE.♥
OOLONG TEA

Batting cage, page 152

Batting centers are a popular form of recreation in Japan.

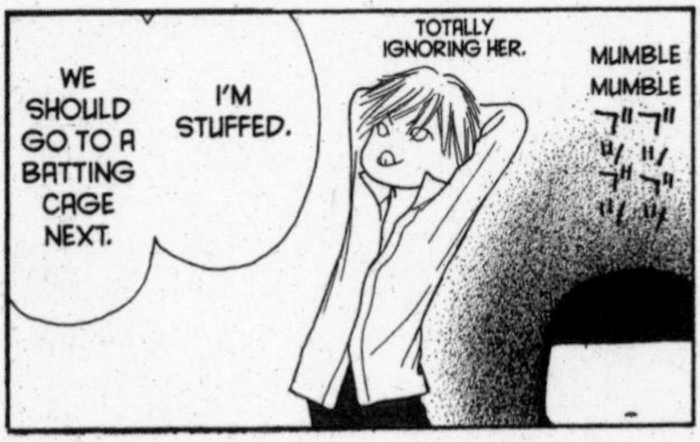
MUMBLE MUMBLE
TOTALLY IGNORING HER.
I'M STUFFED.
WE SHOULD GO TO A BATTING CAGE NEXT.

Preview of volume 12

We're pleased to present you a preview from volume 12. This volume is available in English now!

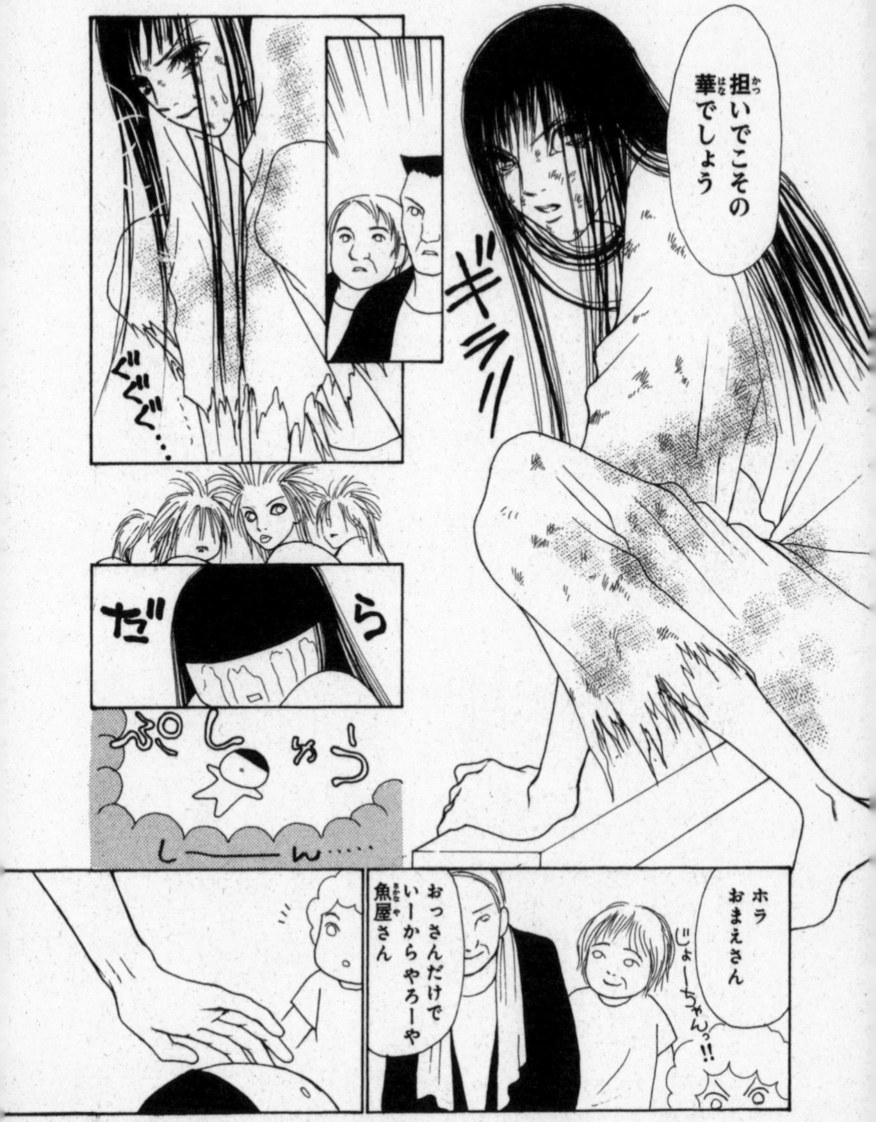
担いでこその華でしょう
ギラッ
ぐぐぐ…
だら
ぷしゅう
しーーん……
ホラ おまえさん
じょーちゃんっ!!
おっさんだけでいーからやろーや 魚屋さん

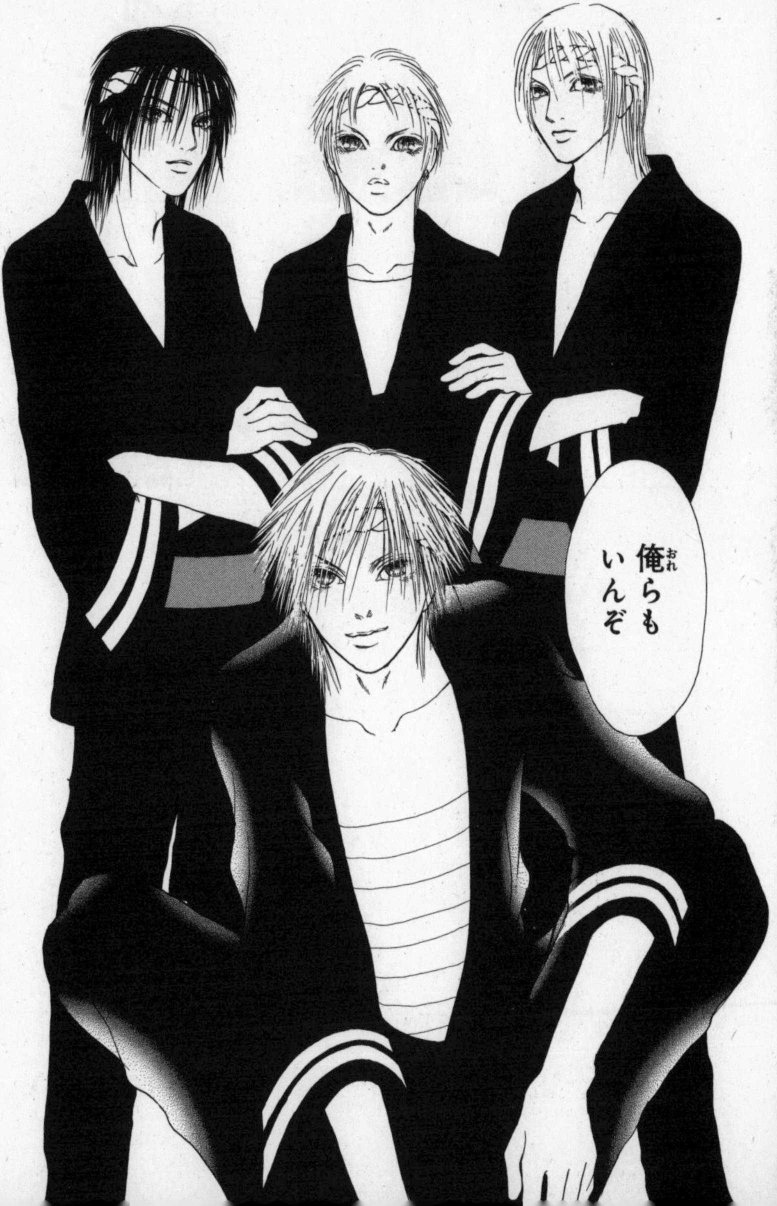
俺(おれ)らもいんぞ

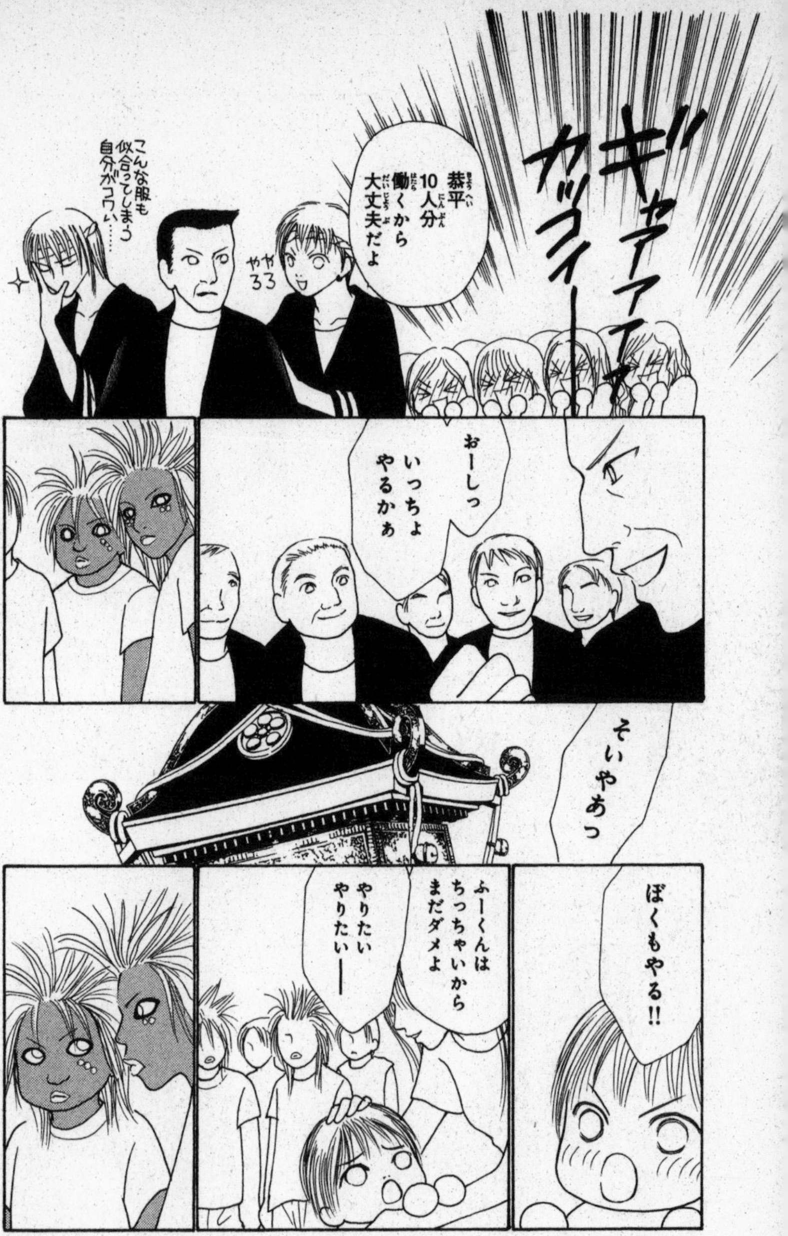
ギャアアアア
カッコイー
恭平10人分働くから大丈夫だよ
こんな服も似合ってしまう自分がコワい……
おーしっ いっちょ やるかぁ
そいやあっ
ぼくもやる!!
ふーくんはちっちゃいからまだダメよ
やりたい やりたいーー

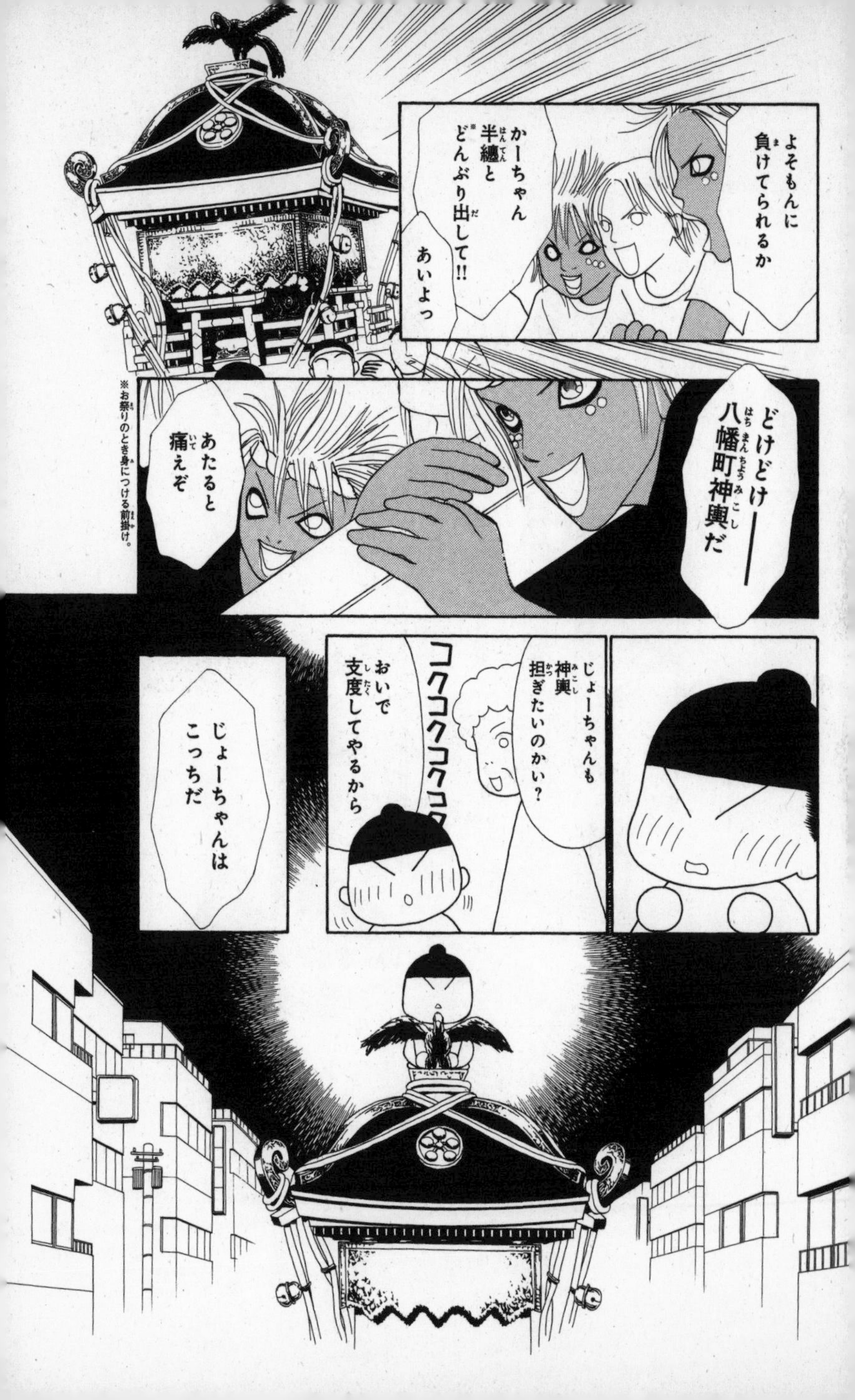
よそもんに負けてられるか
かーちゃん半纏と※どんぶり出して!!
あいよっ
どけどけ――八幡町神輿だ
あたると痛えぞ
※お祭りのとき身につける前掛け。
じょーちゃんも神輿担ぎたいのかい?
コクコクコクコク
おいで支度してやるから
じょーちゃんはこっちだ

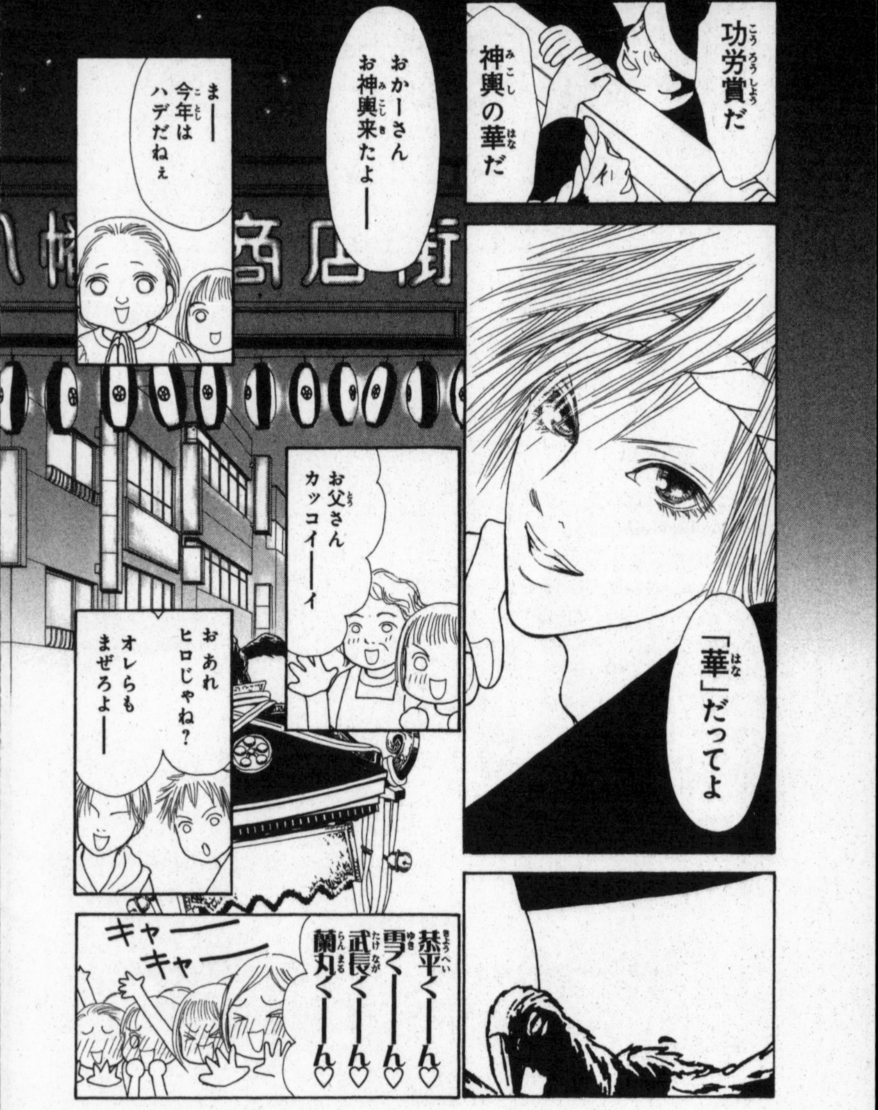
功労賞だ
神輿の華だ
「華」だってよ
おかーさん お神輿来たよーー
まーー 今年はハデだねぇ
お父さん カッコイーーィ
おあれ ヒロじゃね？ オレらも まぜろよーー
恭平くーーん 雪くーーん 武長くーーん 蘭丸くーーん♡
キャーー
キャーー

FREE COLLARS KINGDOM

フリーカラーズキングダム

TAKUYA FUJIMI

THOSE FEISTY FELINES!

It's hard to resist Cyan: He's an adorable catboy, whose cute ears and tail have made him a beloved pet. But then his family abandons him, leaving the innocent Cyan to fend for himself.

Just when Cyan thinks he's all alone in the world, he meets the Free Collars, a cool gang of stray cats who believe that no feline should allow a human to imprison his Wild Spirit. They invite Cyan to join them, and the reluctant housecat has to decide fast, because a rival gang of cats is threatening the Free Collars' territory! Can Cyan learn to free his Wild Spirit—and help his new friends save their home?

Special extras in each volume! Read them all!

VISIT WWW.DELREYMANGA.COM TO:
- Read sample pages
- View release date calendars for upcoming volumes
- Sign up for Del Rey's free manga e-newsletter
- Find out the latest about new Del Rey Manga series

RATING   OT AGES 16+

 **DEL REY MANGA**

The Otaku's Choice

TOMARE!

止まれ

[STOP!]

You're going the wrong way!

Manga is a completely different
type of reading experience.

To start at the beginning,
go to the end!

That's right! Authentic manga is read the traditional Japanese way—
from right to left. Exactly the opposite of how American books are
read. It's easy to follow: Just go to the other end of the book, and read
each page—and each panel—from right side to left side, starting at
the top right. Now you're experiencing manga as it was meant to be!